The archaeology of political structure

NEW STUDIES IN ARCHAEOLOGY

Series editors

Colin Renfrew, *University of Cambridge*
Jeremy Sabloff, *University of Pittsburgh*

Other titles in the series

Ian Hodder and Clive Orton: *Spatial Analysis in Archaeology*
Kenneth Hudson: *World Industrial Archaeology*
Keith Muckelroy: *Maritime Archaeology*
Graham Connah: *Three Thousand Years in Africa*
Richard E. Blanton, Stephen A. Kowalewski, Gary Feinman and Jill Appel:
  Ancient Mesoamerica
Stephen Plog: *Stylistic Variation in Prehistoric Ceramics*
Peter Wells: *Culture Contact and Culture Change*
Ian Hodder: *Symbols in Action*
Patrick Vinton Kirch: *Evolution of the Polynesian Chiefdoms*
Dean Arnold: *Ceramic Theory and Cultural Process*
Geoffrey W. Conrad and Arthur A. Demarest: *Religion and Empire :
  The Dynamics of Aztec and Inca Expansionism*
Graeme Barker: *Prehistoric Farming in Europe*
Daniel Miller: *Artefacts as Categories*
Rosalind Hunter-Anderson: *Prehistoric Adaptation in the American Southwest*
Robin Torrence: *Production and Exchange of Stone Tools*
M. Shanks and C. Tilley: *Re-Constructing Archaeology*
Bo Gräslund: *The Birth of Prehistoric Chronology*
Ian Morris: *Burial and Ancient Society : The Rise of the Greek City State*
John Fox: *Maya Postclassic State Formation*
Alasdair Whittle: *Problems in Neolithic Archaeology*
Peter Bogucki: *Forest Farmers and Stock Herders*

OLIVIER DE MONTMOLLIN

The archaeology of political structure

Settlement analysis in a Classic Maya polity

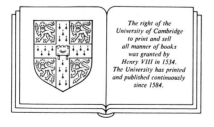

The right of the
University of Cambridge
to print and sell
all manner of books
was granted by
Henry VIII in 1534.
The University has printed
and published continuously
since 1584.

Cambridge University Press

Cambridge
New York   New Rochelle   Melbourne   Sydney

Published by the Press Syndicate of the University of Cambridge
The Pitt Building, Trumpington Street, Cambridge CB2 1RP
32 East 57th Street, New York, NY 10022, USA
10 Stamford Road, Oakleigh, Melbourne 3166, Australia

© Cambridge University Press 1989

First published 1989

Printed in Great Britain by the University Press, Cambridge

British Library cataloguing in publication data

Montmollin, Olivier de
The archaeology of political structure:
settlement analysis in a classic Maya polity–
(New studies in archaeology)
1. Mexico. Chiapos (State). Maya settlements.
Archaeological investigation
I. Title   II. Series
972′.7501

Library of Congress cataloguing in publication data

De Montmollin, Olivier.
   The archaeology of political structure:
   settlement analysis in a classic Maya polity/Olivier de Montmollin.
         p.   cm. (New studies in archaeology)
   Bibliography.
   ISBN 0 521 36232 6
      1. Mayas–Politics and government.   2. Mayas–Antiquities.
      3. Land settlement patterns. Prehistoric–Mexico–Rosario Valley Region.
      4. Indians of Mexico–Rosario Valley Region–Politics and government.
      5. Indians of Mexico–Rosario Valley Region–Antiquities.
      6. Rosario Valley Region (Mexico)–Antiquities.
      7. Mexico–Antiquities.   I. Title.
      F1435.3.P7D4 1989
      972′.32–dc 19   88-16163 CIP

ISBN 0 521 36232 6

To Cathy and Peter

CONTENTS

FIGURES

TABLES

In this study of settlement and politics in a Classic Maya polity I have set out to discuss and exemplify some elements of an anthropological approach to the archaeology of ancient complex polities. To begin, I want to sketch out briefly and rather informally the basic motivations for the work, saving the more detailed formal rationales for later. I see an anthropological approach to archaeology as something more than a simple mining of ethnographic lore in order to fill out archaeological interpretation. I also see it as something other than the uncritical adoption of a single paradigm from social or cultural anthropology (e.g., cultural ecology, structuralism, or post-structuralism). Rather, to my mind, an effective anthropological approach to the archaeology of complex polities requires the adoption of some of the more appealing intellectual traits that characterize the social and cultural anthropology of complex societies. Very broadly, these traits include sustained scepticism about received conceptual tools, respect for the diversity of behaviors and institutions in the record, a sensitivity to issues of social scale, and a sensitivity to the tension between approaches that use abstract formal models as opposed to approaches that use more particularistic substantivist models (the contrast between general comparative and particularizing approaches).

From my chosen anthropological-archaeological perspective, it seems that over the last few years many archaeologists have reached a kind of impasse in their studies of complex polities. Conclusions have been and continue to be drawn about such great issues as state formation or the rise of civilization. But in a more sceptical (and post-heroic) intellectual climate, it seems increasingly difficult to continue discussion exclusively along this track without falling into conceptual routinization. Another major source of worry is (or should be) the methodological problem of linking the conclusions to archaeological evidence. Discussion of methodological problems remains relatively underdeveloped with reference to complex societies, giving a distinct air of unreality or at least arbitrariness to the conclusions reached about them.

Given these difficulties and worries, one tendency might be to strike off in a completely new direction: the new-broom syndrome. Hoping to avoid this syndrome, which often carries with it an evangelical fervor, I prefer instead to react to previous work and to try to bring out some of the alternatives that have not been considered fully in the study of ancient complex polities. From this perspective, an effective research program includes several steps: research history, problem orientation, the archaeological record, fieldwork strategies (data gathering), analytical tools (bridging arguments), drawing conclusions. Each one of these (not necessarily strictly sequential) steps requires a series of choices. What seems to be missing from many archaeological studies of ancient complex societies is a full discussion of the choices made (and especially of the alternatives foregone) at every step of the research program. In light of this, my study attempts to provide such discussion and additionally to do so in a manner which is self-critical. Any fervor or excitement associated with this approach emerges from having to negotiate a problem-solving maze: the video-game syndrome. This contrasts with the excitement that arises from the certainty of having discovered the golden road to understanding, truth or goodness, something more closely associated with the new-broom syndrome.

My use of a specific case study to explore a range of methodological and conceptual options concerning the archaeological study of ancient complex societies stems from a belief that specific case studies are the most effective context within which to examine comprehensively the several steps in a research program. The case study selected need not be perfect nor need it cover all possible options. Rather, the principal requirements are to have a case study which is interesting in its own right, and with reference to the general theme of ancient complex polities, and to set such a case study in the clearest possible context, especially with reference to the options which were not available or not taken up. An alternative approach for a critical (and anthropologically-oriented) discussion of ancient complex polities is to provide an overview of many case studies. While such an approach has great value, I favor the single case approach, in this instance because it allows closer attention to necessary detail and because it provides a more coherent format for tracing through the linkages between different steps in a research program.

Why do I look at a case study in ancient Maya political structure in particular? The ancient Maya have left us an astounding archaeological and historical record. This record has fascinated generations of scholars for its intrinsic and comparative interest. It continues to support a wide variety of interpretations without showing any signs of being wrung dry. Furthermore, the richness of the record makes it especially resistant to one-dimensional or monolithic interpretive approaches. A continuous series of interpretive challenges accompanies the attempt to come to grips with ancient Maya political structure, while keeping due respect for the evidential record. The Maya record provides a good arena for resisting conceptual and/or methodological routinization and for trying out a range of the conceptual and methodological options available for studying ancient complex polities. The Maya record is also a good one for demonstrating the value of an anthropological approach to archaeology. This is because the story of Maya development has been assembled through a variety of anthropological (or anthropologically oriented) disciplines – linguistics, biological anthropology, ethnohistory, ethnology, epigraphy, art history, archaeology – and through a variety of theoretical tendencies within each of these disciplines. The changing conceptions of the Maya presented over time through these different disciplines constitute a veritable museum (or perhaps graveyard) of attitudes and concepts that have prevailed in anthropology over the last century or more.

Framing a study of the Maya to reach the non-specialist (as well as the Maya *aficionado*) is a worthwhile enterprise if it can be done in a way that avoids twin vices. At one end of the spectrum is the *exceptionalist* vice in which the pose is to emphasize the mystery or even the mystique of the Maya compared to other complex cultures (even those of neighboring northern Mesoamerica). At the other end of the spectrum is the *demistificationist* vice in which the pose is to emphasize how the Maya were really just like everyone else, and thus easily insertable into general typological schemes. I have found it a very useful goal to attempt to steer a course between these two poles of particularism and extreme generalization in order to appreciate the particular and generic aspects of ancient Maya polities. More widely viewed, these options are the kind that do emerge and require thinking about whenever specialists in any of the ancient civilizations attempt to present their concerns to a wider audience.

Within the Maya realm, why have I chosen to look at a case drawn from the Rosario Valley in southeastern Mexico? First of all, not much can be done about conceptual and methodological problems without coming to grips with a specific data set. In this case I was fortunate to have the opportunity to assemble such a data set by surveying this uniquely pristine part of the Mexican archaeological landscape, part of an area with extreme marginality after its florescence in the Classic Period (ending around AD 950). The valley and its surroundings had already benefited from studies covering a variety of themes, but not to the point of saturation or staleness. The Rosario Valley itself turned out to have an excellently preserved single-period settlement record, allowing settlement survey and analysis to be stretched to the limit. For example, multiple analytical scales presented a wide set of analytical choices not usually available or exploited in other settlement studies of complex polities. Thus, for these and other reasons, the Rosario Valley provided me with a good and interesting set of materials for trying out a variety of the theoretical and methodological tools which can prove useful in studying ancient complex polities.

To turn these motivations into a formal study, I benefited greatly from the help of many people at various stages in the fieldwork, analysis, and writing. Permission to do the fieldwork was granted by the Instituto Nacional de Antropología e Historia in Mexico. I would like to thank the Institute's director, Enrique Florescano M.; the president of the Consejo Nacional de Arqueología, Joaquín García-Bárcena; and the director of the Dirección de Monumentos Prehispánicos, Angel García Cook, for their gracious help.

Funding and logistical support for the fieldwork were generously provided by the New World Archaeological Foundation (NWAF), the Wenner-Gren Foundation, the Rackham School of Graduate Studies (University of Michigan), and the J. B. Griffin Fund (Museum of Anthropology, University of Michigan). I owe a special debt to the NWAF and to its archaeological staff, Gareth Lowe, Thomas Lee, Pierre Agrinier, Susannah Ekholm, and John Clark, for making it possible to explore the archaeological record of Chiapas to whose understanding they are contributing so much. Thomas Lee especially was helpful and supportive in seeing that the day-to-day running of the project proceeded smoothly, and I thank him for lending his expertise and experience. I owe special thanks to Pierre Agrinier for his constant help and support, for his generous hospitality in San Cristóbal, for his providing the initial opportunities to work in the Rosario Valley, and especially for his friendship.

In the field, I received excellent and always cheerful help from Vicente Pérez Calvo who acted as foreman. I would like to thank him and also the numerous residents of Colonia Chihuahua, Colonia Guadalupe Zapote, Ranchería Santa Marta, and the various smaller ranches in the Rosario Valley who assisted in the survey. More generally, I would like to thank the people of the Rosario Valley for their tolerance in allowing us to walk over their lands. Also assisting in the fieldwork were Nicholas James and Catherine Starr, whose contributions were critically important. I want to thank them for their tireless efforts and for putting up with often difficult conditions. Catherine Starr's contribution was indispensable, not only in the fieldwork, but also at earlier and later stages in the research, and I would like to thank her for generously giving her time and talents.

During the laboratory studies in San Cristóbal, Chiapas, I received valuable help from the NWAF's photographer, Ray Scippa, and from the NWAF's draftsperson, Elizabeth Ross. I also received capable help in processing the ceramics from Artemio Villalobos and from John Lee. Finally, I want to thank John Clark for supervising the analysis of the lithic artifacts.

With particular reference to the initial writing up, I am thankful for the patient and invaluable advice received from the members of my doctoral committee at the University of Michigan: Joyce Marcus, Jeffrey R. Parsons, Kent V. Flannery, and John W. Eadie. I am also grateful for the interest and insightful comments of Henry T. Wright. I owe a special debt to the chairperson of my committee, Joyce Marcus, for her tireless efforts in guiding and encouraging me throughout my graduate studies. While at the University of Michigan, I was able to develop an appreciation for the more appealing intellectual traits of anthropology by studying with these and several other masters of the discipline.

My graduate studies were funded by the Social Sciences and Humanities Research Council (Canada) and by the University of Michigan, for which I am extremely grateful. The final writing was done while working as a Research Officer at the Center of Latin American Studies at the University of Cambridge. I would like to thank its director, David Brading, and the staff, for providing a friendly and interesting work environment.

At various times, I have benefited greatly from discussing various aspects of the research presented here with the above mentioned members of the archaeological staff at the NWAF, and also with Sonia Rivero, Carlos Alvarez, Alejandro Martinez, Manuel Gándara, Barbara Voorhies, Janine Gasco, Nicholas James, Catherine Starr, Michael Blake, and Jeremy Sabloff. I especially want to thank Jeremy Sabloff for taking the time to read and comment on an earlier draft of my book.

Particularly during the final writing stages, my sense of anthropological archaeology and its alternatives has been greatly enriched through contacts with the members of the Department of Archaeology at the University of Cambridge. I feel privileged to have been a part of this lively scholarly community. I also received valuable advice and patient guidance from the editors at Cambridge University Press with a view to sharpening the study's scope and improving its readability. In this respect I am particularly grateful to the archaeology editor, Peter Richards.

As always, none of the people mentioned above should be held accountable for any deficiencies or obscurities in this study. For these I assume sole responsibility.

1

Studying ancient complex polities

The study of political structure in ancient complex polities exercises a powerful attraction on archaeologists working in Mesoamerica and many other parts of the world. Intense interest and energy are invested in trying to describe and understand complex polities which are ancient or traditional in the sense that they often predate and always differ from modern European nation-states (Southall 1965; Giddens 1985). Before proceeding with a study of politics in one or more ancient complex polities, pausing to look at the general reasons for the attraction of such studies proves instructive since these reasons directly affect problem orientation, theory, and methodology. Reasons for studying ancient complex polities revolve around four broad themes: the evocation of great questions (origins of the state, complexity, civilization); the use of data and concepts from political anthropology; the problems encountered in constructing analogies (models); and the vigorous effort and reasoning required for constructing bridging arguments to link theoretical concepts and archaeological data. A number of approaches may be adopted with reference to these four broad themes. My own approach is one of bias in favor of anthropological archaeology which combines a comparative search for general principles with an (intellectual) respect for diversity in political structure and behavior. Such an approach lies towards the relatively more fruitful middle ground of a spectrum. At one end are the highly generalizing approaches in the archaeology of ancient complex societies which deal in political universals and sweeping conclusions about the human condition. At the other end of the spectrum are the highly particularistic approaches which refuse to deal with any comparative generalization and limit themselves to descriptions of single ancient complex polities or cultures.

The first attraction of ancient complex polities as a subject of study is that they provide substantive case material for commenting on some of the seemingly evergreen great questions in anthropology. Such great questions concern the origins of inequality (ranking), the origins of the state, the origins of complexity, the origins of civilization, and the rise and fall of cultures (Service 1975; Steward 1949; Wright 1977, 1986; Wolf 1982; Renfrew and Cherry eds. 1986). Many of these questions are rooted in earlier nineteenth-century concerns with progress and social evolution. Continued concern with these issues on the part of many archaeologists may reflect either academic inertia, at worst, or a conscious desire to continue in an academic tradition, at best. Either way, these concerns are in clear reciprocal relationship with inertia in non-academic political and social thinking on these matters. This consists of the teleological ethnocentrism concerning civilization and development found in nations of the developed world or the teleological dependency thinking concerning the same issues found in the developing world. But the great questions also endure in and around archaeology because some of the subjects they touch on have (often unacknowledged) links to sociopolitical issues of more currently fashionable academic interest. Such issues concern the individual and totalitarianism, social justice, inequalities among nations and classes, and so forth. They are the issues that mobilize radical anti-evolutionist approaches – critical Marxism, post-structuralism, world systems (core-periphery) models, and structuration theory from sociology (Friedman and Rowlands 1977; Miller and Tilley eds. 1984; Spriggs ed. 1984; Hodder 1986; Giddens 1984, 1985).

Thus, on the one hand the great questions can be attractive because they lend the weight of academic precedent to the archaeological enterprise concerning ancient complex polities. On the other hand, the great questions, slightly reformatted, are attractive because they seem to lend current, radical, and wide extradisciplinary relevance to archaeological studies of power and politics in the past. Whatever the underlying reasons, a desire to resolve the great questions as an impetus for studies of ancient complex polities is open to challenge. For one thing, the great questions themselves need much more rethinking and analytical breaking down than they have received. For example, the primary focus on origins in so many of the great questions is rooted in the evolutionary idea of unfolding models of change (Giddens 1984). That a polity's later development is implicit in and must be understood in its earliest form is a doubtful idea which introduces an inappropriately high degree of determinism into models for human history. Ancient complex polities need not be understood only in terms of their remote or pristine origins. The interest and worth of studies of ancient complex polities cannot be measured in terms of their degree of temporal and spatial proximity to the pristine origins of political complexity. Rather, the quality of evidence and the quality of the thinking applied to that evidence are what underlies a study's interest and worth. It is for these reasons that studying late prehispanic Inca political structure and organization in the Central Andes is much more interesting than studying pristine Andean state formation in the Early Intermediate Period. Similarly, studies of the operation of the late prehispanic Aztec polity in Central Mexico evoke a much richer and more interesting set of political puzzles than any studies of the pristine origins of the Mesoamerican state during the Formative Period. Finally, the same applies to Maya politics and settlement which are of interest here. The relatively well-documented and vigorously thought-about workings of complex Classic Maya polities are more interesting to grapple with than the dimly perceived and conceptualized Formative origins of Maya political complexity.

It is also mistaken to adhere closely to the great questions if these lead to the idea that ancient complex polities can only be studied in terms of their relentless transformation from one developmental stage to another. This idea is part of the tyranny of process in which archaeology is viewed as an exclusively diachronic discipline whose sole aim is to chart and explain changes (usually major structural changes in the case of ancient complex polities). As I hope to show through a study of Maya politics and settlement, it is at least as interesting and perhaps more intellectually challenging to construct a study of the more stable structural aspects of ancient complex polities.

Resolving the great questions as an impetus for constructing studies of ancient complex polities is also questionable in the sense that it leads to austere or overgeneralized problem orientation. The simplistic questions which are asked fail to do justice to the richness of available case materials or to the complexity of the puzzles that these present. In fact, a focus on great questions by archaeologists or anthropologists is unnecessarily passive since the great questions are in large part received from outside their disciplines. That is, in their most abstract forms the great questions tend to revolve around general philosophical issues of interest to Western intellectuals and educated laypersons, issues concerning free will and the individual and society. The practice and subject matter of archaeology–anthropology suggests that a passive approach to problem orientation which takes all of its cues from such general philosophical issues is ethnocentric to the point of becoming uninteresting. The non-anthropological discussions lack cross-cultural perspective and rely on essentialist assertions about human nature or else reductionist studies about human capability (e.g., those relating decision-making to brain capacity). On the other hand, the anthropological discipline has to deal with a bewildering diversity of trajectories and political arrangements in human history. These cannot be captured effectively or understood by the broad generalizations about human behavior and institutions found in the great questions. Concerning ancient complex polities, the basis for anthropological archaeology's greatest independent contributions is its ability to document variability in political arrangements, including forms no longer available for study by non-archaeological means.

A second, more positively attractive reason for anthropological archaeologists to study ancient complex polities is that it requires them to delve into political anthropology, one of anthropology's most fertile and interesting subfields. Still relatively underappreciated by archaeologists, political anthropology incorporates within itself practically the full range of social science interpretive frameworks – Marxism, transactional or action theory, structural-functionalism, structuralism, symbolics/semiotics, world systems, cultural ecology – and applies these to extremely varied case material. Compared to a study formulated in terms of the great questions, an anthropological-archaeological study of ancient complex polities which draws on political anthropology has two advantages. First, such a study can better deal with differences as opposed to similarities in political arrangements. Second, it draws on a subdiscipline which is unparalleled in confronting theoretical generalizations about politics, with the widest possible range of documented political structures (institutions) and organizations (behaviors). From my own perspective, these are key advantages for the study of Maya politics where overgeneralization or extreme particularism present clear dangers.

Whether one takes generalizing (great question) or more particularizing (political anthropology) approaches to politics, a third reason that archaeological study of ancient complex polities is appealing is that it raises technically interesting problems concerning analogy (Chapter 2). Analogies are equated here with models or conceptual constructs (of varying complexity) to be confronted against archaeological evidence. Beyond general philosophical aspects (Wylie 1985), the technical problems concern practical aspects of how analogical reasoning can be used to best effect in constructing an anthropological–archaeological argument. Criteria for construction and then application of analogies have to be considered and justified.

The selection and defence of different kinds of substantive (anthropological or historical) analogies presents interesting problems. Substantive analogies may vary widely in their degree of abstraction. At one extreme are relatively specific analogies incorporating single political cases (or institutions). When applied in a direct-historical framework (Steward 1942), such analogies are part of a particularistic approach. Towards the middle of the range are analogies which include composites of political cases informed by moderately abstract political principles. Towards the generalizing extreme of the range are those analogies containing theoretically quite abstract general principles (often only loosely related to either politics or anthropology).

Often ignored as a problem is the justification required for what can be called extradisciplinary theoretical analogies. These are models brought in from non-archaeological or non-anthropological theories. Applications to archaeological analysis of principles from locational geography, information theory, micro-economics, literary criticism, ecology, semiotics, and so forth all require that their substantive relevance to the study of ancient complex polities be defended and not just asserted (Charlton 1981: 130).

When using substantive analogies, archaeologists often push the theoretical component of the case material far into the background. The case material, ethnographic or historical description and interpretation, is treated as a source of relatively raw data. Given the many possibilities and ambiguities associated with the anthropological study of complex polities, to use substantive ethnographic (or historical) interpretive reports as raw data is to assume wrongly that the relation between theory and data is less problematic for ethnographers (or historians) than it is for archaeologists. If one wants to construct and use these kinds of substantive analogies, it makes most sense to inform oneself about the theoretical and methodological issues (and uncertainties) surrounding the ethnographic or historical research that produced the material from which the analogy is drawn. Needless to say, this imposes huge extra efforts on the archaeologist. But these efforts must be interesting for anthropological archaeologists since they go so close to the core of anthropological subject matter.

At the abstractly theoretical end of the spectrum, over-reductionism in constructing analogies becomes a difficulty to be wrestled with. Reductionism problems are especially clear in the use of biological analogies, but not limited to these, as reductionism can become problematic in any broadly generalizing approach (Marxist, structuralist, cultural evolutionist, world-system, or peer polity).

For anthropological archaeology, less generalizing approaches at a more middle range of abstraction are preferable since they stress the institutional variability of political arrangements in human history (examples are structural functionalist, symbolic, or Weberian approaches). Such middle range approaches better avoid the main flaws of reductionism which are triteness and overemphasis on apparent similarities between cases. The contrast between the two classes of approaches is akin to the familiar one between formalism in economic anthropology which emphasizes universals of economic behavior (Halpernin 1985) and substantivism which stresses the variable institutional matrix of the economy (Halpernin 1984).

A focus on the technical problems of constructing analogies (models) may seem less aesthetically pleasing than a focus on well-turned, finished analogies because it interposes considerable legwork before resounding conclusions can be arrived at. However, for those archaeologists who have an intellectual curiosity about how studies are put together rather than a more utilitarian interest in the end product or formal conclusions of such studies, such problems must be of central interest. The formulation of appropriate variables for a study of politics in ancient complex polities is difficult and needs careful thought. Rather than sketching another model for the Maya, the subsequent study of Maya politics and settlement gives extended attention to the conceptualization of political structure and organization (Chapter 2). To advance this kind of enterprise, general programmatic statements in political anthropology provide a helpful guide, confronting high-flown theoretical generalization about political behavior with the particulars of detailed cross-cultural institutional and behavioral case studies (Easton 1959; Winckler 1969; Cohen 1979; Vincent 1978; Goody 1966). On a more specific level, theoretically well-turned case studies in political anthropology are useful for the same reasons (references in Chapter 2).

A fourth and final source of attraction to the study of ancient complex polities consists of the archaeologically fascinating methodological problems of measuring variables on the archaeological record. Ideally, from an anthropological–archaeological viewpoint, such methodological problems should loom into view most clearly once anthropological problem orientations have been set and theoretical models have been formulated. Less ideally, from a more narrowly archaeological position of strict empiricism, focused primarily on the archaeological record and its properties, such methodological problems may precede and altogether swamp theoretical problems. Implicitly following the path of least resistance, most of the work on methodological bridging arguments (or middle range theory – Binford 1977) has been carried out with reference to less complex societies. Consequently, the construction of bridging arguments for theoretical issues concerning ancient complex polities remains a wide-open field (Sabloff 1983). My study of Maya politics and settlement is closely connected to this methodological theme. It explores various ways in which sociopolitical variables can be documented in a complex multiscale archaeological settlement record.

Opposed options for developing bridging arguments concerning ancient complex polities involve differing degrees of generalization. The more generalizing options seek to develop relatively invariant rules for relating political (or other) behavior to archaeological remains, either through cross-cultural analysis (Johnson 1978, 1982; Feinman and Neitzel 1984) or through actualistic studies (Hayden and Cannon 1984). A more particularizing option, adopted here, is one which seeks to treat each case on its own merits, attempting to justify assumptions about the relation between political behavior and material culture by drawing on direct-historical materials to delimit the range of possibilities. As before, with reference to the dangers of reductionism in model building, the contrast between generalizing and particularizing approaches to constructing bridging arguments is akin to that between formalist and substantivist positions in economic anthropology.

To sum up the arguments so far, there are four general reasons why a study of political structure in ancient complex polities proves interesting and ultimately worthwhile. On a substantive and general-interest plane, the first two reasons concern the widely captivating great questions that can be addressed by looking at such polities, and the political anthropology-aided ability to document a wide variety of political regimes. The last two reasons are of more technical interest to specialist practitioners. These reasons concern the anthropologically interesting conceptual difficulties associated with constructing analogies (or models) and the archaeologically interesting methodological challenge of relating models to an archaeological record.

The last two reasons are of particular interest to archaeologists who keep an open mind about their craft and like to think that the varied means of formulating a question and arriving at an answer are worth discussing and exploring. One way of examining such theoretical and methodological issues for ancient social and political systems is to survey the field from a relatively high vantage-point, with passing reference to a variety of cases as brief illustration for the points made (Johnson 1977; Wright 1977; Ammerman 1981; Trigger 1974; Haas 1981, 1982; Hodder 1982:ch. 6; Renfrew 1986). A second way of approaching many of the same issues is to construct a sustained piece of substantive archaeological research and give detailed attention to the conceptual and methodological problems that arise at each stage of the enterprise (Cowgill *et al.* 1984). If the second kind of approach is properly handled, with a measure of self-criticism and an honest exposure of choices, ambiguities, and lacunae in the research process, the general conceptual and methodological problems faced by any archaeologist attempting to understand an ancient complex polity come into view quite clearly, even though filtered through the particular mesh of the specific case examined. The efforts required to shape theoretical questions and to construct relevant analogies are best appreciated in this kind of approach because of the clear grounding in a specific subject matter and research tradition and the need to reconcile this with more general concepts from anthropology (or other disciplines). Also best appreciated in this kind of approach are the practical difficulties and ambiguities associated with confronting ideas and evidence, because of the sustained attention to detail. In contrast, such appreciations are not available generally in a high-vantage survey whose hit-and-run nature militates against critically understanding the full complexity of each example that hurtles past the reader.

In light of these considerations, I have adopted the second approach, using a case study in Maya settlement archaeology to explore and develop some more widely relevant conceptual and methodological themes concerning ancient complex polities. The case study is based on a settlement survey carried out in the Rosario Valley, within the Upper Grijalva Tributaries of Chiapas, Mexico (Figures 1-2; de Montmollin 1985a, 1985b, 1987, n.d.a). In brief, the analysis of settlement patterns characterizes the political structure and organization of the Rosario polity which occupied the valley in the Late/Terminal Classic Period, AD 700-950 (Figure 3). The term *polity* designates a broadly autonomous political entity (Renfrew 1986: 2), with complex state-like political structure. Further details concerning the Rosario polity are provided subsequently (Chapter 3), followed by detailed settlement analysis (Chapters 5–10).

Before turning to the Rosario polity, I continue in a general vein with several further questions concerning problem orientation in studies of ancient political structure. These questions are framed in terms of Maya (and Mesoamerican) studies, but clearly appear in one form or another in many studies of politics and settlement in ancient complex polities. All attempts to formulate archaeological (settlement) studies of Maya political structure immediately run into several interesting conceptual difficulties and choices relating to problem formulation. These concern: analytical scale and level of synthetic generalization; conceptualization of the relation between environmental, economic, settlement, and political variables; and use of bundled continua of variation as opposed to societal typologies in order to conceptualize polities.

A difficult conceptual choice concerns the analytical scale and level of synthetic generalization at which political structure is best characterized. One approach to formulating Lowland Maya political structure has characterized it synthetically, using a very broad brush indeed. This approach deals with Maya political structure in general, as it existed throughout the entire Maya culture (linguistic) area. The characteristics of Maya political structure are reconstructed synthetically by combining scraps of evidence from a variety of sites and localities, on the assumption that political arrangements were broadly similar throughout the culture area. More often than not, the high level of generalization has been required in order to compare Maya to Central Mexican Highland political structure, viewed in an equally synthetic fashion (Sanders and Price 1968; Coe 1961; Wolf 1959). Such an approach has provided valuable comparative insights into the peculiarities of Maya developments in a Mesoamerican context, with the contrasting environments of the Mesoamerican Lowlands and Highlands often playing a large role in the interpretations.

Another approach has given much closer (often particularistic) attention to developments in Maya civilization, largely dispensing with comparisons to the Mesoamerican Highlands, but occasionally bringing into view contrasts among the regional subdivisions within the Maya culture area (Culbert ed. 1973; Adams ed. 1977; Ashmore ed. 1981; Sabloff and Andrews eds. 1986). While it uses a finer brush, the second approach resembles the first in its synthetic quality and use of ideal types. My own study of Maya settlement and politics is similar to this in the sense that the analytical scale has been shifted downward. But compared to the second approach, the analytical scale is even more tightly defined as an individual Maya polity. Additionally, a focus on analysis of the polity's internal variability contrasts sharply with the synthetic reconstructions of political structure that prevail in Maya studies. Such synthetic reconstructions occur at any one of several analytical scales: the whole culture area; a (large) subdivision of the area (Ashmore ed. 1981: fig. 2.1); and a single site (possibly with its sustaining area). Interestingly, the polity scale of analysis is touched on relatively rarely in a systematic way. The non-synthetic single-polity approach which I advocate and use is designed to contribute to an eventual shift in larger scale research emphasis away from synthetic (or patchwork) ideal-type reconstructions. The aim is to move towards a more analytical or variation-sensitive controlled comparison (Eggan 1954) among Maya polities, or indeed among political entities at both larger and smaller scales (entities such as districts within polities or alliances of several polities). Therefore, the approach which I favor is focused relatively specifically in its analytical scale, but not ultimately non-comparative (in a nominalist sense).

A second conceptual difficulty in formulating a study of Maya political structure concerns whether or not to use a chain of reasoning which specifies that environment determines subsistence which determines settlement which determines political structure. Many discussions of the Maya have relied implicitly on such an ecologically determinist form of reasoning, recognizable as part of the mainstream cultural–ecological approach (Blanton 1983). In compressed (and idealized) form, the sequence of arguments runs as follows. One begins by determining the demographic and productive possibilities of the reconstituted ancient environment at a given level of technology (usually with estimations of carrying capacities). From this, one determines the likely nature of the settlement system, almost always by inferring least-effort or cost-benefit logic among the individual settlers. Finally, one deduces from the causally prior environmental and settlement factors the size, complexity, and integration permitted the political system. For brevity, this chain of reasoning can be referred to as the *environmental to political chain of reasoning*. Variations on the environmental to political chain of reasoning have underlain many broad scale and synthetic characterizations of Maya political structure, its developing complexity, its ongoing operation, and its tendency to collapse. An early and still striking example is one side of the polemic about whether or not complex civilization could develop and endure in a tropical-forest setting, the idea that Maya civilization was doomed to failure because of the deficiencies of its environmental setting (Meggers 1954). Several discussions concerning social stratification and urbanism have used the same chain of reasoning (Coe 1961; Kurjack 1974; Webb 1973; Haviland 1966a, 1968; Vogt 1964a; Sanders and Price 1968).

An a priori reason for mistrusting the environmental to political chain of reasoning is that it has a virtually built-in tendency to attribute disproportionate explanatory importance to the environmental head of the chain. Following from this, a privileged place is given to environmental, demographic, and agronomic questions. This severely skews the problem orientation and prejudges the relative importance of environmental, demographic, agronomic, settlement, political, and other variables in the operation of ancient complex societies.

Viewed in terms of methodology, the environmental to political chain of reasoning clearly moulds itself to schemes which assign increasing levels of difficulty for archaeological interpretation as one moves up a ladder of inference leaning against a layer cake of environmental, subsistence, sociopolitical, and ideological spheres (Hawkes 1954). However one may feel about the validity of such schemes, it is ironic that due to the trends of Maya research history and the qualities of the Maya archaeological record, we probably have fuller archaeological evidence bearing on the more difficult rungs of the ladder. More poorly supported speculation is required for reconstructing Maya subsistence and economy than is required for reconstructing aspects of Maya political structure and even ideology. Reinforcing this is the possibility of supplementing archaeological evidence with epigraphic and ethnohistoric sources, which provide lines of evidence that generally bear more closely and usefully on ideological and sociopolitical matters than they do on questions of subsistence and environment. Thus, using the environmental to political chain of reasoning in this case fails to do practical justice to the nature and the relative strengths of the evidence. But the issue goes beyond just playing or not playing to the strengths of the evidence. Even if one were to concede the theoretical ground to some form of techno-environmental determinism and grant the validity of operating with such a chain of independent and dependent variables, dependent variables still have to be as fully studied as independent variables. Because this has not been done, political structure has received somewhat cursory treatment, at least in part because of implicit or explicit placement at the dependent end of the environmental to political chain of reasoning.

In light of this, while developing a problem orientation, I have chosen to avoid most of the tactics associated with the environmental to political chain of reasoning. Instead, I focus first and foremost on political problems and variables, as they can be understood through a study of the settlement record. For a Classic Maya polity (and for many other ancient complex polities), a reasonable supposition is that political structure and organization powerfully determines settlement patterning, rather than the other way around. This supposition will be discussed subsequently (Chapter 5). If one accepts it for the moment, its implication is that political themes cannot be addressed as a simple by-product of a study of environment acting on subsistence acting on settlement.

A third choice in developing a problem orientation concerns whether to use societal typologies or continua of variation to conceptualize polities. In brief, my argument is that the societal typologies often used in Maya and Mesoamerican studies are best avoided. This is not for reasons of particularism, but because of the clumsiness of the typological approach for characterizing polities and studying political questions. The alternative approach selected here uses *bundled continua of variation*. This involves evaluating a polity in terms of the positions it occupies along a series of thematically related continua of variation (Easton 1959). Continua of variation are aligned with reference to higher-order social theoretical principles. Analytical variable-by-variable study is emphasized, rather than synthetic type building. The continua of variation selected here cover the following subject matter: polities of segmentary and unitary tendencies, pyramidal and hierarchical political regimes, dimensions of variation in political stratification systems, mechanical and organic modes of economic solidarity, and segmenting and non-segmenting political organizations (Table 1). The contrast between bundled continua and societal types for conceptualizing polities is an essential one in archaeological studies of ancient complex polities, arising at or near the outset of the research process and strongly shaping subsequent methods, analyses, and conclusions. Because of this importance the reasons for choosing bundled continua of variation instead of societal typologies require detailed discussion (see Chapter 2).

2

Thinking about Maya political structure

Societal typologies

An effective study of political structure and organization[1] in ancient complex polities cannot go very far without a good initial conceptualization of such polities. Societal typologies or bundled continua of variation are two principal approaches to meeting this requirement. Along with other Americanist archaeologists, students of Maya politics have usually opted for the first approach. There are numerous attempts to classify Maya sociopolitical systems as belonging to one or another societal type. Some have tried to decide whether the Maya had theocratic as opposed to secular-militaristic government (Wolf 1959; Webster 1976a). Contrasts are drawn between theocratic (lowland) Maya and secular-militaristic (highland) Central Mexican cultures or between the theocratic Classic Maya and the secular-militaristic Postclassic Maya. Others have adopted a cultural-evolutionary typology (Service 1971), discussing whether the Maya had a chiefdom or a state level of development, and trying to determine when and why the shift from one to the other might have occurred (Sanders and Price 1968; Marcus 1976). Whether the Maya had an urban or non-urban form of civilization has also intrigued Mayanists (Haviland 1966a; Kurjack 1974) as has the question of whether the Maya had egalitarian, ranked, or stratified social structure (Rathje 1973; Haviland 1966b; Vogt 1983). An energy-capture view of cultural evolution has been used to categorize the Classic Maya as a Low Energy Society, contrastable with High Energy Societies in Central Mexico (Sidrys 1978). Other studies have placed the Maya in a Durkheimian typological framework, contrasting the Maya's mechanically solidary socioeconomic system with organically solidary socioeconomic systems and contrasting *societas* with *civitas* (Coe 1961, 1965). Finally, there have been attempts to class the Maya as a feudal type of social organization, contrasted with centralized or bureaucratic societies (Adams and Smith 1981).

How do the various societal-typology approaches deal with change or stability in Maya political structure and organization? There are three major approaches to the theme. One approach equates developmental change with the movement from one type to another. Examples are the change from ranked to stratified society and the change from chiefdom to state during the Classic Period. Another example is the change from a Classic theocratic orientation to a more secular-militaristic (even mercantile) Postclassic orientation (Wolf 1959; Rathje 1975). A final example is the transition from vacant Classic ceremonial centers to (Mexican-influenced) Postclassic urban centers. A second approach to Maya political structure stresses its stability, for example, the Genetic Model of Maya cultural development (Vogt 1964a). From a perspective emphasizing stability, Maya society continues to be typed as theocratic, non-urban, chiefdom-like, and mechanically solidary, but without changing from one type to another. Studies that stress Maya immutability often do so in order to contrast it with relatively greater dynamism and propensity for change in Highland Mesoamerican politics. Thus, Maya immutability is relative rather than absolute. A third typological approach for relating Maya political structure to change or stability proposes a cycling from relatively large and complex forms of political structure to relatively small and simple forms, and back again. Such non-linear cyclical interpretations are the most interesting, being based on an appreciation of Postclassic ethnohistoric sources (Freidel 1983a; Farriss 1984) or African analogs (Sanders 1981: 367–369).

In general, societal typologies operate at a high level of cross-cultural abstraction. The types are so idealized, simplistic, and categorical that much variability has to be suppressed (Service 1971; Fried 1967; Friedman and Rowlands 1977; Claessen and Skalnik eds. 1978). For example, in studies comparing the Maya Lowlands and Central Mexican Highlands, Maya political structure is characterized in an extremely broad manner, with uniformity across the Maya area (Sanders and Price 1968; Coe 1961). This gives useful comparative insights into the broad lines of evolutionary developments in the starkly contrasting environments of the Mesoamerican Lowlands and Highlands. But use of highly generalizing societal typologies in such studies is a barrier to understanding synchronic and diachronic variability among the polities involved.

In contrast to such broad brush abstraction, recent comparative efforts by Mesoamericanists have taken advantage of an increase in archaeological and environmental information to produce more detailed and dynamic comparisons of changing structure and organization in smaller more tightly defined areas. The salient example is a comparative study of prehispanic change in the Maya Lowlands, Oaxaca, and Highland Mexico (Blanton *et al.* 1981). This study tries to deal with specific polities rather than broad culture areas (as homelands for civilizations). Naturally enough, this study also shifts the emphasis away from trying to discover whether the polities belong to a small number of fixed societal types and onto a consideration of the polities' internal variability along several dimensions of variation. Besides this comparative study, a few single-region studies feature a similar focus on specific polities rather than culture areas, and on continua of variation rather than societal types (Blanton *et al.* 1982 for the Valley of Oaxaca; and Steponaitis 1981 for the Formative Valley of Mexico).

A review of the several general conceptual difficulties associated with societal typologies drives home the point that these are not a particularly effective tool for formulating research concerning ancient politics.

For comparative purposes, whole political systems hardly can be classified in the relatively straightforward way that some archaeological artifacts can be classified. Much greater difficulties arise in isolating, defining, and measuring attribute levels of a society as compared to a projectile point. While this is self-evident to the point of triteness, one still senses that among Mayanists and other Americanists there has been a (varying) degree of implicit projection of a typological mode of thinking developed for artifacts into societal classification (most clearly evident in MacNeish's comparison of Mesoamerican societal types – 1981).

Simply locating a society's boundaries to treat it as a unit for classification is difficult. This is in large part an analytical scale problem. Variables of interest for political analysis may operate at different scales and no all-purpose fixed units of analysis have a priori meaningfulness independent of the particular political (or other) variables selected for study. Perhaps for the sake of convenience, scale of study problems are glossed over in societal typological approaches. In any case, such problems may be insoluble when multivariate societal types include a blend of variables operating at different scales.

A tendency in societal typologies to reify society rather than treat it as a collection of persons and groups can cause problems, especially for political analysis (a point raised by Cowgill 1975; Webster 1976a; and others). When an entire social system or subsystem is treated as a monolithic entity for policy and decision-making purposes it becomes difficult to conceptualize the cleavages, oppositions, and accommodations among people and groups which are at the core of political analysis. In fairness, societal reification problems, associated with a position of methodological holism (Ahmed 1976), are not peculiar to societal-typology approaches. Methodological holism also weakens systems and structuralist thinking. Yet, reification problems are intractable particularly in societal typologies because of the classification and characterization of whole societies which are treated as actors in a play.

Even less helpful is the elevation of societal types from parts of an heuristically useful analytical step to an end in themselves. Such an unwarranted reification of the types occurs when identifying chiefdoms or states becomes the central research problem. This tendency is fueled by methodologically-oriented programmatic discussions of all-purpose archaeological correlates for such types (Peebles and Kus 1977; Crumley 1976).

Societal typologies require categorical (polar) thinking. This is a limiting way to conceptualize what may often turn out to be a continuum of variation in variable values between polar extremes (Easton 1959: 239; Steponaitis 1981: 321; and others). To allow detection of continuous as well as discontinuous variation it makes more sense to treat each of the constituent variables in a societal type in terms of continua of variation rather than polar-opposite categories. If variation turns out to be discontinuous (categorical), this can still be detected in the form of clustering along a continuum.

Within a societal-typology framework, it becomes all too easy to identify a set of contrasting types in a temporal sequence and then to be at a loss to deal with the mechanisms and events associated with the change from one type to another (McGuire 1983: 92). In fairness, such a problem is not unique to societal typologies, but has to do with the more general problems associated with using static time-segments to deal with processual problems (Plog 1973).

Some societal-typology approaches entail automatic causal independence for physical-environmental variables outside the political system. This makes it difficult to appreciate processes within the system or to evaluate how independent or dependent political variables might be. Techno-environmental determinism results when the typological approach is applied to political phenomena and not to physical-environmental phenomena since the inability to deal with continuous change is limited to the political phenomena. To avoid being forced into this position, one must abandon purely typological approaches for dealing with political structure. Alternatively, to get around the inability to monitor continuous (or discontinuous) political change without necessarily abandoning societal typology, one might consider Catastrophe Theory (Renfrew 1978). Continuous change in sociopolitical variable states is seen to lead to relatively sudden shifts in societal structure. Radically different archaeological patterns (equated with different societal types) in successive archaeological periods can be said to have undergone an internal catastrophe process, without necessary pressure from extra-societal environmental factors. Renfrew has illustrated this reasoning with reference to the Classic Maya collapse (Renfrew 1978: 212–215).

Societal types are defined by reference to variables and their particular levels. States have the following variable levels: specialized government with a monopoly of force, (economically) stratified society, a market-based exchange system, and a given minimum population size. Chiefdoms have the following variable levels: redistributive economy, ranked society, ancestor worship, and rulership lacking a monopoly of force (Flannery 1972; Service 1971). The variables cover a wide range of phenomena, although for states and chiefdoms it is reasonable to expect that they should fall within the general province of politics. To form part of a coherent type, the variable levels must be functionally related to one another. When types are treated as received entities, their descriptions are used as *real* definitions. A real definition "begins with a concept...that is somehow received from the cultural milieu and is then explored – we try to define it properly" (Service 1985: 226). Variable levels in the type definitions can be assumed to co-vary. To take just one example, whether an economically stratified social structure necessarily entails a specialized government with a monopoly of force is not treated as a research question. The relations, because they are built into the real type definitions, become parts of monolithic explananda (Steponaitis 1981: 321). How invariant relations are taken to be depends on how widely (cross-culturally) one applies the typology. As noted by increasing numbers of archaeologists, empirical variability in ancient complex political arrangements suggests that the several variable levels in existing multivariate societal types will not necessarily co-vary in the way specified by the type definition (Blanton *et al.* 1981: 23; Wenke 1981: 86; Athens 1977: 357, 361; Feinman and Neitzel 1984: 77, 78; Dunnell 1980: 47; Hill 1977: 100–101; Haas 1982: 12; Tainter 1977: 330–331; Sanders *et al.* 1979: 300–301; Coe 1974: 116–118; Hodder 1982: 153–154; and others). From this perspective, use of multivariate societal types eliminates potentially interesting research questions, leading to a kind of multivariate trap. The more variables in a type definition, the more damaging the trap. In other words, the richer and more polythetic the type, the more questions are eliminated from consideration.

One solution to difficulties raised by the multivariate trap is to work with types defined on the basis of the fewest possible variables (Hill and Evans 1972: 267–268; Hill 1977: 101; Sanders *et al.* 1979: 295–296). Chiefdoms and states may be distinguished according to their scale and number of components (Carneiro 1981), their levels of administrative hierarchy (Wright 1977), or their relative tendency to fission (Cohen 1981). It may be stressed that chiefdoms and states are political forms (as defined by Wright 1977) rather than more multivariately defined types of societies (Blanton *et al.* 1981: 23). Such solutions are analytically promising, taking us in the direction of eliminating the multivariate quality of societal types (but without wholly eliminating other problems associated with the typological approach).

Another way out of the multivariate trap is to proliferate types to better accommodate the variability of political arrangements in the ethnographic, historical, and archaeological record (Feinman and Neitzel 1984: 42–43). For example, the segmentary state type (Southall 1956) was developed to fill the middle ground between state and acephalous/segmentary political types (Fortes and Evans-Pritchard eds. 1940). Similarly, the chiefdom type (Service 1971) was designed to be inserted somewhere between earlier *societas* and *civitas* types (White 1959). Subsequently, others have tried to refine the early state as a societal type, producing the notions of inchoate, typical, and transitional early states (Claessen and Skalnik eds. 1978). Further types have been defined (with the aid of numerical taxonomy applied to an ethnographic sample) to better account for variability in African, as opposed to Polynesian, middle range hierarchical societies (Taylor 1975). The Polynesian chiefdom type has been variously subdivided (Sahlins 1958; Goldman 1970; Renfrew 1974; Helms 1979). Finally, complex and simple chiefdom types have been defined to account for variation near the boundary between chiefdom and state types (Sahlins 1968; Earle 1978; Steponaitis 1978; Peebles and Kus 1977). Typological refinement of this kind is helpful. It takes us some way towards continuum-oriented rather than categorical thinking about politics. However, the old and new types remain stoutly multivariate so that the multivariate trap continues to be a problem.

When using real multivariate societal-type definitions, it becomes legitimate to document only some of the attribute states, prior to inferring the existence of other definitionally appropriate states. The procedure is similar to reconstructing an animal's appearance from a fragment of its skeleton, but the parallel is quite specious. We do not have, and never will have, an osteology of societies or polities. While such extrapolation is convenient, it remains a specious solution for filling out a partial archaeological record (Yoffee 1979: 25; Feinman and Neitzel 1984: 44, 72; Tainter 1977: 330).

To balance against this litany of problems, a more optimistic view of the potential of societal typologies is that one day we will have worked out many more necessary relations among variable levels. This will then lead to deployment of a more airtight, exception-proof, and trustworthy set of well-defined societal types. But the discovery of ever more accurate societal types is not a captivating problem orientation. A more compelling research aim is to characterize political variables within polities and to investigate how these variables relate to one another (letting types fall where they may). This takes us from real to *nominal* definitions of political phenomena. A nominal definition "begins by first observing things and then classifying them – we give them names after observation"(Service 1985: 226; also Hill 1977: 100). In a wider sense, contrasting attitudes underlying the use of real versus nominal definitions for political phenomena match the attitudes underlying all-purpose versus problem-oriented typologies and strategies in archaeology (Hill and Evans 1972).

Still on an optimistic (but more minor) note, societal typologies have a useful heuristic function. They can guide the selection of appropriate comparative archaeological case material or analogies. But even this function is weakened by overly broad (catch-all) types which incorporate comparisons that are too generalizing to be interesting for anthropological archaeology.

To sum up, several difficulties make it advisable to avoid societal typologies when formulating studies of ancient complex polities. These difficulties concern: resistance of societies to typological analysis, choosing scale and locating boundaries for societal types, reification of society, reification of societal types, categorical thinking, conceptualizing processual change as a sudden jump from one fixed categorical type to another, a priori techno-environmental determinism, real definitions and elimination of research problems, and unwarranted extrapolation from documented variable levels to undocumented variable levels. Consequently, we had best avoid research problems that take the following form. Had polity X achieved a state type of sociopolitical structure by the end of period Y? How and why was statehood attained or not attained?

Bundled continua of variation

As we have seen, some difficulties are circumvented by breaking down multivariate societal types into their constituent variables and viewing these as continua of variation. This leads to an alternative and more useful conceptualization of social or political phenomena which can be referred to as *bundled continua of variation.* Using bundled continua of variation to characterize a polity is a departure in the study of ancient Maya politics. While societal typologies used heretofore to characterize ancient Maya political systems contain some interesting political variables, these variables have not been analytically separated and/or reconstituted as a number of continua bracketed by polar extremes (Table 1).

In an early overview of political anthropology, a political scientist, David Easton, has given the clearest general account of the need to use something like bundled continua of variation (Easton 1959). His approach is interesting for its generalizing aim to illuminate generic features of political structure and for its strong anti-typological strain. The latter clearly anticipates critical discussions of societal typologies by archaeologists. Easton criticized the pioneer typologizing of

Table 1. *Aligned continua of variation*

1	SEGMENTARY STRUCTURE	UNITARY STRUCTURE
a	decentralization	centralization
b	replication	differentiation
c	loose integration	tight integration
d	ascriptive relations (*societas*)	contractual relations (*civitas*)
e	upward delegation	downward delegation
2	PYRAMIDAL REGIME	HIERARCHICAL REGIME
3	GROUP STRATIFICATION	INDIVIDUAL STRATIFICATION
4	MECHANICAL SOLIDARITY	ORGANIC SOLIDARITY
5	SEGMENTING ORGANIZATION	NON-SEGMENTING ORGANIZATION

Africanists in which state versus acephalous political types were contrasted (Fortes and Evans-Pritchard eds. 1940). He also dismissed typological refinements such as the intermediate segmentary state type (Southall 1956). Had the cultural-evolutionary typology (Service 1971) been more visible at the time, Easton would no doubt have criticized it as well. The argument was not against classification as such, but rather against too simple dichotomous classifications based on presence/absence of traits and against rigid classifications masking interesting variability. Easton concluded that it was "useful to place phenomena on a continuum, with the expectation that to do so will make it possible to locate cluster points" (Easton 1959: 239). Recurring clusters of positions along the several continua of variation might emerge and reasons for these would have to be sought. Then, all the societies having shared clusters of positions could be classed together into types (Easton 1959: 239), if this were felt to be necessary.

Mesoamericanists will note a general resemblance between an Eastonian approach and approaches adopted for interpretations of Mesoamerican prehistory (Blanton *et al.* 1981, 1982; Kowalewski *et al.* 1983; Kowalewski and Finsten 1983; Steponaitis 1981). In looking at developments in the Basin of Mexico, the Valley of Oaxaca, and the Maya Lowlands, Blanton and others refer to three *core features* of human societies – scale, integration, and complexity (Blanton *et al.* 1981: 17–22). *Scale* has to do with the number of people incorporated or with the size of the area controlled in a society. *Integration* has to do with the interdependence (actual interchanges) or interconnectedness (potential interchanges) among units within a society. *Complexity* has to do with the extent to which there is functional differentiation among units in a society. These three core features are variables or continua of variation to be studied and measured separately. Levels for each variable are not assigned by definition in a series of polythetic types. Instead combinations of levels in any given society are a matter for investigation. Another study evaluates the relation of scale and boundary permeability to *centralization*. The latter is defined as "the degree to which activities were concentrated in one place" or "the relative amount of flow that is accounted for by a single node" (Kowalewski *et al.* 1983: 43, 35). Here one finds a good example of continuum-oriented thinking, in which the Monte Alban periods are arranged explicitly on a continuous scale of size, centralization, and permeability (Kowalewski *et al.* 1983: fig. 6). The scale ranges from small, centralized, and closed at one end to large, decentralized, and open at the other. Another example of continuum-oriented thinking, in an economic study of ancient Oaxaca, features many quite specific and concrete variables arranged so that their correlated end-states are aligned (Kowalewski and Finsten 1983: 424, table 5). These are then used to produce a scale of increasing political control (Kowalewski and Finsten 1983: 424, fig. 8). A final example of continuum-oriented thinking is the conceptual plan for Steponaitis' excellent study of Formative Period political evolution in the Valley of Mexico (Steponaitis 1981). In his own words:

> political complexity should (whenever possible) be viewed in terms of several analytically separate dimensions. In addition, I wish to show that it is archaeologically feasible to measure directly some of these dimensions along a continuous scale. Although the number of potentially relevant dimensions is large, I will focus on three in particular: (1) the number of levels in the political hierarchy, (2) the degree of centralization at the uppermost level, and (3) the relative amount of surplus food mobilized to support the political establishment. (Steponaitis 1981: 321)

The general reasoning behind these several studies closely resembles that which underlies my own approach. This consists of aligning several major continua of variation (Table 1). The emphasis at the problem-definition stage falls on analytical breakdown rather than moulding of synthetic multivariate types. Evidently, the specific contents and qualities of the variables selected for different studies will differ. The variables used here are not the only ones possible, but they are among the most interesting and accessible for a study of politics in the Rosario polity. Arranging the variables in a bundle of continua also provides a useful framework for comparing the Rosario polity to other Classic Maya polities. The continua touch on the following subject matter (Table 1). The segmentary-unitary continuum deals with the nature and inter-relation of a polity's constituent territorial units (or districts) and their leaders. The pyramidal–hierarchical continuum deals with the decision-making and implementing aspect of political structure. The stratification continuum deals with modes of access to strategic political positions. The mechanical–organic continuum focuses on economic and exchange factors, but it also concerns sociopolitically relevant degrees of conflict-dampening solidarity. Finally, the segmenting to non-segmenting continuum deals with the degree of cohesion among a polity's districts, especially as concerns the political problems of maintaining a polity's politico-territorial integrity and of dealing with its growth.

Beyond the specifics of the continua used (detailed below) the point of general interest for archaeologists studying ancient complex polities is that vigorous efforts are required for conceptualizing these polities. This involves a careful weighing of the relative advantages and disadvantages of alternative approaches such as societal typologies and bundled continua of variation.

When confronted with a bundle of continua of variation, a theoretically useful procedure is to posit which ones would tend to co-vary and specify why (Easton 1959: 239). A consensus of Grand Theory from Durkheimian British structural-functionalism and from North American cultural evolutionism suggests that the continua of variation treated here align themselves as shown in Table 1. Polar positions will co-occur and movement along one or more of the continua will eventually entail corresponding movement along other continua. If a diachronic perspective is available, on a settlement record from successive periods, one traces movement through time along the various continua, testing for theoretically expected inter-relations among changing continua. If a synchronic perspective is available, on a single-period settlement record, then one charts single positions along various continua, testing for theoretically expected co-occurrences of several variable states. The second procedure is most relevant to the Rosario polity's single-period settlement record. Most comparisons are made within the polity, at various territorial scales, rather than between archaeological periods. Further comparisons become possible between Rosario polity settlement and settlement in other polities.

A detailed exposition of the individual continua specifies the ways in which movements or specific positions along the various continua might relate functionally to one another. Additionally, interpretations of the continua presented here are set in a wider context by relating them to other programmatic approaches to political structure and to a range of concepts used in other studies of Maya and Meso-american political structure.

Segmentary and unitary polities
The first continuum, viewed from its extremes, entails a conceptual distinction between segmentary and unitary polities. The major difference is in the degree to which constituent territorial units (districts or provinces) and their inhabitants are differentiated and bound into a network with an important central hub. Three notable subcontinua are incorporated within the segmentary–unitary continuum. They concern degrees of centralization, differentiation, and integration (Chapters 5 and 6). With reference to the Rosario polity's settlement record, we can develop and use several measures of centralization (Chapter 5), differentiation (Chapter 6), and integration (Chapter 6). Two minor subcontinua concern the degree to which *societas* or *civitas* relations dominate politics and the degree to which authority is delegated upward or downward in a hierarchy. These subcontinua are more difficult to document in the settlement record (Chapters 8 and 5).

A segmentary polity has a loose aggregation of districts which are replications of one another in their political structure. Recasting this in terms of the three sub-continua, there are low degrees of centralization, differentiation, and integration. Segmentary political structure of this kind has been fully described for many African kingdoms (Southall 1965; Fortes 1953; Lloyd 1965; Fallers 1956; Mair 1977). A unitary polity has a more tightly integrated set of districts, which are often differentiated in their political structure. There are high degrees of centralization, differentiation, and integration. Such unitary political structure is most often found in Western nation-states (Southall 1965; Giddens 1985).

Association of replication with loose integration and of differentiation with tight integration derives from the Durkheimian contrast between mechanical and organic modes of solidarity (Durkheim 1933). To get a sense of what is involved in movement from one end of the continuum to the other, let us now consider some spatial factors. In a segmentary polity, authority is only slightly concentrated at the center and there are a number of nearly equivalent and competing authority subcenters. In a unitary polity, authority is clearly concentrated at the center and this central authority projects outward strongly and evenly over the entire polity (Southall 1956). Between the two extremes, lie intermediate structural arrangements. If there is a spatial drop in the effectiveness of centralized authority, somewhere on the continuum is a structural arrangement with zonal gradations in centralized authority's effectiveness. For example, a central core-zone has unitary political structure, a peripheral contested-zone has an intermediately segmentary–unitary structure (featuring indirect rule by the central authority), and a fringe area has a barely segmentary structure, where no more than vague suzerainty of the central authority is recognized (substantive examples of this are given by Lloyd 1965). Interesting as it is, for the Rosario polity it proves impossible to explore the spatial dropoff logic because of a spatial plateau effect. Distances within the surveyed study area were too short to have importantly affected delivery of sanctions required for political control. Potential plateau (or scale) effects need to be investigated for each ancient complex polity before spatial dropoff logic can be applied.

Political anthropologists have suggested that principles governing political relations within and among districts in segmentary polities are based on ascription and/or kinship, while principles governing the same relations in unitary polities are more contractual in nature (Fallers 1956; Mair 1962; and others). This fourth subcontinuum relates closely to the *societas–civitas* contrast that so interested nineteenth-century students of early institutions such as Maine, Morgan, and Tonnies (Service 1985). With a greater corpus of ethnographic studies to draw on, more allowance can be made now for a continuum between the polar extremes and for a blending of *societas* and *civitas* relations rather than their mutual exclusiveness (Service 1985). Why does *societas* co-vary with looser integration and segmentariness; and why does *civitas* co-vary with tighter integration and unitariness? The answer is that greater flexibility is afforded by contractual rather than ascriptive relations for building up and centralizing political power and authority (Rosenfeld 1965; Webster 1976a; Mair 1962; Fallers 1956). While this subcontinuum is difficult to characterize with purely archaeological data, it is worth mentioning because of the pervasive and usually unexamined assumption that prehispanic Mesoamerican political and economic relations were contractual (Blanton *et al.* 1981; Sanders 1981; Santley 1984; Feinman 1986; Litvak 1985; Morley *et al.* 1983; Phillips and Rathje 1977; Rathje 1975). In constructing models for

Mesoamerican prehistory, the routine adoption of formalist positions from economic anthropology or of transactionalist perspectives from political anthropology leaves unexamined important questions about the balance of contractual (*civitas*) versus ascriptive (*societas*) relations in ancient stratified polities. So far, the problem has been examined more thoroughly by ethnohistorians than by archaeologists (see papers in Collier *et al.* eds. 1982; Carrasco and Broda eds. 1978; Carrasco *et al.* 1976). These questions are difficult to address with sole reference to the archaeological record, but eventually they will have to be wrestled with by archaeologists. This is required in order to ensure that the fundamental assumptions underlying theoretical edifices are valid. For the Rosario polity, aspects of the *societas–civitas* subcontinuum are touched on when looking at archaeological evidence for political stratification patterns (Chapter 8).

A fifth subcontinuum concerns the degree of upward versus downward delegation of authority. In segmentary polities, authority and stewardship are delegated upward to the central rulers, while ultimate legitimacy is retained by the leadership of the districts, in a kind of confederate arrangement. In unitary polities, ultimate authority or legitimacy is retained by the central rulers and portions of this authority are transmitted downward to local delegates in the districts (Southall 1956; Easton 1959; Lloyd 1965; Goody 1966). Again, variation along the subcontinuum is possible. In this case variation concerns the degree to which authority passes upward or downward. An association of upward delegation with segmentariness and of downward delegation with unitariness follows from the centralization and concentration of power (and authority) which is entailed by a move from segmentary towards unitary structure. This subcontinuum proves particularly difficult to document archaeologically (Chapter 5).

Aspects of the general continuum between segmentary and unitary political structure have a clear place in other approaches to the study of political development. Looking at the whole bundle of subcontinua, a typologically-oriented cultural evolutionist would associate the segmentary end with a chiefdom and the unitary end with a state (Service 1971). Looking at the same bundle of subcontinua from a systems perspective, unitary structure much more than segmentary structure shows the effects of the process of centralization (Flannery 1972). The content of the variation measured in the segmentary–unitary continuum (especially the content of the three principal subcontinua) has some similarity to the content of core features of integration and complexity used by Blanton and others (1981). In Maya studies, Coe has tried to understand in Durkheimian fashion the segmentariness of Maya *unilateral* civilization – intermediate between *societas* and *civitas* arrangements (Coe 1961, 1965). More diffusely, a concept of segmentariness underlies many efforts to portray Maya political structure as loosely integrated. This underlies typings of Maya sociopolitical structure as feudal, theocratic, non-urban, or unstratified. As often as not, Maya segmentariness is contrasted with Central Mexican unitariness.

Pyramidal and hierarchical regimes

The idea of a continuum between pyramidal and hierarchical political regimes is generally relatable to concepts about administrative hierarchies developed for archaeology (Wright 1977, 1978; Johnson 1973, 1978, 1982), but it owes more to Southall's analyses of African polities (1956, 1965; and also Easton 1959). A segmentary state concept, entailing pyramidal political regimes, was first introduced by Southall in his study of the Alur in East Africa (Southall 1956, 1965).[2] The reason for hatching segmentary states was to refine the typology used by Fortes and Evans-Pritchard (eds. 1940) in *African Political Systems* (APS). The APS typology consisted essentially of a two-tone distinction between groups with centralized state polities and groups with acephalous segmentary polities. According to Southall, the APS scheme did not account for an "empirical form" (the segmentary state) "which has a certain frequency, stability, and structural consistency" (1956: 246). As pointed out earlier, a parallel exists with the development of chiefdoms as intermediate between egalitarian (*societas*) and state (*civitas*) organization (Service 1971: 164). In spite of the segmentary state's being presented as a societal type, its definition incorporates continuous variation in a number of important and clearly distinguished sociopolitical variables. One of these concerns the distribution of political personnel and functions across the levels of a hierarchy.

One way of thinking about political offices is to see them as positioned in a vertical arrangement of nested spans of jurisdiction and authority. In pyramidal political regimes, a full set of similar political functions is repeated in the offices at each hierarchical level. In hierarchical political regimes, political functions for offices are clearly differentiated according to the level at which they occur, with a wider range of functions at higher levels (Southall 1956, 1965; Easton 1959). Between these polar arrangements, there is a continuum in the degree of functional specialization for offices according to political level. Also, given more than two political levels in a polity, the degree of functional similarity among offices between different pairs of levels can vary. For example, polities may have internally hierarchical regimes while being joined to other polities in a confederative arrangement. The resulting overall arrangement appears pyramidal for the top two levels and hierarchical for levels below the second one.

Pyramidal political regimes tend to occur in segmentary polities and hierarchical regimes in unitary polities. Pyramidal regimes, with similar and self-sufficient sets of political offices, have mechanical solidarity and thus loose integration among office holders. Hierarchical regimes, with differentiated and interdependent political offices, have organic solidarity and tighter integrative links among office holders. Simply put, sets of office holders who do essentially the same things as other sets and cover an entire necessary range of functions have a reduced need for close and co-operative ties with other sets of office holders at higher or lower levels.

Pyramidal political regimes resemble the "externally but not internally specialized information-processing subsystems[s]," associated with chiefdoms; hierarchical regimes resemble the "externally and internally specialized information-processing subsystem[s]," characteristic of states (Wright 1977, 1978).

Opposed to information theory approaches (developed by Wright and others), the reasoning behind the pyramidal versus hierarchical contrast is less categorical about any necessary constraints in the relation between the total number of levels of hierarchy and the degree of specialization at each level.[3] It is also less categorical about the necessary existence of a causal arrow between increasing amounts of information and structural changes in information-processing capacity (Johnson 1978, 1982, provides a disciplined exposition of this reasoning). In sum, the approach here is less managerial and more political in focus than an information theory approach, with less concern for administrative efficiency as an adaptive necessity. Also in a comparative vein, hierarchical political regimes occur towards the complex end of Easton's continuum, in which political roles fulfill increasingly specific (specialized) functions, while pyramidal regimes occur towards the simple end of the same continuum (Easton 1959:240–243). Finally, the idea of a continuum between pyramidal and hierarchical regimes is relatable to certain concepts and lines of evidence that appear in studies of Maya sociopolitical structure. Descriptions of replication in intrasite patterning, especially for civic-ceremonial plaza layouts (Garza and Kurjack 1980; Kurjack and Garza 1981; Freidel 1981a, 1981b, 1983b; Harrison 1981; Hammond 1981; Fash 1983; Leventhal 1983; Coe 1965; Willey 1981), might be related through suitable bridging arguments to pyramidal tendencies in political regimes. The typing of Maya sociopolitical structure as feudal (Adams and Smith 1981) rests on notions of pyramidality in political regimes (along with companion notions of segmentary political structure and mechanical economic solidarity). Using a fair amount of analytical imagination, certain kinds of archaeological settlement evidence allow one to judge the degree to which political hierarchies within a complex polity were pyramidal as opposed to hierarchical (Chapter 7).

Variation in political stratification
Stratification is a vast topic. Its complexities cannot be unravelled here where the aim is simply to sketch out a few relations between varieties of political stratification and other continua of political variation. As a system of inequalities, stratification has many dimensions of variation (Fallers 1973; M. G. Smith 1977; Balandier 1970), of which the following have been selected for discussion: kinds of values, modes of access to values, and types of actors.

Stratification occurs with reference to various kinds of values. Social stratification has to do with privileged access to prestige and social rewards. Economic stratification concerns distribution of economic rewards (especially access to critical material resources). Finally, political stratification involves unequal distribution of political rewards and access to offices (M. G. Smith 1977). My principal focus is on the last kind of stratification. Variation also occurs in the modes of access to the rewards distributed in a stratification system, varying from strict ascription to complete achievement (or contract). Referring to access to broad societal strata, one useful scheme places caste, estate, and class systems along an ascription to achievement continuum (Balandier 1970:90). A similar continuum exists for access to specific political offices, i.e., from determinancy to indeterminancy of succession principles (Goody 1966; Burling 1974). Finally, stratification as a system for organizing inequality can have as its actors corporate groups or individuals (invoking the contrast between group and individual stratification systems).

These and other dimensions of variation are important in actual cases of stratification. For example, access to a group which is corporately attached to a political office may be ascriptive. Yet, within the group, access to the attached office itself may be indeterminate enough to involve a large measure of achievement. Such group stratification arrangement appears in many African kingdoms (Goody 1971; Lloyd 1965; M. G. Smith 1960) and possibly in some Mesoamerican polities (Carmack 1981; Van Zantjwick 1985).

Let me sketch out a few hypothetical relations between forms of political stratification and the political continua already reviewed. Here the political system is viewed as a set of political offices and these are rewards (values) in a political stratification system. The main focus is on ascriptive group stratification. Ascriptive group stratification is more congruent with segmentary than with unitary political structure. This is due to the local ascriptive and/or kinship bases for political relations in segmentary polities compared to the more flexible individual (contractual) bases for political relations in unitary polities, relations which are more easily manipulated and controlled from the center (Fallers 1956). Ascribed groups linked to political offices have the potential to constitute self-contained foci of loyalty for their members (and/or outside clients) and to compete with a polity's central focus (Fallers 1956, 1973). Groups with secure corporate ties to political offices and territories are often relatively self-sufficient within a pyramidal regime. Looking ahead, with reference to the following two continua, ascriptive group stratification is congruent with economic autarchy (mechanical solidarity) and with a tendency to fission (a segmenting organization). If the groups corporately tied to political offices are organized on the basis of unilineal descent, and if elite marriages tend to be more polygamous than commoner marriages, it is almost structurally inevitable that an explosive growth will occur in the number of candidates for office (Goody 1966). This particular kind of population growth and pressure (on offices) is certainly more critical for helping to promote fission than a generalized society-wide population growth pushing on a limited material-resource base.

The relations sketched above are hypothetical and certainly not invariant. Ascriptive groups in a political stratification system may have weaker local bases and lesser political or economic self-sufficiency. In that case they fit more readily with unitary political structure and non-segmenting organization. Even full-blown ascriptive group stratification can occur in centralized and non-segmenting polities, if there is consistently more indeterminacy in the succession to political office at the political hierarchy's lower levels compared to its highest level. Meddlesome tactics of divide and rule, applied from the top, can keep districts from fissioning away, in a situation akin to the systemic pathology of meddling (Rappaport 1977; Flannery 1972).

My review of the relation between stratification and other sociopolitical features is based mostly on Africanist studies. Consequently, it privileges political as against economic stratification. Such a bias is useful because it better matches what we know about the relative importance of political and economic stratification in (ethnohistorically documented) ancient Mesoamerican and Maya polities. Furthermore, the political bias serves as a needed counterweight to the attitude of a legion of Mesoamericanists and Mayanists who follow Fried (1967) on stratification and define it in unilaterally economic terms, tracing political developments as responses to the need to maintain and/or intensify economic stratification (for the Maya case – Sanders and Price 1968; Webb 1973; Webster 1977; Rathje 1973; and many others). With archaeological settlement evidence and bold analytical contortions, it becomes possible to investigate questions of group versus individual political stratification, ascription versus achievement in access to political office, and the balance between political offices, contenders, and subjects (Chapter 8).

Mechanical and organic solidarity
For many studies of complex societies that are built from the economy upward, the relations of mechanical versus organic economic solidarity to political development are centrally important. In contrast to this, the focus here is primarily political, both for theoretical reasons (Chapter 1) and because of practical factors. The latter concerns the fact that the evidence from the Rosario Valley which bears on economic questions is weaker than the evidence which is relevant to political questions. Consequently, issues of mechanical versus organic economic solidarity are addressed in a relatively cursory way, mostly for the sake of plugging a yawning gap (Chapter 9).

A contrast between mechanical and organic modes of solidarity (or economic integration) is loosely derived from Durkheim's classic studies concerning the division of labor in society (Durkheim 1933; Coe 1961). A basic assumption here is that economic specialization promotes exchange which promotes interdependence. Exchange acts as a societal bonding agent, a general idea traceable to Mauss' work on gift exchange. But the idea that exchange promotes social solidarity has been explicitly questioned. "Economic exchange does not in itself promote social solidarity or stability, but rather is fundamentally a dissociative, conflict relation which must be carefully regulated" (Foster 1977: 3). This follows the substantivist argument from economic anthropology that economic exchange is a threat to the social fabric (Polanyi 1944; Sahlins 1972). Still, that specialization and exchange promotes social solidarity continues to be the reigning assumption behind most Americanist archaeological discussion about the mechanical versus organic continuum. Starting from this assumption, economically determinist arguments follow. Mechanical arrangements with economically autarchic districts, limited exchange, and independence of districts are less solidary and cohesive (especially as the system's scale increases) than organic arrangements with a great deal of economic specialization among districts, extensive exchange, and interdependence of districts. Furthermore, mechanical economies are associated with segmentary polities and organic economies with unitary polities. That these kinds of relations are necessary is a useful hypothesis, but substantivist critiques of the assumed linear relation between exchange and social solidarity suggest that some rethinking is required.

Another important continuum at the interface between sociopolitical and economic spheres concerns degrees of inter-relation between the spheres. Combining themes from substantivist economic anthropology and evolutionary political anthropology, one might expect closely co-ordinated movement from segmentary to unitary structure, from mechanical to organic economic solidarity, and from more to less inter-relation between economic and sociopolitical spheres. The last process is sometimes characterized as one of increasing disembeddedness of the economy from society (Polanyi 1977: ch. 4–5).

To propose increasing separation of political and economic structure and organization on an evolutionary road towards increasing political size and complexity (from chiefdom to state, for example) demands a belief in Adam Smith's unseen hand. This is the idea that individual economic self-interest produces the best economic results for the collectivity (a position of pure methodological individualism – Ahmed 1976). The unseen hand is what gives increasingly complex and delicate (i.e., organic) economic organizations the capacity to regulate themselves, free from political direction. Opposed to this is the argument that increasingly complex and unitary governments become increasingly involved with economic activities of their subjects for purposes of integration and control (Johnson 1973; Wright and Johnson 1975; Blanton *et al.* 1981). Without seeking a resolution of the issues raised, I hope that this brief overview has established the need to be sceptical about necessary co-variation. between increasingly unitary polities, organic economies, and an increasing economic disembeddedness.

Mesoamericanists have applied Durkheim's mechanical-organic contrast to issues of political and economic structure, often using classical notions of a general evolution from segmentary, mechanical, and economically embedded arrangements to unitary, organic, and economically disembedded arrangements (Coe 1961; Sanders and Price 1968; Webb 1973; Parsons and Price 1971; Price 1978). Such arguments anchor themselves in environmental conditions and follow the chain of reasoning that environment determines subsistence which determines settlement which determines political structure (Chapter 1). More recent studies may be less unidirectionally evolutionist, but they still display a strong (albeit implicit) reliance on the unseen hand (Blanton *et al.* 1981; Kowalewski and Finsten 1983; Feinman *et al.* 1984; Feinman 1986). These studies draw a picture of (sometimes cyclical) fluctuations in political scale, centralization, integration, and degree of economic embeddedness. A market economy involving individual household actors is presented as the natural state of affairs which is more or less distorted by political interference. Underlying all of this is the unexamined assumption that underlies most Mesoamerican archaeological discussions, the assumption that political and economic relations were primarily contractual (*civitas*).

Segmenting and non-segmenting organizations

A contrast between segmenting and non-segmenting polities is central to many studies of ancient complex political organization (Cohen 1981; Carneiro 1981). It proves difficult to appreciate with the single-period settlement evidence of the kind recovered in the Rosario Valley and many other surveys (Chapter 4). Despite methodological difficulties, the segmenting versus non-segmenting continuum's importance is such that these difficulties must be faced and an attempt made to trace the links between it and other continua (Chapter 10). Political anthropologists have proposed that segmenting versus non-segmenting tendencies are entailed by contrasting political structural arrangements of the kinds reviewed in the first four continua (Southall 1956; Easton 1959; Fallers 1956; Mair 1962; Fortes 1953; Goody 1966, 1971; M. G. Smith 1960). Polities with segmentary structure are placed at the segmenting end of the continuum, being relatively unstable and exhibiting a tendency to break apart into their districts which are politically self-sufficient as parts of a pyramidal regime. Polities with unitary structure are at the non-segmenting end of the continuum, being relatively stable with districts that are politically interdependent as parts of a hierarchical regime. As always, with such high-flown generalizations, the absolute functional worth of the associations cannot be taken as demonstrated, but they do represent a provisionally useful hypothesis.

The brittleness of segmentary polities relates to several factors: lack of functional interdependence among sets of office holders (pyramidal regime), low levels of centralization of power and authority, divisive effects of ascriptive/kinship bases for access to sociopolitical offices and groupings, and economic autarchy of districts. Conversely, stability and cohesiveness of unitary polities stems from their more highly integrated and organic structure. Political *stability* refers to the ability to prevent the loss of control over districts. Political *durability* refers to the capacity to preserve over time the same general complexity of political structure and organization, without falling back to simpler forms. Because they are less tightly integrated and less pathologically hypercoherent (Flannery 1972) than unitary polities, unstable segmentary polities may be more durable or shock-proof than more stable unitary polities. Loss of one or a few districts through secession and breakage of a few links among districts is not sufficient to throw segmentary polities badly out of joint. Vertical hierarchical arrangements remain, even though a few pieces drop away. Hypercoherent unitary polities, with critically important linkages among their districts, are correspondingly more vulnerable to total collapse if linkages are damaged. Greater stability and lesser durability can thus go hand in hand.

A noteworthy spatial property of segmenting polities is that districts on the edges are most easily separated to form new polities or join a competing polity, since centralized control decreases moving outward from the center. In unitary polities, centralized control is exercised more evenly throughout the polity's territory and crumbling at the edges is more easily prevented (Southall 1956). Such principles will apply only at suitably large spatial scales, in the absence of a plateau effect (such as occurs in the Rosario polity) in which distances are too short to matter politically.

So far, discussion has covered adherence or lack of adherence of already constituted districts, taking a relatively static view. A more dynamic approach also considers addition of existing districts, usually at the edges. Given the proposed greater durability of segmentary polities, it follows that such an additive process could be less disruptively realized in segmentary as opposed to unitary polities. A facilitating strategy is to create loose pyramidal-style links between the polity core and newly incorporated marginal districts. This is one way of producing concentric zonation featuring a spatial drop in the effectiveness of centralized control. Such a pattern was mentioned earlier as one of the intermediate positions along the subcontinuum between decentralization and centralization.

Also in a more dynamic vein, one can look at reconstitution of existing districts. Reconstitution may be promoted by growth in political scale (e.g., information needing to be processed, size of the subject population, or size of the group of contenders for office). Two relevant processes have been described by Goody (1962) with reference to domestic group cycling. One of these is *cleavage*, which consists of further internal subdivision of units while cohesion is maintained among new and old units. In segmentary polities, growth in political scale leads to cleavage and multiplication of replicated districts. More districts are added without major qualitative change in the relations among them (setting up the potential for fission). In unitary polities, growth in political scale can also be accommodated through cleavage, but with structural modification in the relations among districts. The second process of reconstitution is *fission* or subdivision without maintenance of cohesion, leading to new and separate units (polities in this case). Such fission and cleavage processes are roughly akin to the systems processes of segregation and centralization (Flannery 1972). But, inspired in the first instance by Southall's study of segmentary states (1956, 1965), the reasoning here is less categorical about a necessary need for greater complexity engendered by increased scale, compared to the information theory approaches so often linked to systems thinking (Johnson 1978, 1982).

Distinguishing between political stability and durability has general relevance to the study of ancient complex polities. But it is particularly important when trying to understand the political trajectory of Lowland Maya polities. The brittleness of Lowland Maya political structure has often been noted (Coe 1961; Sanders and Price 1968; Webb 1973; and others). Maya unilateral civilizations or chiefdoms are portrayed as both politically unstable and not very durable. Late Classic Lowland Maya political structure has also been cited as a possible example of pathological hypercoherence leading to collapse, with emphasis on low political durability (Flannery 1972). But the jury is still out on these issues. Much work remains to be done towards building an understanding of the relative degree of durability and stability of Classic Maya polities. Some of this work falls under the wide umbrella of Maya collapse studies (Culbert ed. 1973). But the problems will become more interesting and perhaps tractable when the position of Maya polities on the segmenting to non-segmenting continuum and their tendencies towards collapse are compared to those of the many other Mesoamerican polities that collapsed. This has yet to be done in a detailed manner. Earlier broadly comparative generalizations hold the field (Sanders 1973; Sanders and Price 1968; Coe 1961). With reference to these issues, evidence concerning the Rosario polity's political structure is used to investigate (indirectly) the manner and causes of its collapse, and the findings are placed in the context of the general Classic Maya collapse (Chapter 10).

Research questions

Using the theoretical framework just presented, I can address several issues raised in previous studies of Maya political structure. At the same time, an Eastonian bundled continua framework leads to research problems with wider anthropological relevance. This is because the framework is based explicitly on theoretical principles from political anthropology (at a middle range of abstraction). Such a framework strips away some of the mystery attached to the ancient Maya (Marcus 1983a) because it helps to disentangle generic and particular features of their political arrangements.

With the general theoretical framework serving as a guide, I have drawn up a series of research questions substantively linked to the problem of Classic Maya political structure. Each of the five sets of questions derives from one or more of the continua. Each question is addressed in one or more of the subsequent analytical chapters (Chapters 5–10). A discussion of controlled comparison at the end of this section explains how a case study of a small polity on the fringe of the Maya Lowlands relates to such broadly framed questions about Classic Maya political structure.

Question 1: To what degree did Classic Maya political structure feature a decentralized, replicated, and loosely integrated arrangement of constituent districts?

The first question is framed with reference to the segmentary versus unitary continuum. Degrees of centralization, differentiation, and integration in the Rosario polity are determined by reference to its settlement record (Chapters 5 and 6). The issue of segmentariness and especially of centralization (Chapter 5) is among the easiest to address with available archaeological evidence.

Question 2a: To what degree did Classic Maya political regimes feature a pyramidal arrangement (replication of political functions at the different hierarchical levels)?

Question 2b: If there was a tendency towards pyramidal regimes, what were their scale limitations (in terms of the size of the political community, the number of districts, and the number of hierarchical levels)?

Question 2c: What were the implications of a pyramidal regime for political stability (tendency to fission)?

The second set of questions stems from a joint consideration of the pyramidal–hierarchical and segmenting versus non-segmenting continua. Structural issues raised in Questions 2a and 2b are addressed by examining political settlement hierarchies and by comparing population sizes of the polity's several constituent territorial units (Chapter 7). Question 2c is the most difficult because it requires processual evidence not available in a single-period settlement record. However, some processual implications can be derived from a static structural view of settlement patterns (Chapter 10).

Question 3a: To what degree were Classic Maya political systems characterized by group political stratification (corporate groups linked to political offices), and to what degree were they characterized by ascription in access to offices?

Question 3b: Was ascriptive group stratification, if present, closely linked to a segmentary (decentralized, undifferentiated, and loosely integrated) arrangement of districts?

Question 3c: Was ascriptive group stratification, if present, closely linked to growth in the number of districts, through simple cleavage processes, and was this arrangement linked to a higher tendency to fission?

The third set of questions centers on variations in political stratification linked to two other continua – between segmentary and unitary structure and between segmenting and non-segmenting organization. The issues raised by the questions are only infrequently considered by Mesoamericanists. Nevertheless, rigorous studies of structurally similar complex polities in Africa clearly suggest that relations between candidates and political offices are critical for determining the growth, contraction, and degree of stability of political systems (Lloyd 1965, 1968; Goody 1966; Southall 1956; Fallers 1956, 1973; Mair 1962, 1977; Balandier 1970). Question 3a is addressed with close reference to household-scale settlement remains, their disposition in space, their qualitative distinctions, and their relation to political centers with civic-ceremonial buildings (Chapter 8). The answer to Question 3a is then confronted with earlier findings (Chapters 5 and 6) to address Question 3b (Chapter 8). Question 3c, most difficult because of its processual nature, is addressed along with other thorny issues related to the dynamics of political organization (Chapter 10).

Question 4a: What was the degree of mechanical versus organic economic solidarity that characterized Classic Maya polities?

Question 4b: If there was markedly mechanical economic solidarity, how closely was this associated with segmentary political structure?

The fourth set of questions arises from a joint consideration of the mechanical–organic solidarity and the segmentary–unitary continua. Such questions are important for further evaluation of arguments that use a linear causal chain to link the Maya's undifferentiated physical environment, mechanical economy, and absence of political complexity. Beginnings of an answer to Question 4a emerge when comparing the environmental composition of the polity's several districts (Chapter 9). The answer to Question 4a can be supplemented with earlier findings (Chapters 5 and 6) to answer Question 4b. While evidence is sketchy, efforts to address the questions are worthwhile because economically determinist views of Maya political structure continue to be very influential. It also makes for a more complete argument to give at least some attention to a political system's economic underpinnings.

Question 5: If Classic Maya political structure was markedly segmentary, did this entail segmenting polities, with strong secessionist tendencies among districts?

The final question emerges from consideration of both the segmentary–unitary and the segmenting versus non-segmenting continua and has a direct bearing on the Classic Maya collapse (Culbert ed. 1973). The processual nature of the issues dealt with in the segmenting versus non-segmenting, continuum brings a higher level of difficulty, but Question 5 may be attacked indirectly by inferring likely processual consequences of static structures (Chapters 4 and 10).

The research questions are phrased so as to apply to the Classic Maya in general, yet the answers are drawn from one of a group of small polities on the southwestern edge of the Lowland Maya heartland (Chapter 3; Figures 1–2). This imbalance is purposeful. It does not result from a belief that Rosario polity settlement and politics are typical paradigms for all Classic Maya polities. Rather, the generally formulated questions are paradigmatic of the kind of queries that could be applied to other Maya (and eventually Mesoamerican) polities. In other words, it is the theoretical approach which is paradigmatic rather than the substantive result.

In spite of the caution about a priori extrapolation, it is still interesting to consider to what degree substantive results from the Rosario polity might be extendable to other Maya polities. This requires a brief analysis of cultural–historical information about how the Rosario polity's inhabitants may have fitted into the wider mosaic of Maya development. Generally speaking, a Late/Terminal Classic settlement climax followed by Postclassic collapse parallels settlement trajectories in many other parts of the Maya Lowlands (Ashmore ed. 1981). Additionally, relations between Tenam Rosario and much larger centers in the neighboring Usumacinta Lowlands (Figure 1) may have resembled those between a colony and its metropolis (further details in Chapter 3). That the Rosario polity may have been a colony is intriguing because in some cases colonial sociopolitical structure adheres strictly to the idealized norms of the colonizing society (sixteenth-century New World Spanish settlement [Foster 1960]; provincial Inca settlement [Morris and Thompson 1985]). If such a pattern applies to the Rosario polity, this makes it a relevant model for settlement and political norms elsewhere in the Maya Lowlands. But, this is not equivalent to claiming that the Rosario polity had a wholly typical pan-Maya form of political structure. To search for such a thing is to fall again into a typological trap and to miss the insights gained from a study of variation.

The Rosario polity lay on the margins of Lowland Maya political development and its single period of major occupation generally coincided with maximal Maya development (in the Late Classic Period). This makes it a good example of an area utilized during a civilization's maximal expansion phase and then virtually abandoned. Such circumstances give a particular vividness to the polity's settlement (and other archaeological) patterning. Furthermore, its valley has remained relatively marginal with respect to subsequent developments which might have blurred the record left during the settlement apogee. As a place where the wave of Maya development broke and then receded forever, the Rosario Valley is comparable most specifically to the Puuc Zone in the Yucatan Peninsula (Kurjack and Garza 1981).

Rather than searching for key cases in the Rosario polity, or elsewhere, from which to extrapolate widely, we need general questions such as those listed here to organize research into a whole series of polities. A subsequent step, and a most interesting one, is to take a set of polities and compare them in terms of what kinds of answers they are providing to the standardized set of questions. Such a step-by-step procedure is by far the most logical way to attack some of the general questions about political structure and organization raised in setting out the theoretical orientation. All of this relates to the well-known problem of matching scale of problem to scale of analysis. The solution advocated here is to set the problems on a rather grand scale and to begin the research effort on a relatively small scale, working towards the accumulation of small-scale case studies which are valuable both individually and as potential components in wider controlled comparisons (Eggan 1954; Vogt 1964a). Eventually, the controlled comparisons lead towards conclusions for the grand-scale problems.

Fortunately, there are a multitude of scales to work at and controlled comparison can also be used within the Rosario polity. To take a concrete example, a problem that has been set is to determine to what degree Classic Maya political structure was segmentary (Question 1). For the Rosario polity, and most importantly of all, for its districts, one can measure relative degrees of segmentariness (Chapters 5 and 6). One can also measure where the Rosario polity's districts are positioned on some of the other continua. Controlled comparison (essentially a study of concomitant variation) is then available for testing the expected linkages between positions along continua. The Rosario polity's districts provide what are, in effect, several even smaller case studies. With a set of answers from internal comparisons in the Rosario polity, the ground is laid for comparison with other polities of roughly the same scale. And so one goes on building an understanding of the relations between various aspects of political structure, at increasing scales of analysis.

Models, analogies, and contexts of discovery

It proves useful to review as many as possible of the choices made in constructing a theoretical framework for the study of politics in an ancient complex polity. Since the procedures for model building in this sphere have few agreed-on standards, no criteria should be left unexamined. Discussing the mechanics of erecting a theoretical framework is even more appropriate when the framework is in some senses tailor-made rather than acquired off the rack (from the range of ready-made conceptual apparel such as societal typologies and their associated multivariate or univariate explanatory schemes).

The procedure of measuring sociopolitical variables and trying to understand their relations to one another corresponds generally to a functionalist mode of analysis. It derives from suggestions for systems approaches in political anthropology (Easton 1959). Continua of variation are used to avoid the *cul de sac* into which societal typologies have led. Using several continua avoids a two-tone format in which only two simple models are tested, with one found to be correct and the other wrong. Even the severely restricted amount of complexity that archaeologists can perceive in their data need not be reducible to such an impoverished two-tone format.

For a division of society into analytical units, actual sociopolitical groupings have been used: households, communities, districts, polities, etc. (Blanton *et al.* 1981: 15–16). Such divisions seem better fitted to a study of politics in ancient complex polities than are the analytical divisions of societies into behavioral subsystems, cross-cutting sociopolitical groupings – for example, subsistence, technological, social, projective or symbolic, and trade and communication subsystems (Renfrew 1984: ch. 9). Such a choice makes sense if one accepts that politics conventionally involves the interaction of individuals and groups rather than behaviors which cross-cut these.

In developing points of political–theoretical interest it is inadvisable to use archaeological testability as the sole criterion. Instead, several variables are selected because they fit together as a set, both in (middle range) political theory and in the political practice revealed in a number of ethnographic and ethnohistoric cases. The variables have different degrees of testability. As indicated earlier, some research questions are easier to answer than others, given single-period settlement evidence. For some of the continua there are fairly convincing archaeological tests, for others, only moderately convincing tests, and for yet others, (currently) no tests at all. Besides the archaeological record's absolute limitations, other factors that constrain testability are limits of imagination in devising tests and failures in collecting relevant archaeological material.

Few would defend totally untestable models but it does not follow that totally testable models are required. Calling for totally testable models is a form of categorical yes/no thinking. Given the feeble quality of available bridging arguments for political studies of ancient complex polities, virtually all totally testable models must leave out large amounts of interesting subject matter. Consequently, it is more attractive, useful, and honest to include at least some archaeologically intractable subject matter in problem formulation. This is especially true if there are theoretical or empirical reasons for believing that the intractable subject matter relates closely to more archaeologically accessible matters. Covering a fuller range of subject matter reduces the simplification and austerity found in so many rigorous archaeological models which suffer from the dilemma of increasing triviality accompanying increasing methodological rigor. Here, one thinks of "Archaeology with a Capital S" (Flannery 1973) or of narrowly focused actualistic studies. At the same time, fuller coverage of subject matter at the problem formulation stage usefully brings into view the aspects of a problem which are not currently resolvable through archaeological testing. Knowing the currently untested (or untestable) propositions makes it easier to direct further productive research (Cowgill provides a very perceptive discussion of these issues – 1983: 314–316). Initial knowledge of a problem's fullest possible dimensions also prevents the final conclusion that a problem has been solved and can be filed away when all that has been done really is to cut it down to archaeologically manageable size through impoverishment of its content. Unlike election manifestos, discussions of anthropological–archaeological problems benefit from less certainty and more exposing of ambiguities. Loose ends are not always a bad thing and aims should exceed the means of achieving them. This could only be a drawback when an archaeologist is unaware of the lack of fit between aims and means. And this is best avoided when there is suffcient self-criticism to allow recognition of ambiguities and open-ended questions in one's own work.

In setting up the problem, I have consciously avoided a dogmatic falsificationist approach. Dogmatic falsificationism in archaeology is the research goal of rejecting grand and usually quite complex theories (e.g., Wittfogel's irrigation hypothesis) by reference to single archaeological case studies (examples are discussed by Gándara 1981). In the present case, it is difficult to imagine onto what famous theory gunsights might be trained from the confines of the Rosario Valley. The great prime-mover explanations (Flannery 1972) are one possible target. But their formulation in terms of the great questions (origins of the state, origins of complexity, and so forth) make them problematic targets (for reasons outlined in Chapter 1). Another possible set of targets are the past and current models advanced to account for Classic Maya political structure. But, many such models are presented sketchily and loosely accommodated to data so that it is not yet possible to design research solely with a view to rejecting them. A more positive and useful approach builds on convergences, where variables formulated here have some resemblance to variables embedded in existing models. An understanding that model building (and testing) in this and other studies is still in its infancy leads to the conclusion that, beyond its intrinsic failings, dogmatic falsification is premature.

An excursion into the context of discovery (Hill 1972: 95) leads to the question of how I selected the sources from which the theoretical framework draws particular inspiration. Most of the conceptual baggage and terminology used for setting out the problem orientation is drawn from Africanist political anthropologists. Such a derivation may be justified on a number of counts, by defending the appropriateness of a chosen set of analogies. The general idea for model building through analogies is that the better documented present helps us to interpret the more poorly documented past (Wylie 1985; Ascher 1961; Binford 1967; Hodder 1982). To use present documentation about the relation between behavior and its material correlates in order to increase understanding of the past, the logical step required is to argue that similar behaviors consistently produce similar (and distinguishable) static material patterns. This is the well-known rationale for general analogy, where virtually any relatively well-documented situation can be used to help in understanding the archaeological record of virtually any area or time. Beyond this, there are standards of relevance that make a good analogy. An analogy's worth revolves around similarities between its contexts of discovery and validation, as measured on various axes, for example: Time, Space (straight distance or environment), and Culture (subsistence, sociopolitical structure, ethnic/linguistic identity, or cultural isolation). These criteria are broadly similar to those discussed by Ascher (1961) and Becquelin (1973). Which of the axes of similarity is stressed will depend on theoretical perspective. Cultural ecologists will favor environment, subsistence, and sociopolitical structure axes (Price 1974), while cultural historians will favor ethnic/linguistic identity and cultural isolation axes (Vogt 1983). This account of the role of problem orientation in evaluating the worth of analogies makes more sense than the idea that greater closeness along all or any axes makes for a generally better and more convincing analogy (Hodder 1982: ch.1).

Taking the example of political structure in the Rosario polity, let me trace how one follows the rules for good analogy. On the time axis, analogies from the Spanish conquest period are better than analogies from the (ethnographic) present, as less time has expired, with less chance for cultural alteration. This rule makes particular sense if one has a cultural-historical model in mind where culture drift is a major contributor to change (Vogt 1964a). On the space axis, analogies from a nearby society are best if one works with a cultural–historical diffusionist model; analogies from a society in a closely similar environment (semi-tropical *tierra caliente* lowlands) are preferable if a cultural–ecological framework is used. On the culture axis, analogies from societies with similar paleotechnic subsistence–agricultural systems are favored, again in a cultural–ecological framework. On the same axis, analogies from societies at a similar state level of sociopolitical development are better than analogies from band or tribal societies, if the problem orientation involves cultural evolutionary typology (Price 1974). Finally, and still on the cultural axis, analogies from genetically related ethnic groups (Maya peasants in Mexico and Guatemala) are better than analogies from unrelated or distantly related groups. Such analogies are even better if the groups are isolated and relatively uncontaminated by contacts with other cultures. The cultural–ethnic criterion over-rides most others in ethnographic analogies from Chiapas proposed for the Lowland Classic Maya. This is because these analogies are formulated within a theoretical framework that uses a Genetic Model of Maya cultural development (Vogt 1964a, 1983; Holland 1964; Gifford 1978).

Since I have constructed a political theoretical framework to operate on a reasonably high level of abstraction (somewhere in the middle register) and in a functionalist mode, my primary criterion for evaluating analog material is closeness on the culture axis in terms of sociopolitical structure. In this light, Africanist political anthropology proves a useful source of insights in a context of discovery. One reason for this is that such studies touch on ancient or at least non-modern complex polities. These are arguably similar in sociopolitical structure to ancient (especially Lowland) Mesoamerican societies. Broad similarities apply to basic structural factors (core features – Blanton *et al.* 1981: 17–22) such as scale, complexity, and integration. They also apply to a range of sociopolitical institutions (group stratification, vertical rather than horizontal political cleavages, estates, corporate segments, etc.) and economic arrangements (tributary modes of production – Wolf 1982).

Much of my claim for similarity on the Mesoamerican side has to rest on an appreciation of ethnohistoric (rather than archaeological) evidence and cases. The nature of such an appeal to ethnohistoric evidence is slightly unusual and worth setting out. An appeal to ethnohistory is required because of the problems concerning direct archaeological documentation for institutional components in the comparison. Even so, the idea is not that Classic (archaeological) societies are rigorously similar in every way to Postclassic (ethnohistoric) societies. Rather, evidence from Postclassic societies is used to set some limits on models and interpretations for Classic societies. For example, in Postclassic societies one can document the absence of a fully professional bureaucracy (in Weber's sense, Gerth and Mills 1946: ch. 8; Giddens 1985) or the absence of a fully capitalist economic order (Polanyi 1944; Wolf 1982). A historical–evolutionary logic validates the argument that such institutional arrangements are very unlikely to occur in predecessor Classic societies. This historical–evolutionary logic must be broadly correct. No one can argue that fully-blown capitalist societies predated noncapitalist societies in the New World historical record.

The lesson from all this is fairly simple. Administrative (information-processing) efficiency models from studies of modern corporate and government bureaucracies (Johnson 1978, 1982) or microeconomic models from studies of capitalist (free market) economies (Rathje 1975; Santley 1984; Feinman *et al.* 1984) are poor conceptual tools for a study of ancient complex Mesoamerican polities. This is part of the general substantivist position that modern (western) governments and economies are inappropriate contexts of discovery for studies of archaic and/or ancient societies.[4] Subsequently, variations of this circuitous, but valid, argument linking Mesoamerican ethnohistory and archaeology become useful for the selection of plausible interpretive frameworks, setting limits on the possibilities (Chapters 5, 7, and 11). Viewed in wider perspective, what I have just sketched out is an argument against the relevance of some extradisciplinary theoretical analogs – information theoretic and microeconomic models (Chapter 1).

In sum, the generic similarity to Mesoamerican ethnohistoric (and by extension archaeological) cases makes Africanist material and literature an appropriate context of discovery. But why not simply, and more directly, use Mesoamerican ethnohistoric cases as a source of analogy? The reasons for going to Africanist cases and discussions are twofold. First, they are more fully documented than Mesoamerican cases. Second, Africanist political anthropology includes some of the most systematic treatments of ethnographically specific and/or ethnologically general principles concerning political structure. Thus, one can benefit from comparatively higher levels of theoretical sophistication. Most of the political continua I have used have been handled explicitly by Africanists in a comparative (and sometimes diachronic) framework. Using Africanist political anthropology as a context of discovery is not just a matter of playing to the strengths of the evidence, but also to the strengths of how the evidence has been thought about.

To clear up any doubts, let me reemphasize that the theoretical framework is constructed at an intermediate level of abstraction. Specific African institutions are not used as models for the Maya (i.e., as substantive analogies from specific cases,

Chapter 1). Rather, middle range generalizations about political structure arrived at by Africanists with reference to their material are transposed for use in the study of Maya settlement and politics (i.e., as substantive-theoretical analogies derived from composites of cases and general structural-functionalist theory, Chapter 1). *Middle range* is used here in its original rather than its more recent Binfordian sense (Raab and Goodyear 1984; and Chapter 11). In the following discussion, *analog* refers to something generally equivalent to a middle range theoretical construct rather than a concrete ethnographic description of a specific institution.

In concluding my discussion of conceptual choices, I return to the irrepressible issue of archaeological testability. Most of the notions from general and Africanist political anthropology in the theoretical framework were not developed with attention paid to archaeologically relevant material signatures. Thus, there may be some point to the complaint that this is all fine as political anthropology but of little archaeological use. A necessary response to such a complaint is to develop testable implications for as many continua as possible (Chapters 4–10). While this is a difficult and often interesting undertaking, it is only a necessary means to an end, not an end in itself. To repeat an earlier argument, developing perfect test implications (or totally testable models) cannot be the sole aim of interesting and useful research about political structure in ancient Maya (or other) polities. The subjects that we set ourselves are generally much too multifaceted and interesting to be reduced to archaeologically testable constructs. Approaches to the testability problem vary along a spectrum. At the positivistic extreme is the requirement that every analog be archaeologically testable or else we cannot talk about it. At the anti-positivistic extreme is the contention that all analogs are untestable anyway so that one (subjective) opinion is as good as another. The most constructive positions probably lie between these extremes. From the middle ground it appears that ideally analogs should be distinctively relatable to patterns in the archaeological record. But it is also clear that a host of important and interesting analogs occur where such a linkage is ambiguous (through equifinality) or not visible.

The issue of testability cannot be considered in complete isolation and things become clearer when we look at the wider issue of what analogs are used for. In the earlier New Archaeology (positivistic and scientific in method and orientation), the production of analogs was firmly placed in the context of discovery, and the analogs had to be tested against the archaeological record in a context of validation (reviewed in Wylie 1985: 85; Leone 1982: 180–181; Binford 1967; Hill 1972: 95). Relative worth of competing analogs could then be evaluated against the archaeological record with sets of crucial test implications. Following the logic of this position, it is not critical that analogs meet criteria for quality (temporal, spatial, and cultural closeness), since bad analogs will presumably lose out to better ones in the testing process (see Binford's negative comments [1967: 36, 49] on Ascher's steps for strengthening general analogy, at the source [1961]). A principal criterion for an analog's worth becomes its archaeological testability. It does save effort, however, to follow the standard criteria for good analog building, to avoid time-consuming testing of patently inappropriate analogs.

As Wylie (1985) notes, Binford and others have shifted from the earlier New Archaeology position in order to emphasize that archaeological data are not directly accessible for testing processual analogs. The solution to this problem consists of actualistic studies to build middle range (meaning methodological) theory (Binford 1977, 1983a, 1983b). In a Maya context, some (but not many) archaeologists have come to share a concern for middle range theory (Tourtellot 1983; Freidel and Sabloff 1984; Sahloff 1983; Binford and Sabloff 1982). Such concerns have identified important difficulties in handling the archaeological record. Yet many archaeologists (including the author) continue the earlier tradition of trying to test analogs directly against the archaeological record, assigning a more secondary (means to an end) role to middle range studies. To put the best face on it, this position stems from an interest in substantive theoretical issues which over-rides interest in methodological issues. The problem of balancing methodological rigor and substantive interest in archaeological research is difficult and not resolvable in any absolute sense. The whole issue revolves around the very relative concept of the quality of one's problem orientation.[5]

In a less positivistic and more humanistically oriented form of archaeology, being able to find a good analog that seems to account for much of the existing archaeological evidence is tantamount to explaining or rather understanding that evidence (a position reviewed by Hill 1972: 63, 102, 103; and Leone 1982: 181–182). From this perspective, there is little need to develop an explicit set of standards for archaeologically testing every last part of the analog. Nor is there much need to render variables into testable form. Thus, the analogs can be seen as explanatory sketches which account for the data in a rather loose and informal way. A strong tendency to work with analogs that are tightly bound synthetic packages of variables and a corresponding reluctance to analytically break down the analogs into their component variables are consistent with the failure to render variables into testable form. In this approach, it is critical to follow the best possible procedures in selecting analogs. This requires evaluation along axes of similarity (above) or testing for relational coherence (Wylie 1985: 94–95). The importance of these efforts is due to the fact that the final understanding achieved is only as good as the analog from which it derives. There is no separate context of validation for testing and discarding analogs. The non-positivistic approach may entail direct-historical (Steward 1942) or folk-culture (Clark 1951) views on proper analogy, with a stress on cultural continuities and similarities. In a Maya context, the non-positivistic approach still characterizes the practice of most archaeologists (according to Sabloff 1983). In light of this, any sustained concern with testing constitutes something of a departure (Chapter 4).

Where should one stand with reference to the polar positions that place analogs in a context of discovery or else deny separate contexts of discovery and validation for analogs? Again, the middle ground is least restricting to intellectual curiosity. The positivistic position is attractive as an ideal. When tempered by a sceptical view of the archaeological record's potential and a reasonable (but not overwhelming) interest in methodological arguments, the aim of archaeologically testing analogs promotes disciplined and attractively modest (rather than assertion-based) archaeological research. Confronting ethnographic analogs with the archaeological record gives one solution to the problem, most familiar from earlier hunter-gatherer archaeology, that our knowledge of the past may be unduly limited by our knowledge of the present (Freeman 1968). Such are the attractions of aiming for a positivistic ideal. In contrast a too rigid adherence to positivistic practice is best avoided because of the stultification that results from requiring complete archaeological testability and completely unambiguous analyses and solutions. Elements of the non-positivistic or humanist position are worth adopting when they help to broaden substantive, theoretical discussion, reducing its austerity. But when the humanist position is taken to presentist extremes, proclaiming that reconstructions of the past are entirely subjective creations of the archaeologist (Leone 1986) it needs to be checked. This can be done through positivistic testing (to the limits of the possible) and through anthropologically informed attention to the substantive qualities of particular bodies of evidence. All of this moves us towards the middle ground between extreme positivistic and non-positivistic positions. It places us in a much more interesting and useful position for grappling with the astoundingly rich interpretive puzzles in the archaeological and historical records left by ancient complex polities.

Numerous conceptual choices have been reviewed. A theoretical framework and set of research questions have emerged. The next step is to narrow the focus and to fill in some detail about the Rosario polity in its local and Maya setting (Chapter 3). This is necessary background for considering some of the widely faced methodological problems and choices that occur when the theoretical framework comes to be confronted with the Rosario polity's single-period settlement record (Chapter 4).

3

The Rosario polity

With a theoretical framework in hand, a range of methodological problems need to be tackled before analytical procedures can be developed and applied towards the goal of characterizing political structure and organization in the Rosario polity. But discussion of methodological problems and application of analytical techniques only make sense with fairly specific reference to the properties of a given archaeological settlement record. To introduce the Rosario settlement record, I now provide a brief sketch of the Rosario polity in its local and wider Maya context.

The Rosario polity occupies a small valley within the Upper Grijalva Tributaries of Chiapas, Mexico (Figures 1 and 2). The Upper Tributaries lie on the southwest edge of the tropical rainforest Usumacinta Lowlands, a core area of Classic Period (AD 300–950) Maya political and cultural development, with major centers such as Yaxchilán, Bonampak, and Piedras Negras (Figure 1). The surveyed part of the Rosario Valley covered just under 53 sq km, estimated to have been almost the entire extent of the Rosario polity's densely settled core. Within this, there was an estimated (maximum) population of 20,000 in the Late/Terminal Classic Period, AD 700–950 (Figures 3 and 4). Adding on (cursorily examined) peripheral area gives a total polity area of 100–150 sq km. Consisting primarily of rugged hills separating the Rosario polity from neighboring polities, most of the peripheral area was very sparsely settled. The Rosario polity core has several nested districts. Two *sections* correspond to upper and lower valley halves. Seven *pockets* consist of further divisions of the sections, corresponding to small sub-basins (Figure 5). A political settlement-hierarchy has four discrete levels of centers that include civic-ceremonial plazas (Figure 5, Table 2).

Viewed in light of wider reconnaissance (Lowe 1959; Lee 1984), the Rosario polity appears to be one of at least seven or eight polities in the northern Upper Grijalva Tributaries (Figure 2). Territorial dimensions of the other polities are roughly similar to those of the Rosario polity. In this particular context, the term *polity* denotes a broadly autonomous political entity (Renfrew 1986: 2), with state-like political structure. But the Rosario polity's autonomy was most probably not absolute. Tenam Rosario, its capital, may have exercised dominance over neighboring polities and the Rosario polity may thus have been the core area for a larger aggregation, covering about 1,300–1,500 sq km of the northern Upper Tributaries (Figure 2). Two main lines of evidence support this. First, Tenam Rosario has a civic-ceremonial zone which is larger, more elaborate, and better

40

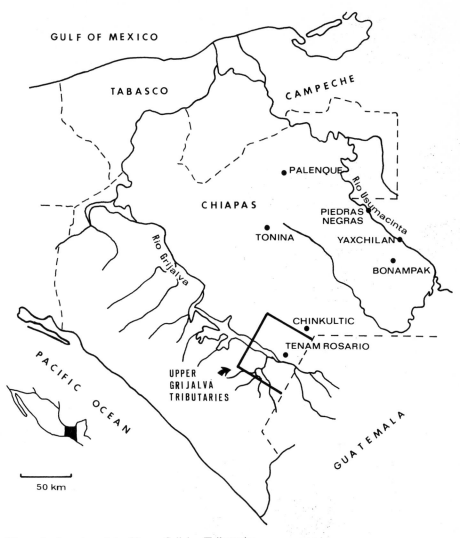

GULF OF MEXICO

TABASCO

CAMPECHE

PALENQUE

CHIAPAS

Rio Usumacinta

PIEDRAS
NEGRAS

TONINA

YAXCHILAN

Rio Grijalva

BONAMPAK

CHINKULTIC

TENAM ROSARIO

UPPER
GRIJALVA
TRIBUTARIES

PACIFIC OCEAN

GUATEMALA

50 km

Figure 1   Location of the Upper Grijalva Tributaries

planned than the civic-ceremonial zone of any other known contemporaneous center in the Upper Tributaries (Chapter 7). Second, Tenam Rosario's known sculptural and iconographic corpus is without equal in the Upper Tributaries (Agrinier 1983; Ayala 1984).

A number of definitional comparisons better qualify the term polity as used here and give a sense of how the Rosario polity fits into some of the schemes currently used by archaeologists to conceptualize political structure. At 1,300–1,500 sq km, the Upper Tributaries aggregation (of which the Rosario polity forms the hypothetical core) falls within the size range for Early State Modules (Renfrew 1975) or Classic Lowland Maya realms (Hammond 1974). With its four levels of political settlement-hierarchy, the Rosario polity core is a state according to

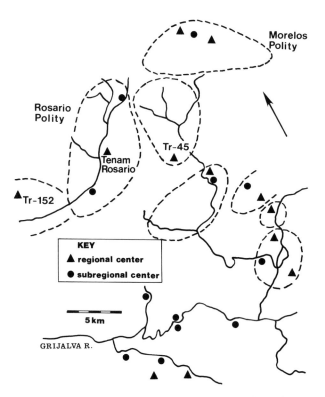

Figure 2   Classic polities in the northern Upper Tributaries

administrative-hierarchy criteria (Wright 1977). The core's maximum estimated population (20,000) falls within the lower end of a population size-range criterion for states (Sanders and Price 1968: 85). Finally, the Rosario polity amply meets sociopolitical stratification requirements for classification as a state (Fried 1967; Service 1971; Friedman and Rowlands 1977). This can be judged from the variable size and quality of its residential architecture, its monumental civic-ceremonial buildings, and its multilevel political settlement hierarchy. These comparisons are not intrinsically important (i.e., as part of a taxonomic exercise), but they do show where the Rosario polity is located in a wider set of archaeological frameworks for describing complex political structure.

Let me now turn to a variety of locally relevant and rather practical reasons which prompted selection of the Rosario Valley in particular as an arena for study of Classic Maya settlement and politics. Results of extensive prior research in the valley and its immediate surroundings were available, thanks to the efforts of archaeologists working with the New World Archaeological Foundation (Lowe 1959; Lee 1984; Agrinier 1983, 1984). As is so often the case, the prior work facilitated problem-oriented research, since exploratory time-space definition had already been accomplished and the general outlines of cultural development in the Rosario Valley and in the Upper Tributaries were already known.

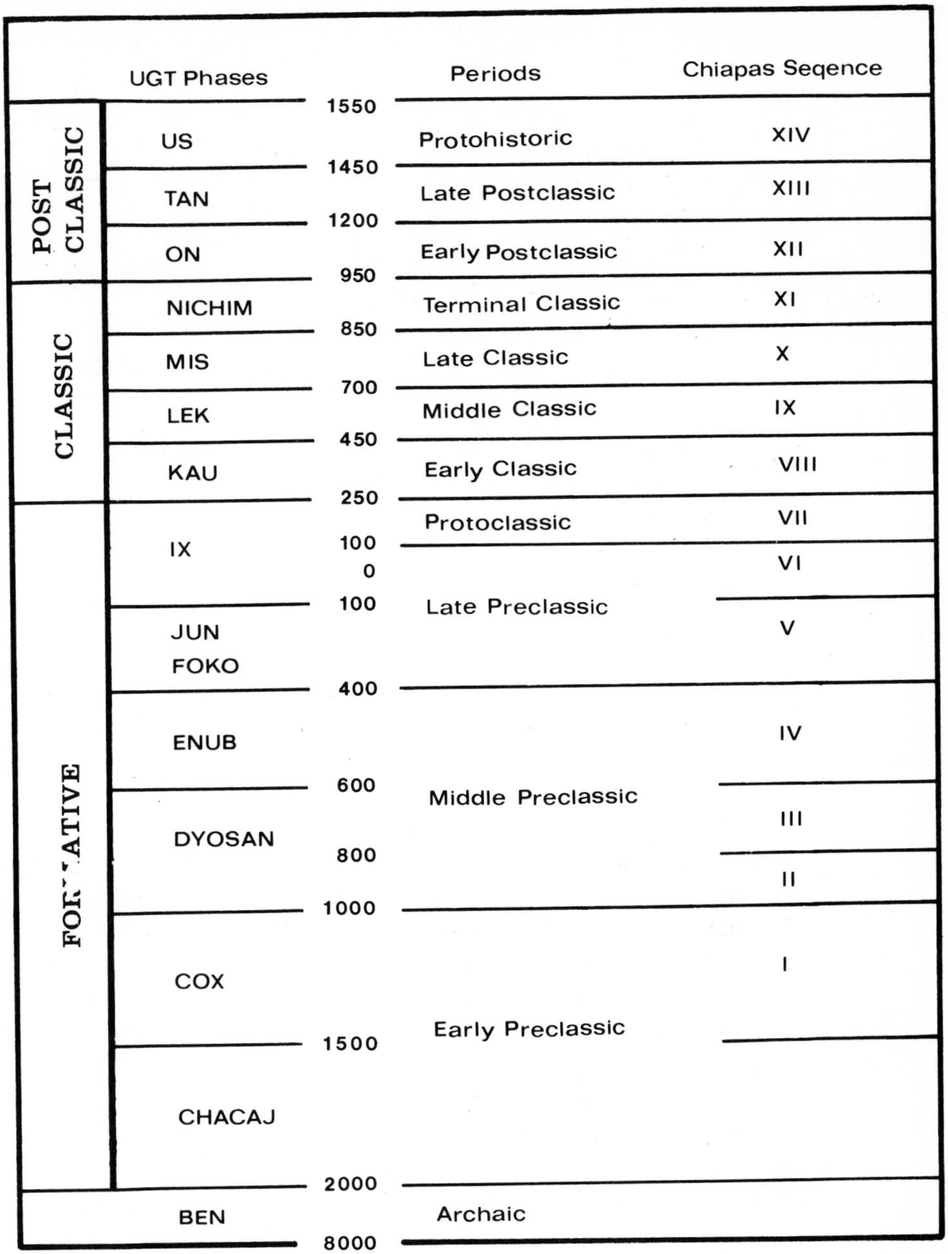

	UGT Phases		Periods	Chiapas Seqence
POST CLASSIC	US	1550	Protohistoric	XIV
	TAN	1450	Late Postclassic	XIII
	ON	1200	Early Postclassic	XII
CLASSIC	NICHIM	950	Terminal Classic	XI
	MIS	850	Late Classic	X
	LEK	700	Middle Classic	IX
	KAU	450	Early Classic	VIII
FORMATIVE	IX	250 / 100	Protoclassic	VII
		0		VI
	JUN	100	Late Preclassic	V
	FOKO			
	ENUB	400		IV
	DYOSAN	600	Middle Preclassic	III
		800		II
	COX	1000		I
	CHACAJ	1500	Early Preclassic	
	BEN	2000 / 8000	Archaic	

Figure 3 Chronology

Earlier reconnaissance within the valley and excavations at the sites of Tenam Rosario and El Rosario showed a marked settlement climax in the Late/Terminal Classic Period followed by a near-total crash in the Early Postclassic Period (Figure 3). This made it likely that the valley was a good place to attempt a synchronic characterization of Late/Terminal Classic settlement and politics, relatively free

Key

- - - - **river**

——— **valley floor edge**

▬▬▬ **survey edge**

TENAM ROSARIO

EL ROSARIO

1k

Figure 4   Rosario polity: Late/Terminal Classic settlement

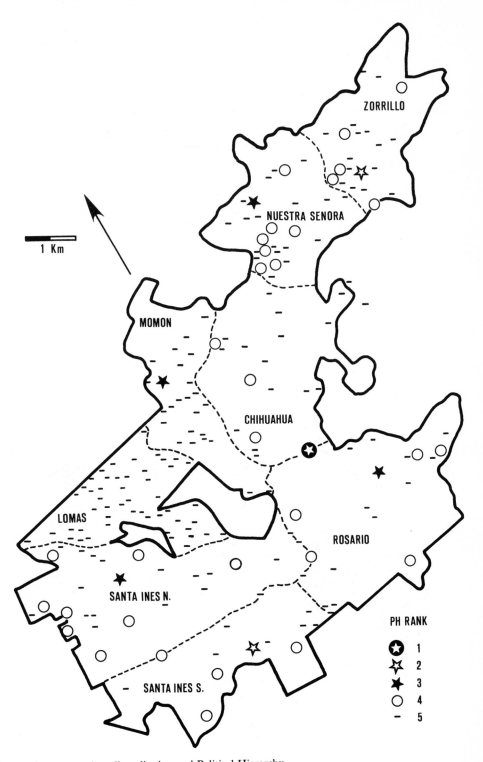

Figure 5   Rosario polity: districts and Political Hierarchy

from overburden caused by subsequent settlement activities. From another vantage, the single-period settlement record was and is a drawback, since it is difficult to trace developments through a succession of archaeological periods. Earlier and later archaeological periods are better represented in other parts of the Upper Tributaries and neighboring Comitán Plateau (Lee 1984; Bryant 1984; Blake 1985; Alvarez 1982). Thus, diachronic settlement developments may be more readily appreciated at a larger scale, incorporating several valleys. But within the Rosario Valley itself, chronological problems importantly affect settlement analysis, especially with respect to contemporaneity and equifinality (Chapter 4).

A prosaic but important reason for selecting the Rosario Valley for settlement survey was the excellent visibility and state of preservation of a wide range of architectural remains. Aspects of the valley's physical setting which contribute to its excellent settlement record are reviewed subsequently, along with fieldwork methods (Chapter 4). Suffice it to say here that the settlement record's high quality made it clear that detailed recording of architectural data would be possible. This in turn would provide a data base appropriate for analysis of settlement form and contents carried out with qualitative sociopolitical questions in mind. It would be possible to go beyond relatively simple quantitative demographic issues.

The initial tracing of potentially valid sociopolitical boundaries around the valley was aided by topographic factors and by prior knowledge of major centers in the Rosario and neighboring valleys (Figure 2). Survey limits could be set towards the half-way point between Tenam Rosario, the centrally located capital, and each of two contemporaneous and more or less equally ranked centers (Tr-152 and Tr-45). Given such presumed ancient boundaries to work with, the relative ease with which surface archaeological features could be recorded made it possible to plan (and achieve) near-complete coverage of a meaningfully bounded political unit, the Rosario polity's core zone. Complete rather than interval coverage was required for the study of sociopolitical structure and organization, given the importance of appreciating territorial arrangements and full sets of intersite relations.

Beyond the local and practical reasons for choosing the Rosario Valley as a setting for studying politics and settlement, cultural-historical factors suggested that the Rosario polity was an interesting example of Maya political structure. The Rosario polity's Late/Terminal Classic settlement climax followed by Postclassic collapse has clear parallels with settlement history in many parts of the Lowland Maya area (Ashmore ed. 1981). This makes the Rosario polity another victim of the celebrated Maya collapse (Culbert ed. 1973; Lowe 1985). More specifically, relations between Tenam Rosario and much larger centers in the neighboring Usumacinta Lowlands may have resembled those between a colony and its metropolis (Figure 1). Agrinier has proposed that relatively strong, elite iconographic and architectural style links existed between Tenam Rosario and Yaxchilán during the Late/Terminal Classic Period (Agrinier 1983). Such a proposal is supported by an analysis of the inscription on Tenam Rosario's Stela 1, some of whose glyphs bear close stylistic resemblances to glyphs found at Yaxchilán (Ayala 1984). Furthermore, in a study of Rosario Valley ballcourts, Agrinier detected a locational pattern whereby the principal ballcourt at Tenam Rosario is approximately aligned with the ballcourts at the two secondary (section) capitals. An imaginary line extending this alignment eastward passes between Bonampak and Yaxchilán in the Usumacinta Lowlands, the proposed metropolitan heartland (Agrinier n.d.). If it did indeed take place, a colonizing and control-seeking move from the Usumacinta zone southwestward towards the Upper Tributaries could have been a reaction to military pressures coming from the Putun Gulf Coast zone to the north (Agrinier 1983). A positive attraction for Usumacinta elites may have been the Upper Tributaries' cotton-growing (J. Marcus, personal communication 1985) or salt-producing potential.

Whatever the precise motivating factors in the metropolis, that the Rosario polity may have been a colony is intriguing for more general reasons. In some cases colonial sociopolitical structure adheres strictly to the idealized norms of the colonizing society. The planned urbanism and orthodox Catholicism in the sixteenth-century New World Spanish empire is much more rigorous than anything found in the Iberian metropolis (Foster 1960). The imposed Inca imperial administrative centers in the provinces are more tightly planned than any centers in the Cuzco metropolitan heartland (Morris and Thompson 1985). Since this is in large part a blank-slate phenomenon, strict adherence to norms might diminish with time through a process of political drift and the organic buildup of settlement. If the Rosario polity's hypothesized colonial regime was relatively short-lived, spanning some part of the Late/Terminal Classic Period (over no more than 250 years), unadulterated metropolitan norms may have had relatively little time to become blurred. This sets up the possibility of comparing more sharply defined colonial structural patterns in the Rosario polity with fuzzier metropolitan patterns (Chapter 11). If one accepts the preceding hypothetical arguments, it follows that the Rosario polity contains a relevant model for political and settlement norms aspired to elsewhere in the Maya Lowlands.

I have already compared some of the conceptual choices made in setting up a study of the Rosario polity to choices made in other studies of ancient Maya (and Mesoamerican) politics (Chapters 1 and 2). But, to provide a fuller understanding of the Rosario polity in a Maya research context, I need to specify how its study fits into the interdisciplinary stream of research bearing on Maya political structure. While focused on Maya issues, the following observations touch on problems common to all fields where an archaeological record for ancient complex polities may be supplemented by rich epigraphic, ethnohistoric, and ethnographic records.

A key point is that my analysis is framed first and foremost in terms of archaeological settlement evidence and what it can tell us about some fairly general principles of political structure and organization among the Classic Maya. This needs saying because there is an extensive set of basically non-archaeological studies about Classic Maya politics which draw on epigraphic evidence and use this to fashion particularistic and synthetic reconstructions of the emic aspects of Maya politics (references in Fox and Justeson 1986; Morely *et al.* 1983; Schele and Miller 1986). This kind of reconstruction is not attempted here. Compelling negative reasons for this are a scanty local epigraphic record (Agrinier 1983; Ayala 1984) and the author's lack of expertise in epigraphic matters. A positive reason for not delving into epigraphy is to avoid getting sidetracked from a central goal of critically stretching the analytical lengths to which archaeological settlement evidence may be taken in pursuit of political questions. This is a widely neglected goal in archaeological studies of Maya settlement and politics (see Ashmore ed. 1981), and one which receives no particularly direct help from detailed epigraphic studies (except insofar as these improve chronological resolution). Additionally, to this outsider, Maya epigraphic studies appear to be in a self-congratulatory phase concerning great substantive advances and have yet to mount a concerted and self-consciously critical attack on issues in political theory and how they relate to the mounting quantities of (decifered) epigraphic evidence. It stands to reason, however, that when required advances have been made on all fronts, future generations of studies of ancient Maya politics will have to combine critical and sophisticated handling of archaeological (settlement and excavation) evidence with equally critical handling of epigraphic evidence. Then, and only then, will the several kinds of evidence illuminate political structure and organization at several differing levels of emic and etic abstraction.

Another branch of studies which touches on ancient Maya politics uses ethnohistoric sources. Ethnohistory does enter more directly than epigraphic studies into my concerns with archaeological settlement evidence and politics. Because there is virtually no locally relevant ethnohistory in the right Classic Period time range or even for the subsequent Postclassic Period (Blake 1985), ethnohistoric materials are not used to construct very specific direct-historic analogs. However, ethnohistoric materials from elsewhere in the Maya area do contribute to the construction of analogs for archaeological study of Maya settlement and politics in the Rosario Valley. Examples of this are the ethnohistorical materials from Yucatan bearing on forced settlement (Chapter 5) and the ethnohistorical materials from Highland Guatemala concerning group stratification (Chapter 8). Beyond this, the major role for ethnohistoric materials and interpretations is rather indirect. As discussed earlier, ethnohistory provides a kind of negative check for discarding irrelevant analogs or models (Chapter 2). Such a check is particularly valuable when the archaeological record itself does not independently or unambiguously allow one to detect such irrelevancies. The ethnohistoric check is carried out by applying a kind of evolutionary-historical logic. The logic is that clearly modern political or economic institutions should not precede clearly premodern or traditional institutions in any given sequence. In other words, non-market economies or archaic administrative structures ethnohistorically documented in the Postclassic Period preclude the possibility of finding market economies or fully professional (Weberian) bureaucracies in the earlier archaeologically documented Classical Period. In turn, this allows one to discount as irrelevant the extradisciplinary theoretical concepts such as the models and analytical techniques which assume existence of modern institutional forms (e.g. information-theoretic approaches, market-based locational analysis, methodological individualism, and so forth).

Ethnographic studies of Maya politics do not bear on the issues dealt with here in any obvious way. The simple reason for this is that analogies drawn from political conditions in ethnographically recorded closed corporate peasant communities (Wolf 1982) are structurally inappropriate for shedding light on ancient complex polities (Chapters 2 and 5). Another fairly straightforward reason for the lack of impact is the relative underdevelopment of political anthropology in Mesoamerica (especially compared to advanced development of this subfield in other areas such as Africa). In a much more subtle way, however, Maya (and Mesoamerican) ethnography does have an impact on a study of ancient Maya politics such as this one. This is because many of the conceptual and analytical themes that run through this study have been wrestled with in the Maya ethnographic arena. A few of these themes are methodological individualism versus holism, analytical scales, controlled comparison, synthetic typological approaches versus analytical functionalism, and positivistic versus relativistic and/or humanistic approaches to research. Awareness of these themes in a closely familar (and a very richly documented) ethnographic setting has led me to consider their potential importance in archaeological studies and to appreciate that there are few clear-cut solutions. A more general observation derives from this. It is that in anthropological archaeology at its most useful, the link between ethnography and archaeology is not just a straightforward mining of the ethnographic case material and ready-made conceptual categories by archaeologists. Beyond this, anthropologically trained archaeologists may pay close attention to ethnography (especially of their own or closely related research areas) in order to inform themselves and form critical judgments on a wide range of theoretical, methodological, and analytical issues affecting the study of complex polities.

As a minor afterthought, it strikes me that Maya ethnoarchaeological studies do not yet have a central role to play in the study of ancient Maya politics. Existing ethnoarchaeological studies (e.g., Hayden and Cannon 1984) do not bear very directly on politics and they tend to be carried out at inappropriately small (subpolity) scales. None of this detracts from their relevance for other issues, including lower-order small-scale bridging arguments that enter into the study of ancient complex polities.

To conclude, my sketch of the Rosario polity provides a springboard from which to plunge through a careful examination of its settlement record. At the bottom lies a full-blown portrait of the Rosario polity's political structure and organization (Chapter 11). On the way down there are many interesting currents to explore (Chapters 4-10).

4

Linking Maya politics and settlement

Bridging arguments for ancient complex polities

Archaeological studies of ancient complex polities often rest on a base of weakly developed bridging arguments for linking theoretical concepts to data in the archaeological record (Chapter 1). Bridging arguments are indeed difficult to develop for such complex subject matter. Furthermore, devoting a lot of attention to them detracts from the time available for pondering what seem to be more fascinating great questions (Chapter 1) and substantive details associated with civilizations. However, there can be no doubt that building bridging arguments has a fascination of its own, requiring intricate problem solving and vigorous imagination on the part of the archaeologist (well exemplified in Binford's Palaeolithic studies – 1983a, 1983b).

In looking at bridging arguments and their uses it makes sense to distinguish "between theory treated methodologically as a means of investigating *another* theory and theory treated substantively as the theory to be investigated" (Bailey 1983: 177). From this perspective, constructing bridging arguments is a methodological means to an end. For example, alternate notions about politics (behavior) are related through bridging arguments to distinguishable settlement patterns (material culture). From a different perspective, the distinction between substantive and methodological theories begins to blur. What look like bridging arguments take on a more intrinsic theoretical interest. For example, an argument that links settlement-density patterns (seen in material culture) and sociopolitical patterns (behavior) becomes the central focus of theoretical interest (Fletcher 1981). This seems to be the trend in certain forms of ethnoarchaeology where material culture is the main archaeological subject matter (Hodder 1982) and the call is for theoretical work to develop generalizations about the role of material culture in creating political structure and organization.

The dichotomy in approaches to bridging arguments proves useful for viewing the purposes to which settlement studies in particular may be put. First, one can take an instrumental view, in which the distribution of ancient settlement over the landscape is taken to inform us about past political, social, economic, or ideological structures and processes. A clear example is the conventional notion that dispersed settlement is an indicator of low levels of centralized political control, while nucleated settlement is an indicator of high levels of control (Chapter 5). Thus, settlement reflects political structure and provides a tool for studying political centralization, its determinants, its relation to other aspects of society, and so forth.

In this view, settlement evidence and its analysis provide one of the means used towards the end, which is to study ancient politics.

As will be shown throughout, there is nothing particularly straightforward about this instrumental use of settlement evidence. There are many methodological difficulties concerning how well the settlement record reflects processes of short-term change (contemporaneity) and whether the same settlement forms always reflect results of the same developments (equifinality). Problems revolving around bridging arguments are so major that they may become all-important, leading to a shift in the position occupied by settlement research in archaeological study.

Results of such a shift are evident in a second approach to settlement research where one may take a more isolated theoretical interest in the relation that settlements have to other variables in a sociocultural system. Consider again the idea that dispersed settlement is associated with low degrees of centralized political control. Problem orientation shifts from a primary interest in political centralization to the reasons why there is a link between degree of settlement nucleation and political centralization. What was a methodological (means to an end) problem becomes the central or substantive problem for research. Such a shift is unfortunate because interesting problems shared with anthropologists and other social scientists are shunted aside in favor of a very narrow focus on the relation between behavior and material culture. A tendency towards elevating methodological activity into the final goal of archaeology unites cultural ecologists (Binford 1983a) and structuralist/contextualists (Hodder 1982). How this happens has been perceptively analyzed by Bailey. "Structuralist archaeologists...wish to deny the validity of this distinction [between methodological and substantive theory] and...assert that the methodological theory by which they give meaning to the archaeological record and the substantive theory in terms of which they explain past behavior are one and the same" (Bailey 1983: 177–178). On the other side of the divide, a positivistic "emphasis on methodology is also vulnerable to the charge of induction and a belief that reconstructing the past without clearly specified a priori substantive aims will somehow lead to a uniquely correct view of past reality" (Bailey 1983: 178).

Within its severe limitations, the second approach to settlement studies can be interesting, but it has not influenced Mesoamerican and Maya settlement studies up to now. Defending the second approach, one could argue that it is a prerequisite for constructing good bridging arguments. One needs to understand why certain relations exist between behavior and settlement before one can infer behavior from settlements (e.g., Hodder 1982: 117–139). This is a fair argument, and archaeologists working with settlement evidence could worry more than they do about bridging arguments. But a perception that bridging arguments need sharpening does not give grounds for shifting the focus of research away from substantive questions about human history (at various levels of abstraction) and entirely onto a methodological domain (covering the mechanics of the relation between thought/behavior and material culture).

The second approach would be better justified if it could be shown that settlement patterns have a uniquely strong determinant effect on political structure.

It would then be possible to study the nexus between settlement and political behavior with certainty of touching on central issues in political life. However, a much sounder working assumption for most ancient complex polities is that settlement is more clearly determined by social, political, and ideological factors than it is a determinant for these. So the first of the two approaches to settlement studies continues to be most viable.

More specifically, studies of Maya settlement are no exception to a general pattern of weakly developed bridging arguments (Sabloff 1983). As a rule, the fairly informal attempts to relate Maya settlement patterning to properties of political structure have used an environmental to political chain of reasoning (Chapter 1). One example is the argument that lowland tropical forest environments do not allow much more than undifferentiated swidden agriculture, which itself requires low population densities in a dispersed settlement pattern (as determined by least-effort convenience), a pattern which, in turn, allows only a relatively low level of centralized political control or sociopolitical stratification (Coe 1961; Culbert 1974; Sanders and Price 1968). Such an argument has now been revised as a result of work modifying our appreciation of environment and agriculture (Harrison and Turner eds. 1978; Flannery ed. 1982), and because of studies which have shifted perceptions about the degrees of dispersion in Maya settlement patterns (Haviland 1966a; Ashmore ed. 1981; Kurjack 1974). Yet virtually none of the revisionist work has been done outside the environmental to political chain of reasoning. Instead, revisions attempt to consolidate the chain of reasoning by bringing environmental and agronomic variables into line with increasingly better-known settlement and political variables. Each link in the chain requires bridging arguments. Of all the links, the one of central interest here is the close relation between degree of dispersion in settlement patterns and degree of centralized political control. Subsequently, I attempt to systematize and expand this line of argument (Chapter 5).

More specifically still, I have used several continua of variation (Table 1) to construct a theoretical framework for studying politics and settlement in the Rosario polity (Chapter 2). The importance of trying to develop expected material manifestations for as many as possible of the continua has been stressed. Totally testable models are fine as an ideal, but austere and even uninteresting in practice. From this it follows that a good procedure is to construct theoretically interesting models and questions and then archaeologically try to document as many elements as possible, acknowledging that certain elements in each model are as yet archaeologically untested or untestable (Chapter 2).

To provide bridging arguments for the several continua and their variables, a general strategy is to take the end points of each continuum and set out archaeological (settlement) expectations for it. The specific bridging arguments appear subsequently (Chapters 5–10). A wide range of settlement data are available for constructing bridging arguments (Chapter 5). In some cases, sites or civic-ceremonial plazas can be compared with reference to attributes of size, number and spatial arrangement of buildings, range of building types, and nature of the

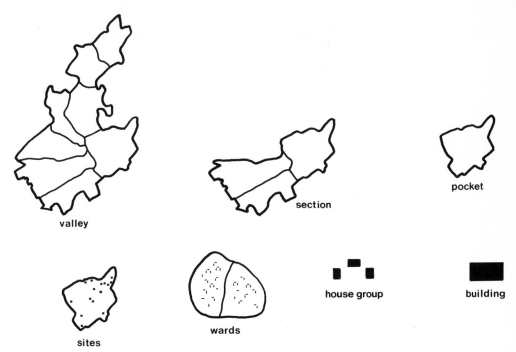

Figure 6   Settlement scales

hinterland. In other cases, territorial divisions may be compared with reference to attributes of areal size, environmental makeup, population, distribution of population across political hierarchy levels, and number of political hierarchy levels. The settlement record's complexity is a tremendous asset, providing many scales to work at.

To construct bridging arguments with relevance to the Rosario polity, I need to work with patterning of settlement and architectural remains from a single archaeological period. Therefore, contemporaneity difficulties loom large as one of the two major generic difficulties in comparing elements in a single-period settlement distribution. The other difficulty concerns equifinality (Hodder and Orton 1976: 239–240), the possibility of different growth patterns for superficially similar settlement configurations. Additional difficulties arising in both single-period and multi-period settlement analysis are: inappropriate scale of coverage, uneven preservation and visibility (affecting recovery), and uncertain form to function arguments. Such difficulties require general attention before constructing specific bridging arguments. An interesting feature of such a general examination is that contemporaneity and equifinality vary in quality and intensity depending on the (spatial) analytical scale chosen. Analytical scales for the Rosario polity are nested divisions (Figure 6): valley, section, pocket, sites, intrasite divisions (wards), domestic housegroups or civic-ceremonial plazas, and individual domestic or civic-ceremonial buildings (compare a slightly simpler scheme in Flannery ed. 1976).

Survey setting and fieldwork methods

Looking at difficulties associated with employing settlement data to test ideas about politics in an ancient complex polity such as the Rosario polity is more useful when there is a clear sense of the conditions (survey setting) and procedures (fieldwork methods) that governed data gathering. The survey setting, the Rosario Valley, lies on the northern edge of the mountainous Upper Grijalva Tributaries Subregion (Lowe 1959) which occupies a downfold between the Cuchumatan Mountains and the edge of the Chiapas Highlands or Mesa Central (Figures 1 and 2). The Upper Tributaries are in *tierra caliente* (with an Aw tropical savannah climate). Much the greater part of the surveyed valley surface had been cleared of its original Tropical Deciduous Forest vegetation. Such conditions, more similar to Highland Mexico than to the Maya Lowlands, were highly favorable to a fieldwalking survey. Present valley population is small, about 2,400 people within the 53 sq km survey area, concentrated in two hamlets. The two major land-use modes – *minifundista* subsistence maize cultivation and large land holdings with commercial cattle grazing, and maize and cotton farming (Agrinier 1984) – have had little adverse impact on the archaeological record. This gives the valley a degree of architectural preservation close to that found in the currently lightly settled Maya Lowlands and much superior to that found in the presently overcrowded and archaeologically ravaged Mexican Highlands.

Modified Highland Mesoamerican strategies of total coverage fieldwalking were used in the Rosario Valley survey (Sanders *et al.* 1979; Blanton *et al.* 1982). While details of data gathering activities may be consulted elsewhere (de Montmollin n.d.a), this discussion is limited to generalities. The major modification to Highland strategies was the much greater use of architecture (rather than sherd scatters and their densities) to define sites. Possibilities afforded by the valley's settlement record allowed this. Even very modest architecture was sufficiently well preserved to be detected, due mostly to absence of deep plowing sufficient to obliterate it. Soil buildup was usually so shallow that few buildings or features are likely to have been masked. Finally, relatively small amounts of surface ceramics (in the absence of deep plowing) made it unfeasible to rely on these for site definition.

A systematic full-coverage approach, providing an overview of all or most of a polity's core area, was required to answer research questions (Chapters 2 and 3). It was useful to record all the constituent territorial units and as complete as possible a set of sites for classification into various hierarchical schemes. Analysis was not aimed primarily at producing ratio information about population density or differential intensities of land use, making a sampling program inappropriate. This contrasts with most other Maya settlement studies which do focus on ratio information (e.g., Greater Tikal [Puleston 1973]; Peten Lakes district [Rice and Rice 1980a]; Peten savanna [Rice and Rice 1980b]; Tikal-Yaxha transect [Ford 1982, 1986]). A compelling argument for full (versus intermittent sampling) coverage is that it better allows locational analysis (Cowgill 1986). But this argument is not centrally relevant to the Rosario case because of a kind of plateau effect in which distances within the surveyed Rosario Valley are so small that they preclude the relevance of the travel-energy-saving logic that underlies locational analysis.

A focus on mapping and surface collection with no excavation was partly a function of time constraints. One possibility, limited test-pitting, would have been of only slight use for addressing the research questions and would not have provided a solution to the key problem of defining chronologically finer-grained segments within the Late/Terminal Classic Period (see below). As things now stand, excavation data from prior seasons allow conclusions about the construction history and function of some (46) Late/Terminal Classic Period domestic buildings at two sites – Tenam Rosario and El Rosario – and about four civic-ceremonial buildings at one site – Tenam Rosario – (Agrinier 1979, 1983; de Montmollin 1984). This must serve as the sample of buildings for which there is something more than a surface knowledge. Slightly farther afield, one can draw on excavation information from Ojo de Agua (Bryant and Lowe 1980) or from Los Cimientos (Rivero 1978), in immediately neighboring zones.

Visibility of architectural remains was good over most of the survey area, the poorest conditions being associated with small patches of secondary regrowth, tall grass, or weed-choked maize. Forested areas most often had sufficiently thin undergrowth to allow detection of buildings. Throughout the survey area, there was a degree of preservation sufficient for satisfactory recording of buildings. While destruction of these was increasing because of deep plowing (in parts of the valley bottom zone) this left at least rubble and sherd scatters to indicate building location (and often general size).

Contemporaneity

Let us now turn to some of the methodological difficulties associated with linking single-period settlement data to political themes. Contemporaneity is the first of these and one of the most serious. Concerning contemporaneity, my aim was not to develop a snapshot of what the settlement and political system was like at one instant in time. Such a research aim has been effectively criticized by Binford (1981) who refers to it as the Pompeii premise. Rather, single-period settlement is analyzed in order to bring out settlement manifestations of broadly consistent structural principles which would underly equally broad and general organizational trends. Thus precise or instantaneous contemporaneity problems lose their urgency.

But using single-period synchronously lumped data (a settlement palimpsest) to address processual questions involving changes within the period under examination always remains difficult. Cross-period comparisons are not necessarily a solution. Single-period contemporaneity difficulties still exist within approaches that compare static patterns from successive archaeological periods. The processual quality of settlement studies covering a number of time periods (Sanders *et al.* 1979; Blanton *et al.* 1982) may be more apparent than real since they essentially provide linear chains of single-period settlement palimpsests. Much discussion of the contemporaneity problem concerns how to manipulate and link up the sequence of palimpsests, offering no approaches to directly overcoming the palimpsest effect

(Schact 1984; Plog 1973). Of course, the palimpsest problem is not resolvable in any absolute sense. All that can be done is to refine chronological control to the point where the palimpsests under study have reasonable temporal proportions. But what is reasonable? Setting aside practical difficulties, ultimately this depends on problem orientation, on the temporal dimensions of the kind of change under investigation (Bailey 1983). Perhaps it is more reasonable when looking at politics to use a time scale of one human generation (30 years) rather than 10 generations (300 years or so, the estimated length of the Late/Terminal Classic Period). This would certainly aid appreciation of succession to political office. But, I will be arguing that generational or shorter time spans (while nice) are not absolutely indispensible for settlement study of consistent structural principles in a political system (principles covered by the continua in Chapter 2).

Direct solutions to contemporaneity difficulties are simple to state but their execution, besides being difficult, produces fresh problems. Increasing the power of a dating instrument through ceramic analysis (to bring out more chronologically sensitive variation) raises practical problems for wide coverage areal survey. Most of these surveys necessarily depend on rapid surface collections for site dating. The small size of such surface collections and their loosely controlled recovery prevent a refined chronological typology from working effectively (Cowgill 1986). One solution is to spend a lot more time on the surface collections, both to expand their size and systematic provenience (Lewarch and O'Brien 1981). This brings us into an area of conflict between extension and intensity of coverage in a situation of "limited good," something which has received explicit attention in most of the serious survey work carried out in Mesoamerica (Sanders *et al.* 1979; Blanton *et al.* 1982; and see especially discussion in Kowalewski and Finsten 1983). A second solution to the contemporaneity difficulty is to abandon regional coverage and concentrate on small-scale excavation to monitor process (producing a few bright spots on the archaeological landscape while consigning the rest of it to darkness). In practical terms, this kind of solution stands at one extreme of the continuum between extension and intensity of coverage. At the other extreme, all research would be survey. Both of the direct solutions to the contemporaneity difficulty are vigorously advocated from what can be called a *processual* position (Wright *et al.* 1980). This commendably seeks an appreciation of short term change in the archaeological record:

> If large site excavations are not undertaken with greater attention to representative sampling, comprehensive recovery of daily debris, and the development of very fine scale – seasonal to decadal – chronologies, we cannot hope to understand the emergence of social stratification, competition among elites, and other such processes. (Wright 1986: 359)

Based on settlement survey results, my analysis of the Rosario polity stands towards the extension end of the coverage continuum. As there is no reason to believe that process is everything, and since much may be learned from sociopolitical statics, my problem orientation has been tailored without apology to (chronological) limitations of the archaeological data. A processual stance (that archaeology is process or it is nothing at all) is only one of many that can be adopted and there is no sign yet that it can replace insights provided by a more static (or *structural*) approach that works within chronological possibilities of regional data sets.

In focusing principally on structural (rather than organizational) aspects, one can utilize peculiarly archaeological analytical concepts of *cultural time* and *stationary state* (Chang 1967). Cultural time is:

> an archaeological interpretation of the relationship between scientific time and archaeological form... It has nothing to do inherently with the archaeological material, for the material's physical time is the archaeologist's own biological time. Nor does it have anything to do with prehistoric peoples, who have long since perished together with their own time. (Chang 1967: 25)

The concept of stationary state underwrites the use of segments of cultural time in studying the past.

> An archaeologically synchronic unit is one in which changes occurred within the bounds of constancy and without upsetting the overall alignment of cultural elements. It is a stationary state in which generalizations as to behavior and style from most of its parts or its most significant parts can be applied to its entirety... Points of time within a "cultural type" or "stationary state" have identical value with reference to one another. (Chang 1967: 33)

Of greatest interest here is the peculiarly archaeological approach to time and process, contrasting with the more concrete aims proposed in the processual approach where the idea is to precisely monitor specific past events (Wright *et al.* 1980).

Let me drive home exactly how the structural approach (incorporating notions such as cultural time and stationary state) actually relates to the processual approach (monitoring the flow of events). The notion of stationary state which underlies the structural approach is a relative one. The length of the time segments utilized depends on what one defines and/or manages to identify archaeologically as significant change (Bailey 1983). Looked at in this way, processual archaeologists are not making qualitatively distinctive divisions of the archaeological record's temporal dimension. Rather, the difference is quantitative. Processualists are much more exacting, fine-grained, and particularistic in what they consider to be the chronological span for significant change. For clear practical reasons exactitude and particularism on the temporal dimension translates into a much smaller scale on the spatial dimension (single households, pits, middens), leaving little or no chance to acquire regional data bases. This is due not just to an image but to a situation of limited good. As with the temporal dimension, the question of proper scale on the spatial dimension must be a relative one dependent on problem orientation (Foley 1981: 197–198; Toumey 1981). Small spatial (and thus social) scales required in processualist approaches severely restrict the range of political questions that can effectively be studied (de Montmollin n.d.b).

For a regional structural study, neither of the direct solutions to contemporaneity difficulties (chronological refinement or an excavation-based stratigraphic focus) are available. Nevertheless, passivity about contemporaneity difficulties is not the sole option. To indirectly reduce contemporaneity difficulties one may reason that settlement from the single archaeological period is mostly relevant to the period's final part. According to Chang's (1967) terminology, the period's final part is a unit of cultural time with stationary state, of indeterminate length but shorter than the whole period. Such a growth-to-late climax-followed-by-crash (or climax–crash) assumption about settlement development is most convenient and useful for relative dating of sites falling within the Late/Terminal Classic Period. Indeed, this is the basic assumption used for working with the later Classic Maya settlement record (Ashmore 1981: 63–64). The climax–crash assumption also surfaces in general discussion of the contemporaneity problem, as one of the options for estimating population when single-period sites are very numerous in the settlement record (Schact 1984: 686–687). The upshot of adopting a climax–crash perspective is a shortening of the length of the time segment or unit of cultural time under study. In this case, the reduction is from the 250–300 year span of the entire Late/ Terminal Classic Period to a shorter span at its end. A simple climax–crash assumption says nothing about the kind of growth (steady, episodic, linear, exponential) that leads up to the climax state. Growth patterns within a period are difficult, if not impossible, to comment on with purely survey data and an absence of readily usable intra-period chronological markers. The climax–crash assumption is simply that there was some kind of growth, since the climax state was most probably not achieved right at the beginning of the period.

We can make other kinds of assumptions about the chronological relations of the sites dated to within a period. One possibility is growth to a maximum at mid-period followed by slow decline in the latter part of the period (Plog 1973). Other possibilities are maximal development at the start of the period followed by decline throughout, maximal development at the start of the period followed by continued high development throughout the period until a sudden crash at the end (the implausible variant of the climax–crash assumption, equivalent to Plog's synchronistic paradigm – 1973: 192–193), and maximal development poles shifting sequentially through different parts of an area during the course of the period. Why is the climax–crash assumption more plausible than the others? As mentioned, it seems more plausible to have some sort of growth throughout a period as opposed to full development at the beginning followed by stasis. In the Rosario Valley, dense Late/ Terminal Classic settlement is followed by very sparse settlement in the Early Postclassic. This suggests a collapse rather than a protracted and gradual winding down of settlement and polity. How relatively sudden the collapse was is more difficult to tell from settlement pattern evidence alone. The pristine nature of the architecture at many sites argues against a slow winding down, which should result in considerable disturbance and stone robbing. The same evidence also weakens the notion that there were distinct development poles sequentially abandoned during the period. Again, one would expect great amounts of disturbance and stone robbing at abandoned sites, with variation in the degree of disturbance depending on how early in the period the sites had been abandoned. Such variation is absent in the settlement record. Finally, the reasonably regular spacing of major centers (Figure 5) suggests a contemporaneously operating arrangement at a maximal point of development. In a system of sequential centers, there would be less of a tendency to respect spacing principles.

So far, my discussion of contemporaneity difficulties has touched on regional-scale patterns. But the nature and severity of contemporaneity difficulties varies with spatial scale. With reference to demographic estimates and their possible distortion by palimpsest effects, it has been argued that the contemporaneity problem is less severe at larger regional scales in the Basin of Mexico (Sanders *et al.* 1979: 65, 73). The reasoning is twofold. First, small site occupations tend to be more short-term and transitory than larger site occupations. This is not a question of analytical scale, but concerns size differences within a single category, the site scale of analysis. Second – in contrast to smallish areas such as the Cuatitlan region – "For much larger areas, like the Basin of Mexico as a whole, where there is a great increase in community sample size, the problem of intraperiod contemporaneity would seem to be less serious" (Sanders *et al.* 1979: 73). In this case, the reference is to a shift in analytical scale since regions are nested within the Basin. The second line of reasoning is a little bit unclear and it might make more sense to specify that because of the increase in community sample size, a larger area coverage reduces the chances of stumbling across a particularly high proportion of small (and therefore ephemeral) sites.

What is the relevance of all this for the Rosario Valley? The issue of contemporaneity for settlement patterns is paramount and a climax–crash assumption is a plausible solution. Because they focus on demographic issues, Sanders and others take a different view of the contemporaneity problem. They see it as a difficulty in showing "that all sites assigned to a particular chronological phase were in fact all occupied throughout all of the time period in question" (Sanders *et al.* 1979: 65), using a synchronistic paradigm (Plog 1973: 192–193). In spite of the scale difference between it and the Rosario Valley (about 3,500 sq km versus 50 sq km), observations from the Basin of Mexico on size-determined variation in the contemporaneity problem's severity are potentially extendible to the Rosario Valley settlement record. Especially noteworthy is the idea that some of the very smallest sites in the Rosario Valley might represent relatively short-term occupations (de Montmollin n.d.a: ch. 7). Would coverage of the whole valley instead of one of its smaller constituent territorial units lessen the contemporaneity problem by reducing the chances of finding a particularly high proportion of small (ephemeral) sites? As it turns out, small sites are so relatively rare in all constituent territorial units (excepting the anomalous peripheral Midvalley Range) that this argument has low relevance.[1]

Contemporaneity at subregional scales (site, ward, and housegroup) revolves around the same basic question. Are we looking at a blurred palimpsest or are the patterns in the distribution maps relatable to the (precrash) climax condition of the settlement unit? But there are shifts in the kinds of arguments that can be mobilized.

If the climax–crash assumption can be defended at some of the smaller settlement scales, it becomes possible to address new issues in settlement interpretation specific to those scales. For example, one can hypothesize the existence of a regular developmental cycle for domestic units (occupying housegroups). One can then explore through bridging arguments whether the operation of such a cycle is a determinant of variability in housegroup form. If this can be shown, one can then go on to evaluate the effects of domestic cycling on political structure and organization (Chapter 8). Similar lines of interpretation are feasible at other scales such as the site and district (Chapter 10).

To come to grips with contemporaneity difficulties at the subregional scale, a concrete example proves useful. The example is El Rosario (Figure 7), the most closely studied site in the survey area (de Montmollin 1984). El Rosario is a representative case for many other valley sites, at least those towards the larger end of the demographic size continuum. In a detailed architectural survey carried out at El Rosario (before the general valley survey), sustained attention was given to problems of chronological control, as a precondition for carrying out synchronic studies of its community structure. From this site, one can draw on a relatively large selection of excavated buildings and features to check statements based on survey data. However, this skewed sample cannot be used to validate assertions about contemporaneity which are meant to cover the whole universe of buildings.

The basic proposal is that the bulk of the buildings at El Rosario functioned simultaneously at the community's moment of peak extension, immediately prior to its abrupt abandonment at the end of the Late/Terminal Classic Period. In other words, the climax–crash perspective is applied to a community development pattern (as it was earlier to a polity-wide development pattern). El Rosario is treated as a unit of cultural time, which contains synchronic variability free from the noise provided by extreme diachronic variability. Several arguments support this proposal.

To begin rather simply, El Rosario is a single-component site, with occupation limited principally to the Late/Terminal Classic Period, a claim founded on the uniformity of diagnostic ceramic materials and general architectural style. Thus, the site lacks a palimpsest of successive or intermittent occupations from various archaeological periods; but this says nothing about contemporaneity difficulties within the single occupation period. One possibility is that some or all of the site's six wards (Sections A to F in Figure 7) were founded and abandoned successively during the period's span of eight to ten generations. Were this the case, structural analysis requiring synchronicity for comparison of remains across the site would indeed be misapplied to a chronologically composite set of wards. Surface architecture evidence can be used to support the counter-argument that the six wards were occupied simultaneously (in a climax–crash framework). The site's six

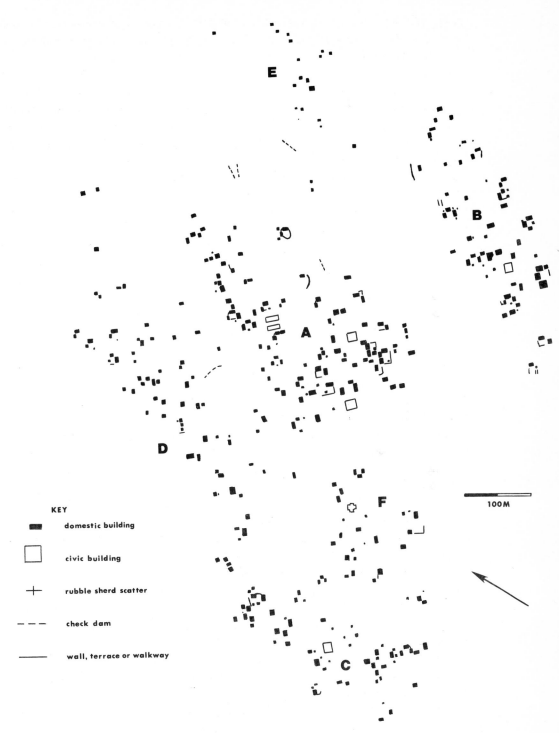

Figure 7   El Rosario (RV163)

civic-ceremonial buildings, located in four of the six wards, are roughly aligned in a capital-T formation (Figure 7). As such a disposition is not determined by topographic factors, it seems to be a result of community-scale planning. Such planning is more likely to have been done for a community in the process of growing to reach its final (six-ward) form than for a community that shifted its center of ceremonial and demographic gravity every generation or so. Another pattern supporting the idea that wards were contemporaneously occupied is the similar state of decay in housemounds across all of the wards. The significance of this is that a sequential founding and abandonment of wards, with discernible amounts of stone robbing in the abandoned wards, should have produced different degrees of decay among the several wards.[2] Finally, tenuous support for climax contemporaneity among wards (and perhaps smaller-scale units) is the rigorous similarity in the orientation of buildings across all wards, 40–50 degrees west of magnetic north (Figure 7). The same orientation holds across virtually all the Late/Terminal Classic Period sites in the survey area. However, its remarkable universality may weaken uniform orientation as a contemporaneity indicator.

Even if one accepts that all wards were broadly in use towards the end of El Rosario's occupation, there remain contemporaneity difficulties at smaller scales. A possibility is that significant numbers of housegroups were abandoned at the point of peak settlement (as suggested by ethnoarchaeological cautionary tales). Again, arguments hinge on surface evidence. Formal planning in the spatial dispositions among housegroups is not present and cannot be used as an argument for climax contemporaneity. Nevertheless, parts of some wards display intense crowding among housegroups, with no clear signs of overlapping, surely indirect evidence for climax contemporaneity. Naturally, such an argument can only be extended to similarly crowded parts of sites elsewhere in the valley. An argument used at the ward scale also applies at the housegroup scale. The non-stone-robbing pattern is more congruent with climax contemporaneity than with sequential founding and abandonment.

For the smallest relevant settlement scale, the individual building, I shift from a focus on El Rosario as a paradigm to a more general focus on Maya settlement. In Maya settlement studies, a number of interesting arguments have been made both for and against contemporaneity of individual house remains on single-period settlement maps. Indeed, the issue receives much greater attention in Maya than in Highland Mesoamerican settlement studies, for reasons traceable to long-held assumptions about greater reliance on swidden agriculture and thus greater settlement shifting in the Maya Lowlands. These assumptions are in need of re-examination (see discussion below). Comments here draw mostly on Puleston's useful review of Maya Lowland settlement (1973: 151–164; with further references there to Haviland's studies at Tikal – 1963, 1969, 1970).

Before looking at pro and con arguments about domestic building contemporaneity in Maya settlement, some of these arguments' general features are worth noting. The time span considered falls within a single period and temporal divisions of the ceramic sequence are not fine enough to impinge on contemporaneity questions. Although most of the arguments are phrased in terms most closely relevant to the housegroup scale, none of them directly addresses the contemporaneity problem at this scale. Rather, arguments are treated as relevant to larger settlement scales (ward, site, region) through extrapolation based on an implicit assumption that what applies in the smaller units in a nested arrangement can be used to shed light on the larger units. Such extrapolation can be accepted on practical grounds for resolution of contemporaneity problems, but the theoretical implications of simple extension from small social building blocks (households) to whole communities and societies require much more thought than they have received (Chapter 11). At any rate the contemporaneity arguments are discussed here as they apply at the housegroup and individual building scales. The arguments are unclear about the particular growth pattern envisaged, but virtually all of them implicitly support a climax–crash view. I begin with a set of arguments in favor of contemporaneity or residential stability for dwelling structures within a period.

1 Architectural alterations within a ceramic phase are frequent; dividing the number of these into total phase length gives a figure that corresponds reasonably to a house lifespan (Haviland 1970: 191).

2 Earlier house floors are included in subsequent alterations, which suggests that there was no substantial period of abandonment before alteration, no period long enough for the floor to deteriorate from exposure to the elements (Haviland 1970: 191).

3 Some domestic middens next to houses show evidence of continuous deposition (Haviland 1970: 191).

4 It is very rare to find disturbed burials in building platforms and from this one can infer continuous occupation without loss of information as to the location of prior burials (Haviland 1970: 191).

5 Physical permanence of residential architecture in prehistoric times (i.e., formal stone substructure platforms, plaster floors, paved patios) suggests enduring use, in contrast to relatively more ephemeral architecture known from historic or modern times, from which many shifting settlement analogies are drawn (Puleston 1973: 163–164). Similar lines of reasoning are used with reference to the range of variability within prehistoric housing at Dzibilchaltun: "Less substantial architecture may represent shorter occupations, but ruins that indicate considerable investment of energy likely were not abandoned for centuries" (Kurjack 1979: 12).

6 Spatial evidence for intensive food production (i.e., kitchen gardens) and for the relative crowding of buildings suggests inhibition of mobility and continuous occupation (Puleston 1973: 160–161).

Further arguments (not mentioned in Puleston's review) are even more directly keyed to establishing contemporaneity for buildings within a housegroup.

7 Certain excavated features such as patio floors can be used to link up two or more buildings within a housegroup, providing a powerful argument for contemporaneous occupation.

8 Specific connecting facilities (such as raised stone-lined walkways) may be

discernible by excavation or even by surface survey and they can then be used to establish contemporaneous occupation for the linked buildings.

9 Boundary walls which surround adjacent housegroups are good indicators of contemporaneous occupation (Kurjack 1979: 12).

10 Formal arrangement of buildings around a patio area is not incontrovertible evidence for continuing simultaneous use, but it might be pressed into service because it is so easy to detect in survey.

11 An equally tenuous but still necessary basis for arguing housegroup-scale contemporaneity is a common focus of the larger domestic buildings on a small domestic altar.

Now I review a set of arguments that challenge the notion of contemporaneity or residential stability for dwellings within a period. The main burden of these arguments is to suggest that few of the individual dwellings that appear on a single-period palimpsest map were in simultaneous use at any one time during the period, including its final span.

1 A shifting swidden cultivation system linked to shifting settlement produces single-period settlement maps which represent a palimpsest of successively occupied or intermittently occupied buildings, housegroups, and settlements. Swidden requires frequent settlement shifts because households and communities have to keep moving around to avoid inefficiencies of land exhaustion immediately adjacent to their settlement (Sanders 1962, 1963, 1967; Willey and Bullard 1965; Coe 1961). The argument linking swidden and shifting settlement is central not only in methodological debates about contemporaneity, but also in substantive discussions about the nature of Maya civilization. In the latter case it appears as a link in the environmental to political chain of reasoning (Chapter 1). Being so central, it deserves extended attention. The automatic link between swidden and shifting settlement, in particular, needs to be questioned. First, as a general point, a cross-cultural ethnographic sample has been used to challenge the necessary connection between swidden agriculture and shifting settlement (Harris 1972). Second, direct-historical ethnographic analogies from modern Yucatan which have illustrated the link between shifting settlement and swidden are problematic at the source. Much of the ethnographic work (summarized in Sanders 1967) was conducted in or near a frontier zone created by the nineteenth-century Caste War, with little account taken of such an unusual context. Fuller historical settings for the ethnographic variability in this region have been brought out by recent work with a longer diachronic perspective (Jones ed. 1977; Bricker 1981: ch. 8; Farriss 1984). None of the new studies support the notion that swidden agriculture was a prime determinant of shifting settlement for the Yucatec Maya. There are much more compelling geopolitical reasons for the settlement shifts observed. Thus, relative stability, one of the main differences between settlements associated with swidden and settlements associated with intensive agriculture, begins to blur. Consequently, debates about whether swidden agriculture was really important for the ancient Maya (Harrison and Turner eds. 1978) become less relevant. Even within the economically-determinist limits of the environmental to political chain

of reasoning and of the (Maya) swidden hypothesis, a pattern of rapidly shifting settlement determined by swidden agriculture is less plausible than it once seemed.

2 Residential abandonment always followed burial, with consequent frequent shifts of dwellings (Thompson 1971, drawing on ethnohistorical sources).

3 Residential instability is and was a Maya cultural trait (Thompson 1971; Vogt 1964a, 1964b, 1983). Vogt's arguments are based on a Genetic Model of Maya cultural development which posits great diachronic continuities in Maya culture including settlement patterns (Chapter 5, note 11).

4 Presumably because of the requirements of swidden agriculture, there were many cases of dual commoner residence related to an infield-outfield system. The implications of this are that many of the buildings in the distribution maps were only intermittently or seasonally occupied field (or *milpa*) houses. Dual residence of this kind is proposed as a possibility for Tikal. But the possibility is rejected on the basis of settlement evidence for the equally high construction quality and close spacing of possible outlying field houses compared to urban houses (Puleston 1973: 159–160). Another proposal is that Classic dual residence systems existed because these are present in modern Zinacantan and the Genetic Model of Maya cultural development posits no intervening change (Vogt 1983: 101–103, 111). A study of dual residence and possible *milpa* houses at Classic Coba comes to essentially the same conclusions as for Tikal (Folan, Kintz, and Fletcher 1983: 193–194). Finally, there is a possibility that a dual residence system existed in the Classic Copan Valley (Webster 1985a: 50; Fash 1986: 93).

Arguments against residential stability tend to propose great cultural continuity, allowing appeal to the authority of analogies from Maya ethnography or ethnohistory (used in a context of validation). Arguments in favor of residential stability are based on behavioral inferences from the patterning of remains discovered in archaeological excavation (no. 1, no. 2, no. 3, no. 4, and no. 7) or else on inferences drawn from archaeologically recorded surface settlement configurations (no. 6, no. 10, and no. 11). Some of the arguments (no. 5, no. 8, and no. 9) may or may not require solely survey evidence, depending on visibility conditions.

I can now consider whether the climax–crash framework applies within most of the housegroups in the Rosario Valley by considering how these fit into the scheme of pro and con arguments just reviewed. The sample of excavated buildings (46) is incalculably small relative to the total number of ostensibly Late/Terminal Classic buildings recovered in the survey (4,300). Therefore, my arguments must necessarily rely on survey evidence. Two arguments in favor of residential stability from Tikal, relative physical permanence of prehispanic domestic architecture (no. 5) and relative crowding inhibiting mobility (no. 6), are readily applicable. Rosario Valley sites are generally quite densely packed with domestic buildings. Densities are usually much greater than at Tikal or any other mapped Lowland site (compare the Rosario Valley all-site average of 8 buildings per ha to the suburban Tikal average of 1 building per ha). The quality of prehispanic house-platform construction in the Rosario Valley far exceeds that found in modern traditional housing in the valley or in the adjacent Chiapas Highlands (home of the analogy-generating Tzotzil and Tzeltal Maya groups – Vogt 1969). Concerning arguments no. 8 and no. 11, connecting walkways or housegroup altars are much too scarce to have much bearing. Argument no. 10, formal arrangement around a patio, is widely relevant since such formality occurs in 1,199 multibuilding housegroups out of the valley's 2,429 single and multibuilding housegroups.[3] This argument is especially useful since it is wildly impractical to excavate every last multibuilding housegroup in order to ferret out the details of its construction history. Finally, argument no. 9, boundary walls around housegroups, is not usable because these features are so rare (although they are more common at some Upper Tributaries sites – Rivero 1983).

An argument against contemporaneity that may apply in the Rosario Valley concerns dual residence (no. 4). Tiny and peripherally located sites may have contained field houses or seasonal facilities, used in addition to more substantial home-base residences in the larger more centrally located sites. This question has been fully considered elsewhere (de Montmollin n.d.a: ch. 7). In brief, the answer is that buildings broadly interpretable as field houses comprise a tiny proportion of all the buildings in the survey area (about 0.02 %). The general question of field houses is best separated from the question of dual elite residences which sometimes crops up in Maya settlement studies (Adams and Smith 1981: 343, 348; Leventhal 1981: 207; Freidel and Sabloff 1984: 161). Dual elite residence is a possibility for the Rosario Valley (Chapter 7). But, given the much smaller numbers of elite as opposed to commoner dwellings (Chapter 8), likely cases of dual elite residence are not numerous. Like the fields houses, the elite second houses would thus contribute little to methodological problems of overcounting (for demographic estimates). In contrast, the possibility of a dual elite residence system has much greater impact on substantive interpretations of political centralization and integration (Chapter 7).

Because they use ethnographic/ethnohistoric analogs in a context of validation, and thus should be avoided, the other arguments against residential stability (no. 1, no. 2, no. 3) cannot be applied directly to the Rosario settlement record. Such arguments would require sets of archaeological test implications to become useful in this context. Since the converse of the arguments in favor of contemporaneity has given us some required implications, it is most economical to refer to them.

In conclusion, my review of contemporaneity difficulties as they apply to the Rosario settlement record (at various scales) relies on a (static) structural rather than a (dynamic) processual approach. Because of this, contemporaneity difficulties are dealt with circuitously rather than head-on. Contemporaneity difficulties clearly show the inextricable linkage between the state of methodology (observational theory) and the possibilities that are truly available for addressing substantive theoretical problems. In large part, my substantive theoretical approach to political structure and organization is keyed to structure (versus organization) because of having to wrestle with the chronology of a regional settlement record. A degree of bottom-up methodological determinism of this kind is acceptable for two principal reasons. On a positive note, social statics are a legitimate area of substantive theoretical interest. It may even be impossible to analyze any political system, without appreciating its structure (seen in a freeze-frame). On a negative note, purely processual approaches cannot give adequate appreciations of sociopolitical phenomena at a large regional scale. The substantive sociopolitical implication for such a methodological spatial-scale problem is clear. Larger-scale structural approaches are required to avoid the problems of strict methodological individualism associated with small-scale processual approaches. Strict methodological individualism is the assumption underlying interpretations of large sociopolitical systems made purely in terms of their smallest-scale (individual or household) components (Ahmed 1976; de Montmollin n.d.b; problems of methodological individualism and spatial scale are reviewed in Chapter 11).

With respect to the Rosario polity, I need to infer process (organization) from structure. This is exemplified by the way the Classic Maya collapse is handled (further details in Chapter 10). Viewed through the lens of a climax–crash assumption, the static Late/Terminal Classic settlement record shows patterning relatable to structural principles. The structural principles exist in the time immediately preceding the political–organizational crash whose results are evident in the subsequent Early Postclassic Period. A relevant question is whether the linkage of particular structural principles and political collapse is accounted for by (middle range theoretical) generalizations from political anthropology. If not, rethinking of the generalizations may be in order.[4]

Equifinality

Equifinality is a second key methodological difficulty in settlement studies (Hodder and Orton 1976: 239–240). Ideally, one wants to know something about the developmental runup to the static patterns seen in maps of regions, sites, wards, housegroups, and buildings. In practice, this knowledge is difficult to acquire with the surface examination allowed by settlement survey. Several general solutions to equifinality difficulties are on offer. One solution is to create a finer chronological instrument permitting the handling of more and shorter time segments. Practically, this kind of solution should be most effective for the larger regional scales of settlement analysis. At these scales individual sites in a region are redated (within what was formerly seen as a single period). Comparing several regions reworked in this way allows the identification of newly distinct development trajectories (Tolstoy [1975] has a famous example of this from the Formative Basin of Mexico). This can be done with existing surface ceramic collections; it does not necessarily require new excavation or more intensive controlled surface collection techniques. Taking advantage of improvements in chronological instruments at the intrasite scale is another matter. In practical terms, there has to be a shift in surface collection tactics, from rapid unsystematic "pickup" to more controlled systematic "pickup" aimed at covering all parts of a site. Moving down to the housegroup or individual building scale, collections have to become ever more controlled, entailing huge increases in time and effort and cutting down the possibilities for expansive total coverage survey. As mentioned with reference to contemporaneity, a chronological refinement solution has yet to be attempted in the Rosario Valley.

A solution to equifinality at the individual building scale is to search for cuts into buildings which might provide a glimpse of construction development prior to the final superficially visible form. Such a crypto-excavation approach, seeking to take advantage of looting or quarrying activities, has little relevance in the Rosario Valley with its virtually pristine archaeological record. The most forthright solution is to excavate, but this is awkward since the crux of the equifinality problem is that things are not as they seem on the surface. This clearly rules out extrapolation from a small number of excavated buildings to the thousands of buildings that are routinely recorded in Maya settlement surveys. Unfortunately, this difficulty applies even when sophisticated sampling strategies govern the selection of buildings for excavation (Rice and Rice 1980a, 1980b; Ford 1982, 1986).

As with contemporaneity, one finds a polar contrast between processual and structural approaches to dealing with equifinality. A processual approach attacks equifinality difficulties directly (in the ways already mentioned). A structural approach sets aside equifinality. For example, developments leading up to final settlement forms are left in a black box. Effort then shifts to understanding the relation between structural principles (from the single-period settlement record) and a dramatic final event in the record such as a political collapse.

Just as regions or sites can have variable developmental histories which are imperceptible on single-period settlement palimpsests, so can wards, housegroups, and individual buildings. The paradigmatic site of El Rosario displays examples of equifinality difficulties at these smaller scales. Equifinality at the individual building scale looms very large. Do surface forms represent a single construction effort or the end result of a series of efforts? The problem involves both domestic and civic-ceremonial buildings, although the ensuing discussion refers primarily to domestic buildings. Resolving this question is important, for example, if one wishes to compare domestic building volumes as indicators of family-level labor investment and control over labor (Kurjack 1974). We cannot equate the ability to mobilize labor for constructing a large platform in one episode with the ability to mobilize labor for an equally large platform in two or more episodes (Arnold and Ford 1980; Haviland 1982).

Equifinality difficulties disappear if the comparison of building dimensions refers to the extent to which the buildings once projected information about the relative sociopolitical status of the inhabitants. Such an approach draws inspiration from the active view of material culture (Wobst 1977). In this case, buildings not only passively reflect things done to them, but also actively function to project information. Blake (1984) has applied this reasoning to ethnoarchaeological data from modern Maya communities and to the settlement record from El Rosario. Within the terms of this approach, final (and contemporaneous) building forms are validly comparable.

Volumetric studies are even more common for civic-ceremonial than for domestic buildings (Freidel and Cliff 1978; Sanders 1974; Rathje 1975; Cheek

1986). Comparative volumes of civic-ceremonial buildings may represent several things: the relative ability of rulers to draw in tribute, the absolute amount of surplus labor available in the population for construction of communal or civic-ceremonial facilities, or projected information about the relative sociopolitical status of rulers controlling the civic-ceremonial buildings. The third (projective) approach draws on the active perspective mentioned with reference to domestic buildings and using it bypasses equifinality difficulties. But, for the first two approaches equifinality looms just as large for civic-ceremonial as for domestic buildings.

Clearly, survey information is of no direct use for resolving equifinality difficulties. Thus, I come out of the structural closet and refer to excavations carried out at El Rosario and Tenam Rosario (Agrinier 1979). At El Rosario, only two of the (25) excavated dwellings (from four of the six wards) had more than one construction stage. In central Tenam Rosario (Section E) all five of the excavated dwellings had multiple construction stages. In peripheral Tenam Rosario (Section T) all ten of the dwellings had single construction phases (de Montmollin 1985a: ch. 4). Excavation at El Rosario and part of Tenam Rosario supports the idea that the final surface form of many or most domestic buildings was the one they had throughout their use-lives.[5] If most buildings had a single major construction phase they can be compared in terms of relative labor investment measured through mound volume, without too many equifinality difficulties. Nevertheless, in most cases comparative volumetric labor-investment analyses are probably a doomed enterprise in settlement studies. Such analyses must be used sparingly or only in conjunction with other approaches. They might even be abandoned in favor of a projective approach (Chapter 5).

Are the excavation-based findings from El Rosario and Tenam Rosario very extendible to the many other sites and buildings in the polity? Generalizations derived from a comparison of the number of building stages at central Tenam Rosario versus El Rosario are relevant to this question. Preponderance of multistage buildings at central Tenam Rosario may be due to unusual space limitations on the narrow mesatop it occupies. This would promote a tendency to accommodate growth by expanding existing buildings. Horizontal spread through adding on new buildings would be inhibited. The markedly higher sociopolitical status of the residents at Tenam Rosario (Agrinier 1979; Chapter 8) could also account for multistage buildings. But the crowding factor seems more important. This is because differences in the number of construction phases cross-cut modest and elaborate buildings at both sites, discounting status as a clear-cut determinant.

These findings are quite preliminary for at least two reasons. The set of excavated buildings is small (and unbalanced between the two sites), and not explicitly chosen to discover the determinants of variation in numbers of construction stages. Another unknown and uncontrolled factor is relative length of occupation. Greater numbers of construction phases could result simply from longer periods of residence. It is not possible to determine whether Tenam Rosario was occupied longer than El Rosario. At any rate, if one accepts these preliminary findings, it appears that space limitations are an important determinant for structural alterations to dwelling platforms, with another possible determinant being the higher sociopolitical status. These observations serve as guidelines for hypothesizing about whether unexcavated buildings at other sites had multiple construction phases. Another guideline is the commonsense (but untested) idea that the volumetrically largest housemounds are most likely to have had multiple construction stages.

Equifinality difficulties emerge at the larger housegroup scale. Did a multibuilding house group come to have its final number of buildings by additions over time or through one initial construction episode? Direct excavation evidence of the kind needed to tackle this question is unavailable (horizontal clearing of whole housegroups). Even if a few excavated examples were available, equifinality difficulties would inhibit wide extrapolation from these. Obviously, it is impractical to fully excavate all the (1,199) multibuilding housegroups in the polity. Approaches to the housegroup-scale equifinality issue using survey data turn out to be quite circuitous. The effort is worthwhile because it relates to politically important substantive themes concerning the determinants of housegroup size and composition. Two of these themes are domestic cycling and sumptuary status restrictions on domestic-group size (Chapter 8).

As settlement scales get larger, it becomes increasingly difficult to conceptualize and find evidence relating to equifinality questions. Here, I provide a few brief simplistic examples. Demographic differences among sites may be attributed to structural political constraints or to the fact that the sites had reached different stages in a growth cycle when they were abandoned (Steponaitis 1981: 341, 345). Different settlement densities among districts (of equal size and resource endowment) may be attributable to structural differences in land use (de Montmollin 1985c) or to the districts' having reached different stages in a demographic filling-in process when abandoned. Differences in the degree of population concentration around capital centers for different districts may be interpreted as structural differences entailed by a particular kind of political regime or as different stages in a centralization cycle reached by the districts before abandonment. These and other relatively larger-scale equifinality problems are particularly intractable.[6] In spite of the difficulties, the themes of cycling at various settlement scales are worth pursuing (Chapter 10). They are not only methodologically important (as possible determinants for observed settlement variation) but also substantively important as aspects of political organization in ancient complex polities.

Scale of coverage

General methodological contemporaneity and equifinality difficulties have been examined as they occurred (and sometimes differed) at various scales of settlement analysis. Analytical scale (scale of coverage) is also closely linked to problem orientation. To set up effective bridging arguments (whether based on excavation or survey) we need suitable scales of spatial coverage for chosen research questions

(Chapter 11; de Montmollin n.d.b; Bray 1983; Blanton *et al.* 1982; Toumey 1981). What constitutes a suitable scale is relative but perhaps a good rule of thumb would be to have a sufficient number of causal factors operating within rather than outside the arena for study.

For the Rosario Valley, the scale of coverage was designed to encompass the core of a territory politically controlled from the capital Tenam Rosario (Chapter 3). Further extension of coverage into peripheral areas and into neighboring polities would open up further worthwhile analytical possibilities. But, for the moment, total area covered does prove broadly adequate for the proposed research into the Rosario polity's political structure. Further spatial divisions of the study area (within what has been rather loosely called the regional scale to denote a level above the site scale) are the sections and pockets (Chapters 3 and 5; Figure 5). These are particularly valuable as they allow controlled comparison of several smaller political regimes nested within the overall Rosario polity (there are numerous examples of this in Chapters 5–10). Still smaller political segments may be studied at the site scale while issues of sociopolitical stratification are appropriately studied at the ward, housegroup, and individual building scales (Figure 6). Scale of coverage shifts with the requirements of various lines of analysis prompted by various research questions. In keeping with a focus on settlement patterns and social statics, much closer attention is given throughout to issues of spatial scale than to the issues of temporal scale. The latter are more centrally important for processual (excavation-based) approaches (Wright *et al.* 1980).

Preservation and visibility

Uneven preservation and visibility of sites, buildings, etc. is another complicating factor to be accounted for in constructing bridging arguments. Preservation and visibility difficulties occur at several settlement scales. At the largest scale, preservation and visibility of archaeological remains were good throughout the valley, for reasons mentioned earlier in discussing the survey setting and fieldwork methods. At the site scale and smaller, evidence from El Rosario provides paradigmatic examples of the possible effects of uneven preservation and/or visibility factors on recovery and interpretation of settlement remains.

To come to grips with preservation for El Rosario (and other sites), we need some idea of the degree to which settlement patterning has been disturbed by post-occupation cultural activities. Best possible preservation would result from a clear or relatively abrupt abandonment of dwellings followed by a period with little modification of the ruins by humans. Let us see if there was ideal preservation at El Rosario (and by extension, other sites). Several lines of evidence bear on the question.

First, the absence of excavated and surface ceramic material postdating the Late/ Terminal Classic Period indicates that El Rosario ceased to be occupied by the end of this period and remained unoccupied through to the present.

A second line of evidence is the context of offerings in excavated buildings. This sheds a thin but penetrating ray of light on the manner in which the buildings were abandoned (de Montmollin 1979a, 1979b). Fourteen offering events (excluding burial-associated offerings) were associated with 11 buildings (in Sections A and E). Four terminal (Type IV) events associated with four buildings occurred immediately prior to building abandonment (the classification of offering events follows W. Coe 1959). These consisted of items placed on floors and subsequently covered by wall fall, never again to be disturbed. Breakage patterns and the material's condition would even suggest that wall material was pushed down on these items soon after they were placed on the floors. While admittedly of limited occurrence (4 of 11 buildings in one ward), such a pattern suggests rather sudden and definitive abandonment of the buildings (de Montmollin 1979a).

The evidence for stone robbing or looting provides a third avenue for evaluating the archaeological record's preservation. Practically no evidence for prehispanic stone robbing or looting of domestic buildings was found. This pattern holds at El Rosario and all other sites surveyed. Looting of civic-ceremonial buildings was proportionately higher although still very modest compared to currently more densely settled parts of Mexico. Most of this looting activity was clearly modern. So, uneven preservation and recovery attributable to looting activities seems a negligible problem, at El Rosario or elsewhere.

A fourth and final line of evidence concerning preservation has to do with modern activities. Agricultural activities on and around El Rosario are of recent origins, confined to cattle grazing, with little adverse impact on housemounds. These conditions are extendable to the vast majority of surveyed sites located in pastures or lightly cultivated maize fields away from modern settlement.

Summing up, all the lines of evidence reviewed so far support the idea that there was a chronologically clear-cut and a definitive end to occupation at El Rosario. A similar pattern of minimal post-Late/Terminal Classic Period disturbance or settlement seems to occur often enough around the valley to support the wider claim that there was a similarly abrupt termination of settlement at many other sites.

Visibility of remains at El Rosario is another important factor affecting recovery chances. To effectively use the El Rosario survey information, fairly precise knowledge is required of what is archaeologically visible and included in the data set, and of what is archaeologically invisible and left out of the data set. To what degree are empty spaces on the site map a product of research technique and visibility factors or a reflection of actual gaps in settlement distribution? My basic contention is that there was excellent archaeological visibility at El Rosario. Consequently the overwhelming majority of buildings (which had some stone materials) were available for recovery through survey techniques (de Montmollin 1985a: appendix B).

The high visibility at El Rosario (and a great majority of other sites in the valley) is attributable to two factors. The first factor is the currently sparse vegetation cover (which also contributes secondarily to a high degree of preservation). Vegetation is extremely unlikely to have concealed or disturbed beyond recognition even the lowest of stone (sub)structures. Even if vegetation was heavier prior to recent clearing, it is unlikely that forest cover was heavy enough to sufficiently churn up remains of buildings to the point of making them unrecognizable. In fact, the tropical deciduous forest on the nearby hilltop at Tenam Rosario, probably a good approximation of the area's original undisturbed vegetation, has not damaged housemounds to any extent. Such observations are extendable to all sites found in the survey area's relatively small tropical deciduous forest zone.

The second factor promoting high archaeological visibility is the thin soil cover above bedrock across El Rosario's more densely settled areas. These areas are on several low, flat-topped ridges separated by shallow unoccupied gullies. In light of excavation experience in which solid bedrock was repeatedly reached, it is clear that soil cover rarely exceeded 20 cm. This depth of soil is insufficient to obscure all traces of a building with stone elements. Most buildings (excavated down to the base of their platform walls or wall footings) were found to be at least 20 cm (usually more) in height, enough to project above the modern ground surface. Furthermore, mounding of stone rubble (platform fill or wall material) was usually present in excavated buildings and such mounding was even more likely to remain unburied than lower basal wall alignments. Thus, during survey the extent of mounded stone rubble could be used to locate and delimit a building if the wall alignments happened to be either buried or disturbed beyond recognition.

Exceptional areas of El Rosario which had deeper soil cover are the shallow gullies separating the flat-topped ridges. Within these gullies very few buildings were recorded. Does this reflect a real gap or failure to recover buildings buried in deeper soils? The first possibility is the likelier one. Land surface in the gullies is less ideally flat for purposes of residential location than the surface on the flat-topped ridges. Gullies experience a heavy runoff during periods of rainfall. Therefore, if the inhabitants were foolhardy enough to place their houses in the gullies, most of these should have had high and still visible platforms or wall footings (sufficient to keep them above the water's damaging effects). Remains of prehistoric check dams between Sections A and E and between Sections E and B (Figure 7) suggest that gullies were set aside for cultivation (possibly arbori-culture) rather than housing (Agrinier 1979). Elsewhere in the survey area, there were many other uninhabited low spots with relatively deep soils between site wards or else between sites, to which the preceding kinds of arguments could be applied.

A nagging issue is the possible existence of totally perishable features and buildings at El Rosario (and elsewhere in the valley). This is referred to as the hidden housemound problem in Lowland Maya settlement studies (Puleston 1973: 164–170; Andrews IV 1965: 60; Tourtellot 1983: 44; Willey and Bullard 1965: 363). If there were buildings at El Rosario ephemeral enough to lack stone materials they were not recovered in survey. Nor were any such buildings recovered in excavation, although not enough testing of superficially open areas was done to make this a particularly decisive point concerning the presence or absence of stone-free buildings. Can it be assumed that stone-free buildings, if they existed, were subsidiary outbuildings, dependencies of dwellings made with stone material? Or, were some, or all, of these ephemeral buildings also dwellings? In the latter case, such dwellings would presumably have been associated with lower ranking folk because of their abysmal quality and minimal labor cost.

Two arguments refute the idea that any undetected and unrecorded ephemeral buildings functioned as dwellings. First, in the site's densely packed areas (the central parts of Sections A, B, C, and D – Figure 7), there is little space left for (ephemeral) buildings in addition to those recorded. A second, more widely applicable argument, is partly functional. This is that some degree of stone footing was required in all relatively permanent general-purpose dwellings to protect them from the damaging effects of runoff provoked by heavy rains. Such damaging effects include temporary flooding of living floors, undermining of earth and/or cane walls, and deterioration of these walls through upward seepage. Consequently, the sparsely packed areas on the site map can be interpreted as just that, rather than as areas with a few recorded dwellings among any number of unrecorded stone-free dwellings (used by socially inferior persons). Ephemeral buildings, if such existed, would probably have functioned as temporary shelters and/or storage facilities. To recap, the high-visibility settlement record and the survey technique used were both adequate for recording virtually the entire universe of buildings containing stone material. Furthermore, the recorded buildings include all of the dwellings. Any unrecorded, ephemeral, stone-free buildings which may have existed functioned as temporary subsidiary outbuildings.

Summing up, near uniformly good preservation, visibility, and recording exist not only for El Rosario, but also for other sites throughout the survey area. Overall, the Rosario polity's settlement record has a high degree of preservation and visibility, allowing unusually full recovery of architectural evidence. This evidence proves adequate for an effective construction of the kinds of bridging arguments required in a study of political structure in an ancient complex polity.

Form to function

Form to function arguments are difficult to construct in archaeology, especially so when a heavy reliance is placed on surface architecture. Form to function problems are by no means absent for excavated evidence. But excavation documents an association of artifacts (of better-known function) with what are usually functionally more enigmatic architectural features. In this way it helps to strengthen arguments about the function (or status) of those architectural facilities with a convincingness that is unavailable in survey techniques (Tourtellot 1983).

Form to function problems have many relevant dimensions. For example, functions can be apportioned to individual domestic buildings in a housegroup, based on their architectural form and size (and perhaps their associated artifacts). Size, shape, and architectural style are bases for attributing function to the various forms of civic-ceremonial buildings. Proximity is a general, locational and contextual, as opposed to formal, principle that is useful for attributing social and political function to buildings. For example, small building-clusters are interpreted as extended family housegroups, larger building-clusters are interpreted as lineage-unit wards, and still larger building-clusters are interpreted as communities (sites). The closeness of certain domestic buildings to civic-ceremonial buildings is taken to indicate greater access to or control over related civic-ceremonial activities for the inhabitants of those domestic buildings. These are some of the most common and generic features of form to function arguments, at least for Maya studies (see also Ashmore 1981: 40–42). At the moment, having identified and sketched out the general problem, I can leave the matter. Subsequently, I discuss specific (detailed) form to function arguments as they become necessary in the analysis.

From the preceding extended discussion of difficulties associated with constructing bridging arguments, there emerges one really major theme. This is the close-knit web of relations that link qualities (and possibilities) of the settlement record, fieldwork methods, bridging arguments (observational theory), and problem orientation (substantive theory) (Figure 49). Earlier (Chapter 2), I stressed that problem orientation had to be given some autonomy with reference to archaeological testability, because totally testable models tend to be austere relative to the conceptual richness of anthropological–archaeological theory and data. To rephrase and expand this observation in terms of the above factors, ideally one works towards achieving a close congruence between qualities of the settlement record, fieldwork methods, arguments of relevance, and problem orientation, but since the world is not yet perfect, the last factor should not be totally constrained by the limitations of the first three (an argument taken up again in Chapter 11).

We now have a substantive theoretical framework (Chapter 2) as well as some sense of the general methodological difficulties associated with linking such a framework to an archaeological settlement record (discussed above in this chapter). The next steps in analyzing the ancient complex polity that occupied the Rosario Valley consist of taking each of the continua (Table 1) and trying to generate some specific archaeological settlement correlates (or measures) for various points along the continua (Chapters 5–10). This necessarily requires further methodological effort (construction of specific bridging arguments) on the way to producing substantive results: a documentation of the Rosario polity's positions on the various continua and answers to the research questions.

5

Centralization

Analytical tools

Several analytical tools help us to arrive at the archaeological measures needed for examining political structure in the Rosario polity. Narrowing the earlier focus on general methodological difficulties (Chapter 4), my methodologically oriented discussion of analytical tools is geared even more specifically to the Rosario settlement record's qualities and possibilities. Nevertheless, the choices faced and the logic used for constructing analytical tools are common to many settlement studies of politics in ancient complex polities. The needed analytical tools consist of: a territorial subdivision of the valley, functional classifications of buildings, a site classification of dwellings, a hierarchical political classification of civic-ceremonial plazas, and a size classification of sites. Particular emphasis is placed on the widely relevant analytical importance of the relationship between political and size classifications of settlements.

Territorial subdivisions

The survey area is readily divisible into smaller districts defined topographically by ranges of low hills or constrictions in valley-floor width – i.e., one *section* in each valley half, and within each section a set of sub-basins termed *pockets* (Zorrillo, Nuestra Señora, Chihuahua, Momón, Rosario, Santa Inés North, Santa Inés South). Another district, the Midvalley Range, has a different character, covering part of the range of hills that bisects the valley. Because its settlement pattern is so different (de Montmollin n.d.a: ch. 5), the Midvalley Range is left out of most comparisons. A consistency in the number of political hierarchy levels within equivalent topographically defined districts (four levels in each section, three levels in five of seven pockets – Figure 5) suggests a correspondence of topographic and political boundaries and reinforces the district's analytical validity.

Functional classifications of buildings

Many formal and locational (contextual) criteria make it quite easy to separate domestic buildings from civic-ceremonial buildings (de Montmollin n.d.a: ch. 6). Within the set of domestic remains one finds dwellings, connecting walkways, subdwelling-size buildings, outdoor altars, burial slabs, circular buildings, patio walls, residential and agricultural terraces, check dams, and *chultunes* (subterranean storage pits). Precise functional identification of the various kinds of platforms and enclosures within the domestic dwelling category is, as elsewhere in the Maya settlement record, quite difficult (Tourtellot 1983). For the Rosario settlement record, a surface-based classification of small mounds as dwellings rather than (non-residential) outbuildings relies on simple size and locational–contextual criteria. Detailed distributional studies of architectural attributes among the small mounds at El Rosario were used to develop and support the criteria (or low-level bridging arguments) used for the distinction between dwellings and outbuildings (details in de Montmollin 1981). Additionally, functional identification problems can be sidestepped altogether by stressing relative comparisons. In these comparisons the results are not affected by functional attribution errors when these are distributed evenly across the units compared (this is similar to the defence of cross-period population estimates from settlement data). Dwellings are a straightforward and workable population indicator. They may be aggregated into housegroups by applying a number of locational and formal criteria (de Montmollin n.d.a: ch. 5). Civic-ceremonial buildings and features include pyramids, ranges [very long domestic buildings], high platforms, outdoor altars, ballcourts, pyramid annexes, basal platforms, tombs, and cruciform platforms. These classes are even more easily distinguished from one another than the domestic building classes. Civic-ceremonial facilities are clearly arranged around plazas. A political settlement-hierarchy can be constructed by analyzing variability in the numbers and kinds of civic-ceremonial buildings around the plazas associated with different sites (below).

Site classification

Population is apportioned among a set of sites produced by clustering a spread of domestic dwellings in a consistent and thematically meaningful way. As is the case for much of the Classic Maya settlement record (Ashmore 1981), it is relatively easy to group housemounds into discrete housegroups. Less typically, the Rosario settlement record has a sufficient degree of housegroup clustering to facilitate assembly into larger-scale settlement units which serve as correlates for ancient communities. The site-communities are generally larger social groupings than the nuclear or small extended families associated with individual domestic buildings and housegroups.[1] In the field, a marked topographic divide and/or about 100 m of building-free area were taken to mark the edges of a site. The topographic criterion has sociological relevance on the assumption that relatively more closely related groups would tend to settle on the same eminence or else on the same side of a stream or gully. The 100 m figure is not entirely arbitrary because it corresponds to a clearly noticeable settlement gap, in the context of Rosario Valley domestic settlement densities. There is a contrast here with other Lowland Maya settlement records (or at least maps) which have much more widely dispersed buildings and where analysts use correspondingly more generous distances to represent a gap between sites. For example, Harrison uses 1,000 m (1981: 262), and a glance at the Tikal map (Carr and Hazard 1961) shows that many Rosario Valley sites would fit comfortably into this large urban site's intrasite gaps. No pan-Maya spacing principles exist (except in the very general sense that settlement tends to be more dispersed than in Highland Mesoamerica).

While reasonable (problem-oriented) criteria are desirable, sites need not be viewed as absolute objective entities. Criteria for determining site boundaries may be varied according to analytical need. Alternative approaches to that used here include further lumping or splitting of the domestic settlement distribution. Using several sets of site definition criteria helps to cover better the range of possible sociospatial arrangements (de Montmollin n.d.a: ch. 5, ch. 6). But, as in the functional attribution of small mounds, the search for absolutely valid site-definition (community) criteria can be analytically underplayed since comparisons are unaffected so long as site definition errors are distributed evenly across the cases compared. In light of this and to avoid complicating matters unduly, my subsequent analysis uses the (arguably reasonable) site-definition criteria given above. Still another approach to site-definition problems is to give up on domestic site definition and interpret the distribution of single buildings and housegroups solely with reference to civic-ceremonial plazas (seen as islands in a sea of houses – Willey 1981: 401). Given the tendency of Classic Maya domestic settlement to sprawl, for some kinds of locational analysis the clearest (most usable) spatial patterning will be discernible among plazas, not domestic settlement (e.g., Marcus 1976; Flannery 1972; Hammond 1974). Such an approach also makes analytical sense since locational techniques from cultural geography often concern the distribution of service-providing centers (Johnson 1977) and for the Maya these are most likely to have been plazas. A current drawback for Maya plaza-distribution studies is that they are still carried out with little knowledge of population sizes and distributions in areas between the plazas. This makes it deceptively easy to simply assume that population was efficiently distributed among plaza centers rather than investigating whether this was indeed so. Thus, a plaza-centered approach proves useful for some lines of analysis (Chapters 7 and 8), but not for others. For fullest possible understanding, the attempt to define wards and sites above the housegroup scale should not be abandoned, however difficult the attempt proves to be. Sites remain an important analytical tool because they constitute a theoretically indispensible (community) social scale of analysis for any study of an ancient stratified sociopolitical regime which features corporate restrictions on individual household autonomy. The last point raises the recurring issue of methodological individualism versus methodological holism which underlies settlement study of ancient complex polities (Chapter 11).

Political settlement hierarchy

Clearly, for a study of politics we need a classification that produces a hierarchy of political centers: locales for public political activity above the domestic level. Such locales are indicated clearly by civic-ceremonial buildings (notably pyramids, ballcourts, and ranges) disposed around plazas. Units in the Political Hierarchy (abbreviated to PH) are referred to as centers (not sites) and they are spatially

Table 2. *Political Hierarchy (PH)*

Level	Functions	Attributes
PH1	polity capital	multipyramid plazas, two ballcourts (Figure 9)
PH2	section capital	at least one multipyramid plaza, one ballcourt (Figures 10 and 11)
PH3	pocket capital	no multipyramid plaza, one ballcourt
PH4	local center	no multipyramid plaza, no ballcourt
PH5	basal community	no civic-ceremonial buildings

Note : There is usually a one-to-one relation between PH centers and domestic sites (only four PH centers lack contiguous domestic settlement). The relation between PH centers and individual plazas is not necessarily a one-to-one relation, except for single-plaza sites (24 cases) or plazas isolated from domestic settlement (4 cases). When a site encompasses two or more plazas (11 cases), these are treated collectively and given the PH ranking of the most elaborate plaza. The logic underlying the use of a domestic settlement site in common as a criterion for close relationship between plazas is that plazas within the same community (site) are more closely related than plazas in separate communities. This over-rides a possible spatial criterion for determining relations between plazas, for which no social logic can be found.

Two centers, RV30/37 and RV200, function at both PH2 and PH3 levels. What portion of these centers' associated residential population or civic-ceremonial architecture pertains to political affairs at the section as opposed to pocket level cannot be judged.

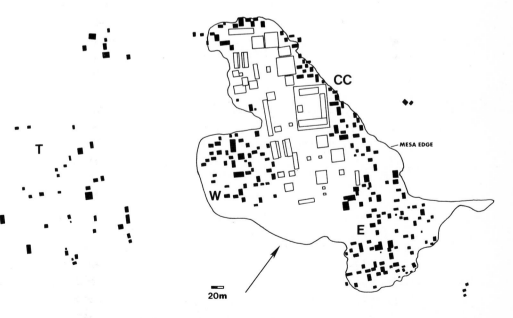

Figure 8   Tenam Rosario [Key: see Figure 7]

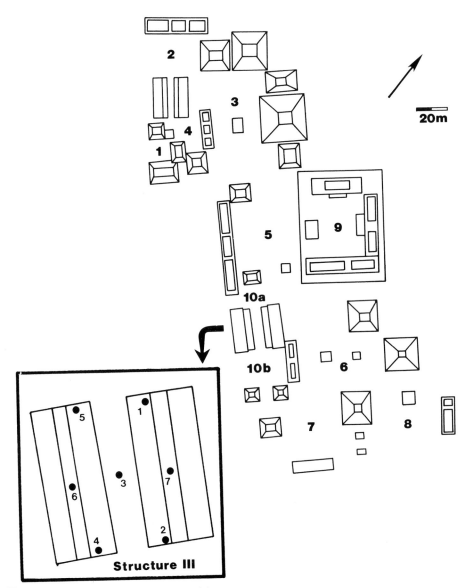

Figure 9   Tenam Rosario: civic-ceremonial zone

associated with, but not equivalent to, sites which are the residential population aggregates. Using civic-ceremonial buildings to represent the presence of politically important persons or activity is a well-worn procedure in Mesoamerican and Maya settlement analysis (Blanton *et al.* 1982; Spencer 1982; Freidel and Sabloff 1984; Adams and Jones 1981; and others). The ethnohistoric sources do not contradict the underlying idea that range and importance of ritual/governing activity and personnel would correspond to the relative number and size of civic-ceremonial buildings at a center (although cautionary tales can always be found). Additional

Figure 10   RV30/37 [Key: see Figure 7]

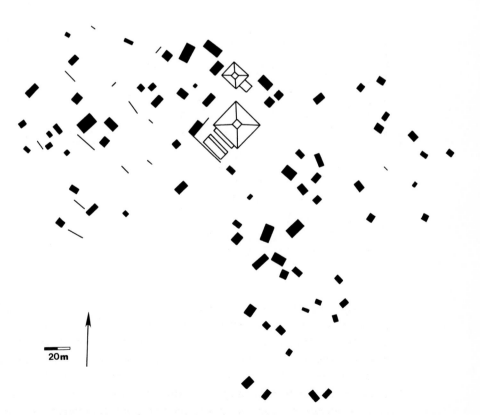

Figure 11   RV200 [Key: see Figure 7]

lines of archaeological evidence would be useful to evaluate an assumed relation between architectural impressiveness and ritual/governing importance. Artifactual remains in the form of offerings and burials associated with civic-ceremonial buildings are most pertinent here. But since the Rosario polity data are derived from surface survey, excavated artifactual evidence is not available and primary reliance has to be placed on surface architectural remains and their distribution (Chapter 7). The assumption that religious/ritual and political activities were inextricably linked in Mesoamerican polities is a virtually unassailable one. It underlies the use of what are clearly ceremonial buildings to represent loci of political activity. Turning now to the specifics, the PH for the entire valley has five levels (PH1-PH5), defined according to a variety of criteria (summarized in Table 2).[2] The PH1 center, Tenam Rosario, has many more civic-ceremonial plazas than any subordinate political center (Figures 8 and 9). Its complex civic-ceremonial layout is noteworthy as it seems to represent a microcosm of its hinterland's politico-territorial structure (Chapter 7). PH2 centers are clearly preeminent in their own districts – RV30/37 (Figure 10) in the upper section and RV200 (Figure 11) in the lower section. Four PH3 centers serve as capitals for smaller districts or pockets (RV6 in Nuestra Señora, RV131 in Momón, RV163 in Rosario, RV93a in Santa Inés North). The two PH2 centers do double duty as capital centers for their own pockets, and Tenam Rosario may double as a capital for the apparently acephalous Chihuahua Pocket. PH4 includes the lowest ranking centers with civic-ceremonial buildings, while PH5 includes all residential sites which lack civic-ceremonial facilities, i.e., basal communities below the political hierarchy's lowest (PH4) rung. Just outside the survey area, two centers (RV53 and RV175) fall somewhere between the PH1 and PH2 levels. Their locations suggest a special function of controlling access between the Rosario Valley and the Comitán Plateau (RV53) or the San Lucas drainage (RV175). Another PH4-like center outside the survey area (Tr-5) also seems to be located to control a pass between the Rosario Valley and the San Lucas drainage.

Site size classifications

With a well preserved settlement record, several site-level demographic size indicators may be used. These are the number of dwellings, the number of housegroups, the number of intrasite divisions or wards, and the site area. For various reasons, the first of these is preferable (de Montmollin n.d.a: ch. 9). Since housegroup size varies little (between 1 and 4 dwellings) and since the average number of dwellings per housegroup is relatively constant among sites and districts (1.7 dwellings per housegroup), the number of housegroups is redundant as a demographic counting unit for intravalley comparisons. Using it will change neither the shape of site-size distributions nor the site-size rankings. Counting numbers of wards for demographic size estimates is not viable since these vary greatly in the number of dwellings they contain. Counting wards proves much more important for understanding the relative political complexity of sites (Chapter 7). Since dwellings are well preserved throughout the settlement record, site area

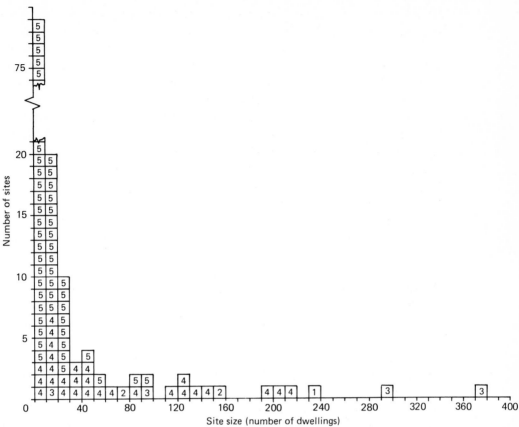

Figure 12 Sizes of PH-ranked sites – polity [Key: 5 = PH5; 4 = PH4; 3 = PH3; 2 = PH2; 1 = PH1]

makes little sense as a demographic indicator (being a last choice indicator anyway). Site area is more useful for estimating and then comparing residential densities among sites (e.g., number of dwellings per ha). The variability in site residential densities found within the valley (de Montmollin n.d.a: ch. 9) is more interesting than any average densities. The latter probably have limited extendability to other archaeological cases (for purposes of generating population per site-area indices). As is already apparent from the discussion of site definition, it proves difficult to argue for any pan-Maya, much less universal, constancy in settlement densities (see also Fletcher 1981; De Roche 1983).

Having shown why dwellings are the most appropriate demographic indicator for site size, let me now look at the specific site-size patterns for the Rosario Valley. Overall, the distribution is heavily skewed to the right (Figure 12).[3] Fairly dramatic discontinuities occur towards the larger end of the distribution. Occasional multimodality in the continuous portions and some clear breaks allow division of the distributions into discrete classes. The number and limits of such size classes vary depending on the regional settlement scale used (Figures 12-14). Such site-size classes are indeed worthwhile when they provide a basis for a site hierarchy derived

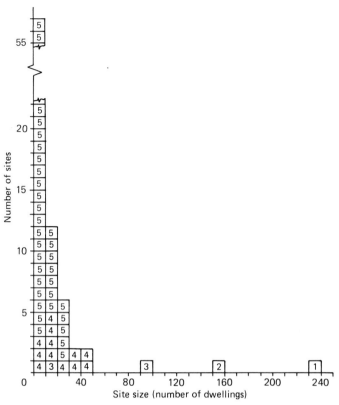

Figure 13   Sizes of PH-ranked sites – upper section [Key: see Figure 12]

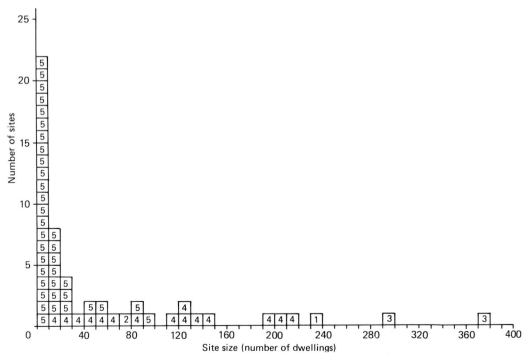

Figure 14   Sizes of PH-ranked sites – lower section [Key: see Figure 12]

completely independently from any civic-ceremonial architectural variables. The analytical advantages of this for a study of politics appear subsequently in my discussion of the distribution of political functions across a political hierarchy (Chapter 7).

Settlement size and political importance

In contrast to the approach used here, many Mesoamerican and Maya settlement studies analytically conflate site-size classifications and classifications of centers according to political importance. A few partial to complete exceptions to the practice of conflating site-size and political importance may be found in Highland Mesoamerican settlement studies (Blanton *et al.* 1982; Steponaitis 1981; MacNeish *et al.* 1972). But Highland Mesoamerican settlement studies much more frequently take site demographic size as a sole indicator of its political importance (Sanders *et al.* 1979; Brumfiel 1976; Earle 1976; Parsons 1971; Redmond 1983; and others). The implications of such conflations are important and worth pursuing in greater detail. These implications are even more clearly seen in Maya settlement studies which usually deal with more detailed architectural evidence (of more direct relevance to the issue than Highland Mesoamerican sherd scatters). In Bullard's influential Lowland Maya settlement classification scheme, the classification of structural remains (into house ruins, minor ceremonial centers, and major ceremonial centers) addresses variability in individual building or building-group function, which mostly has to do with degrees of political importance (Bullard 1960: 357–362). The scheme also includes a separate classification into levels of settlement organization. This classification comprises a nested arrangement of clusters, zones, and districts, and deals with population and its spatial distribution (Bullard 1960: 367–370). According to Bullard, a correspondence exists between the two classifications (Bullard 1960: 367), but this is a hypothesis for testing rather than an established fact. The clear implication is that the two settlement classifications should not be blended into one even more multivariate classification. Unfortunately, this kind of blending has been done by virtually all the Mayanists who have adopted or modified Bullard's scheme.

A recent overview of Classic Maya settlement taxonomy also notes the need for a scheme that uses not necessarily equivalent hierarchies of increasing settlement size and increasing organizational complexity (Ashmore 1981: 43). However, the ensuing description of settlement types goes on to blend hierarchies of settlement size and organizational complexity, above the housegroup scale (Ashmore 1981: 51–54). A similar logic underlies many substantive settlement typologies which blend demographic, status, political, and spatial variables. Examples are the site typologies for the Copan Valley (Willey and Leventhal 1979: 81–83; Leventhal 1981), the Motagua Valley (Leventhal 1981: 194–196), Northern Belize (Hammond 1975a), Southern Quintana Roo (Harrison 1981: 268–269), and the Maya Lowlands in general (Willey 1981: 402–403). Supplementing any conceptual confusions leading to blended classifications are the measurement difficulties posed by sprawling domestic settlement remains in the Maya Lowlands and an enduring lack of wide areal-survey coverage which might help to make some sense of this spread (Rice and Puleston 1981: 148).

In a more programmatic vein, Marcus has pointed out forcefully the need to consider a variety of separate settlement classification schemes in Lowland Maya studies (Marcus 1983a: 466). Emically derived conclusions that "the Maya view of which sites were secondary, tertiary, and quaternary generally, *but not always*, conformed to site size differences" (Marcus 1983a: 464) lead to etic insights that "there are some dangers in the asssumption that size and political importance are isomorphic" (Marcus 1983a: 466). This is a fair procedure when trying to understand Maya politics, which were certainly shaped by what the Maya were thinking. Beyond this, the basic typological issue is that settlement classifications are analytical tools, whose nature and constituent variables vary with the questions being asked. One needs to be clear about what each variable is measuring before moving on to assemble multivariate constructs. All-purpose, polythetic, and multivariate classification schemes for discovering the definitive or correct Classic Maya site types are too narrowly empiricist (Binford 1986) to be useful as analytical tools. The settlement typology issues raised here are similar to those I discussed earlier with reference to societal typologies (Chapter 2). It helps to keep in mind the useful distinction between troublesome real definitions for synthetic discovered types and more useful nominal definitions for analytical problem-oriented types (Service 1985: 226).

Why make such a fuss about avoiding analytical conflation of settlement size and political importance? Separating size and political importance variables has at least three positive advantages. First, it avoids a possible blending of discrete and continuous variation. For example, the Rosario polity's PH levels are discrete (Table 2), as political hierarchical levels should be, while its site-size distribution happens to be rather continuous (Figure 12). Second, separation is conceptually interesting since it sets up the possibility of identifying a range of possible arrangements for the distribution of population with reference to loci of political activity (as in a forced settlement model, below). This is in contrast to the rather banal assumption, forced on us by a size-political importance conflation, that only locationally efficient arrangements are possible. Third, separation maximizes analytical sharpness and flexibility. It allows us to analyze dwellings and their distribution with reference to centers of varying political importance, without falling into circular reasoning. We no longer need to say that dwellings tend to be concentrated in politically important sites which are themselves important because of their size (number of dwellings).

Against the backdrop of frequent assumptions that site size equals political importance, it proves instructive to compare the site-size distribution and the PH for the Rosario Valley (Figures 12–14). A fairly good correspondence emerges between relative position in each classification, but least clearly at the polity-wide settlement scale (Figure 12). This is because of a heterogeneous pooling of sites at the polity scale which is produced by differences in average site size (across all PH levels) between the upper and lower sections. A clearer correspondence occurs at smaller settlement scales such as sections (Figures 13 and 14) or pockets (de Montmollin 1985a: ch. 7), with their more homogeneous site pools. Although results support the site size equals political importance assumption, the correspondence is not invariably close. The lack of correspondence becomes important if analysis requires a careful look at individual cases, especially in the PH's upper reaches. To take just one example, it would be mistaken to attribute paramount political importance to the polity's demographically largest site, RV93a, which is only a third rank (PH3) center. One might want to use these findings as a cautionary tale. But for my subsequent analysis, methodological aspects of the relation between site size and political importance are not centrally important as I need not rely on absolute regularity in the relationship between these two variables (as part of a bridging argument). In fact, it is the irregularities in this relationship which turn out to be substantively interesting and can be studied in their own right (instead of effacing them within a methodologically-required generalization about necessary equivalences between size and importance).

Forced settlement and centralization

With analytical tools in hand, I am now in a position to construct some archaeological tests for various theoretical notions. The first of these is the centralization subcontinuum which is part of the more general continuum between segmentary and unitary political structure (Table 1). Centralization is also one of the easiest and most rewarding political variables to study archaeologically, as a variety of arguments and measures are available.

One interesting interpretive option for understanding degrees of centralization lays special emphasis on forced settlement as a determinant of settlement nucleation. Here, forced settlement refers to the (political) imposition of settlement choices on inferiors by their political superiors, with the superiors using a variety of coercive, remunerative, and/or normative means. That political control is facilitated by proximity is an important assumption required for consistently relating settlement distribution to political centralization. There are several ideas about why proximity is important in political systems. Proximity may be a solution to the problem of minimizing transport costs for tribute prestations (Steponaitis 1978, 1981) or transport costs for conveying information (Blanton 1976; Alden 1979). Or both of these cost factors may apply within a tribute-flows-in while information-flows-out framework (Spencer 1982: 19). All of these ideas emphasize strict formalist economics and abstract managerial information-processing issues. An alternative set of ideas is that proximity is important because it minimizes the effort of delivering (normative, renumerative, or coercive) sanctions, while it maximizes the effectiveness (at whatever cost) of supervision effected on political inferiors by their superiors. This last set of ideas is closer to what one finds in action theory political anthropology (Winckler 1969; Vincent 1978) and it is more appropriate for a study of politics in ancient complex societies.

Whatever the reasons underlying a close connection between settlement proximity and political control, an examination of population distribution across a hierarchy of political locales is sure to vary in its implications depending on whether one looks at elite or commoner population. For simplicity's sake, total dwelling distribution is equated here with subject population distribution. But potentially this is deceptive since there were clearly elite dwellings within the total pool of dwellings (these receive separate consideration in Chapter 8). Nevertheless, a separate set of analyses using a pool of dwellings from which elite dwellings have been subtracted produces virtually identical proportional results to those for the general pool of dwellings. Therefore, the simplifying assumption is not a worrisome source of distortion. More straightforwardly, the hierarchy of political locales is represented by the PH (Table 2).

A hypothetical and abstract sketch of the relationship between political control and settlement distribution has the following properties. If subject population is highly dispersed with reference to political control centers, this creates control problems for the various segments of the elite or ruling group. But because the elite group is internally segmented (and potentially conflictive), the problem of controlling subject commoners is not part of a horizontal class conflict (contra Fried 1967; Haas 1981, 1982; Gilman 1981). Nor is controlling subject commoners the only or necessarily the major political control problem for the members of the various elite segments. Intra-elite problems may be more important (Service 1975, 1985; Wright 1986; and for the Maya case, Farriss 1984: ch. 6, ch. 8). A push and pull of subject population around political control centers occurs, as the rulers practice a forced settlement policy opposed by the subject population's dispersal tactics. Since the ruling group itself is hierarchically segmented there is also a potential for push and pull of elite population around poles of superior control. Higher-ranking rulers use forced settlement policies against lower-ranking rulers, while lower-ranking rulers use dispersal tactics against higher-ranking rulers. Also likely is competition between equally or differently ranked elite segments for control of commoner subject population.[1] Out of all these properties, I have selected for emphasis here the forced settlement exerted by rulers on subjects. A subsequent analysis considers forced settlement within the elite ruling group (Chapter 8).

In sum, forced settlement refers to the (political) imposition of settlement choices on subjects by their political rulers. An important assumption is that, given the choice, subjects would settle at a distance from ruling centers to lessen the degree of control to which they were exposed. The means used by rulers to effect forced settlement involve a mix of coercive, remunerative, and normative sanctions (arranged from least to most voluntaristic). Therefore, forced settlement refers not just to coercion, as actual or threatened violent physical interference. Rather, it refers to the broader phenomenon of manipulation or self-interested interference in others' behavior (however this may be achieved). At any rate, specifying the precise mix of coercion and voluntarism in forced settlement cases may be difficult, if not impossible, to do archaeologically (or even ethnohistorically), without interviewing the participants. Therefore, it is best left in a black box. What can be done in settlement archaeology is to appreciate the relative degree of spatial inconvenience to subjects (particularly agriculturalists) caused by their settlement at a political center rather than in its hinterland. But it is impossible to infer how coercive or voluntaristic political relations were solely from the degrees of (spatial and thus material) inconvenience to subjects. This only tells us about coercion, not about normative sanctions. To leave out normative sanctions requires a risky assumption that coercive sanctions are always stronger and more effective than normative (or even remunerative sanctions). Not everyone would agree that such an assumption is risky. For example, the assumption is used by Webb (1973) for the Classic Maya, and by all other archaeologists who use an a priori contrast between unstable theocratic chiefdoms and more stable secular-militaristic states in their research. Nevertheless, it remains very problematic to assume outright that material sanctions are always more persuasive than normative sanctions. This is especially true for political regimes such as those found in ancient Mesoamerica where we know that the efforts put into ideological/religious affairs by the participants were absolutely and proportionally enormous.

The abstract notion of forced settlement in the preceding hypothetical sketch can be illustrated and filled out by reference to a concrete example. A well-known historical case of forced settlement is the Spanish imperial policy for resettlement of New World Indian populations into new towns to enhance political and religious control. The policy was known as *reducción* or *congregación* (Cline 1949; Farriss 1984: ch. 5). In this case, dispersal tactics were adopted by many of the subject Indians to escape Spanish control, which became increasingly coercive and oppressive as total tribute demands remained high in a context of demographic decline among the Indian tributaries.

It seems fair to say that such a dispersal tactic was present among commoners in some prehispanic Maya (and Mesoamerian) cases. Some preconquest ethnohistoric examples are reviewed subsequently. What is much more difficult is to specify correctly the key locus of decision-making and implementation for the prehispanic dispersal tactics. At one extreme is the idea that all subject households were autonomously devising and implementing their own political and economic strategies, including residence strategies. This is equivalent to the idea that there was no top-down forced settlement at all. Similar ideas implicitly underlie some parts of the intriguing Mesoamerican regional studies carried out by Blanton and others (1981, 1982). In those studies, the effective presence and absence of top-down politically forced settlement alternates through the sequences in tandem with the relative dominance of political (state) and market forces. Household autonomy in a free-market system is equated with a natural state of affairs, which itself is natural given the authors' firm grounding in formalist economic anthropology (and free-market microeconomics). To my mind, it makes more sense to move towards the other extreme which downplays household autonomy in residential (and other political) decision-making. This is equivalent to taking a substantivist perspective (Polanyi 1957; Carrasco 1978, 1982) and is more suitable for strictly stratified (and definitely precapitalist) Classic Maya (and other Mesoamerican) polities. From this perspective, top-down political control over subject settlement may vary in its intensity (as Blanton and others suggest), but the locus of decision-making for dispersal always lies firmly within corporate supra-household groupings of subject commoners and/or factions of higher- and lower-ranking rulers. The latter attempt to subtract commoners from the influence of higher-ranking rulers and thus add them to their own followership.

Since a small number of conquering Spaniards relied heavily on forced settlement to control a large number of subject Indians, the Spanish imperial example also raises the interesting question of whether there is a close relation between a high degree of reliance on forced settlement and bi- or multi-ethnic conquest situations. I can pursue this question by reviewing some archaeological examples from Mesoamerica where forced settlement seems a likely contributor towards producing the observed population distributions. In a more general way, my discussion of the archaeological examples also makes the point that a forced settlement concept has potential use in helping to interpret Maya and Mesoamerican settlement patterning in other than purely economic terms.

A dramatic example of possible forced settlement is the concentration of Basin of Mexico population into the city of Teotihuacan (Sanders *et al.* 1979: 105–129; Millon 1981: 208, 217, 219–222). Virtually the entire regional settlement and political system, including most of the population (80–90 %) and several levels of political hierarchy, came to be concentrated within the capital (possibly quite rapidly at first). And much of it remained there until its collapse (Millon 1981; Cowgill 1983; Cowgill *et al.* 1984). The extreme inefficiency of this population distribution for the farmers living at Teotihuacan (at least two-thirds of the city's population [Millon 1981 : 220]) suggests some degree of compulsion (even coercion) in a forced settlement policy. I assume here that coercive sanctions are more likely to have been important for producing this outcome than either normative or remunerative sanctions. Compulsion is also indicated by the initial resettlement's apparent rapidity (Millon 1981: 221). Conversely, the arrangement greatly facilitated control by rulers from the very top of the political hierarchy (Millon 1981 : 222). Unlike the Spanish imperial example, nothing clearly suggests a foreign multi-ethnic conquest situation. Although Teotihuacan did have apparent pockets of foreigners from Oaxaca, the Maya area, and the Gulf coast, these foreigners were not running the show.

Another possible example of forced settlement from Highland Mesoamerica is the Late Formative settlement pattern in the Oaxaca Valley (Blanton 1978). Compared to Teotihuacan, concentration of population into Monte Alban is much less extreme. This is evidenced by comparative rank-size graphs (Kowalewski 1983) or by the estimate that 31 % of the Late I Period valley population was resident at Monte Alban (Feinman *et al.* 1985). But the presence of many people in an agriculturally unfavored part of the valley does suggest inconvenience, compulsion, and perhaps even a degree of coercion for the proportionally large number of subject farmers at Monte Alban. On the other hand, for the rulers at least, Blanton has argued that settling at Monte Alban was initially a voluntaristic, politically confederative process (Blanton 1978). As with Teotihuacan and unlike the Spanish case, evidence is lacking for foreign conquest or multi-ethnic structure.

More sketchily documented archaeologically are two possible examples of forced settlement from Yucatan – the drawing-in of population from a wide area into Early Postclassic Chichen Itza (Freidel 1981b: 313–314) and into Middle Postclassic Mayapan (Freidel 1983b: 46; Pollock *et al.* 1962). Both cases are taken to be examples of "political interference in 'natural' demographic patterns" (Freidel 1981b: 314). Ethnohistoric sources (Roys 1962; Thompson 1970: ch. 1; Willey 1986) suggest foreign conquest and ethnic diversity, but it is difficult to distinguish between foreign elite migration and conquest, local emulation of more prestigious exotic elites, or elite intermarriage (see especially Lincoln 1986, for Chichen Itza). Mayapan-related ethnohistoric sources specifically suggest concentration of ruling elite groups from around the peninsula into the capital, which can be distinguished from a policy of forced settlement applied to subjects (suggested archaeologically by Mayapan's apparently predominant size).

There is additional ethnohistoric evidence from Yucatan which bears on the issue of prehispanic politically enforced nucleation. Consider the following statement by one of Bishop Landa's informants, Gaspar Antonio Chi.

> As for these vassals, there were no towns expressly assigned (to them to live in)... with others, and they were considered to have licence... were free to marry and dwell (wherever they wished. The reason for this was that they might) multiply (saying that if they restrained them,) they could not fail (to decrease in number). (Chi 1941[1582]: 230)

The statement is meant to be an indirect condemnation of Spanish *congregación* policy, through an implicit comparison of that policy with conditions in the Mayapan period, which was viewed by Chi and other members of the early colonial Maya elite as a kind of golden age. The thrust of the statement is that there were relatively fewer political constraints on (subject population?) settlement during the Mayapan period. This seems to contradict the argument just made that there was a striking degree of subject population nucleation into Mayapan. Since Chi's implicit aim was to criticize the Spanish forced settlement polity, his equation of prosperous times with absence of forced settlement in Mayapan times can be taken with a grain of salt. What is more generally important about Chi's statement is the indication it gives that politically forced nucleation was an issue in the political value system of the early colonial Maya elite, and that they were disposed to interpret both colonial and prehispanic times in terms of the relative strength of this phenomenon.

A more positive reference to prehispanic Yucatec forced nucleation is found in the following statement provided by the Spanish *encomendero* (appointed tribute receiver) of Tetzal in Mani province:

> nunca fueron sujetos los de tetzal a nadie sino que cada uno bibia como queria despoblados hasta que bino napuecamal que los junto y fundo

pueblo... despues, deste muerto tubieron por prencipal a holpophau este los mudo deste pueblo y poblo a tahbuleh. (Relaciones de Yucatán I: 297)

those of Tetzal were never subject to anyone, rather, each person lived as he wished away from any towns, until Napuecamal came and joined them together and founded a town... afterwards, after his death, their leader was one Holpophau who moved them from the above town and founded Tahbuleh. (author's translation)

The statement clearly implies that the Spaniards' informants were cognizant of prehispanic processes whereby scattered and autonomous populations were gathered together for purposes of political control and whereby settlements were shifted as a result of political decision making.

Another apparent reference to prehispanic forced settlement is found in the Probanza of Don Pedro Paxbolon, a contact period Chontal *cacique* in Acalan. In the context of a brief dynastic history, it is stated that an early Chontal ruler "arrived to assemble the pueblo of Tanodzic" (Scholes and Roys 1968: 383). This could be interpreted as a (peaceful) nucleation of a dispersed local population by new foreign rulers (Scholes and Roys 1968: 79).

Finally, there is some (emic) terminological evidence concerning forced settlement in the major sixteenth-century Maya–Spanish dictionaries: the Motul Dictionary (Martinez H. ed. 1929) and the San Francisco Dictionary (Michelon ed. 1976):

bakte uinic – hombre que está bajo el poder de otro [a man who is under the power of another]   (San Francisco: 385)
bak – cercar rodeando..., asir [to fence in by encircling..., to seize] (Motul: 132)
bakte – juntamente [jointly]
bakte – él que está a cargo de otro [one who is under the charge of another]
bakte – él que ésta así debaxo del gobierno de otro [one who is thus under the governance of another]   (Motul: 133)
baktecunach – aiuntar, congregar muchas cosas en uno [to join, to congregate many things into one]   (Motul: 133)
baktehal – juntarse o congregarse [to join together or come together] (Motul: 133)

A semantic link between the condition of subordination and the action of joining or congregating emerges strongly from this set of definitions. To sum up this brief and incomplete review, ethnohistoric evidence suggesting the existence of forced settlement processes in prehispanic Yucatan is thin, but positive.[5]

Relative hypertrophy at Teotihuacan, Monte Alban, Chichen Itza, and Mayapan occurred at a much greater scale than anything we might expect at Tenam Rosario in the Rosario Valley, making these structurally distant comparative examples. But on a general level the examples are interesting as more or less extreme cases of settlement nucleation in the Mesoamerican archaeological and ethnohistorical record. They lie more or less close to one end of a cross-cultural continuum for ancient complex polities. At one end are the cases where all of the population is settled into the capital (e.g., some ancient Greek city-states, called primate states by Renfrew 1982: 281). At the other end are the cases where virtually none of the population resides at the capital (e.g., earlier ideal-type descriptions of Lowland Maya vacant civic-ceremonial centers, now found to be empirically unwarranted). My general argument is that much variation in settlement nucleation may be profitably interpreted in terms of the degree to which forced settlement was being used as an instrument of political control.

Analytically speaking, it is most useful to view these cases as arrayed along a continuum. The alternative strategy of using an absolute quantitative cut-off point for establishing the presence or absence of forced settlement makes much less sense. A single variable (proportion of the total regional population settled at a capital site) has values in a continuous function. This single-variable perspective is also the antithesis of multivariate settlement typology-building (which results in the kinds of typologies which attempt to contrast true cities and ceremonial centers [Willey 1974; Sanders and Price 1968]). An excellent general example of a variable-by-variable analysis of Mesoamerican sites is Marcus' comparative overview of Mesoamerican cities (Marcus 1983b). Since, in effect, she is working with nominal definitions (Service 1985: 226), her analysis brings out the complex variability in the data set much more effectively than an essentialist approach, which seeks to identify true cities versus non-cities, using real definitions (Service 1985: 226).

To better support the relevance of a forced settlement model, other possible determinants of settlement nucleation besides the relative strength of forced settlement have to be considered and discounted. These are: religious attraction, household-scale economic attraction, household-scale attraction of administrative managerial services, and defense needs. Since each case must be weighed on its own merits, my discussion focuses closely on the Rosario polity and its settlement pattern.

A crucial role for religious or ideological attraction into major centers is evidenced by the fact that civic-*ceremonial* buildings are selected as the identifying attributes for determining political importance of centers. But from a theoretical vantage which privileges political analysis, ideology and religion fall under the rubric of normative sanctions, which are but one aspect of political control (along with other aspects such as coercive and remunerative sanctions). Therefore, religious attraction is part of forced settlement, not in opposition to it.

Economic attractions on individual households, such as the pull of markets or employment prospects, are not likely determinants for the Rosario polity's population distribution among its political centers. Most simply, I have constructed the hierarchy of control centers with purely civic-ceremonial architectural evidence. None of this evidence indicates loci of economic activities.[6] No evidence of specialized economic activities was found (e.g., market places or storage complexes or multihousehold craft-production centers), evidence of the kind needed for constructing an economically based settlement classification. My analyses of general population distribution around the valley indicate that it does not correspond to the most efficient and convenient pattern from an individual household perspective (Chapter 9; de Montmollin 1985c). Household proximity to productive fields is not maximized. While the distributions may be interpreted in several ways (de Montmollin 1985c), at a minimum they suggest that complete economically based household-level autonomy in settlement decisions is unlikely. Similar interpretations are possible for other studies which chart the (changing) relations between settlement and resources in various much larger regions of Mesoamerica (Blanton et al. 1982; Steponaitis 1981; Gorenflo and Gale 1986; Bell et al. 1986). More programmatically, a substantivist interpretation (Polanyi 1957; Carrasco 1978) takes the Rosario polity's sociopolitical structure, with its high degree of stratification (probably a system of estates if not castes – Balandier 1970: 89-90), as an unlikely arena in which to find individual subject households acting as small maximizing firms and autonomously implementing their economic strategies (including deciding where to live). Nor is it remotely likely that there was a free labor-market determining population distribution. Since the precise locus of residential decision-making (household-level or above) and the relative merits of substantivist versus formalist approaches are critically important but very difficult to get at archaeologically, some forays into ethnohistory are required to begin to sort out these issues. The basic idea is that the Rosario polity is generically similar to ethnohistorically documented Postclassic Mesoamerican political systems, as these are interpreted from a substantivist perspective (Carrasco 1978, 1982). An opposed idea that the Rosario polity was class-mobile and that commoner households autonomously made (economically based) settlement choices may also draw comparisons to the same ethnohistoric cases, this time interpreted from a more formalist perspective (M. E. Smith 1979; Santley 1986). Or it may draw comparisons with more general cases of peasant societies (viewed in terms of patron-clientism and game theory). Since I find greater value in the substantivist interpretations of the ethnohistorical material and little of value in the allusions to generic peasant societies, I make the following argument. If Mesoamerican Postclassic societies are not interpretable in formalist terms as capitalist socio-economic systems, then the logic of a historical-evolutionary development from pre- or non-capitalist to fully capitalist systems (Polanyi 1944; Wolf 1982) makes it extremely unlikely that earlier Classic predecessor societies might be interpretable in formalist terms. The reasoning here is not necessarily that Rosario society is similar in every way to later Postclassic societies. Ethnohistoric examples are not used in a context of validation. Instead they help to set some limits on what is possible, given what we (as substantivists) know about the historical specificity of capitalist economic systems and the inextricable linkage of microeconomic or formalist analysis with such systems.

To what degree was there a voluntary and autonomous flow of individual subject households into political centers because of the attraction of administrative services they provided? Based on my substantivist interpretation of the Rosario polity as having a social order which gave limited decision-making autonomy to individual subject households concerning residential location (see above), my answer to this question is that voluntaristic subject household-scale attraction to political services was relatively unimportant. Here, I skirt the treacherous sands of debate about consensus versus conflict in political development (Cohen and Service eds. 1978). Concerning the Mesoamerican archaeological examples cited, debate has raged about the degree of coercion as opposed to voluntarism that governed the dramatic in-gathering of population into some of the major centers. For Teotihuacan, Millon (1976) argues for voluntarism and normative forces while Sanders and others (1979) argue for political coercion based on dire economic necessity. For Monte Alban, Blanton (1978, 1980) argues for voluntarism and confederative arrangements, while Santley (1980) and Willey (1979) again argue for political coercion based on dire economic necessity. Yet, it may not be necessary or really possible to join such a polar debate or to determine the precise degree of coercion which determined the distribution of Classic Maya subject population around political centers. It may not even be necessary to worry about whether the Maya had functional or fungal elites (Rathje 1983). Since ancient sociopolitically stratified societies are the objects of study, it must be allowable to conclude that there was enough top-down political control exercised over where commoners lived to give more relevance to forced rather than individual household voluntaristic settlement. As specified above, forced settlement includes a mix of coercive, remunerative, and normative sanctions. Even so, my argument against the importance of household-scale voluntarism probably lines up towards the conflict (rather than consensus) end of the interpretive continuum. But it discards the idea that sociopolitical cleavages had a horizontal class structure, an idea frequently associated with conflict interpretations (Fried 1967; Gilman 1981; Haas 1981, 1982). Instead, my argument adopts the idea that there were vertically running cleavages between internally stratified sociopolitical segments (Service 1975, 1985; Wright 1977 1986).[7]

Defense is another possible determinant affecting population distribution in the Rosario polity. A standard argument is that peaceful conditions allow dispersed settlement while nucleated settlement (usually into defensive localities) is required by conditions of insecurity and warfare (Webster 1976b). But, alternately, dispersed settlement might be a defensive adaptation under certain conditions of warfare (Palerm 1954), or warfare may be an elite activity with little impact on the bulk of commoner settlement (Freidel 1986). Each case needs to be examined on its own merits, with these (and other) possibilities in mind. For the Rosario polity, virtually all the relatively nucleated and politically important sites are in the valley bottom and situated without obvious defensive advantage. Consequently, defense needs do not seem to have been a crucial determinant for differences in settlement nucleation within the polity.

Based on the preceding arguments for the small impact of religious attraction, household-scale economic decision-making, household-scale political decision-making, and defense needs on the Rosario polity's settlement distribution, my general conclusion is that differences in degrees of political forced settlement are the most likely major determinant for variations in the degree of nucleation at political centers. While the same may well have been the case for many other complex settlement systems in Mesoamerica or elsewhere, the only real way to find out is by developing appropriate analytical tools and arguments and applying them to individual cases (measuring population and identifying the poles of political importance). Even so, a forced settlement model is not the only way of relating politics to settlement. As an elite policy, forced settlement entails more direct than indirect supervision of subject population. In subsequent analysis, I deploy tribute flow arguments which deal with more indirect control policies.

Paramount and cross-level forced settlement

Before starting the forced settlement analysis, I need to re-emphasize an important methodological difficulty. The problem is that only the cumulative effects of continuously occurring forced settlement policies may be studied, given the need to use single-period settlement distribution maps. Although it entails grave interpretive problems (Chapter 4; Binford 1981), this approach is practically required in order to maintain a regional perspective on settlement. Of the artificial solutions to contemporaneity problems (Schact 1984; Plog 1973), the climax–crash assumption, common in Classic Maya settlement studies (Ashmore 1981), is the one I have selected for use here.

Now let me turn to the·mechanics of testing for degrees of forced settlement in the Rosario polity. Units of comparison are the core's districts (sections and pockets) and their populations grouped into sites and arrayed across a hierarchy of political centers (PH). This provides a scaled-down version of the controlled comparison that can and should be carried out eventually between the whole Rosario polity and other Maya polities. Two measures are used.[8]

Paramount Forced Settlement: The proportion of population residing at the (PH3, PH2, or PH1) capital centers.

Cross-level Forced Settlement: The proportion of population at each of the PH levels.[9]

In an innovative discussion of the abstract systems properties of centralization, scale, and permeability, Kowalewski and others have presented a battery of archaeological measures for these systems properties (Kowalewski *et al.* 1983: 41). One measure of centralization is a computation of the proportion of total regional population residing in a region's largest center. In keeping with a focus on abstract systems properties, such a measure monitors the "relative amount of flow that is accounted for by a single node" (Kowalewski *et al.* 1983: 35), or "the degree to which activities were concentrated in one place" (Kowalewski *et al.* 1983: 43). The place of interest is a priori the largest site (that the largest population center is always the most important political center admits no exceptions). The measure of paramount forced settlement which I use for the Rosario polity is broadly similar, except for two changes. A procedural change is that nodal sites are selected only with reference to architectural evidence of political importance (in the PH). A conceptual change is that a high or low proportion of population resident at a center is taken to represent high or low degrees of direct elite control over population

Table 3. *Proportion of population at different PH levels (percentages)*

	PH1	PH2	PH3	PH4	PH5	nonPH5	Dwellings
Polity	0.06	0.05	0.23	0.42	0.23	0.67	4,360
Upper section		0.14	0.24	0.24	0.38	0.62	1,120
Zorrillo			0.48	0.22	0.30	0.70	332
Nuestra Señora			0.05	0.64	0.31	0.69	258
Chihuahua			0.00	0.20	0.80	0.20	128
Momón			0.41	0.00	0.59	0.41	243
Lower section		0.03	0.25	0.53	0.20	0.80	3,001
Rosario			0.38	0.37	0.26	0.74	794
Santa Inés North			0.30	0.53	0.17	0.83	1,223
Santa Inés South			0.12	0.73	0.15	0.85	641

Note : In the hierarchies with PH2 centers, dwelling totals from these are counted twice since they occur at two hierarchical levels (PH2 and PH3). Grand totals for these districts are thus slightly inflated above their actual values, which are: 961 for the upper section; 2,922 for the lower section, and 4,122 for the polity. With single counting of the dwelling totals from PH2 centers, the pattern differs only slightly in the sense that there are no longer relatively equal proportions of PH3 population in the upper and lower sections, the upper section now has relatively less PH3 population.

rather than high or low amounts of matter, energy, or information that flow through that particular node.

Paramount forced settlement measures chart the proportion of population residing at the individual PH3, PH2, or PH1 centers, compared to the total population in the political catchment controlled from these (Table 3, Figures 15 and 16). Such measures allow a close focus on centralization as practiced by highest-level rulers (not considering effects of centralization by lower-ranking rulers in the same district). Horizontal or vertical comparisons allow judgements about the relative effectiveness of forced settlement centralization as practiced by equally or differently ranked rulers. The low degree of paramount forced settlement for the whole valley is remarkable, especially compared to the levels of paramount forced settlement reached in some of the districts (Table 3, Figure 16). For Tenam Rosario to have matched the level of population concentration at the PH3 center in Zorrillo, it would have required almost 2,000 dwellings. Such a pattern suggests a decentralized structure for the overall regime since rulers at its capital had less effective direct control over polity-wide subject population than had rulers at some PH3 centers over their subject pocket populations.

Cross-level forced settlement measures are slightly more complicated and chart the proportion of population associated with each of the PH's five levels. Why use such a measure? The relative amount of population found at each of the levels in a political hierarchy should have a close relation to the relative degree of forced settlement centralization exercised at that level. Vertical comparisons of these forced settlement measures within pockets and sections allow a closer look at how

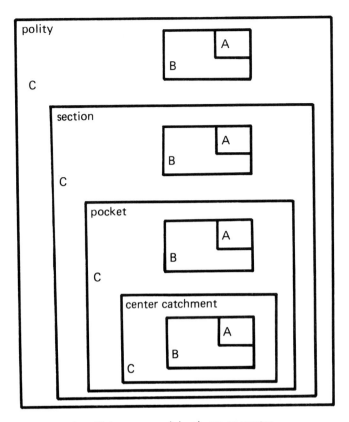

A = Civic–ceremonial volume at center

B = Number of dwellings at the site
associated with 'A'

C = Number of dwellings outside the
site associated with 'A', in 'A''s
tribute catchment

Forced settlement = B/B+C

Tribute drawing index [TDI] = A/B

Tribute load index [TLI-1] = A/B+C
[TLI-2] = A/C

Tribute base size [TBS] = B+C or C

Figure 15   Centralization indices

subject population is divided among differently ranked and competing sets of rulers within the same district. Additionally, proportion of population at PH5 sites can be used as an indicator of loose population living beyond the immediate reach of rulers associated with civic-ceremonial plazas.

Five pockets have structurally comparable three-level hierarchies (Chihuahua and Momón have only partial hierarchies). The five are far from having identical forced settlement configurations (Table 3). As mentioned, paramount forced settlement varies greatly. Aggregate forced settlement at PH4 centers also varies

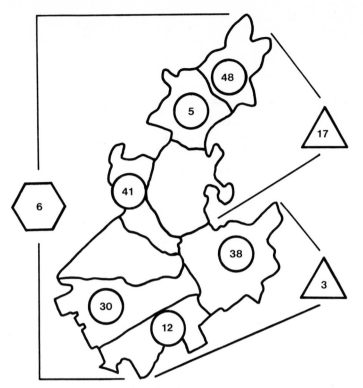

Figure 16a   Paramount forced settlement

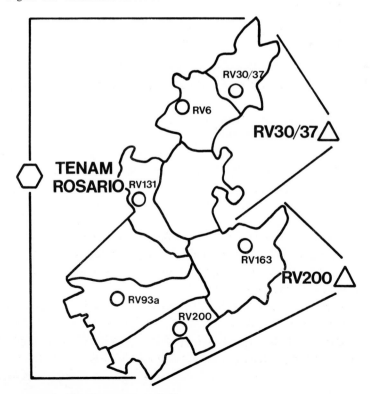

Figure 16b   Key for paramount indices

Table 4. *Forced settlement at individual PH3 and PH4 centers and individual pyramid-plazas (percentages)*

	Controlled by PH3 paramount	Controlled by PH4 centers	Total – all PH4 centers
Zorrillo	48 [28 10 10]	12 9 1	22
Rosario	38 [10 10 7 10]	18 16 2 *	37
Santa Inés North	30 [4 27]	18 11 9 7 4 3 2 [11 7] [5 2]	53
Santa Inés South	12	32 30 10 [16 16]	73
Nuestra Señora	5	17 16 12 7 6 5 2 [9 8]	64

Note : Figures are percentages of the territorial unit's total population (dwellings) at a center or plaza. Any discrepancies between totals and subtotals are due to rounding error.

[ ]   population percentage controlled by individual plazas in the center on the line above
*   less than 1 %

from one pocket to another, as does the proportion of population at the PH5 level. One finds a dichotomy between Zorrillo and Rosario (with high PH3 control, moderate aggregate PH4 control, and almost 1/3 uncontrolled PH5 population) and Santa Inés South and Santa Inés North (with moderate to low PH3 control, high aggregate PH4 control, and less than 1/5 uncontrolled PH5 population). Only Nuestra Señora (unusual in several respects) fails to fit the pattern.

A negative relation between PH3 control and aggregate PH4 control is understandable as a tradeoff. For example, low PH3 and high PH4 control corresponds to relatively greater decentralization (population is controlled from a greater number and locational spread of political centers). To better understand this one needs to stop treating the PH4 centers as an aggregate and address specifics of population associated with individual PH4 centers (Table 4) or individual plazas (for multiplaza centers). Since in practice it is difficult to delineate political catchments for PH4 plazas (Chapter 7), proportions of population at individual PH4 centers and plazas are calculated with reference to the total for their pockets (Table 4). Besides avoiding practical difficulties, such an approach is justified by the plausible idea that rulers at individual PH4 centers (as a group) compete with rulers at higher-ranking centers to draw in subjects from the entire population of a common district. To provide insights into the relative degrees of centralization exercised by various subgroups in the polity's internally segmented ruling group, results (Table 4) can be compared in several ways: the total PH3 population percentage versus the aggregate PH4 percentage, the total PH3 population percentage versus the average population percentage associated with individual

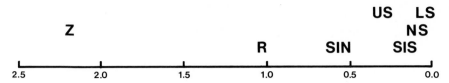

Figure 17   PH3/PH4 and PH2/PH3-PH4 continuum [Key: US = upper section;
LS = lower section; Z = Zorrillo; NS = Nuestra Señora; R = Rosario; SIN = Santa Inés North;
SIS = Santa Inés South]

PH4 centers, and the average population percentage associated with PH3 pyramid plazas versus the average population percentage associated with PH4 pyramid plazas. Concerning the first comparison, one finds a broad range in the degree of centralization, from high in Zorrillo to very low in Santa Inés South and Nuestra Señora. The second comparison gives an indication of the relative centralizing effectiveness of individual PH4 centers versus their PH3 capital. Rosario and Santa Inés North come closer into line with Zorrillo as more centralized pockets (where the PH3 center clearly overshadows any of the individual PH4 centers). By contrast, PH4 centers in relatively decentralized Santa Inés South and Nuestra Señora tend to overshadow their PH3 centers. The third comparison gives a rough indication of the relative strengths of forced settlement centralization practiced from individual PH4 and PH3 plazas. Results follow the general trends seen in the second comparison, except that Rosario reverts to the relatively more decentralized pattern seen in the first comparison. From the three comparisons, one sees a reasonably clear range of variation in the pattern of cross-level forced settlement among the pockets. The degree of forced settlement centralization in pockets can also be re-expressed as the proportion of PH3 forced settlement to the total PH4 forced settlement (Figure 17).

Bringing in PH5 sites and their uncontrolled population illustrates that four of five pockets show a positive relation between low PH3 control and a low percentage of PH5 population (Table 3).[10] Such a pattern can serve as a test implication for a tentative hypothesis that a powerful PH3 center (controlling a large proportion of the population) dampens development of competition among subordinate PH4 centers, a competition that expresses itself in the forced settlement of most available PH5 population into competing PH4 centers. By contrast, absence of a PH3 center allows such competition to develop.

The other set of hierarchies available for comparison comes from the two sections which contrast very clearly with one another (Table 3). Upper and lower section configurations are towards the centralized and decentralized ends of the range, respectively. As with the pockets, this can be re-expressed numerically as the proportion of PH2 forced settlement to the total PH3/4 forced settlement (Figure 17). Extending hypothetical ideas about contrasting pocket hierarchies to the section hierarchies, it may be that the upper section has a hierarchy with a powerful PH2 paramount center that dampens development of competition among subordinate (PH3 and PH4) centers and diminishes forced settlement of PH5 population into these. In contrast, the lower section's relatively less powerful PH2 center presides over a set of competitive subordinate (PH3 and PH4) centers which have drawn in a large proportion of PH5 population.

As interim conclusions about the degrees of forced settlement centralization in the Rosario polity and its districts, let me compare values at different hierarchical levels and trends of change in these from one level to another. Increasing paramount forced settlement values going down the hierarchy are to be expected in a system tending towards segmentary structure since these denote greater centralization and concentration of power away from the political system's apical positions. In contrast, a unitary structure should produce decreasing paramount forced settlement values down the hierarchical levels, congruent with a concentration of power towards the political system's apical positions. As it turns out, paramount forced settlement measures show a quite variable pattern of rise and fall down PH levels (Tables 3 and 4),[11] indications of a tendency towards segmentary political structure within the polity. The districts are far from uniform in the degree of centralization that they show. Lack of uniformity with reference to paramount forced settlement is interesting in the sense that possibly it reflects some of the internal cleavages within the political elite in the Rosario polity.

Finally, forced settlement centralization may be appreciated through a slightly different method. The idea is to look at the relative amount of population that is drawn into the orbit of Tenam Rosario and then to compare this to the population drawn to the vicinity of PH2 centers in each section. This is similar to a technique developed by Kowalewski and others for measuring centralization by looking at regional distribution of population as one moves outward from the primary site (Kowalewski *et al.* 1983: 41). Tenam Rosario's hinterland includes at the very least Chihuahua, probably Momón, and possibly Rosario. Its total population ranges from 383 (Chihuahua only) to 1,485 (adding in Momón and Rosario). Compare population figures of 590 (Zorrillo and Nuestra Señora) to 961 (entire upper valley) for the upper section PH2 center and figures of 2,000 (Santa Inés North and South) to 2,922 (entire lower valley) for the lower section PH2 center. Results still suggest a low degree of centralization polity-wide. One difference (from earlier results) is that the relative positions of the lower and upper section PH2 centers are reversed. But, population drawn into the orbit of major sites is less useful than paramount forced settlement or cross-level forced settlement as a measure of centralization, particularly at the relatively small intravalley scale used here. The hinterland population measure as a centralization indicator would make more sense for larger-scale intervalley comparisons.

Tribute flow and centralization

Another interesting approach to settlement evidence and centralization of power at different levels of a political hierarchy has to do with tribute flow (Steponaitis 1981: 322, 331). The argument runs as follows. Political power is closely relatable to control over human and material resources and finds expression in access to tribute exacted from inferiors. Relative degrees of power are thus systematically associated with relative amounts of tribute drawn in. A measure for the degree of political centralization is the ratio of the amount of tribute going to the superior site in a political unit compared to the average amount of tribute going to sites in the level immediately below (Steponaitis 1981: 322). Amounts of tribute may be characterized by comparing population size to catchment productivity ratios for sites (as Steponaitis does) or by comparing ratios of civic-ceremonial (and elite) architectural components to non-elite residential architectural components (as I do). Catchment productivity analysis is relatable most closely to tribute as foodstuffs, while architectural analysis is related most closely to tribute as labor service and/or provision of construction materials.

Any procedure which combines architectural and settlement analysis is likely to raise hackles, given well known methodological pitfalls associated with trying to compare and interpret numbers and masses of buildings that are known only from their surface appearance (see Chapter 4 – contemporaneity, equifinality, and form–function difficulties). A mitigating factor in the following analysis is that the population figures derived from dwelling counts are used for comparative purposes with errors spread (evenly?) among the units compared and thus cancelled out. Form to function problems for domestic buildings do not seem overwhelming (Chapter 4; de Montmollin 1981). And again, since results are used for comparative purposes, any errors in functional attribution will have relatively little impact on accuracy as long as the errors are evenly distributed. Contemporaneity difficulties for civic-ceremonial buildings are roughly the same as those for domestic dwellings (although perhaps made worse by the former's smaller numbers). Equifinality difficulties for civic-ceremonial buildings open a very old can of worms involving labor investment arguments applied to possible or probable multiconstruction stage edifices. For the building-to-building comparisons to be most enlightening, one needs not only a rough contemporaneity at a climax–crash point, but a roughly similar sequence of civic-ceremonial architectural development at each of the buildings being compared. Unfortunately, there is no easy (non-excavation based) tactic to lessen the degree of dubiousness associated with an analytical procedure which treats surficially measurable architectural mass as a rough indicator of command over labor effort. In the absence of appropriate excavations, an assumption of climax–crash contemporaneity and roughly similar developmental sequences may be adopted to warrant comparison of civic-ceremonial building construction volumes as indicators of tribute-drawing success, in a direct labor investment approach.

To use civic-ceremonial mass as an indicator of political power and importance, while circumventing at least equifinality if not contemporaneity difficulties, one may shift assumptions. Civic-ceremonial architectural mass in its final maximal form can be used as a rough relative indicator of the associated rulers' ability to draw in tribute of all kinds (not just corvee labor). In such an indirect projective approach, the relative size of civic-ceremonial buildings associated with rulers serves to project information (Wobst 1977) to archaeologists and to participants in the ancient political system about these rulers' tribute drawing power and political authority. While it is generally preferable to the direct labor investment approach, the indirect projective approach is considerably more vague about the linkage between civic-ceremonial architectural mass and tribute drawing power. So, if stratigraphic data are available from civic-ceremonial buildings allowing more direct resolution of equifinality difficulties, it is just as well to use both approaches.[12]

Tribute drawing and tribute imposition

A Tribute Drawing Index (abbreviated to TDI) measures degrees of tribute drawing centralization. The number of domestic dwellings is an indicator of local (i.e., on-site) tribute providers and civic-ceremonial architectural mass is a relative indicator of the tribute received there (a slippery combination of the direct labor investment and the indirect projective approach). The cubic meters of civic-ceremonial architectural mass at a center divided by the number of dwellings at the associated site gives the TDI (Table 5, Figures 15 and 18).

Leaders at a high TDI site with a relatively low proportion of local population to tribute had relatively high success in pulling in tribute from outlying populations (off-site tribute providers). For this interpretation of comparative TDI to make sense, there has to be a roughly equivalent tribute drawing rate within the centers and their sites which are being compared. Relatively high TDI is an indicator of a relatively high degree of political centralization exercised over a hinterland.

Such tribute drawing centralization differs from forced settlement centralization strategies, being at an arguably higher level of political sophistication because it features a greater degree of control at a distance. To clarify the difference, we can take the example of two centers with equal civic-ceremonial masses (e.g., 5,000 cu m), and thus equal amounts of tribute received (or better, tribute drawing potential). The first center has 500 residents in its associated site, the second has 50 residents. Given equal total populations in the catchments or spheres of influence (e.g., 1,000 people), the first center shows a greater degree of centralization as measured by its rulers' ability to concentrate population at one locus (e.g., 0.50 versus 0.05 of catchment population). The first center shows greater forced settlement centralization in its associated site. But, given a major simplifying assumption that there were equal rates of per capita tribute extraction at the two centers, the second has a greater degree of centralization as measured by greater per capita ability of its rulers to draw in tribute from outside (e.g., the second center has a TDI ten times greater).

If civic-ceremonial masses are fairly equivalent among centers and if the total population figures within relevant catchments are also equivalent, then forced settlement and tribute drawing centralization will tend to vary inversely. They will be on the opposite sides of the same coin (as assumed in the above example). But, if civic-ceremonial masses and/or total populations vary greatly (which they do), the inverse relation does not always hold.

The aggregate TDI value is higher in the upper section, suggesting that it had a higher level of tribute drawing centralization. But horizontal comparison is not as enlightening as vertical comparison of TDI values within each section (below).

Table 5. *Tribute Drawing Index (TDI) values*

District and PH rank	Civic-ceremonial volume [tribute]	Dwellings [population]	TDI
Polity			
PH1	50,371	239	210.7
PH2	5,418	238	22.8
PH2/3, PH3	10,238	1,022	10.0
PH3	4,820	784	6.1
PH4	11,290	1,850	6.1
all	71,900	3,111	23.1
all (excluding PH1)	21,529	2,872	7.5
Upper section			
PH2	3,142	159	19.8
PH2/3, PH3	5,145	272	18.9
PH3	2,003	113	17.7
PH4	2,335	264	8.8
all	7,480	536	14.0
Zorrillo			
PH2/3	3,142	159	19.8
PH4	335	72	4.6
all	3,477	231	15.1
Nuestra Señora			
PH3	857	13	65.9
PH4	1,310	166	7.9
all	2,167	179	12.1
Chihuahua			
PH4	690	26	26.5
Momón			
PH3	1,146	100	11.5
Lower section			
PH2	2,276	79	28.8
PH2/3, PH3	5,093	750	6.8
PH3	2,817	671	4.2
PH4	8,955	1,586	5.6
all	14,048	2,336	6.0
Rosario			
PH3	1,812	300	6.0
PH4	1,352	291	4.6
all	3,164	591	5.4
Santa Inés North			
PH3	1,005	371	2.7
PH4	3,589	647	5.5
all	4,594	1,018	4.5
Santa Inés South			
PH3	2,276	79	28.8
PH4	2,122	465	4.6
all	4,398	544	8.1

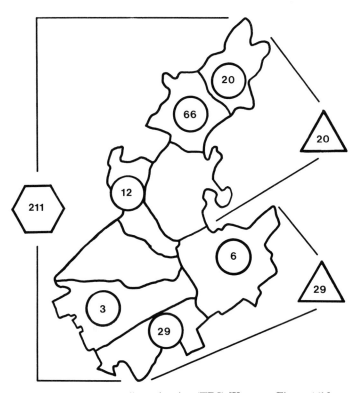

Figure 18   Paramount tribute drawing (TDI) [Key: see Figure 16b]

Overall, average TDI values are fairly uniform across the three lower-valley pockets, with slightly more variable values among the upper-valley pockets. All pockets except Chihuahua are in the same general range. As with sections, horizontal comparison of aggregate TDI values is not readily interpretable.

Vertical TDI comparisons are clearly more interesting. If TDI declines down PH levels, this could indicate an increasing ability of rulers at higher-ranking sites to draw in relatively greater proportions of tribute from outside sources. In other words, degree of tribute drawing centralization and relative concentration of political power declines as one moves down the PH.

Vertical comparisons of TDI values across PH levels also may be related (tenuously) to the subcontinuum between upward and downward delegation of authority. Declining TDI values down the PH would be compatible with a unitary system of downward (top-down) delegation of authority. Conversely, equal or increasing TDI values down the PH would be more congruent with an upward delegation. The reasoning is that authority flows outward from where power is most concentrated.

With these arguments in mind, let me look at actual TDI values moving down the PH (Table 5, Figure 18). Tenam Rosario is clearly in a class by itself as concerns its high TDl. The two PH2 centers have a TDI generally higher than virtually all other subordinate centers (including all but one PH3 center). TDI decreases across all levels. While PH3 centers have disparate TDI values, these are almost always superior to the TDI of all PH4 centers. Such a pattern supports the conclusion that the polity had a unitary political structure since the tribute drawing centralization is progressively greater towards the top and center of the hierarchy. This pattern is also congruent with a downward delegation of authority.

Moving to a smaller scale, the same pattern (declining TDI) holds clearly in the upper section, while in the lower section TDI values decline from PH2 to PH3 levels, but are roughly equivalent at PH3 and PH4 levels (Table 5). This suggests that the lower section had more segmentary than unitary structure, at least at the lower hierarchical levels. The pattern of roughly equivalent TDI values at PH3 and PH4 levels in two of the lower section's three pockets may reflect a more competitive, evenly matched, and less centralized regime compared to the upper section (a conclusion also arrived at in studying and comparing degrees of cross-level forced settlement). At the yet smaller pocket scale, the unitary pattern of declining TDI values all the way down the hierarchy is found in Zorrillo, Nuestra Señora, Rosario (by a slight margin), and Santa Inés South. The pattern is reversed for PH3 and PH4 sites in Santa Inés North. Comparisons cannot be made in mono-level Chihuahua and Momón. So the polity-wide pattern occurs clearly in all (comparable) pockets but Santa Inés North.

Tribute drawing centralization focuses from the top down on rulers' ability to extract (outside) tribute. Another way to look at tribute flow uses a more "from the bottom up" perspective, by focusing on the size of the burdens imposed on tribute providers (with greater burdens indicating greater centralization). A Tribute Load Index (abbreviated to TLI) is the measure used. To calculate TLI, one divides civic-ceremonial architectural mass at a center (or centers) by the number of dependent dwelling buildings to get a per capita (or per dwelling) measure of tribute load (Figure 15). Inputs into the TLI are definable in various ways,[13] each of which has different implications (below).

As with the TDI, absolute value of the TLI is not particularly crucial. In concrete terms (cubic meters of civic-ceremonial construction per dwelling), these quantities seem much too small to have mattered energetically, even in the unlikely case that efforts required were expended in a single event, and not distributed piecemeal over part or all of the Late/Terminal Classic time span. Total civic-ceremonial building volume (71,900 cu m) divided by the number of dwellings (4,300) gives a figure of 16.7 cu m per dwelling. However imperfectly, this suggests that civic-ceremonial construction activities were energetically slight in their impact on a rather large population.[14] For TLI, interest lies in comparing its relative values in different parts of the polity and across PH levels.

Certain ways of calculating the TLI make more sense than others. Tribute flow has to be regulated tightly and structured by a political hierarchy. From this it follows that calculations which encompass average values from different centers are less useful than calculations focused on individual centers (as nodes for tribute reception) and on these centers' specific and smaller catchments (as fields for tribute provisioning).

Some general principles of tribute obligation in stratified polities are relevant here. A polity's residents are responsible for tribute payment at: their own center, all higher-ranked centers in their own district, and no lower-ranked centers (in whatever district). In other words, tribute payments will only flow up the political hierarchy (excepting the use of tribute in redistribution from superiors to subordinates). The first kind of obligation may or may not apply, but there is a very high probability that the second and third obligations have to apply and a reasonable analysis of a hierarchical tribute collection system must take account of them.

An assumption needed for calculating TLI is that all civic-ceremonial centers draw at least some tribute from outside their own associated site boundaries. Preliminary support for this assumption comes from analysis of the TDI, in which the general tendency for TDI values to decline down the PH is congruent with a pattern whereby rulers at higher-ranked centers draw in tribute from subordinate centers and sites. The only other thing such a pattern might indicate is a higher per capita tribute load for residents of higher-ranking centers which seems less plausible in a stratified society.

With the three principles of tribute obligation (outlined above) and with nested hierarchies of districts and political centers, tributary catchments necessarily get smaller moving down the rungs of the PH. For the PH1 center the catchment is evidently the whole Rosario polity core. For each PH2 center the catchment includes one section. PH3 centers have tribute catchments encompassing their respective pockets. Tribute catchments for PH4 centers are much more difficult to determine but may be approximated by drawing Thiessen Polygons around the plaza(s) (Chapter 7).

The number of dwellings in a tributary catchment is an indicator of the Tributary Base Size (abbreviated to TBS) for the center to which the catchment belongs (Figure 15). TBS can be calculated in two ways: including all the dwellings in the catchment (assuming that all provide tribute), or including all dwellings in the catchment except those at the center (assuming that the inhabitants at the center are by and large exempt from tribute).

Estimating the numbers of dwellings contained in tributary catchments for individual centers (Table 6) presents problems not encountered in calculating the TDI. In the latter index, one only deals with numbers of dwellings at a center's associated site and all (but one) of these centers were completely mapped. Center catchments could not be as completely mapped, because survey coverage did not dramatically overspill the valley's topographical and/or political boundaries and many Thiessen Polygons run up to the survey limits causing undercounting of dwellings for some site catchments. The undercounting shrinks TBS and increases TLI values (Chapter 7). Yet, undercounting is probably slight on most sides of the valley (as survey margins were lightly settled, except on the southwestern downvalley side). Any unrecorded civic-ceremonial centers outside the survey area would alter polygon shapes but these are unlikely to exist (judging from informant questioning about the survey edges). Again, the exception to this is along the downvalley edge. In spite of such difficulties, it appears that differences noted in TBS (Table 6) have more to do with actual differences than with varying completeness of recording.

Presently, no attempt is made to be more subtle about the various ways in which tribute requirements might be apportioned among various categories of inhabitants. A more refined and difficult approach takes variation among dwellings as indicative of sociopolitical differentiation. For example, one might draw a distinction between elite tribute-receiving and non-elite tribute-providing groups (Chapter 8).

Viewed instrumentally, TBS calculations provide information needed for the TLI. But TBS may be used more independently as an indicator of tribute drawing potential or political power at a center. Viewing TBS in this way makes most sense at the lowest hierarchical levels (PH4 centers and their catchments). In contrast to PH4 centers, higher-ranking centers and their catchments have competing authority centers (and their catchments) nested within them, making tribute-paying mobilization of the entire catchment population from the highest-ranking center more of a problem. Let me now review differences in TBS among various catchments (Table 6). Since the two TBS measures (with or without the dwellings at the center) show the same general trends, they are not treated separately. The lower section has a TBS at least three times greater than the upper section. The imbalance may have been even greater as the large center at RV53 probably had control over some upper valley residents, and incomplete survey in Santa Inés South and North has led to undercounting of dwellings in the lower valley. The lower valley would have been a much more important source of subject manpower and total tribute for Tenam Rosario. If there was a policy of extracting equal aggregate amounts of tribute for Tenam Rosario from both sections, then clearly the burden on the upper-valley residents would have been much greater. The dual symmetrical layout at Tenam Rosario (Chapter 7, Figure 9) might support the latter possibility. However, one of the two replicated plazas at Tenam Rosario has roughly twice the architectural mass of the other (Chapter 7; de Montmollin 1988), which might indicate reduced disparities in tribute rates if it were supported by the more populous lower section. At a smaller scale, TBS in lower-valley pockets tends to be much larger than in upper-valley pockets (by at least two orders of magnitude), although TBS is not uniform among pockets within sections.

Horizontal TBS disparities may be evaluated in light of relative differences in total civic-ceremonial architectural mass for the centers that head the various catchments. Quite simply, differences among TLI values (Table 7) indicate a poor proportional match between civic-ceremonial architectural mass and TBS for centers. Conclusions drawn from this will vary according to whether one adopts the direct labor-investment approach or the indirect projective approach to civic-ceremonial architectural mass. In terms of the direct labor-investment approach, differences in tribute extraction rates will explain the evident failure of mass to proportionally match the TBS. Using the indirect projective approach, the fact that the TBS is not proportional to mass shows that TBS is not a faithful indicator of

Table 6. *Tribute Base Size (TBS) values*

PH rank	Center	Dwellings in catchment (*)	Dwellings in catchment, outside center
PH1	RV164	4,299	4,060
PH2	RV30/37	961	802
	RV200	2,922	2,843
PH3	RV30/37	332	173
	RV6	258	245
	RV131	243	143
	RV163	794	494
	RV93a	1,223	852
	RV200	641	562
PH3 average		582	412
PH4			
Zorrillo	RV14	54	14
	RV15	5+	5+
	RV34	50	21 c
	RV38	8	8 c
	RV43	8	5
average		25	11
PH4			
Nuestra Señora	RV1	38	7
	RV4	46	5
	RV8	12	0
	RV9	17	12
	RV20	43	27
	RV46b	51	7
	RV110	40	22 c
average		35	11
PH4			
Chihuahua	RV118	45	37
	RV127	33	15 [c]
	RV145	60	60
average		46	38
PH4			
Rosario	RV157	128	0
	RV165	79+	76 [c]
	RV166	171	29
	RV169	18	0
average		99	26
PH4			
Santa Inés North	RV86	114	32
	RV89	114	3
	RV91	27	0
	RV93b	223	8 c

Table 6. (*cont.*)

PH rank	Center	Dwellings in catchment (*)	Dwellings in catchment, outside center
	RV177	183	54 [c]
	RV203	32	0
	RV205	69	18
	RV208	139	139 [c]
average		113	32
PH4			
Santa Inés South	RV192	137	70
	RV195	193	0
	RV196	206	1
average		179	24
PH4			
SIN/Ros	RV158	184	137 c
PH4			
SIN/SIS	RV194	136	0 c

Note : PH4 centers are grouped according to the pocket to which they belong. However, the Thiessen Polygon boundaries that are drawn around each center to delimit a catchment may cross over into adjacent pockets, incorporating dwelling structures from these (Figure 38). Except for Tenam Rosario, multiplaza centers have their catchments divided among the plazas (Figure 38), although the figures are lumped by center in Table 6.

(*)   equivalent to Political Span [PS] (see Chapter 7)
c catchment completely within survey area (Figure 38)
(c) as c, but touching on unsurveyed parts of Midvalley Range

power exercised at the center. In other words, political power exercised from centers can vary somewhat independently of the population sizes of their tribute catchment areas.

Let me now look at implications of variation in the TLI. The index is calculated in two ways: a minimal view of tribute load assumes that it is distributed less onerously among all inhabitants of a catchment (TLI-1); a maximal view assumes that it is laid more onerously only on those inhabitants not privileged to live within the center's associated site (TLI-2). Actual tribute load conditions probably lie somewhere between the two extremes, with a complex web of obligations distributed among tribute payers in ways forever beyond the capability of archaeologists to decipher.

As with the TDI, it is most interesting to interpret changes in the TLI across PH levels (Table 7, Figure 19). A drop in the TLI moving down the PH is an indicator of unitary structure, with decreasing tribute imposition centralization at lower hierarchical levels. Conversely, increase or equivalence in the TLI going down the PH indicates a more segmentary structure. At a polity-wide scale, there is a sharp

Table 7. *Tribute Load Index (TLI) values*

PH rank	Center	All dwellings in catchment – TLI-1	Dwellings in catchment, outside center – TLI-2
PH1	RV164	11.7	12.4
PH2	RV30/37	3.3	3.9
	RV200	0.8	0.8
	average	1.3	1.4
PH3	RV30/37	9.5	18.2
	RV6	3.3	3.5
	RV131	4.7	8.0
	Upper section average	6.2 [4.0]	9.2 [5.2]
	RV163	2.3	3.7
	RV93a	0.8	1.2
	RV200	3.6	4.0
	Lower section average	1.9 [1.4]	2.7 [2.1]
	Polity average	2.9 [1.9]	4.1 [2.8]
PH4	Zorrillo average	2.7	6.3
	Nuestra Señora average	5.3	16.4
	Chihuahua average	5.0	6.2
	Upper section average	4.6	9.5
	Rosario average	3.4	12.9
	Santa Inés N. average	4.0	29.9
	Santa Inés S. average	4.0	14.1
	borderline average	5.9	13.8
	Lower section average	4.2	15.8
	Polity average	4.2	13.9

[ ] PH3 centers only, without PH2/3 centers

drop in both TLI-1 and TLI-2 from the PH1 center to the PH2 centers. Comparing horizontally, the upper section PH2 center imposes a higher tribute load than does the lower section center. Decreasing TLI between the first and second hierarchical levels indicates that the Rosario polity was centralized and unitary in the sense that there was greater tribute imposition centralization for the overall polity than for the two constituent sections and certainly greater centralization than for all but one of the constituent pockets (the exception being Zorrillo for TLI-2 only). In general, the pattern matches that found for TDI values and differs sharply from the pattern found with reference to forced settlement. Such a contrast provisionally indicates that the Rosario polity was more effectively centralized by indirect means (tribute drawing and tribute imposition) than by direct means (forced settlement). TLI values for PH3 centers are variable. The four pure PH3 centers[15] tend to have equal or slightly greater TLI values than the PH2

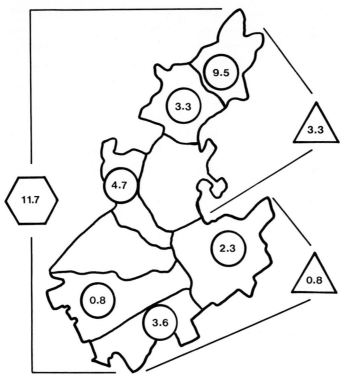

Figure 19a   Paramount tribute imposition (TLI-1) [Key: see Figure 16b]

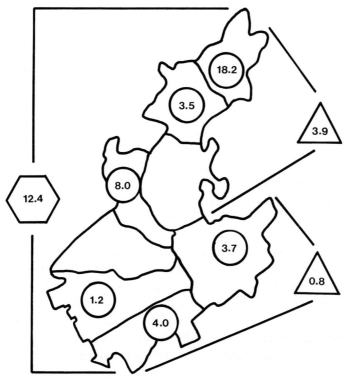

Figure 19b   Paramount tribute imposition (TLI-2) [Key: see Figure 16b]

centers, breaking the trend of dropping TLI values down the PH. Overall, this indicates a situation of strong centralization at the polity-wide scale, then weak centralization for the two constituent sections, then relatively stronger centralization again for the pockets (compared to sections). There is extreme variability among TLI values for individual PH4 centers. But on average these values are higher than for PH3 centers. Thus, the segmentary-looking pattern already seen with reference to the relation between the sections and their constituent pockets is reproduced within some of the individual pockets (Nuestra Señora, Rosario, Santa Inés South, and Santa Inés North; Zorrillo is the exception).

Patterns of change in TLI values across PH levels also may be related to the subcontinuum between upward and downward delegation of authority. Declining TLI values down the PH would be congruent with unitary downward delegation of authority. By contrast, increasing or unchanged TLI values down the PH would reflect more segmentary upward delegation of authority. The uneven pattern of rising and declining TLI values down the PH levels suggests that there was a complex mix of both upward and downward delegation of authority in the Rosario polity.

Moving from the realm of detailed substantive conclusions, I take now a more general overview of the analyses carried out so far. For the centralization subcontinuum various indices (such as the forced settlement measures, TDI, TLI, and more indirectly TBS – Figure 15) have been checked for similarities and differences in their values in different parts of the Rosario polity. For these particular measures there is a relatively direct notion of what they represent in political terms. This is especially the case for the forced settlement measures where dwellings are reasonably equatable with (subject) population and the hierarchically arrayed centers are equatable with political control points of varying importance and power. The TBS measure also is interpretable quite clearly as an indicator of the subject (tribute-paying) population available to political rulers. TDI and TLI measures are less clear-cut as to what they represent, mainly because they use civic-ceremonial architectural volume to represent tribute flow and political power (Sanders 1974; Blanton *et al.* 1982; Steponaitis 1981; Kurjack 1974; Cheek 1986; and others). It is difficult to arrive at the precise political meaning of variations in the cubic meters of civic-ceremonial construction-fill per dwelling among different centers. Therefore, greater confidence should be placed in forced settlement measures. But even with the disparities in how clearly they are interpretable, it is worth using all the indices, since they measure different kinds of centralization or at least offer different perspectives on the phenomenon of centralization and political control. Forced settlement centralization concerns direct control over subject population, effected by pulling it into the political centers. Tribute-flow measures concern more indirect forms of centralization which involve exercising or projecting power out over a territory beyond the immediate confines of a political center, so as to produce a flow of tribute into the center.

The preceding analyses have taken us some way towards characterizing the Rosario polity's position on the centralization subcontinuum (Table 1) and answering the first research question: To what degree did Classic Maya political structure feature a decentralized, replicated, and loosely integrated arrangement of districts? To more fully address the question, further analysis is required to determine the Rosario polity's positions on the other subcontinua (differentiation and integration) within the segmentary to unitary continuum (Chapter 6). Subsequently, differences and similarities in centralization can be evaluated in terms of their co-occurrence with other factors in order to account for their possible determinants (Chapter 11).

6

Differentiation and integration

Differentiation

Degrees of replication in settlement patterns among the Rosario polity's centers and districts provide insights into degrees of differentiation (along the second sub-continuum contained in the segmentary–unitary continuum, Table 1). Presence or absence of replication (for centers and districts) is judged with reference to values arrived at on the various centralization measures (forced settlement, TDI, and TLI – Figure 15). Other available measures (for districts) are: territorial size, settlement density (and environmental composition), and tributary base size (TBS – Figure 15). A high degree of (horizontal) replication in centralization measures among all hierarchically equivalent units indicates a segmentary polity. Vertical replication of centralization measures across levels of a hierarchy (the PH) indicates segmentary structure, as does increasing degrees of centralization down the PH. Decreasing degrees of centralization down the PH indicate unitary structure. To a very great extent, the differentiation subcontinuum has an analytically residual quality with reference to the centralization subcontinuum. Many of the values examined with reference to differentiation have been generated while investigating centralization (Chapter 5).

At the outset, it appeared that a search for replication in internal layout and composition among sites (and wards) might be a useful way of examining degrees of differentiation in the Rosario polity (de Montmollin 1982a), but it soon turned out that this kind of analysis was inappropriate. Sites are too numerous and richly variable in their internal layout and composition to be effectively compared. Besides practical difficulties of too much detail, there are theoretical objections to the site scale. It is uncertain that all individual sites (communities) are important or relevant political units for analysis which attempts to chart degrees of segmentary versus unitary structure at the polity scale. To meet practical objections, summary attributes (degrees of forced settlement, TDI, TLI, and TBS – Figure 15), which have little to do with the details of individual site layout and composition, are more manageable for intersite comparisons. Theoretical objections to site-scale analysis can be met by focusing on hierarchically superior sites (and their hinterlands). These are more likely to have encompassed political entities relevant to a study of polity-scale political structure. Conversely, hierarchically inferior PH4 sites are best omitted from comparisons. Thus, some intersite comparisons are relevant (and are presented) along with the comparisons made among districts.

Larger-scale settlement units such as districts (pockets or sections) are more appropriate than individual sites for comparing degrees of differentiation when the theoretical focus is on issues of relatively large-scale political structure. A set of differentiated sites (within a district) corresponds to a meaningful political unit with clear relations of superordination and subordination, outside the purely domestic domain. In contrast, individual sites, especially small ones, often encompass no more than a small kinship or domestic unit. The important political concept of territory obviously is better handled at the district scale. Tracing boundaries for districts is no more difficult than tracing boundaries for sites or wards. There is equal uncertainty in all cases. On a practical note, districts are easier to manipulate for comparison of their attributes. Finally, problems of contemporaneity and equifinality may be smoothed out by broadening the territorial inclusiveness of the units compared (as argued in Sanders *et al.* 1979: 65, 73; and Chapter 4). Also, a more general case for the smoothing out of inaccuracies by increasing the scale of study has been made on the basis of an ethnoarchaeological analysis of three Highland Maya communities where the material culture–behavior (or form–function) nexus is clearer at the community scale than at the individual household scale (Hayden and Cannon 1984: 18–19, 181, 185, 188).

For districts, a variety of attributes may be compared: general size (area), horizontally compared between sections and among pockets; settlement (population) density and environmental composition, horizontally compared between sections and among pockets and vertically compared between sections and their constituent pockets; TBS (Figure 15), horizontally compared between sections and among pockets; paramount forced settlement at PH1, PH2, and PH3 centers and aggregate forced settlement, horizontally compared between sections and among pockets and vertically compared between sections and their constituent pockets; tribute drawing centralization (TDI–Figure 15) at PH1, PH2, and PH3 centers and aggregate TDI, horizontally compared between sections and among pockets and vertically compared between sections and their constituent pockets; and tribute imposition centralization (TLI – Figure 15) at PH1, PH2, and PH3 centers and aggregate TLI, horizontally compared between sections and among pockets and vertically compared between sections and their constituent pockets.

Given these measures to work with, it is often difficult to define in an absolute sense what constitutes replication or differentiation. At one extreme, it is highly unlikely that all units compared will show identical values for the measures. And, since the differences are all of degree, it is impossible for any two or more cases to be dissimilar entirely from one another. Thus, one has to judge what constitutes a strong degree of similarity or dissimilarity. Relative differences of one or more orders of magnitude are clearly more meaningful with reference to the simpler measures of population distribution (paramount forced settlement or TBS), since demographic scale is important politically. In contrast, for measures involving civic-ceremonial architectural mass (TDI or TLI), numerical differences (of whatever magnitude) are harder to interpret because of the shaky status of direct labor investment arguments applied to survey data (Chapters 4 and 5) and because of ambiguities in indirect projective approaches associated with evaluating the concrete political implications of differences in cubic meters of civic-ceremonial construction per household. To recapitulate my introductory comments, the rationales for interpreting comparisons are the following. Horizontally, replication suggests segmentary structure and differentiation suggests unitary structure. Vertically, there are three possibilities when looking at centralization indices: replication suggests segmentary structure; differentiation with consistent increase in values down the hierarchical levels also suggests segmentary structure; differentiation with consistent decrease in values down the hierarchical levels suggests unitary structure.

Area

The areas of what are (initially) topographically defined districts might not seem to be an appropriate attribute when the aim is to examine political structure. Nevertheless, a political component does enter into the delineation of districts. This is suggested by their often similar political settlement-hierarchies (see PH, in Chapter 5). If two adjoining (topographic) pockets were really one single political unit, this should produce some sort of hierarchy spanning both of them. What comes closest to this is combined Momón/Chihuahua (Figure 5), but it is preferable to interpret Chihuahua's lack of a PH3 center in terms of its dependence on the capital, Tenam Rosario, rather than in terms of its being subsumed into the Momón Pocket. Thus, the districts represent a political as well as a geographical partitioning of the landscape.

Accepting that pockets are viable units for political analysis, there is no apparent geographical reason for a one-to-one correspondence between pockets and topographical sub-basins. Given this lack of geographical determination, factors affecting whether a pocket covered only one or else two (or more) sub-basins might be political norms and/or functional requirements governing the ideal territorial size for viable districts. For the various districts, I first consider degrees of replication in areal size. Then I look at determinants of and degrees of replication for such variables as population density, environmental composition, and total population size.

Horizontal comparison alone makes sense, since area diminishes by definition as one moves down the nested hierarchy of districts (Figure 20). The two sections have similar size. The replication still holds, although more tenuously, even when unsurveyed valley bottom from the lower section is added in. The uneven proportions of sloping valley-edges covered in upper and lower sections make the area comparison slightly suspect, but a tendency towards equal size is still broadly valid. Among the pockets, areal size replication occurs within each section, but not across them. Upper-section pockets have a five to seven sq km size range and lower-section pockets a nine to eleven (or more) sq km range. For a better replication, further subdivision of lower pockets or else a merging of adjoining upper pockets is required. As mentioned earlier, a basis for further subdivision or grouping is not readily apparent. There is no replication of fully developed settlement hierarchies within any single lower pocket (one possible basis for subdivision). Perhaps a better

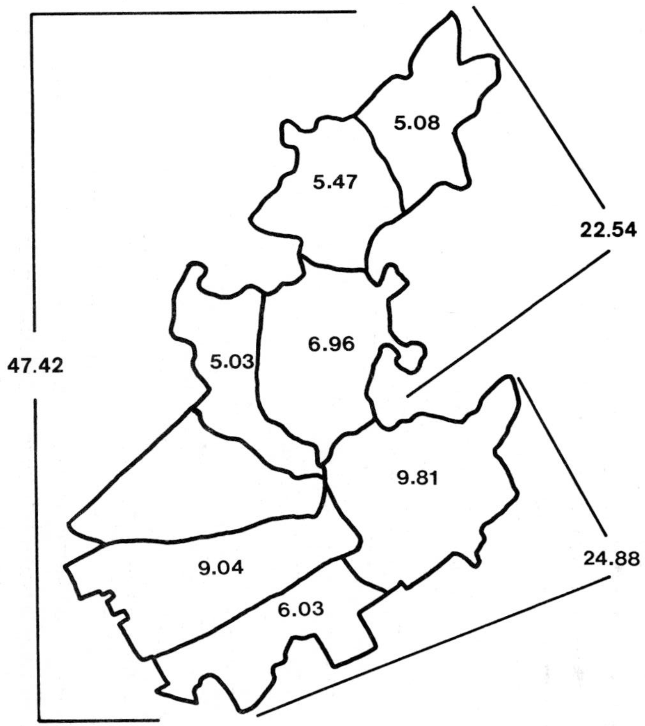

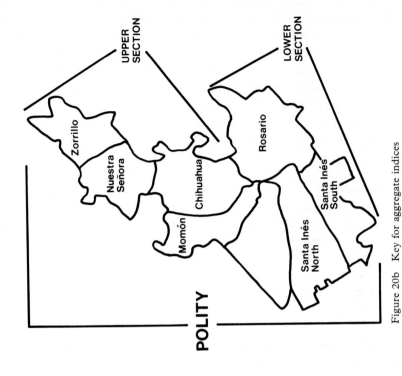

Figure 20a   District areas (in square kilometers; polity total does not include Lomas and fringe areas; projected areas, including unsurveyed area, are: lower section – 29.76; Santa Inés North – 11.22; Santa Inés South – 8.73)

Figure 20b   Key for aggregate indices

argument could be made for merging Zorrillo and Momón or else Momón and Chihuahua, to produce somewhat more standard arrangements with reference to PH3 centers. Combined Zorrillo-Nuestra Señora has an area of 10.55 sq km and combined Momón-Chihuahua has an area of 11.99 sq km, closer to the area size-range for lower pockets. However, there is no compelling reason for such manipulations of the settlement record and it remains best to leave the upper pockets as defined. Thus, a reasonably good degree of area size-replication for pockets within each section is a possible (but very indirect) indicator of segmentary structure within each section.

Population density and environmental composition

Population density and environmental composition may be horizontally compared between sections and among pockets and vertically compared between sections and their constituent pockets. The need to compare environmental composition becomes apparent through a rather complicated argument aimed at discerning whether there are political determinants of population density and total population size (TBS) for districts. Initially it seems rather more likely that population density would be subject to environmental (or economic) rather than political determinants. Population density also might depend on a demographic growth cycle. Yet there are at least some possible political determinants for density. When the total population size in each of several districts is subject to political constraints, their settlement densities can vary in light of such political constraints. A political imperative to maintain equivalent populations in districts is to be expected most readily in a segmentary political regime, as it helps to maintain the balance between politically equal constituent districts. Such a balance is all the more necessary in a segmentary regime with greater potential for competition among autonomous districts. Generically similar arguments have been made in Earle's study of ancient Hawaiian politics and economics:

> Theoretically there is a spectrum in the possible pattern for the
> distribution of population. At one extreme, population can be distributed
> such that each community is approximately equal in size. This pattern is
> characteristic of acephalous societies where the communities are politically
> autonomous and in direct competition. Small communities must either
> recruit additional members or risk defeat in battle...Without strong
> community leadership, large communities tend to segment. At the other
> extreme, population is distributed with respect to resource availability.
> Because population is closely adjusted to resources, community self-
> sufficiency is enhanced; however, variability in community population size
> (according to resource availability) requires an organizational mechanism to
> guarantee the viability of smaller communities. (Earle 1978: 160)

This is sound general reasoning, not limited to communities in acephalous types of political systems, but also extendable to districts in complex polities. However, it is not necessary to see resource availability as a sole determinant of differences in

Table 8. *Implications of political or economic determinants for comparative*
population densities

	Same-size district	Unequal-size district
Equal		
relative	P =	P ≠
resources	E =	E =
Unequal		
relative	P =	P ≠
resources	E ≠	E ≠

= similar population densities
≠ unequal population densities
P political determinants of settlement densities: aim is to maintain total district population
within a small range of variation (especially likely in a segmentary political system)
E economic determinants of settlement density: aim is to match population and resources as
evenly as possible

population size (see discussion of Rosario Valley densities, environmental
composition, and TBS, below). There is a different perspective on district size,
used by Alden with reference to complex political systems in the Basin of Mexico.
From this perspective, strong variation in the demographic size of districts or
clusters denotes the end product of a period of intense competition with expansion
of some clusters at the expense of others. In contrast, a small range of variation in
the population size of clusters is the end product of a period of low competition,
associated with efficiency in administration (Alden 1979: 195). I do not use this
perspective because of its inappropriate dependence on administrative efficiency
arguments (Chapter 7), and instead rely on the first idea that equally populous
districts are the outcome of balanced competition while unequally populous
districts (perhaps matched to differential resource availability) are allowed in a
more centralized political system.

   Given a set of districts with equal area, a political imperative to maintain their
population sizes at roughly equal levels would produce equal densities within them.
A political determinant would be more clear-cut if the districts were endowed
unequally with physical resources and thus likely to show unequal densities if
economic determinants were predominant. For districts with unequal area, matters
become more complicated. A political imperative to balance population sizes
produces unequal densities in line with relative areas. However, unequal resource
endowments could also produce this pattern (where economic factors were
important). In the latter case, unequal densities should match closely resource
inequalities, which is not necessarily so for politically determined unequal densities.
Equal resource endowments within districts (of unequal area) produce a pattern of
equal densities with economic determinants and unequal densities with (segmentary) political determinants. Thus, equal resource endowments make it easier
to distinguish effects of political versus economic determinants (Table 8).

Table 9. *Distribution of environmental zones across districts (areas in sq km)*

District	vf	vfe	lh	uh	hill	ms	All
Zorrillo	1.52	0.00	2.64	0.86	3.56	0.00	5.08
Nuestra Señora	1.26	0.00	1.73	2.44	4.21	0.00	5.47
Chihuahua	4.57	0.24	1.05	0.91	2.06	0.09	6.96
Momón	1.10	0.00	2.63	1.09	3.84	0.09	5.03
Upper section	8.45	0.24	8.05	5.30	13.67	0.18	22.54
Rosario	3.34	0.56	5.36	0.43	5.91	0.00	9.81
All Santa Inés	11.14	0.96	2.53	0.37	2.94	0.03	15.07
Santa Inés North	7.10	0.91	0.59	0.37	1.00	0.03	9.04
Santa Inés South	4.04	0.05	1.94	0.00	1.94	0.00	6.03
Lower section	14.48	1.52	7.89	0.80	8.85	0.03	24.88
Polity total	22.93	1.76	15.94	6.10	22.52	0.21	47.42
Midvalley range	0.00	0.00	0.00	4.10	4.42	0.00	4.51

vf   Valley Floor Zone: composed of alluvial soils and colluvium, relatively great subsurface moisture (with a few, small marshy patches and waterlogged areas), surrounds the channels of the Santa Inés River and its main tributaries, running up to the foot of the piedmont (lh, uh), broken up by knolls (vfe), largest uninterrupted stretch at downvalley southwest end

vfe   Valley Floor Eminence Zone: various knolls that rise entirely out of the valley floor (vf), soils are thinner and stonier than on the valley floor

lh   Lower Hillside Zone: extends upward from the edge of the Valley Floor to the edge of the Upper Hillside, lower segment of piedmont, gentle slopes, fairly flat ledges, isolated knolls, with variable degree of slope and depth of soil cover, soils generally shallower and drier than on Valley Floor

uh   Upper Hillside Zone: begins at the first continuous band of steep-sloped large hills bordering the valley, upper segment of piedmont, continues up through the Comitan Escarpment on the north side and through an area of rolling hills on the south side (separating the Rosario and San Lucas Valleys), steep slopes, (larger hilltops classed in the Hilltop Zone), ledges, and high basins, soils generally thinner and rockier than in lower zones

hill   Lower Hillside, Upper Hillside, and Hilltop Zones: largest, flattest, most mesa-like hilltops, widely scattered around the valley

ms   Marsh: larger areas of marsh, around springs, usually on the valley floor

Different effects on population density are expected for a more unitary political regime which allows a greater degree of horizontal differentiation in total population sizes of its districts. However, this line of enquiry is difficult to pursue because of the unconstrained nature of these kinds of political effects on population density and the consequent difficulties in finding their crucial test implications. Minimally, unitary political determinants result in unequal or equal population densities (depending on whether there are districts of equal or unequal area) which results in unequal population sizes. If variability in population densities does not correspond closely to environmental endowments, this indicates that unitary political determinants were important. If the variation in population density does

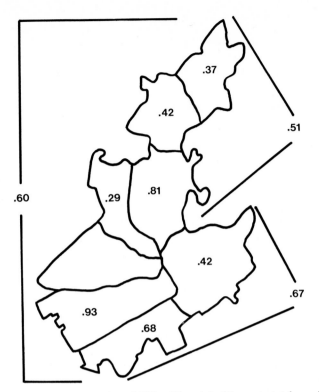

Figure 21   Proportion of Valley Floor (vf–vfe) area to total area [Key: see Figure 20b]

correspond closely to environmental endowments, it is more difficult to distinguish the relative importance of unitary political and economic determinants.

Clearly, the environmental composition of districts must be understood in order to distinguish properly between political and economic determinants of their settlement-density patterns. A separate problem concerns whether district environmental composition is itself a primarily politically or economically determined attribute (Chapter 9). But here I treat environmental composition instrumentally as an attribute whose variability has to be understood and controlled for, as a step towards better understanding of other attributes such as general population density or population density on prime land.

The surveyed valley was divided into several environmental zones (described in Table 9). With the exception of some unsurveyed area in Santa Inés South and North, the entire extent of Valley Floor and Valley Floor Eminence has been surveyed in all pockets making their comparison quite sound. Absolute amounts and relative proportions of Upper and Lower Hillside terrain are affected by how far upslope on the pocket edges the survey was carried. However, since there was a generally equivalent attempt to cover all the flatter more useable ground in each pocket (again with the partial exception of Santa Inés South and North), amounts and proportions of Lower Hillside, Valley Floor, and Valley Floor Eminence are

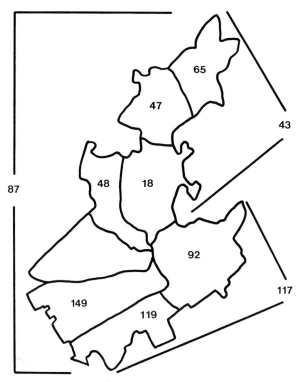

Figure 22   Population densities (in dwellings per square kilometer [Key: see Figure 20b])

legitimately comparable, while the actual amount and proportion of Upper Hillside is less likely to coincide with the surveyed amount.

A convenient (if crude) indicator of a district's relative resource endowment is the proportion of Valley Floor (vf) and Valley Floor Eminence (vfe) area within its total area (minus Upper Hillside and Hilltop). Higher proportions indicate a richer resource base (Figure 21). Pockets break down into roughly two classes – Zorrillo, Nuestra Señora, Momón, and Rosario in the 0.29–0.42 range and Chihuahua, Santa Inés South, and Santa Inés North in the 0.68–0.93 range.

Let us now compare population densities among districts (Figure 22) and try to understand whether political or other factors are producing the patterning, and, if political factors are at play, whether these are segmentary. As a ratio measure, densities should not be overly sensitive to variations in completeness of survey coverage. But for comparing differences in population densities to differences in resource endowments, it is better to recalculate population densities leaving out the Upper Hillside's settlement and area (Figure 23). This reduces the effects of uneven survey coverage in the Upper Hillside. The lower section has a density almost three times greater than the upper section (Figures 22 and 23). This is not congruent with segmentary political determinants (where upper-section density should be higher). As the lower section has a better resource endowment (Figure 21), its higher density is more congruent with economic determinants. Nevertheless, the density difference

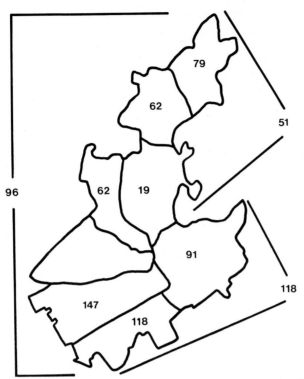

Figure 23   Population densities minus Upper Hillside (in dwellings per square kilometer) [Key: see Figure 20b]

(Figure 23) is far greater (proportionally) than relative differences in resource endowments (131% versus 30%) which indicates that more than, or other than, purely economic determinants were operating. In line with the reasoning I have already detailed, such a lack of constraint on population density is congruent with more unitary than segmentary political structure. Ideally, one should also consider the not mutually exclusive possibility that the upper section was at a relatively earlier stage in a demographic development cycle, not having filled in to its eventual maximal density when the system collapsed (this issue is addressed in Chapter 10).

Within each section, there is some pocket-to-pocket variation in density figures, but this is not extreme, except for markedly less dense Chihuahua (Figures 22 and 23). In the upper valley, Nuestra Señora and Momón have roughly similar densities, with Zorrillo's somewhat higher. Since overall territorial size and relative resource endowment for the three pockets are also roughly similar, it is impossible to differentiate between political and economic determinants, but segmentary political determinants are not precluded. Chihuahua is a case apart. It has a larger area and a better resource endowment than the other three pockets. Given (segmentary) political determinants it should have lower density; given economic determinants it should have higher density. Chihuahua (not counting population from Tenam Rosario) has a density much lower than required to bring its total population into balance with other pockets. Thus, the more likely political determinant is a unitary-like maintenance of Chihuahua as a relatively lightly settled agricultural reserve for the important residents at Tenam Rosario (Chapter 9; de Montmollin 1985c). There are at least two alternative determinants, but they are difficult to document. One alternative possibility is that Chihuahua was at a relatively early position in a development cycle. This seems unlikely because of Chihuahua's central location and relatively good resource endowment. But a relatively early position in a cycle is a more likely possibility for Chihuahua if one views it as part of a lightly settled buffer zone between earlier poles of development (for example, PH2 centers in the upper and lower sections). The second possible factor contributing to Chihuahua's low density is a draining off of its population into Tenam Rosario (through a forced settlement policy). Evaluating this interpretation is methodologically quite difficult (Chapters 4 and 5). For its impact to be so clearly apparent in the Chihuahua settlement record, such a forced settlement polity would have needed to be quite continuous over the latter part of the Rosario polity's development.

If a large part of the population at Tenam Rosario (195 dwellings on the mesatop – Figure 8) belonged to Chihuahua, this pocket's density would have been 49 dwellings per sq km (54 dwellings per sq km leaving out Upper Hillside).[1] This brings it into line with the densities and total populations of other upper pockets and reinforces the idea that Tenam Rosario and Chihuahua belonged together (with Tenam Rosario serving as PH3 center for Chihuahua). Following this reasoning, the original Chihuahua density (minus Tenam Rosario) may be compared to recalculated densities for other pockets (minus their own PH3 centers): Chihuahua = 18, Zorrillo = 34, Nuestra Señora = 45, and Momón = 28. The comparisons suggest that Chihuahua is still exceptional (in this case, because of the demographic dominance of Tenam Rosario).

Within the lower section,[2] Santa Inés North and Santa Inés South have somewhat different resource endowments (Figure 21), but Santa Inés North is clearly larger in area. With (segmentary) political determinants, population density in Santa Inés South should be higher, but in actual fact it is rather lower (Figures 22 and 23). Compared to Santa Inés North, Santa Inés South's resource endowment is 27% less, while its population density is 20% less, something of a match which suggests potential importance for economic determinants and possibly unitary political determinants. Rosario has slightly less area than Santa Inés North and its density should be somewhat higher with segmentary political determinants operating, but the density is appreciably lower (Figures 22 and 23). Thus, total populations differ – 1,589 dwellings (projected) for Santa Inés North and 839 dwellings for Rosario. Segmentary political determinants seem relatively more likely in the case of density differences between Rosario and the areally smaller Santa Inés South. The latter's higher density brings its (projected) total population (1,030 dwellings) relatively closely into line with Rosario's (839 dwellings). The difference may have been even smaller if Rosario was somewhat larger than the area surveyed or if some of the dwellings at Tenam Rosario belonged in Rosario. Rosario

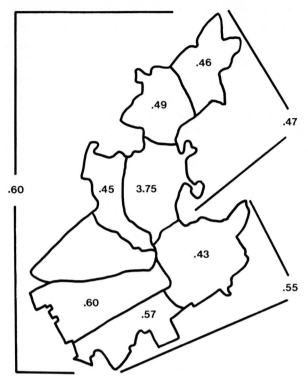

Figure 24 Hectares of Valley Floor (vf–vfe) per dwelling [Key: see Figure 20b]

has a less favorable resource endowment than the other lower pockets (Figure 21). With economic determinants operating, Rosario's density should be lower, as is the case (Figure 22 and 23). But the difference is proportionally less than the resource difference (38 % versus 54 % with reference to Santa Inés North, and 22 % versus 38 % with reference to Santa Inés South). So resource differences cannot account for all of the variation.

In sum, Rosario's total population fails to closely replicate that of Santa Inés North and (to a lesser degree) that of Santa Inés South. Such a pattern may be attributed in part, but not entirely, to economic determinants. It may be that Rosario was at an earlier stage in a developmental cycle, for similar reasons to those proposed for Chihuahua – the existence of a lightly settled buffer zone between earlier poles of development at the valley's upper and lower ends. Two other factors to account for lower than expected density (discussed with reference to Chihuahua) are: the suppression of settlement to "free-up" an agricultural reserve, and the drawing off of population increase into Tenam Rosario (forced settlement). But relative under-settlement in Rosario is much less than in Chihuahua, so that the three factors (to the degree that they did apply) had a relatively smaller impact.

Another settlement-density measure is more directly sensitive to differences in environmental composition (and carrying capacity) among districts. This consists of the hectares (ha) of prime Valley Floor (vf) and Valley Floor Eminence (vfe) available per dwelling (Figure 24). The [(vf-vfe)ha/dw] measure roughly indicates population pressure on favored agricultural resources (bottom lands),[3] and it targets the one resource whose relative abundance clearly varies among districts. Such a measure is also more sensitive to political and/or growth cycle determinants than the simpler density measures used so far (Figures 22 and 23) since it factors out differences in absolute quantities of prime land. Any variation in (vf-vfe)ha/dw among districts reflects a deviation from economically optimal population distribution. One of the contributing factors to the deviation might be a segmentary political imperative of maintaining balance in district population sizes. Another contributing factor to the deviation might be the stage reached in a development cycle. For example, lower than average densities could be found in a district closer to the beginning of a growth cycle, while higher than normal densities could be found in a district closer to the maximal point in a growth cycle.

Aggregate (vf-vfe)ha/dw is not very different between sections, nor is it very variable among pockets (Figure 24). The striking exception is Chihuahua with its much higher (vf-vfe)ha/dw. The overall replication is congruent with optimally regular distribution of population according to resources (bottom lands). District population size disparities allowed by replication in (vf-vfe)ha/dw are more in keeping with unitary political structure and economic efficiency (Chapter 9) than with segmentary political structure.

Summing up, the second set of comparisons suggests that political as well as economic determinants governed differences and/or similarities in district areas, population densities, and eventually total population sizes. Such a conclusion is better supported by comparisons of population densities and resource endowments than by comparison of vf-vfe(ha)/dw values. Finally, since the attempt to detect political determinants of population density and size proves to be so tortuous, other attributes (forced settlement, TDI, TLI) remain more appropriate and clear-cut as indicators of politically relevant tendencies towards differentiation or replication.

Tributary Base Size (TBS)

The degree of differentiation in TBS between sections and among pockets is a useful indicator of degree of unitariness (Figure 25). This takes up the suggestion (made in Chapter 5) that TBS could be an indicator of tribute-drawing potential or political power for rulers at centers. The lower section has a TBS at least three times as large as the upper section's, a lack of replication indicating segmentariness at the polity scale. TBS among all pockets shows a fair degree of differentiation, although replication occurs for three of four upper pockets (or even four of four if one adds Tenam Rosario to Chihuahua) and for two of three lower pockets. Such results suggest separate tendencies towards segmentariness (replicated pocket TBS) within each section.[4] These or any other conclusions about political significance of differences and similarities in TBS rest on the prior analysis which suggested that economic determinants were not the sole factors governing differences or similarities in areas and population densities, and eventually the TBS.

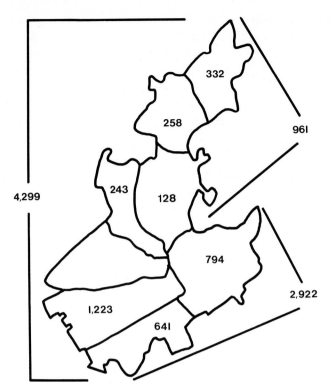

Figure 25   Tribute Base Size [Key: see Figure 20b]

Forced settlement centralization

Paramount forced settlement values for the two sections shows a marked disparity as do those for the pockets (Chapter 5, Figure 16). Altogether, the general absence of horizontal replication indicates unitary structure. Little vertical replication occurs in the paramount forced settlement values. A varied pattern of both increases and decreases (but mostly increases) down the PH suggests a mixture of both unitary and segmentary structure, with most of the arrangements being segmentary (Table 3 and 4, Figure 16).

The proportion of population at all PH1-4 centers versus the proportion of population at all PH5 sites is an aggregate measure of forced settlement centralization within districts. In other words, this compares attached as opposed to uncontrolled population (Figure 26). Such a measure is more likely to show replication than the paramount forced settlement measure, if one accepts that districts are likely to have had similar degrees of overall control exercised by their elites, but not an invariant distribution of control among members of the stratified and internally segmented elite group. The last statement is based squarely on earlier assertions about the internally divided (non-monolithic) nature of Classic Maya elite groups (Chapter 5).

The sections and pockets have divergent aggregate forced settlement values

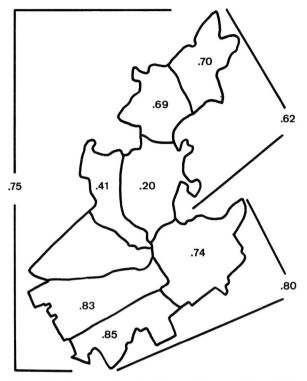

Figure 26   Aggregate forced settlement [Key: see Figure 20b]

(Figure 26). However, two of four pockets in the upper valley and two (or even three) of three pockets in the lower valley show some replication. The replication is difficult to interpret properly in absolute terms, but marked enough to conclude that sections and pockets are differentiated much less on this measure than they were on the measure of paramount forced settlement (perhaps for the reasons outlined above). In a vertical comparison, one finds generally clear replication all the way down the PH (excepting Chihuahua and Momón), which suggests segmentary political structure. Such replication is not an absolute identity by any means and some of the variation has been highlighted already for discussion with reference to cross-level forced settlement (Chapter 5).

Tribute drawing centralization
Chances of finding replication in paramount TDI values may be better than the chances of finding replication in forced settlement values. The TDI seems more directly subject to political factors than forced settlement which is subject to many additional demographic and environmental factors. Horizontal comparisons indicate an apparent absence of replication, such as might be produced by more unitary than segmentary structure (Figure 18). Vertical comparisons show differentiation, with a fairly constant decrease in paramount TDI down the first

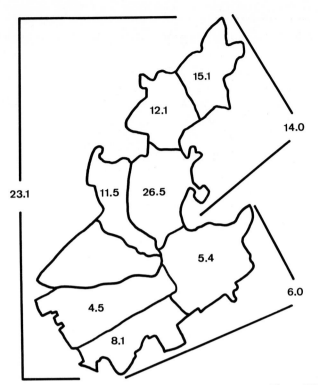

Figure 27   Aggregate tribute drawing (TDI) [Key: see Figure 20b]

three levels of the PH, indicating a tendency towards unitary structure throughout (Chapter 5, Table 5).

As with forced settlement centralization measures, it is feasible to use an aggregate measure of TDI (Figure 27). Horizontally compared, upper and lower sections have distinct aggregate TDI values while pockets show some horizontal replication, but separately within each section (three of four cases in the upper section and two of three cases in the lower section). A vertical comparison shows fairly good replication down the PH (a pattern strengthened at the upper two levels if one subtracts Tenam Rosario and its enormous civic-ceremonial bulk). The general pattern indicates some tendency towards segmentary political structure, as shown by the replication within and across the PH levels.

Tribute imposition centralization

For the reasons suggested with reference to the TDI, TLI values have a greater possibility of showing some replication among districts than do paramount forced settlement values. Vertical and horizontal comparisons of paramount TLI indicate a mixed pattern (Table 7 and Figure 19; Chapter 5). Vertically, there is a decrease in TLI values down the first two levels of the PH, suggesting a tendency towards unitary structure at the polity scale. Between the second and third PH levels, there is either equivalence or increase in TLI values, both of which suggest a tendency towards segmentary structure at the section scale. Horizontal comparison of TLI values shows little replication between sections, suggesting unitariness at the polity scale. Horizontal comparison of TLI values among pockets shows a greater degree of horizontal replication, in keeping with a tendency towards segmentary structure.

In terms of tribute imposition centralization exercised from paramount centers within its districts, the Rosario polity shows a slightly greater degree of both vertical and especially horizontal replication than was the case for either forced settlement centralization or tribute drawing centralization. These replication patterns denote a more segmentary structure among some of the Rosario Valley's districts (notably the sections) with reference to tribute imposition centralization (compared to forced settlement or tribute drawing centralization).

Aggregate TLI values may also be compared (Figure 28). Vertically, between the first two PH levels the tendency is for aggregate TLI values to decrease, which is congruent with unitary structure (at the polity scale). Between the second and third PH levels the trends are mixed, which suggests both segmentary and unitary arrangements at the section scale. Horizontal comparison of aggregate TLI values shows slight replication between the sections (especially for TLI-1, much less so for TLI-2). Horizontally comparing the pockets shows what seems like a fairly small range in TLI-1 values, with two internally more homogeneous groupings (Momón, Chihuahua, Rosario, and Santa Inés North versus Zorrillo, Nuestra Señora, and Santa Inés South). TLI-2 values are more variable. In sum, a sufficient degree of vertical and horizontal replication in aggregate TLI measures exists to suggest a degree of segmentariness in political structure.

The substantive results presented above are summarized briefly in Table 10. Moving from these results onto a more general plane, I want to summarize some of the analytical properties of my handling of the differentiation subcontinuum. First, it is worth re-emphasizing that analysis of the differentiation subcontinuum has been in large part analytically dependent on prior analysis of the centralization subcontinuum (Chapter 5). The focus was on the significance attributable to presence or absence of replication in various centralization and other (population) values which could be compared for the Rosario polity's centers and districts. With reference to the centralization measures, differentiation analysis focused not so much on individual values and what they indicate (Chapter 5) as on the relations among hierarchically arrayed values (in the PH framework). The interpretive rationale for relations among centralization values was the following. Horizontal replication suggested segmentary structure, while its absence (i.e., differentiation) suggested unitary structure. Vertical patterns were more complicated. Replication in values down the PH suggested a segmentary structure which was also suggested by a consistent increase in values down the PH. Consistent decrease in values down the PH suggested a tendency towards more unitary structure. Given four relevant levels in the PH, there was great potential for patterns of alternate decrease or increase in centralization values down the hierarchy, making it less straightforward to interpret the political system as uniformly segmentary or unitary. Generally,

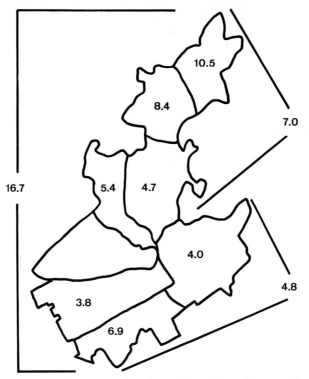

Figure 28a   Aggregate tribute imposition (TLI-1) [Key: see Figure 20b]

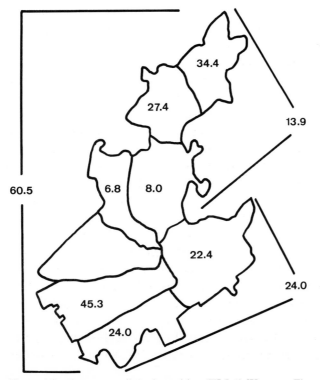

Figure 28b   Aggregate tribute imposition (TLI-2) [Key: see Figure 20b]

Table 10. *Summary of the differentiation subcontinuum*

		Section	
Index	Polity	Upper	Lower
area (H)	S	S /	S
TBS (H)	U	S /	S
paramount forced settlement (H)	U	U	
paramount forced settlement (V)	m	m /	S
aggregate forced settlement (H)	wS	S	
aggregate forced settlement (V)	S	S	
paramount TDI (H)	U	U	
paramount TDI (V)	U	U	
aggregate TDI (H)	U	S /	S
aggregate TDI (V)	S	S	
paramount TLI (H)	U	wS	
paramount TLI (V)	U	S	
aggregate TLI (H)	U?	wS	
aggregate TLI (V)	U	m	

U	unitary
S	segmentary
/	separate norms within each section
(H)	horizontal comparison
(V)	vertical comparison
m	mixed
w	weak

analysis was restricted to the best documented and most appropriate first three levels. This reduced analytical complications and focused attention squarely on patterning at the polity and section scales. The other values compared among districts were area, settlement density (checked against environmental composition), and TBS. For area and TBS, horizontal replication was equatable with segmentary structure, while differentiation was equatable with unitary structure. Settlement density was difficult to interpret and could not be understood independently from area or environmental composition.

Integration

Degrees of integration are measured along the third major subcontinuum incorporated within the segmentary–unitary continuum (Table 1). As there are no particularly direct or exclusive measures for integration, degrees of integration depend on degrees of centralization (Chapter 5) and differentiation (above). A conventional theoretical notion that high degrees of centralization and differentiation occur in well-integrated political systems is useful here (Chapter 2). Thus, districts that score high on the centralization subcontinuum and also show unitary tendencies on the differentiation subcontinuum are better integrated. This is fair enough, but probably too crude. Unlike differentiation, where it was possible to take all the centralization measures and handle them with different ends in mind, analyzing integration requires a more selective approach. When one looks at all the measures used to analyze centralization and differentiation, some seem definitely better than others for tracing degrees of integration. TDI and TLI measures are clearly preferable. Additionally, I preview some subsequent analysis (Chapter 7) to bring in measures of political specialization which are also helpful for analyzing degrees of integration.

When compared vertically, the TDI is particularly good for evaluating degrees of integration, with a special emphasis on the flow of tribute up the PH. Systematic decrease in TDI values going down the PH indicates a regime in which rulers at lower-ranking centers are constrained by their subordinate positions with reference to their tribute drawing activities (and their tribute investment into civic-ceremonial architecture). A decline in TDI values going down the PH means a high degree of integration in the sense that such top-down constraints are clearly effective throughout the hierarchy. Conversely, equivalent or rising TDI values down the hierarchy means a poor degree of integration. Less effective constraints from above equate with a lower degree of connectedness or integration.

Vertical comparison of TLI is also a way to appreciate degrees of integration. The reasoning is the same as for TDI, except that it is rulers' per capita tribute imposition activities (taken to reflect the control that they exercise) which may or may not be limited by subordinate position in a wider political arrangement. Lower TLI values going down the PH indicate greater integration, in which rulers hierarchically above local rulers impose tribute and exercise controls on local subjects more vigorously than do the local rulers (more about this below). All of this indicates a greater degree of vertical connectedness through the hierarchy. By contrast, higher TLI values down the PH indicate closer local control over subjects and hence poor integration.

The two centralization measures which have to do with indirect control (TDI and TLI) are the best for looking at integration since they concern political relations exercised at a distance. In contrast, the measure of direct control (forced settlement) is not as useful. And some measures considered with reference to differentiation (area, density, and TBS) are completely irrelevant.

Declining TDI values across the PH1, PH2, and PH3 levels (Table 5, Figure 18) clearly indicate integration at the polity and section scales.[5] It is impossible to say whether greater integration existed in the lower or upper section. This is because of uncertainties associated with interpreting absolute values for TDI and also because the lumping of diverse pockets into each one of the sections renders synthetic conclusions suspect.

Most pockets show a decrease in TDI values across the PH3 and PH4 levels which indicates integration (Table 5, Figure 18). It may be reading too much into the numbers, but there are tentative indications that individual upper pockets are more integrated than lower pockets. This is because there are large drops in TDI values in upper pockets, while the lower pockets show a range of values (from a large drop in Santa Inés South, through a slight drop in Rosario, to no drop at all, but rather an increase, in Santa Inés North) .

TLI values (Table 7, Figure 19) show a pattern which suggests integration at the polity scale and a relative absence of integration at the section scale (with higher TLI values for PH1 and PH3 than for PH2 centers). The indicators for strength or weakness of integration within individual pockets are as follows. A drop in TLI values from PH3 to (average) PH4 levels within Zorrillo indicates relatively high integration. Conversely, a rise in TLI values from PH3 to PH4 for Nuestra Señora, Rosario, Santa Inés North, and Santa Inés South indicates less thorough integration.[6]

The results of TDI- and TLI-based analyses of integration turn out somewhat differently. A good degree of integration (with possibly stronger integration in the upper pockets) appears when one takes a top-down (TDI) perspective. From this vantage, integration has to do with the ability of rulers at higher-ranking centers to draw in relatively more tribute from outside their centers, which may represent a dependence on lower-ranking rulers and centers to send up tribute. All the differently ranked centers and their rulers are thus strongly integrated into this overall arrangement. A bottom-up perspective is given to us by using TLI which focuses on the tribute burden placed on individual tribute payers and equates the size of this burden with the intensity of power and control exercised by the tribute receivers. From this perspective, there is a high degree of integration within the whole polity with a less clear pattern of integration within the constituent districts. Lower-ranking rulers can set higher per capita tribute rates (and exercise greater per capita control) than can higher-ranking rulers, at least at the third and then the fourth levels of the PH. Poor integration results from a failure of higher-ranking rulers to impose heavier tribute burdens (or controls) on everyone within their catchment, compared to the tribute burden imposed locally within their own nested catchments by subordinate rulers. Thus tribute paying subjects within the catchments of the lower-ranking centers are more heavily controlled by local rulers than they are by higher-ranking rulers (the sole exception to this is Zorrillo).

The general conclusion is twofold. Tribute probably moves up the hierarchy in a well-integrated scheme (as evidenced by declining TDI values down the PH). At the same time, lesser integration is suggested by a degree of local control which outweighs extralocal control from above. The latter occurs at the third (pocket) and fourth (PH4 catchment) PH levels (as evidenced by increasing TLI values down the last three PH rungs).

Another way to appreciate degrees of integration is to analyze political specialization. Political specialization relates to the continuum between pyramidal and hierarchical political regimes (Chapter 7). Vertical political specialization in a hierarchical regime (Southall 1956) is equatable with a relatively high degree of integration. Absence of vertical specialization (replication of political functions) in a pyramidal regime (Southall 1956) equates with a relatively low degree of integration. Also, horizontal political specialization (in either pyramidal or hierarchical regimes, but more usually the latter) is associated with a relatively high degree of integration.

Very briefly, results of subsequent analysis (Chapter 7) suggest that the polity has a generally hierarchical political regime, with vertical differentiation of political functions according to the hierarchical level at which they are performed. Looking at the districts one finds some variation in the degree of vertical political specialization (and thus in the degree of integration) among them. For example, the upper section shows a clearer pattern of vertical political integration than the lower section. Among pockets, Zorrillo has the most vertical political integration, while Santa Inés North has the least. Such results generally match those achieved with the TDI centralization measure and with the TLI centralization measure (except for the TLI measure's showing a drop in integration at lower PH levels).[7] What are the implications of this last divergence? If changes across PH levels for TLI values are an independent way of looking at integration, then it follows (loosely) that there can be differences in degrees of vertical integration among districts, even when all of them have vertical political specialization. Specialization does not invariably entail integration. Others have looked at integration and differentiation (or complexity) and have tried to keep these notions separate to allow for, and eventually test for, the inter-relation between them. The idea behind this is that these phenomena may vary from one another with some freedom for reasons that have to be specified. For the Valley of Oaxaca, Blanton and others (1982: 70, 94) found that the same amounts of vertical differentiation (numbers of levels of administrative hierarchy) are associated with differing degrees of integration or articulation (evaluated through an interaction potential between sites – Blanton *et al.* 1982: 51–53).

The patterning in horizontal political specialization sheds light on the degree of horizontal integration within the polity's districts. Tests (Chapter 7) show no clearly monolithic polity-wide pattern of horizontal political specialization, such as might have been expected given strong vertical specialization. Equating high specialization with high integration translates into a situation where vertical integration is not matched by across-the-board horizontal integration. However, there is a generally strong tendency towards horizontal political integration, which appears most clearly in the larger-scale units. The lower section seems to show a higher degree of horizontal specialization (and hence integration) than does the upper section (Chapter 7). Among pockets, the range from most to least horizontally specialized and integrated runs from Santa Inés North to Santa Inés South to Rosario to Nuestra Señora and finally to Zorrillo (Chapter 7). Concerning possible relations between vertical and horizontal specialization (integration), Rosario and Santa Inés South show a weak positive relation, Zorrillo shows a negative relation (strong vertical integration and weak horizontal integration) as does Santa Inés North (weak vertical integration and strong horizontal integration). Nuestra Señora shows an ambiguous pattern. Such results suggest that the relation between vertical and horizontal integration is not unidirectional.

By way of conclusion, let me summarize some of the general analytical properties of my treatment of the integration subcontinuum. Even more than for differentiation, analyzing integration depends on results of a study of centralization (Chapter 5). Vertical comparisons of changes in TDI and TLI values were the most effective ways to study degrees of integration (since both measures deal with control exercised at a distance). A decline in either measure, going down the PH, would show that rulers at the lower rungs were constrained by higher-ranking rulers (whether in tribute-drawing from outside their site [TDI] or in the general rates of tribute set [TLI]). Higher degrees of constraint from above indicate greater vertical connectedness and integration. Increases in either measure suggest fewer constraints on lower-ranking rulers and thus a lower degree of connectedness or integration. When centralization was the focus of interest (Chapter 5), an increase in TDI or TLI values down the PH was seen as a dispersal of power and control towards the hierarchy's lower levels. Now that integration is the point of interest, an increase in TDI and TLI values down the PH is seen as weakness of linkages between sets of rulers at different hierarchical levels, linkages which should produce constraints on the behavior of the lower-ranking rulers. Results of a study of political specialization (Chapter 7) also allowed me to trace degrees of vertical and horizontal integration (with specialization taken to imply integration and non-specialization lack of such).

Segmentary versus unitary structure

The entire Rosario polity may be characterized as either unitary or segmentary in structure, based on whether it appears to be either centralized, differentiated, or integrated. From my analyses, it transpires that the Rosario polity has a tendency towards unitary structure with reference to tribute drawing centralization, tribute imposition centralization, differentiation of tribute base size, and vertical integration. Against this, there is a slight tendency towards more segmentary structure with reference to paramount forced settlement and aggregate forced settlement. These and other conclusions about the Rosario polity as a whole will eventually gain even more resonance when it becomes possible to compare the Rosario polity along these relative measures to other polities in the Maya area, both near and distant.

At present, my principal focus is on variability among districts within the polity. A consistent structural contrast exists between the sections. The upper section shows a clearly more unitary structure than the lower section in the degree of paramount forced settlement centralization and vertical integration. Differences are not as great with reference to the degrees of tribute drawing centralization and tribute imposition centralization or the differentiation of tribute base size. At a smaller scale, there are marked differences in the degree of unitariness characterizing separate pockets. A spatial alternation of relatively unitary and relatively segmentary pockets occurs, moving from northeast to southwest: unitary Zorrillo, segmentary Nuestra Señora, unitary Chihuahua/Momón/Tenam Rosario, unitary Rosario, and then segmentary Santa Inés North-South. Alternation is most clearly evident with paramount forced settlement centralization. Contrasts at either end of the chain are clearly evident with tribute drawing and tribute imposition centralization and also degrees of vertical integration. With reference to the last measure, the most clearly integrated pocket is Zorrillo and the least integrated is Santa Inés North. Alternance among pockets within the upper section is still evident with tribute imposition centralization. At the pocket scale, there is no clear support for the idea that a segmentary polity can be distinguished from a unitary polity by its having more unitary districts towards its edges, as a function of relatively greater drop in control from the center (Chapter 2). Both unitary and segmentary districts are found at either end of the polity. In sum, there are more complex factors working than differing intensity in the drop of control from a center. Additionally, a plateau effect may be operating in the small survey area, meaning that distances are too short to make travel-time efficiency in delivering sanctions or exercising control an important consideration. This eliminates one of the logical underpinnings for the idea that intensity of control drops off moving outward from the center.

When drawing the above comparisons, it makes sense to take spatial disposition of districts as a framework (or environment) within which to understand the differences and similarities in political structure that appear. Additionally, other factors can be considered in trying to understand differences and similarities among districts: scale differences, different stages reached in a development cycle, and environmental differences. I discuss these other factors in the general conclusions (Chapter 11), after completing my characterization of political structure and organization in the Rosario polity (Chapters 7–10).

7

Political regimes and microcosms

Pyramidal versus hierarchical regimes

The continuum between pyramidal and hierarchical political regimes deals with both the decision-making and decision-implementing aspects of a political system. The practical reason for treating these aspects jointly is that archaeological evidence in the Rosario Valley does not allow anything like a distinction between policy-making (politics) and policy-implementation (administration or bureaucracy) to be made. There are no executive buildings and artifacts as opposed to administrative buildings and artifacts. Taking the argument onto a more interpretive plane, Maya ethnohistoric sources suggest that in the Postclassic Period there were no clearly separable groups of people involved in policy-making as opposed to policy-implementation (with the exception of menial administrative "flunkies" such as the *tupiles* mentioned in a few Yucatec sources). More precisely, this assertion is based on an ethnohistorical survey covering a variety of Contact Period Maya polities (the Yucatec Maya – de Montmollin 1980; the Guatemala Highland Quiche Maya – de Montmollin 1982b; and the Chiapas Highland Maya – de Montmollin 1979c). Once again applying historical–evolutionary logic, one would not expect earlier periods to feature fully professional bureaucratic structures (after Weber, see Gerth and Mills eds. 1946: ch. 8). This logic is a form of substantivism applied to politics instead of economics. It resembles Giddens' discontinuist perspective on the development of the state, one which draws a sharp contrast in terms of bureaucratic structure and efficacy between traditional states and modern nation-states (Giddens 1985). Thus, the lack of evidence for pure administrators or bureaucrats in the Rosario Valley polity may be taken to reflect a genuine absence of such specialized personnel. Given the possibilities of the evidence and the limitations indicated by best available ethnohistoric analogies, I try to avoid using the term *administrative* since it has potentially confusing connotations, to the degree that it suggests the existence of gray and faceless bureaucrats whose sole job is to implement policy. Over and beyond this, an equation of only administration (policy-implementation) with politics and government is incomplete, allowing a narrow and skewed focus on information-processing efficiency considerations as the main motor-force for political development (e.g., Johnson 1978, 1982). A more accurate term to use would be *politico-administrative* as it reasonably suggests combined policy-making and policy-implementation and helps to turn our thoughts in the right direction. However, its double-barreled awkwardness makes such a term unattractive. Therefore, I use the term *political* to refer to policy-making, which also subsumes policy-implementation (where relevant).

Another relevant general ethnohistoric datum is that there is an inextricable link between religious or ritual activities and political activities in Mesoamerican polities. This is such a solidly founded generalization that arguments by example would be gratuitous and the burden of proof falls on those who reject the generalization. This datum further buttresses the assumption that civic-ceremonial buildings are legitimately interpreted as loci of political activity, albeit activity with heavy religious and ritual content. One might coin the triple-barreled term *politico-religio-administrative* to describe buildings or areas having this quality, but that would be reaching germanic levels of terminological pedantry.

To recap an earlier discussion (Chapter 2), pyramidal regimes have a full set of identical political functions repeated at each hierarchical level while hierarchical regimes have political functions differentiated according to the level at which they occur (Southall 1956, 1965; Easton 1959). Between these polar extremes there may occur different degrees of functional specialization according to hierarchical political level. The Rosario Valley's settlement record is analyzed here to address one of the second set of research questions (2a): To what degree did Classic Maya political regimes feature a pyramidal arrangement (replication of political functions at different hierarchical levels)?

Charting political specialization across the levels of a political hierarchy requires archaeological correlates for both features. Such a requirement is potentially very difficult to fulfill. A relatively limited amount of architectural variability among Rosario Valley civic-ceremonial buildings (the prime body of evidence) constrains the amount of functional differentiation that can be inferred. Recourse to the same limited body of data is needed for determining both political specialization and hierarchy, bringing up potential problems of circularity (Chapter 5, note 2). To avoid circularity, it becomes necessary to apportion the various kinds of civic-ceremonial architectural evidence among the two features being compared. This further impoverishes the breadth of data available for documenting each one of them. In spite of such practical (testing) difficulties, it proves worthwhile to examine the distribution of political specialization across a political hierarchy because this offers a preliminary chance to weigh some very commonly made assumptions about the necessary relations between levels of political hierarchy and political specialization at each one of those levels.

Several steps are required in order to investigate whether the Rosario polity (and its districts) had a pyramidal or hierarchical political regime. The first step is to examine the utility of the PH as an independent way of forming a political hierarchy across which variations in political specialization may be charted. As a second step, alternate means of constructing political hierarchies (using other kinds of criteria) must be examined. The third step is to find archaeological indicators of political function. The fourth and final step is to perform cross-tabulations using the indicators of political hierarchy and function in order to test for degrees of political specialization across political levels.

After such tests it becomes possible to give a limited amount of attention to research question 2b: If there was a tendency towards pyramidal regimes, what were their scale limitations (in terms of the size of the political community, the

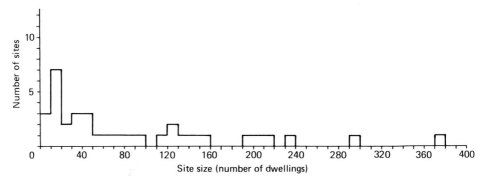

Figure 29   Sizes of sites associated with centers – polity

number of districts, and the number of levels of political hierarchy)? This is done by comparing the degrees of pyramidality in the upper and lower sections which have differing population sizes.

My analysis thus begins with a look at the varieties of political hierarchies that may be constructed using settlement evidence from the Rosario Valley.

I have already reviewed the rationale and contents of a Political Hierarchy or PH (Chapter 5, Table 2). Here, the important issue becomes whether the PH uses criteria that are independent for the most part of other criteria useful for evaluating political function. Two attributes used in the PH bear on political function: presence or absence of ballcourts, and presence or absence of multipyramid plazas (especially those with different sized pyramids, discussed below). Because these are important in what is a small set of relevant attributes, it might seem more efficient to completely discard the PH (for this part of the analysis). This would make available something closer to the entire range of attributes for use in evaluating political specialization. But then the problem arises of finding an alternate means of constructing a political hierarchy. And since all the alternate means (discussed below) are inferior to the PH, it follows that the PH must be retained as at least one of the hierarchies to be used.

Use of a Size Hierarchy (abbreviated to SH) to array settlements according to relative political importance hinges on the notion that demographic size corresponds closely to political importance (Chapter 5). The distribution of site sizes across the PH levels (of their associated centers) shows that size does not increase in a rigorously regular fashion as one moves up the levels (Chapter 5, Figures 12–14). However, the size-importance relation is close enough to allow the use of a SH, especially in the present case when there is a need for a political-hierarchical classification that frees as many as possible of the political attributes for a separate classification of political function. Nevertheless, the SH is given the least weight (compared to the alternative civic-ceremonial volume hierarchy and intrasite complexity hierarchy). An analysis of histograms (Figures 29–31) produces the following size classes (for sites associated with civic-ceremonial centers): Rank 1 (300 + dwellings, 2 sites); Rank 2 (191–240 dwellings, 4 sites); Rank 3 (111–160

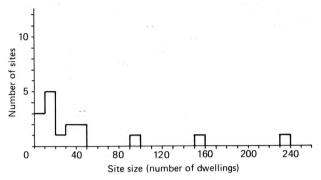

Figure 30   Sizes of sites associated with centers – upper section

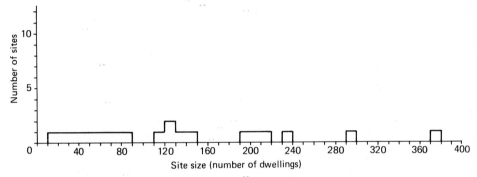

Figure 31   Sizes of sites associated with centers – lower section

dwellings, 6 sites); Rank 4 (61–100 dwellings, 4 sites); and Rank 5 (1–60 dwellings, 18 sites).

Another way of classifying centers into a hierarchy of political importance does not use any obvious political functional attributes. The procedure involves arraying centers (on a histogram) according to the total volume of civic-ceremonial construction that they contain in their plaza(s) and dividing them into size classes to be arranged in a Volume Hierarchy (abbreviated to VH). All the usual problems associated with volumetric analysis arise here (Chapters 4 and 5). Beyond problems already discussed, there is an additional point of contention. This is the idea that a center's civic-ceremonial volume (representing projection of political importance rather than ability to mobilize tribute) is not a relevant indicator of its political function(s). This idea runs counter to the precepts of a school of analysis which equates a center's civic-ceremonial bulk with its relative importance in a political hierarchy and automatically attributes political functional differences to centers according to what rung they occupy in the hierarchy (e.g., Blanton *et al.* 1982). In this kind of analysis, we can see the roundabout way in which civic-ceremonial volume relates to political function. The relation is made possible only through the intervening (information-theory based) assumption that differences in hierarchical position (especially with three or more levels) must automatically entail differences

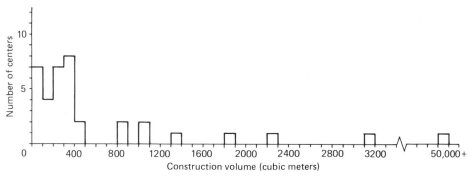

Figure 32   Civic-ceremonial construction volume at centers – polity

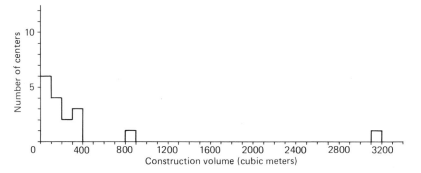

Figure 33   Civic-ceremonial construction volume at centers – upper section

in political function (Wright 1977; Johnson 1973, 1978; Wright and Johnson 1975). Since this is precisely an assumption I wish to evaluate, I cannot accept it at the outset and stick to the idea that civic-ceremonial volume is not an indicator of political function.

For the centers, I have plotted total civic-ceremonial volumes onto histograms (Figures 32–34). Distributions from the different districts could be lumped (Figure 32) without too much distortion to local patterns. Separate histograms (Figures 33 and 34) for the two sections are included so that the moderate differences between them can be appreciated. The final division into five ranks is thus made on the global polity-wide sample (Figure 32): Rank 1 (50,000+ cu m, 1 center); Rank 2 (3,100+ cu m, 1 center); Rank 3 (1,800–2,300 cu m, 2 centers); Rank 4 (800–1,400 cu m, 6 centers); and Rank 5 (1–500 cu m, 28 centers). There is a degree of arbitrariness in lumping a few centers in Ranks 3 and 4, but otherwise the divisions are clear enough.

Centers may also be classed hierarchically by reference to the complexity of their associated sites' domestic settlement layout. This involves considering how many (relatively large) wards there are in each site (wards are defined and discussed in de Montmollin n.d.a: ch. 6). Sites with more wards give their center a higher rank-ing in a Complexity Hierarchy (abbreviated to CH). Why do more wards give

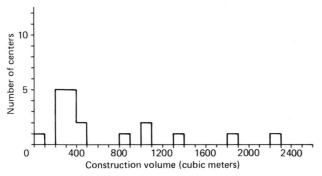

Figure 34   Civic-ceremonial construction volume at centers – lower section

Table 11. *Size and complexity rankings (polity)*

		Size (SH) rank				
		1	2	3	4	5
Complexity	1	1				
(CH) rank	2		1			
	3		1		1	
	4	1	1	2		1
	5/6		1	4	3	14

superiority in a political hierarchy? Wards represent partially autonomous social segments and greater numbers of these present greater sociopolitical complexity. This greater complexity requires political work, especially concerning the management of relations between social groups occupying different wards. Therefore, sites with large, but undivided, populations are politically less important than sites with equally large but internally more divided populations. These arguments are stretched to the limits of plausibility and the CH is far from an ideal framework for evaluating political importance. However, it is worth using because it is quite independent of the civic-ceremonial architectural data used to evaluate political function. That population size enters indirectly into the CH can be seen from a cross-comparison between it and the SH (Table 11). The number of wards at relevant sites[1] ranges narrowly: Rank 1 = 6 wards; Rank 2 = 5 wards; Rank 3 = 4 wards; Rank 4 = 3 wards; Rank 5 = 2 wards; and Rank 6 = 1 ward.

So far I have focused on center (and associated site) hierarchies. A focus on the individual plaza is also viable because of the strong likelihood that each plaza was an authentically discrete locus for political activity. To classify individual plazas by applying criteria used in the PH (Table 2) is difficult since the top two PH levels have ballcourts or two-pyramid plazas distributed in agglutinated arrangements (Figures 9–11). Trying to break these down into individual plazas destroys much of the sense of the PH. Having to omit the PH's top two levels leaves only the lower

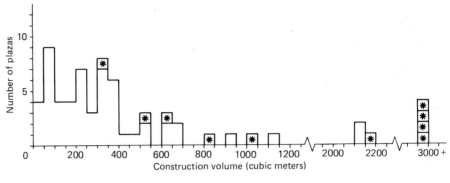

Note: ✱ = Plaza from Tenam Rosario

Figure 35 Civic-ceremonial construction volume in plazas – polity

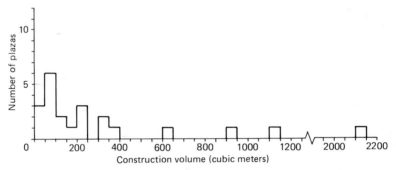

Figure 36 Civic-ceremonial construction volume in plazas – upper section

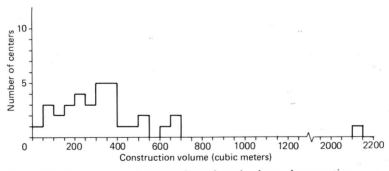

Figure 37 Civic-ceremonial construction volume in plazas – lower section

two levels for comparison, not a useful exercise. Many fewer problems arise if the VH is used to arrange individual plazas. The method for classifying plazas into volume-size ranks is the same as described above for centers (but now based on Figures 35–37): Rank 1 (3,000+ cu m, 4 plazas); Rank 2 (2,100–2,200 cu m, 3 plazas); Rank 3 (800–1,150 cu m, 4 plazas); Rank 4 (451–700 cu m, 9 plazas); and Rank 5 (1–450 cu m, 46 plazas).

Next, I need to evaluate the degree of political-functional specialization at various centers. Two measures are used towards this end – the Structure Diversity Index (abbreviated to SDI) and the Plaza Count Index (abbreviated to PCI). The first measure can also be used for evaluating individual plazas.

Useful clues about political specialization lie in the presence or absence of formally distinctive civic-ceremonial buildings. These buildings include pyramids, ballcourts, high platforms, altars, ranges, and pyramid annexes. Of these, ballcourts must be omitted from analysis involving the PH, but can be used with the other hierarchies (SH, VH, or CH). Altars are left out because of small numbers (and differential preservation problems). Additionally, the pyramid category has been divided into two functional types based on size distinctions (de Montmollin 1985a: ch. 7). One type includes 52 small pyramids (50–500 cu m) and the other includes the 16 large pyramids (525–5,300 + cu m). While arbitrary, this procedure is based on the commonsense notion that there will be somewhat differing political activities associated with civic-ceremonial buildings of substantially different sizes (especially when found at the same center or plaza). The Structure Diversity Index (SDI) is an exercise in summary statistic construction. To compute it, one point is assigned for every civic-ceremonial building type at a given center (up to a maximum of six). A higher SDI value indicates a greater range of political functions. SDI values are charted across political-hierarchical levels. Differentiation across levels suggests a hierarchical regime while replication suggests a pyramidal regime.

That a greater (formal) variety of civic-ceremonial buildings indicates greater complexity in associated political activity is a widely used assumption in Maya and Mesoamerican archaeology. To take just a pair of recent examples, this assumption is used in settlement studies of the Valley of Oaxaca and Cuicatlán Cañada (Spencer 1982: 13–14, 16–19, 25–28), and of Cozumel Island, off the coast of Yucatan (Freidel and Sabloff 1984: 97). Compared to the Rosario settlement record, the settlement records in both Oaxaca and Yucatan have a better selection of variant architectural forms and more direct ethnohistoric analogical sources for functional interpretations of formal architectural differences. Another difference is that neither of the interpretations of the Oaxaca and Cozumel settlement records considers the possibility that there might be variability in the distribution of political specialization across hierarchical levels (along the pyramidal–hierarchical continuum). For Oaxaca, the problem is defined away by an efficiency-driven information-theory perspective. For Cozumel, reference is made to "a general premise in cultural geography that variation in the function of communities showing a tendency towards hierarchical grouping reflects interdependence between these communities" (Freidel and Sabloff 1984: 97). Thus, both studies assume that superordinate centers necessarily have a wider range of functions; in effect hierarchical regimes (Southall 1956) are the only possibility. At least one cross-cultural study of proto-complex societies suggests that non-hierarchical arrangements may be quite common (Feinman and Neitzel 1984; and see Chapter 2).

In contrast, another discussion of Postclassic Yucatec settlement patterns and politics by Freidel provides a more searching examination of the political implications of variability (and replication) in civic-ceremonial architecture at hierarchically arranged centers. Freidel states that:

> Adams and Smith (1981) suggest that the evident replication of architectural forms involved in governance at descending levels of Classic Maya settlement size registers the simple scaling-down of the same kind of political organization at descending levels of power in a system of vertical personal obligations between chiefs. In the first place, architectural replication of this kind has been used elsewhere to document the existence of bureaucratic state organizations... Second, the organization of public, political facilities varies significantly from level to level in Late Postclassic Maya settlements. Third, such facilities do not focus on or reify the personal power of rulers (as in the courts of feudal Europe) in higher-order Late Postclassic Maya settlements. (Freidel 1983b: 47)

In a substantive sense, Freidel challenges the blanket relevance of a feudal interpretation for Postclassic Period Yucatec political structure. He stresses the personalized obligation component of the diffusion of power that is associated with feudalism (Freidel 1983b: 46) and then discounts it in favor of the idea that positions of power were institutionalized in a more bureaucratic arrangement with co-ordination of power (Freidel 1983b: 46–47). Unrestrained patron-clientism of the kind argued against is quite unlikely to have existed anywhere in Mesoamerica, if the ethnohistoric sources are anything to go by. After the development of ranked society in the Late Formative Period, there was probably a clear framework of institutionalized offices within which political activity worked itself out (something recognized by Freidel 1983b: 53). But there is a twofold quality in the argument: presence versus absence of personalized patron-clientism, and concentration versus diffusion of political power across levels of a hierarchy. The latter contrast can be detached from the former and it constitutes a more theoretically and analytically compelling issue to address with reference to archaeological evidence (see Chapter 5, Steponaitis 1981, or Blanton *et al.* 1981 for different formulations of this general problem). In a detailed discussion, Freidel examines vertical (and horizontal) variability in civic architectural distribution and interprets it as reflecting variability in the distribution of political functions and powers across the levels of a political hierarchy. His main point is that vertical variability indicates a more centralized and integrated political system than that proposed in feudal models (Freidel 1983b: 47–63). The logic of this is similar to that underlying the bridging argument I use here: that vertical differentiation of civic-ceremonial architecture indicates a hierarchical regime (Southall 1956) associated with unitary political structure.

Methodologically speaking, Freidel leaves little to chance, arguing not only that vertical architectural replication may not always be a very good indicator of personalized patron-clientism in political structure, but also that such vertical replication (whatever it may mean) does not even exist in the case at hand. That vertical architectural replication is not always an unambiguous indicator of decentralization and diffusion of power is good to keep in mind, although Freidel provides no tale to go along with the caution. At any rate, casting caution aside, I continue to use my bridging argument: that vertical replication indicates a pyramidal regime (Southall 1956) associated with segmentary political structure.

Returning to the Rosario settlement record, the SDI is applicable at the center or single-plaza scale (working at the latter scale changes results for 11 multi-plaza centers but not for 29 single-plaza centers). Most of the analysis uses the center scale since this enriches the available variability, increasing the chances for differentiation in SDI values among the units compared and the chances of finding vertical differentiation (suggesting a more hierarchical than pyramidal regime). A more limited set of tests compares SDI values for individual plazas.

The second measure of political specialization is the number of plazas at a center, expressed by a Plaza Count Index (PCI). This measure is harder to justify than the SDI as a measure of political specialization. It could be argued just as well that the several plazas at a multiplaza center have a replicated set of political functions.[2] Nevertheless, if one accepts that the centers (and associated sites) are well-bounded social units, then the presence of two or more plazas (versus a single plaza) shows a greater degree of specialization with respect to the range of political activities at the entire center. The number of plazas at a given center has been used as an attribute for hierarchically classifying Lowland Maya centers (Adams 1981; Adams and Jones 1981). However, this usage differs from the present one in an important way. Adams uses plaza counts to construct hierarchies of political importance, instead of using them to evaluate the range of political functions at a center already placed in an independently constructed political hierarchy (the approach I use here).

With an analytical toolkit finally in hand, my basic procedure for testing the presence of pyramidal as opposed to hierarchical political regimes is to trace the differentiation of political functions across the levels of a political hierarchy. Many permutations are possible since there are four kinds of hierarchies (the PH, SH, VH, and CH), two measures of political specialization (the SDI and PCI), and two scales (whole center and individual plaza). Since the tools discussed vary in their effectiveness, some tests make more analytical sense than others and have been selected for discussion here: SDI values for centers distributed across PH levels, SDI values for centers distributed across VH levels, and SDI values for individual plazas across VH levels (a fuller set of tests is found elsewhere – de Montmollin 1985a: ch. 11).

Test implications for pyramidal versus hierarchical regimes are straightforward as concerns distribution of SDI values across PH levels. With a pyramidal regime there should be a relative constancy of SDI values at all PH levels (indicating a similar range of functions performed at each level). With a hierarchical regime SDI values should decrease moving down the PH (indicating an increasingly narrow range of functions performed at lower levels). The nature of the test seems to be biased against the possibility of discovering pyramidality because there is a

Table 12a. *Polity – SDI versus PH*

		Structure Diversity Index				
		1	2	3	4	5
Political	1					1
(PH) rank	2			1	1	
	3		2	2		
	4	27	2	3		

Table 12b. *Upper section – SDI versus PH*

		Structure Diversity Index			
		1	2	3	4
Political	1				
(PH) rank	2				1
	3		1	1	
	4	14	1		

Table 12c. *Lower section – SDI versus PH*

		Structure Diversity Index			
		1	2	3	4
Political	1				
(PH) rank	2			1	
	3		1	1	
	4	13		3	

tendency for higher-ranked centers in the PH to have more civic-ceremonial buildings and thus an increased chance of having a greater variety of buildings (measured by the SDI). However, pyramidality might still be found if higher-ranking centers have buildings all of one kind (producing SDI values similar to those for lower-ranking centers with fewer buildings). At any rate, SDI values diminish regularly as one moves down the PH, which indicates a more hierarchical than pyramidal political regime. This applies at the polity (Table 12a) and section (Tables 12b and 12c) scales.

The distribution of SDI values across VH levels is checked to evaluate degrees of pyramidality in a similar fashion as for SDI values and PH levels. At the polity (Table 13a) and section (Tables 13b and 13c) scales, the distribution meets the expectations for a more hierarchical than pyramidal regime even more clearly than was the case using the PH.

Table 13a. *Polity – SDI versus VH*

		Structure Diversity Index					
		1	2	3	4	5	6
Volume	1						1
(VH) rank	2					1	
	3			1	1		
	4			4	2		
	5	26	2				

Table 13b. *Upper section – SDI versus VH*

		Structure Diversity Index				
		1	2	3	4	5
Volume	1					
(VH) rank	2					1
	3					
	4			1	1	
	5	14	1			

Table 13c. *Lower section – SDI versus VH*

		Structure Diversity Index			
		1	2	3	4
Volume	1				
(VH) rank	2				
	3			1	1
	4			3	1
	5	12	1		

Although there is a more restricted range of variation in the SDI, the distribution of SDI values for individual plazas across VH levels still shows a patterning which meets the expectations for a more hierarchical than pyramidal political regime, at both the polity (Table 14a) and section (Tables 14b and 14c) scales.

The single-plaza perspective proves interesting for comparing the capital Tenam Rosario (Table 14d) to the individual pockets, a reasonable comparison in terms of numbers of plazas. With its 10 plazas, Tenam Rosario has as many or more plazas within it as most of the pockets (Zorrillo with 8, Nuestra Señora with 10, Momón with 1, Chihuahua with 3, Rosario with 10, Santa Inés South with 7; only Santa Inés North with 16 has more). A general decline in SDI values down the VH also

Table 14a. *Polity (without Tenam Rosario) – plaza SDI versus VH*

		Structure Diversity Index		
		1	2	3
Volume	1			
(VH) rank	2			2
	3		1	1
	4	4	2	1
	5	42	3	

Table 14b. *Upper section – plaza SDI versus VH*

		Structure Diversity Index		
		1	2	3
Volume	1			
(VH) rank	2			1
	3		1	1
	4			1
	5	17	1	

Table 14c. *Lower section – plaza SDI versus VH*

		Structure Diversity Index		
		1	2	3
Volume	1			
(VH) rank	2			1
	3			
	4	4	2	
	5	25	2	

appears at Tenam Rosario, but the pattern is not entirely clear-cut as there is considerable overlap of SDI values between hierarchical levels (Table 14d). At least as much variability occurs within the capital center as within individual pockets. But the parallels cannot be taken too far, for there are striking and quite obvious differences between these various sets of plazas. Not only are the Tenam Rosario plazas concentrated within the confines of a single center, but they are jammed into an agglutinated arrangement (Figure 9) found nowhere else (except in a minor way

Table 14d. *Tenam Rosario – plaza SDI versus VH*

		Structure Diversity Index		
		1	2	3
Volume	1		6, 9	3, 5
(VH rank	2		10	
	3		1	
	4		2, 4, 7	
	5	8		

Note: Numbers are the plaza numbers for Tenam Rosario
(see Figure 9).

at the two PH2 centers – Figures 10 and 11). Besides these differences in layout and distribution, there are size (volume) differences between some Tenam Rosario plazas and pocket plazas. Nevertheless, setting differences aside and concentrating on the equivalent numbers of plazas, it is possible to view Tenam Rosario's civic-ceremonial zone as representing something like a standard number of plazas from one pocket all jammed into one spot. Beyond this, the range and complexity of civic-ceremonial architecture at Tenam Rosario is such that it repays much more extended examination as a possible political microcosm of its hinterland (see discussion below).

A general conclusion from this set of tests (and from additional tests reported elsewhere – de Montmollin 1985a: ch. 11) is that the Rosario polity has a more hierarchical than pyramidal regime. Concerning research question 2b, about possible scale limitations associated with pyramidal regimes, such limitations do not apply when one compares the relatively more pyramidal lower section to the upper section (or the more pyramidal pockets to the less pyramidal ones). Indeed, the more pyramidal regimes tend to have larger populations. In case the Rosario polity's districts are too small in scale to make effective comparisons of this kind, one would want eventually to compare the whole Rosario polity to other polities on this score.

Information-processing efficiency
Following the axioms of information-processing efficiency approaches (Johnson 1978), a hierarchical regime could have been assumed a priori from the existence of three or more levels of political hierarchy. Nevertheless, the procedures carried out here are valuable because they have allowed a somewhat more sceptical test of the assumption. The tests have also brought out local or smaller-scale differences in the degree to which hierarchical political regimes are evidenced, and such differences are usefully compared to other differences in political structure. Furthermore, results showing a strong tendency towards a hierarchical political regime in the Rosario polity are not a definitive demonstration of a preponderant role for

information-processing efficiency principles as determinants of political structure. In fact, there are other ways of testing for the presence and strength of these principles. A first way is to compare political spans for various civic-ceremonial facilities around the valley. Political efficiency as a strict determinant of settlement distribution should produce some uniformity in the spans, while lack of uniformity suggests that political efficiency was not the overriding determinant for arranging people in the political landscape. A second way of testing for the importance of information-processing efficiency principles is to use a form of intrasite analysis. One looks not just at raw numbers of people, but at the complexity of their arrangement in space, with the archaeological correlate for this taken to be the number of wards present at a site. Intensity of political activity is (roughly) charted archaeologically by weighting civic-ceremonial facilities at the center associated with the site. Efficiency arguments propose a regular positive relationship between complexity of site (domestic) layout and the number and variety of political facilities (i.e., the intensity of political activity) required in order to manage the heightened information flow produced by this complexity. Rosario polity sites can be compared to see whether there is a constant relationship between their complexity and intensity of political activity.

If the distribution of political facilities around the Rosario polity was determined closely by information-processing efficiency considerations, one should expect to find a fairly even distribution of political facilities with reference to population, or vice versa. The amount of population controlled from a political facility is termed its *Political Span* (abbreviated to PS). Major differences in sizes of PS could serve to raise some doubt about the notion that information-processing efficiency was the prime motivator structuring the political system. To look at PS and its degree of replication, the same set of bridging arguments is brought into play. Various civic-ceremonial buildings (plazas, pyramids, range structures, or ballcourts) represent the political facilities (Figures 38 and 39). The information-producing component is represented by population (dwellings).

Discussion of PS covers the same evidence considered for TBS (Chapter 5). With TBS, the focus is on people as tribute providers to rulers at a center. With PS, the focus is on people as producers of information to be processed or as recipients of political services from rulers at a center. In looking at TBS, the question was one of how many people were providing tribute to support the rulers at a general set of centers. Because PS focuses more closely on political activity, more specific interpretation of civic-ceremonial centers is required. That different kinds of buildings represent different kinds of activities becomes relevant (see the SDI). Looking at PS values in this more specific way, a political facility may be equated with any of the following: a whole center, an individual plaza, a pyramid, a ballcourt, or a range building.

There are two ways to calculate numbers of dwellings associated with individual political facilities (whether centers, plazas, or individual buildings). On the one hand, numbers of dwellings pertaining to individual facility hinterlands are

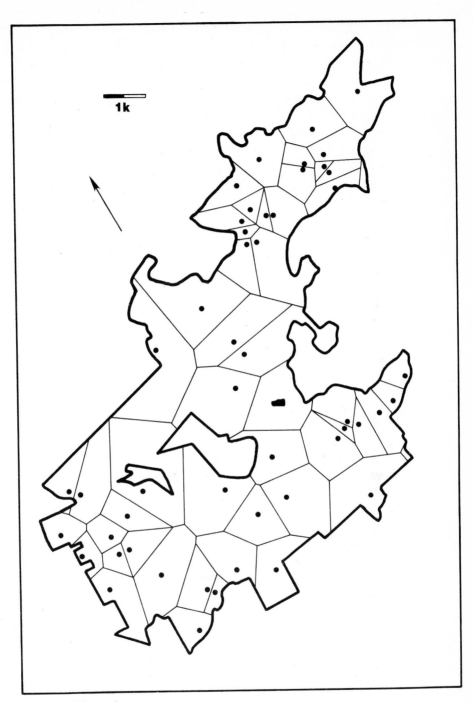

Figure 38   Plaza polygons

Figure 39   Distribution of civic-ceremonial buildings (buildings at Tenam Rosario are not itemized, see Figure 9)

calculated. On the other hand, districts are used and average numbers of dwellings pertaining to the several political facilities within these are calculated.

In a previous attempt to define territorial segments and dwellings falling under the tributary control of civic-ceremonial centers (the TBS), unweighted Thiessen Polygons were constructed around pyramid plazas (Chapter 5, Table 6; Figure 38). Here, TBS may be equated with PS (for pyramid-plazas). Such a method was only necessary for lowest-ranking centers, since higher-ranking centers could be associated with (less arbitrarily defined) districts. In such a nested hierarchy approach to partitioning territory between centers of different political weight, the implication is that subjects fall under the jurisdiction of a series of centers. This is a plausible arrangement for tribute extraction systems in stratified societies (especially if they have more hierarchical than pyramidal regimes). However, this idea may be modified, giving local centers first call on their immediate subjects for tribute, with a mechanism for passing up tribute to higher-ranking centers. In other words, a highly ranked center has more complete access to tribute from the subjects in its immediate hinterland than it does from more distant subjects (who are also under the wing of subordinate centers). Since earlier analysis has suggested that there was a more hierarchical than pyramidal political regime in the polity, we may envision a nested arrangement where ever more important centers, with ever wider ranges of political functions, have ever more inclusive PS. From this perspective, it becomes relevant to compare the PS values of hierarchically equivalent centers to see whether they resemble each other or not (representing information-processing efficiency or its absence).

Alternatively, the political hierarchy's nested quality may be disregarded and all the centers treated as equivalent units controlling only the subjects within their own polygon catchments. No subjects fall under more than one center; there is no meddling from above. Such a view of PS is more compatible with pyramidal regimes and segmentary political structure because these forms feature relatively greater autonomy for constituent centers. Even with hierarchical regimes (as in the Rosario polity), this is probably an accurate view at least concerning mundane aspects of political activity handled locally, irrespective of rank. This perspective allows horizontal PS comparison for all centers, without separation according to rank.

The second approach to calculating numbers of dwellings associated with civic-ceremonial centers deals with aggregate values at a larger scale. For example, ratios of dwellings to plazas, dwellings to pyramids, dwellings to ranges, or dwellings to ballcourts are calculated for individual districts. Such an approach destroys variation in the data base (having to do with uneven distribution of dwellings within districts). But compensating advantages concern the greater ease of comparison afforded by reducing the number of cases (e.g., from 67 plazas to seven pockets). Also, the approach is less susceptible to effects of technical problems such as uneven or incomplete survey coverage and the essential arbitrariness of Thiessen Polygon approaches. The last point becomes clearer when the elements that enter into construction of Thiessen Polygons are considered.

The general conceptual problems associated with using Thiessen Polygons need to be reviewed briefly before considering the more narrowly technical problems. The logic of Thiessen Polygons depends heavily on least-effort efficiency assumptions, a reductionism which should be bothersome. But, in defense of this logic, it might be argued that use of polygons in modelling is licensed by limitations of the archaeological data (for putting least-effort assumptions to a searching test). With some uneasiness then, Thiessen Polygons (and their efficiency assumptions) are applied to the problem of calculating PS for low-ranking centers in the Rosario polity. The general least-effort logic is that spatial strictures associated with Thiessen Polygons relate to frictional effects of distance on movement of information or tribute – a political (versus economic) efficiency approach to location (Blanton 1976; Steponaitis 1978, 1981; Spencer 1982). Getting away from strict least-effort principles, the spatial strictures may also relate to the need for political control and supervision (as in forced settlement, Chapter 5) or to the need for defensive security.

Using Thiessen Polygons raises several technical problems. The procedure used here gives equal weight to all plazas, justifiable from some, but not all, points of view. Since the Rosario Valley record affords better means of defining territories for higher-ranking sites (i.e., by reference to districts), this obviates the need for further technical exercises using weighted Polygons for hierarchically unequal centers. Another technical problem concerns the use of straight-line distances, rather than topographically modified travel-time distances (Johnson 1977: 485–487). But in the Rosario survey area, distances (and travel times) are so slight that this difficulty pales into insignificance. A more important technical problem stems from the restricted nature of survey coverage (see discussion of TBS in Chapter 5). The drawback is that many (29 of 40) of the Thiessen Polygons touch on the survey limits, with two problematic consequences. First, parts of the Thiessen Polygon boundaries are uncertain. Second, an unknown degree of undercounting occurs for the dwellings within polygons that extend beyond survey limits. Fortunately, these problems are mitigated by two factors. First, it is unlikely that many additional civic-ceremonial plazas were located close to the survey limits, except on the southwest downvalley side (known exceptions are RV53, RV175, Tr-5, and Baxac). Thus, Thiessen Polygon boundaries have probably not been overextended greatly, if at all. Second, it is not likely that there was much domestic settlement along the survey edges. These generally consisted of rough steep terrain or else flat, but exceedingly dry, zones (the latter especially on the south side). Again, the exception is on the survey area's southwest edge. Thus, Thiessen Polygon catchments which touch survey edges probably do not have a serious undercounting of their dwellings (with undercounting on the southwest edge cancelled out by the probable presence of civic-ceremonial centers just outside the survey limit). Whatever the effects of such mitigating factors, great interpretive weight should not be put on comparisons of individual plaza catchment contents. The list of problems associated with a plaza-by-plaza calculation of catchments (for TBS or PS) highlights the possible worth of the alternative approach which uses

Table 15. *Number of dwellings per pyramid-plaza, ballcourt, and range building*

	Dwellings per pyramid-plaza	Dwellings per ballcourt	Dwellings per range building
Upper section	46		481
Zorrillo	42	332	
Nuestra Señora	21	258	
Momón	243	243	
Chihuahua	43		
Tenam Rosario	34		
Lower section	122		731
Rosario	99	794	
SIN	111	1223	
SIS	128	641	
Polity	78		

aggregate values for districts to produce average ratio values. Boundary and coverage problems are much less important and distortions should "come out in the wash" at these larger scales.

My search for replication in PS (as an indicator of information-processing efficiency determinants) begins with horizontal comparison of individual plaza catchments (Figure 38). Marked variability appears in PS measures (Table 6). Thus, the patterning does not suggest information-processing efficiency determinants as a dominant factor. A decrease in variability does occur when plazas are considered separately by section. PS tends to be generally smaller in the upper section, but these are still not very uniform.

Since TBS and PS are essentially equivalent, I can refer to aspects of the earlier analysis of TBS (Chapters 5 and 6) when comparing plaza catchments in a nested hierarchy. Analysis of degrees of differentiation in TBS (Chapter 6) showed sufficient differentiation in the TBS/PS for PH2 and PH3 plazas to cast doubt on information-processing efficiency as a major determinant.

Average values (dwellings per plaza) for districts (Table 15) show a certain amount of uniformity within each section, but not between them, so that information-processing efficiency is not a convincing determinant at the polity scale.[3] In considering PS for ballcourts, the two ballcourts at Tenam Rosario are omitted since they probably had a catchment which encompassed catchments of the other ballcourts. Because ballcourts outside Tenam Rosario are distributed with close one-to-one reference to the pockets (Figure 39), Thiessen Polygons may be discarded and the ballcourt PS defined as coinciding with the pocket to which it belongs (Table 15). There is some replication within the two sections[4] and efficiency considerations may have had some effect on distribution of ballcourts within each section. But the replication pattern is not strong enough to indicate clearly that information-processing efficiency was a prime determinant, especially

Table 16. *Polity – SDI versus CH*

	Structure Diversity Index						
	0	1	2	3	4	5	6
Complexity 1				1			
(CH) rank 2		1					
3			1				1
4	1	1		2	1	1	
5	1	3		1			
6	17	14	1	1	2		

at the polity scale. In calculating PS for ranges, Tenam Rosario ranges are left out, and, since ranges are few and unevenly scattered (Figure 39), it seems simplest to examine them in the context of whole sections (Table 15). Results show a lack of replication between sections indicating that information-processing efficiency was not a major determinant affecting range distribution.

I now turn to the second method for evaluating the importance of information-processing efficiency considerations in the Rosario polity. This involves a form of intrasite analysis. A measure of site complexity has already been presented in the form of a Complexity Hierarchy (CH), in which sites with greater numbers of wards are classed as relatively more complex. More complex sites produce more information needing to be processed (i.e., for mediating relations between partially autonomous social segments in separate wards). The reasoning is not that raw population produces information, but rather that population segments are important producers of information. The segments are akin to what Johnson calls basal units (Johnson 1982). With information-processing efficiency as an important determinant, one would expect more complex sites to have more elaborate civic-ceremonial facilities. Such an expectation may be tested by tracing the distribution of SDI values across CH levels (Table 16). Sites without civic-ceremonial facilities or only modest civic-ceremonial elaboration tend to rank low on the CH. This lends some support to the notion that an information-processing efficiency imperative was operating. However, there are rather numerous exceptions to what would be ideal for information-processing efficiency. Especially important in this sense are the sites with high complexity but low civic-ceremonial elaboration.

Results of this last test of the importance of information-processing efficiency determinants are more positive than those for tests using PS. Overall, however, the two tests do not lend much weight to the contention that information-processing efficiency was a critically important factor. Thus, existence of a more hierarchical than pyramidal political regime in the Rosario polity does not seem to entail automatically a preponderant role for information-processing efficiency principles. And, clearly, information-processing efficiency cannot be invoked easily as an explanation for the polity's particular kind of regime.

Table 17. *Presence/absence of horizontal political replication*

Test	Replication	No replication
Centers		
SDI vs PH	Z, C, R	NS, SIN, SIS
PCI vs PH	Z, C, R	NS, SIN, SIS?
SDI vs SH	Z, C, R	NS, SIN, SIS
PCI vs SH	Z, C, R,	NS, SIN, SIS
SDI vs VH	Z, C, R, SIS	NS, SIN
PCI vs VH	Z, C, R, SIS	NS, SIN
SDI vs CH	Z, R	NS, SIN, SIS
PCI vs CH	Z, R	NS, SIN, SIS
Plazas		
SDI vs VH	Z, C, R, SIS	NS, SIN

Note: Momón is not considered as it has only one case. Chihuahua is not considered for CH, as it has only one case.

Z = Zorrillo; NS = Nuestra Señora; C = Chihuahua; M = Momón; R = Rosario; SIN = Santa Inés North; SIS = Santa Inés South

Horizontal political specialization

Another noteworthy aspect of political regimes is their degree of horizontal political specialization. A weak degree of horizontal replication (indicating high specialization) would be most congruent with a hierarchical regime. But, strong horizontal replication (indicating low specialization) is not incompatible with a hierarchical regime since it is defined only with reference to vertical differentiation (and specialization). In a case where there was a hierarchical regime with horizontal replication, it could be argued that the regime was integrated less organically than one with both vertical and horizontal differentiation.

The archaeological correlates used to search for hierarchical versus pyramidal regimes also serve in an examination of horizontal political specialization (SDI and PCI as indicators of political functions and the PH, SH, VH, and CH as indicators of political importance). As earlier, the SDI, PH, and VH are selected for discussion here (with fuller analysis in de Montmollin 1985a: ch. 11). A first approximation of the degree of horizontal specialization appears in the cross comparisons of (center and plaza) SDI values with the PH and VH (see above, Tables 12–14). Since there is a spread of SDI values at each hierarchical level, this distinctly suggests horizontal political specialization (at the section and polity scales). The spread can be reduced in some, but not all, cases by going down to the pocket scale with more homogeneous sets of centers or plazas (results summarized in Table 17).

The SDI as a functional indicator (for centers) is not entirely ideal for examining

Table 18. *Comparison of vertical and horizontal*
political specialization within pockets

Pocket	Vertical specialization	Horizontal specialization
Zorrillo	yes	no
Nuestra Señora	almost	almost
Rosario	no (almost?)	yes
SIN	no	yes
SIS	no (almost?)	yes

Note : Vertical specialization is present when there is no
overlap in SDI values between different VH levels and almost
present when there is a small amount of overlap; horizontal
specialization is present when there is absence of replication
in civic-ceremonial building types at the same VH level.

degrees of horizontal political specialization as it is a simple count that does not
differentiate in any detailed way between specific kinds of civic-ceremonial
buildings (and functions). A more direct way to chart horizontal replication is to
examine specific arrangements of civic-ceremonial buildings at each plaza, working
at the pocket scale. Detailed results are tabulated and discussed elsewhere (de
Montmollin 1985a: ch. 11). Generally, polity-scale trends suggest a combination of
vertical specialization with strong tendencies towards horizontal specialization.
But, the relation between vertical and horizontal political specialization within the
pockets shows a mixed pattern (Table 18). While the comparisons should be viewed
with caution because of the small numbers of cases, the benefit of looking directly
at pocket-scale political hierarchies is that they give an idea of the local-level
variability that goes into making up the larger-scale patterns.

In sum, the whole range of tests shows no monolithic pattern of horizontal
political specialization, such as might be expected under the assumption that a
necessary relation holds between vertically specialized hierarchical regimes and
horizontal specialization.

Tenam Rosario as a political microcosm

A detailed analysis of the civic-ceremonial zone at the capital center of Tenam
Rosario suggests some interesting political links between it and its hinterland (de
Montmollin 1988). Tenam Rosario is located strategically on a hilltop in the valley's
center and it is distinguished clearly from the other centers by the large number and
relative elaboration of its civic-ceremonial buildings and plazas (Figure 9).
Although my analysis here concentrates on the civic-ceremonial zone, some
background information about its residential component proves helpful. The
capital's demographic size is much less impressive relative to its civic-ceremonial
elaboration. The 239 dwellings rank it third among valley sites (with only about six

percent of the valley total). Surface appearance of Tenam Rosario housemounds suggests larger and better constructed dwellings than at other sites, an impression confirmed by excavations there and at El Rosario (Agrinier 1979). On average, housegroups are larger at Tenam Rosario (2.1 dwellings versus 1.7 valley-wide), an interesting contrast possibly attributable to social differences (with larger higher ranking households), to differences in domestic cycling, or to some combination of these factors.

While the civic-ceremonial zone borders very closely on the surrounding residential zone, there is a strict separation between them (as evidenced by the fact that none of the adjacent residential and civic-ceremonial buildings face one another). The close proximity seems to result from the need to squeeze as many buildings as possible onto the limited space at the mesa top's north end (Figure 8). This pattern is exceptional compared with other hinterland sites where single civic-ceremonial plazas are scattered within residential zones and where housemounds may be oriented onto civic-ceremonial plazas. The only other examples of interlocking plazas in the valley are much simpler in comparison (at RV200, Figure 11, and perhaps at RV30/37, Figure 10, both PH2 centers).

Tenam Rosario's civic-ceremonial zone covers an area of 3.21 ha at the mesa top's north end (Figures 8 and 9). All of the ten plazas are contiguous so that many civic-ceremonial buildings bound more than one plaza, but usually with a clear primary orientation onto only one plaza. Overall, the civic-ceremonial zone shows clear coherence and planning in its layout. Besides any specific interpretations of it (see below), the planning is interesting generally in light of the hypothetical notion that a colonial polity (such as the Rosario polity may have been) will tend to reproduce the normative patterns of its metropolis with particular clarity (Chapter 3). Thus, Tenam Rosario's strict planning may be related to its having been a colonial foundation, on a blank slate.

There are important similarities and differences in the contents and layout of individual plazas (full description of individual plazas in de Montmollin 1985a: ch. 11). Six plazas have one range building primarily oriented onto them (Plazas 2, 3, 5, 6, 7, and 8). In three of these cases (Plazas 3, 5, and 6), one or more pyramids have primary orientation onto the plaza. In these same plazas, which are lined up northwest to southeast down the civic-ceremonial zone's backbone, range buildings all face northeast. Of these three, Plazas 3 and 6 are most similar, with pyramids on all sides except the southwest side, which has the range building. These two plazas symmetrically flank Plaza 5 on its northwest and southeast sides. The other three plazas with range buildings (Plazas 2, 7, and 8) have no pyramids with primary orientation onto the plaza and the range buildings face in three different directions (excluding northeast). The resulting impression is that these plazas have been added on to the edges of a basic plan represented by Plazas 3, 5, and 6. Four plazas (counted here as three) are end zone enclosures for the two I-shaped ballcourts (Plazas 2 and 4 for ballcourt structure VIII; Plazas 10a and 10b for ballcourt structure III). Each has a different composition and plan. More symmetrical is the pattern whereby each of the ballcourts (along with its attached end plazas) blocks off the southwest side of one of the two large identical plazas (Plazas 3 and 6) which flank Plaza 5. Plaza 9 has a unique plan, a housegroup-like arrangement of three range buildings and one high platform set atop a massive basal platform or mini acropolis. This plaza (the only one of its kind in the Rosario Valley) occupies a clearly pivotal position. The detailed review of similarities and differences among individual plazas reinforces the initial conclusion that the civic-ceremonial zone shows a high degree of coherence and planning in its layout, which can now be related to its hinterland's politico-territorial structure.

At Tenam Rosario, there is a strong pattern of dual replication involving Plazas 3 and 6 and the two ballcourts. This duality is crowned clearly by an apical feature consisting of the mini acropolis. In a formal sense, the dual quality corresponds to the hinterland's territorial division into two sections. Additionally, the three or four small peripheral plazas have a close correspondence with the number of pockets (i.e., the four which have exclusively PH3 sites). Formal numerical correspondences between Tenam Rosario's civic-ceremonial layout and its hinterland's politico-territorial arrangement raise the interesting possibility that the capital contained a political microcosm for its wider setting – a reproduction writ small in the civic-ceremonial zone of the encompassing politico-territorial system's structure.

While this does not prove the point for Tenam Rosario, political microcosms at capital sites seem to crop up elsewhere in the archaeological and ethnohistorical record (de Montmollin 1988). A confederation model for the origins of Monte Alban stems from an interpretation of settlement structure at the disembedded capital compared to the three-part territorial structure (i.e., the three arms) of the surrounding Oaxaca Valley (Blanton 1978: 38–40). As intrasite civic-ceremonial data from earliest Monte Alban cannot be drawn on, and only general settlement clusters (based on distributions of ceramic material) are available, this example requires further elaboration. Internal civic-ceremonial structure of the Quiche capital at Greater Utatlan has been related to an ethnohistorically reconstructed tripartite territorial division of the Quiche Basin (Carmack 1981: 76, 166–168, 255–256). A quadripartite structure of elite housing at the capital site of San Gervasio has been linked to a hypothesized four part territorial division of Cozumel Island (Freidel and Sabloff 1984: 160–161). And, with reference to earlier and related material, a correspondence has been pointed out between Mayapan's civic-ceremonial layout and the ethnohistorically indicated territorial structure of the Yucatan peninsula, ruled from that site (Proskouriakoff 1962: 90; also Freidel 1981b: 329). Viewed from a methodological perspective, all these examples have intrasite and regional settlement data of varying quality, with the principal unifying criterion being an explicit linkage between analyses of the two kinds of data. This kind of linkage sheds valuable light on political questions (there is further comparative discussion of political microcosms in Chapter 11).

In contrast to the other cases of political microcosms which involve relatively acephalous systems with balanced ruling groups, Tenam Rosario's archaeological record suggests a more centralized and hierarchical elite political order. The unique and apical character and position of the civic-ceremonial facilities incorporated in

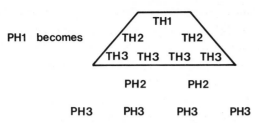

Figure 40a Tenam Rosario disembedded from its hinterland hierarchy [Key: PH = Political Hierarchy; TH = Tenam Hierarchy]

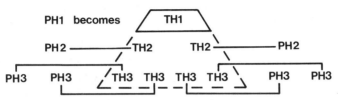

Figure 40b Tenam Rosario embedded in its hinterland hierarchy

Plazas 5 and 9 at Tenam Rosario preclude interpretations suggesting balanced confederacy or dual rulership.

Also supporting the idea of a relatively centralized political order at Tenam Rosario is the clear hierarchical ordering of its civic-ceremonial plazas and of its hinterland's territorial divisions. Looking once more at the Tenam Rosario plazas with hierarchy in mind, they can be related to three discrete levels of political activity: Tenam Level 1 – Plazas 5/9, the unique acropolis-palace complex; Tenam Level 2 – Plaza 3 and Plaza 6, each with its respective ballcourt, on either side of Plazas 5/9; and Tenam Level 3 – Plazas 2?, 4?, 7, 8, and 1, located around the edges of the Tenam Level 1 and 2 plazas. These Tenam Levels may be fitted into the hinterland's political hierarchy in one of two ways. From one perspective, all Tenam Levels are hierarchically above political facilities at PH2 centers (Figure 40a). This adds two levels to the PH, between PH1 and PH2, and produces a six level hierarchy. From a second perspective, only Tenam Level 1 is hierarchically above the PH2 centers. Then, Tenam Level 2 and Tenam Level 3 would be equivalent to the PH2 and PH3 levels in the hinterland (Figure 40b), reasoning that the numerical equivalence between Tenam Rosario plazas and subordinate centers parallels political hierarchical equivalence. This second view is formally quite congruent with the concept of Tenam Rosario as a microcosm.

Interesting structural and organizational possibilities emerge if one takes the second view of how the three Tenam Levels intermesh with the hinterland PH (Figure 40b). One possibility is that the political practitioners at different rungs of the Tenam Rosario hierarchy are relatively detached from the practitioners at hierarchically equivalent centers elsewhere in the valley, with Tenam Rosario structurally equivalent to just another pocket. Note, in this respect, that there are ten plazas at Tenam Rosario arranged in three levels and an average of eight plazas in the seven pockets (range 1–16) arranged in two levels. A big difference, of course, is that Tenam Rosario plazas form an agglutinated mass. A second possibility is that political practitioners at different rungs in the Tenam Rosario hierarchy (and residing at Tenam Rosario) had particularly close relations with the practitioners residing in the equivalent centers out in the hinterland. A third possibility, closely related to the second, is that there was an alternating movement of the same political practitioners between the Tenam Level 2 plazas and the equivalent PH2 centers and between Tenam Level 3 plazas and the PH3 centers. The last possibility is congruent with a system of dual elite residences, as proposed by others for the Classic Maya (Adams 1981; Vogt 1983).

This discussion has to be tempered by the realization that more evidence and analysis is required to show whether there were specific links between the hinterland's districts and particular plazas at Tenam Rosario. With reference to a similar problem, Blanton has considered how to demonstrate special links between the three initial settlement clusters at Late Formative Monte Alban and the Oaxaca Valley's three arms (Blanton 1978: 38–39). His ceramic arguments concerning distinctions in the relative popularity of ceramic types are not feasible for the Rosario case because of: absence of systematic collections from Tenam Rosario's civic-ceremonial zone, limited understanding of micro-regional typological variability, and problems with using a civic-ceremonial context for evaluating relative popularity of types. Another attempt by Blanton to demonstrate special links between Late Classic Period Monte Alban *barrios* and the civic-ceremonial buildings on its main plaza uses volumetric architectural analysis, showing a rough match between the variability in volumes of mounded buildings in the 14 *barrios* and the variability in volumes of their possible representative mounded buildings on the main plaza (Blanton 1978: 68–69, fig. 4.5). Although bridging arguments required for volumetric exercises are shaky (Chapters 4 and 5), I can apply a variation on Blanton's reasoning to note that Plaza 3's construction volume is more than twice that of Plaza 6 (9,930 cu m versus 4,769 cu m), while the lower section has about three times more housemounds than the upper section (2,922 versus 961). This makes it tempting to associate the more voluminous Plaza 3 with the more populous lower section and the less voluminous Plaza 6 with the less populous upper section.

Let me pursue a little farther the idea that there is a correspondence between Plaza 3 and the lower section and between Plaza 6 and the upper section. The number of dwellings per Tenam Plaza pyramid is quite different for each section: 487 for the lower section and 320 for the upper section. While this does not invalidate necessarily the hypothesized correspondences, it is not as convincing in support of them as a result with more similar values might have been. Along similar lines, let me compare section pyramids per Tenam Plaza pyramids: 4.5 for the lower section and 8.0 for the upper section. These disparate values also do not lend much support to the idea of close linkage between Plaza 3 and the upper section and Plaza 6 and the lower section. However, the requirement that there should be a uniform relation between numbers of pyramids in each section and numbers of pyramids in the corresponding Plaza at Tenam Rosario is perhaps not appropriate since the two sections are structurally quite different concerning the relative numbers of pyramids they have (Table 15).

Another (sketchy) line of evidence for links between individual Tenam Rosario plazas and hinterland capital sites is replication of plaza plans. Loosely following an ethnic plaza plan approach (de Montmollin 1988), replicated plaza plans could be taken to suggest close links between their users. In this case the small-scale comparison means that these are less likely to be ethnic rather than functional or sociopolitical links. Only one case of really strong replication occurs, in the very generic resemblance between the layout of the main plaza at the upper section PH2 center, RV30/37 (Figure 10), and the two Tenam Level 2 plaza/ballcourt arrangements (Figure 9). The arrangement of civic-ceremonial buildings at the lower section PH2 center, RV200 (Figure 11), does not match Tenam Rosario or RV30/37 plaza patterns. The other civic-ceremonial plazas around the valley are too simple in composition and layout to bear much comparison to Tenam Rosario plazas, precluding any linkage on the basis of formal layout similarities between PH3 plazas and Tenam Level 3 plazas.

The spatial arrangement of Tenam Rosario's political microcosm has interesting implications. Hierarchically less important plazas are more peripherally located, with a quasi-concentric drop in importance, quite distinct from the hinterland's territorial hierarchy which is clearly nested. The quasi-concentric arrangement in the capital's civic-ceremonial zone gives a neater expression to the concept of hierarchy than does the politico-territorial arrangement of the polity which it microcosmically reproduces. Seen in crudely functional terms, this would be another integrative and centralizing quality of Tenam Rosario's civic-ceremonial layout. A concentric dropoff pattern can be effectively contrasted with the pie-shaped division of Quiche territory radiating outward from Greater Utatlan (Carmack 1981: fig. 4.1), or perhaps the three-armed division of the Oaxaca Valley radiating outward from the three Late Formative *barrios* at Monte Alban (Blanton 1978). Both of these cases show a more straightforward correspondence between the divisions at the capital and within its territory.

In relation to the analysis of civic-ceremonial patterning at Tenam Rosario, some wider-ranging resonances in the design of Tenam Rosario's two second-order plazas (Plazas 3 and 6) emerge. In each of these, the pattern of pyramids on the north, east, and west sides – with a residential range building on the south side – is reminiscent of the plan for the Great Plaza at Tikal; the ideological implications of this layout have been discussed by Guillemin (1968). Strangely enough, the tendency in both Plaza 3 and Plaza 6 for the associated ballcourts to be set more or less below the southwest corner is matched rather specifically in standard Late Postclassic Period, Central Quiche plaza plans, whose ideological co-ordinates are unusually well-documented (see especially Carmack 1981: ch. 7, 8, 9; Fox 1978: ch. 2, 1987: ch. 8). It is difficult to know what to make of such generic parallels having to do with position and layouts and very generally defined types of buildings. Large differences in scale and style of construction for individual buildings exist among all three cases. What is more, orientations of buildings at Tenam Rosario (and in the Rosario Valley generally) are distinct from those at either Tikal or Quiche sites. At any rate, these similarities are worth pointing out as a pattern to provoke curiosity and thought (see Chapter 11, note 5, for further discussion).

In light of some of the arguments made here concerning Tenam Rosario's microcosmic plaza layout *vis-à-vis* its political hinterland, Pierre Agrinier has made an intriguing restudy of the principal ballcourt at Tenam Rosario (Agrinier n.d.; and see Structure III on Figure 9). According to his insightful interpretation, the ballcourt's seven carved circular discs are arranged also in a manner that broadly suggests microcosmic replication of the Rosario polity's politico-territorial structure. Of the seven carved discs:

> four were placed on top of benches, and two in the playing walls; each one represents an armed personage... The seventh disc was located in the center of the playing alley and is intricately carved with a [worn] glyph band circling the edges. (Agrinier n.d.: 8–9; and see Figure 9)

Following a microcosmic logic, the three discs set across the ballcourt (nos. 6, 3, and 7) can be equated with the political centers (and their rulers) pertaining to the lower section (RV200), the whole polity (Tenam Rosario), and the upper section (RV30/37), respectively. This makes locational sense because the alignment of the discs corresponds closely to the direction of a line drawn across the ballcourts at each of these centers (Agrinier n.d.). The three discs set along the ballcourt range closest to the lower section (nos. 5, 6, and 4) can be linked to political centers and rulers pertaining to Santa Inés North (RV93a), Santa Inés South (RV200), and Rosario (RV163). There is a rough locational logic to these equivalencies in that the relative placement of the pocket capitals and the discs is the same, although they are not strictly aligned (in the way that discs no. 6, 3, and 7 are aligned with their respective centers). Finally, the three discs set along the ballcourt range that lies closest to the upper section (nos. 1, 7, and 2) can be linked to political centers and rulers belonging to Momón (RV131), Zorrillo (RV30/37), and Nuestra Señora (RV6), respectively. In this case the locational logic for the equivalencies begins to break down since RV30/37 should lie between RV131 and RV6 to match the order of the discs, while the actual placement of the centers is RV131, RV6, and RV30/37 (west to east).

The functional implications of such an arrangement for the ballcourt have been summarized effectively by Agrinier:

> at Tenam Rosario, the personages of the main ballcourt do not seem to be representing gods, but humans of high rank, possibly the highest ranking members of the global political territory. It is not inconceivable to consider the Tenam Rosario ballcourt as having been used as a decision-making instrument presided over by the seven top men of the entire polity. (Agrinier n.d.:10)

Agrinier's proposals concerning the principal ballcourt at Tenam Rosario bring up, once again, the interesting problem of a seeming mismatch between idealized architectural models (or microcosms) of a political system and the system's on-the-ground appearance. Earlier, I argued that Tenam Rosario's microcosmic concentric-plazas arrangement was a clearer (spatial) expression of the concept of centralized hierarchy than was the actual nested territorial arrangement of sections and pockets out in the hinterland. Somewhat similarly, the layout of discs on the main ballcourt is a clearer expression of centralized hierarchy than the actual nested territorial arrangement out in the hinterland. The discs that correspond to the pocket/section capitals (disc no. 6 for RV200 and disc no. 7 for RV30/37) are unmistakably distinguishable from the discs corresponding to the pocket capitals (nos. 1, 2, 4, and 5). Discs nos. 6 and 7 are not only placed centrally with reference to the other pocket discs, but they are also in clear (and probably privileged) alignment with disc no. 3 (representing apical rule at Tenam Rosario). By contrast, out in the hinterland, the pocket/section capitals are *not* centrally located in their sections. Furthermore, the immediate hinterlands around RV30/37 and RV200 can be seen also as pockets, not immediately distinguishable from the other pockets in their sections. In other words, RV30/37 and RV200 can be seen as both pocket and section capitals (a pattern which contains potential hierarchical ambiguities).

In wider perspective, the notion that single civic-ceremonial buildings may serve as microcosms is not by any means foreign to Mesoamerica (see the analysis of the Templo Mayor in Tenochtitlan by Van Zantjwick [1981]). The possible presence of both a single-building microcosm and an encompassing plaza-plan microcosm at Tenam Rosario gives a nested pattern of a microcosm within a microcosm. In fact, the linkage between the two microcosms is an interesting, but open, question. At the moment, what seems clear is that a microcosm pattern occurs in Structure III, but not in the other ballcourt (which has only a single associated carved disc – Agrinier 1983). Assuming (reasonably) that the two ballcourts and several plazas were in contemporaneous operation at some point, this introduces an imbalance between the two second-ranked plazas. Interestingly, the relative elaboration and complexity of Plaza 6's ballcourt contrasts with relative unimpressiveness in the number and size of its civic-ceremonial structures as compared to those associated with Plaza 3, which has the simpler ballcourt.[5]

Finally, it proves interesting to place Tenam Rosario in a somewhat broader context, looking at settlement outside its hinterland in the Rosario polity core. To do this one can consider the neighboring regional centers in the Upper Tributaries Subregion. These are the centers with which Tenam Rosario may be compared most readily in a horizontal fashion. In Lee's reconnaissance of the Upper Grijalva Tributaries, many major Late Classic sites were located, described, and classified into the following types: small hamlets, large hamlets, subregional centers, and regional centers (Lee 1974: 7, 1984; Lee *et al.* n.d.). At least ten regional centers occur in an approximately 1,300–1,500 sq km portion of the Upper Tributaries, extending south and east from the Rosario polity (Figure 2).[6] As a class, regional centers are relatively more elaborate when compared to the rest of the Late (Terminal) Classic sites in the Upper Grijalva Tributaries. Equally important, each of these regional centers is most prominent in a distinct territorial segment.

Table 19. *Upper Tributaries regional centers*

Center	Plazas	Pyramids	Ballcourt	Range	Other	Civic area (hectares)
Tr-44	4	4–5	2	—	6	0.80
Tr-50	3	2	1	2	4–5	1.04
Tr-77	3	4	1	—	dws	1.40
Tr-45	4	6	1	3	6	?
Tr-66	5	9	—	—	4	1.92
Tr-76 AA	2	2	1	—	2	0.40
Tr-76 BB	2	1	—	—	3	0.24
Tr-74	4	6	1	1–2	dws	4.68
Tr-152 A	3	5	—	1?	—	2.85
Tr-152 B	1	2	—	—	—	0.48
Tr-152 C	7	13	1	6	2+	3.90
Rosario polity centers						
RV164	10	17	2	9	10	3.21
RV30/37	3	5	1	1	2	0.58
RV200	2	2	1	—	1	0.29

Note : Information is abstracted from maps and descriptions in Lee *et al.* (n.d.). Number of plazas includes ballcourt end-zone plazas (usually counted as one plaza)

dws   plaza-associated dwellings

The relative, locationally determined quality of these regional centers' prominence means that there is some formal variation among them. Territorial segments generally correspond to small tributary river basins or portions of larger river basins, analogous in the last case to pockets (Lee 1974: fig. 4; redrawn and modified here in Figure 2).

An important feature of macro-settlement patterning is the tendency of several of the regional centers to be aligned in a broad southeast to southwest arc, roughly parallel to the present course of the Panamerican highway. Quite reasonably, this pattern is taken to be an indicator that the regional centers were once aligned along an ancient communication route which cut across the major tributary river valleys (San Lucas and Santa Inés) to join up the Cuchumatan Mountains to the Comitán Plateau (Lee 1974).

Variability among the ten or so regional centers is interesting and provides some useful points to help place Tenam Rosario and the PH2 centers in a broader regional context (Table 19). It does not follow necessarily that the PH will be adequate to account for variability in all parts of the Upper Tributaries, far from it. But since hierarchical relationships among centers are studied currently most completely in the Rosario Valley, it makes sense to work from the known to the relatively unknown and thus use PH as a measuring standard. Of all the other centers in the Upper Tributaries, only Ojo de Agua (Tr-152) comes close to matching the civic-ceremonial elaboration at Tenam Rosario. Evidently, Ojo de Agua has a much longer construction history (back to the Late Formative and Early Classic Periods – Bryant 1984) and its facilities are spread out over a much wider area. Consequently, Ojo de Agua seems to display less coherence and patterning in the layout of its civic-ceremonial zone(s) compared to purely Late/Terminal Classic Period Tenam Rosario. Because of Tenam Rosario's preponderance, there is good reason for believing that the rulers living there in the Late/Terminal Classic Period had political powers and responsibilities extending beyond the boundaries of the Rosario Valley itself. If one adheres to the hypothesis that colonial centers are clear reflectors of normative principles from the metropolis (Chapter 3), the exceptional degree of formal planning in Tenam Rosario's civic-ceremonial layout gives reason for thinking that it may have been a key center of colonial control (from Usumacinta zone centers such as Yaxchilán) within the Upper Tributaries. This is in addition to the iconographic and architectural similarities that make Tenam Rosario look like a far flung dependency of Yaxchilán (Agrinier 1983, n.d.; Ayala 1984). The regional centers outside the Rosario Valley have a degree of civic-ceremonial elaboration which places them between the PH1 and PH2 levels. In this sense they would perhaps resemble RV53 and RV175, the two centers immediately outside the Rosario Valley survey area, which do not fit neatly into the PH. One supposes that many of these centers were capitals for polities of roughly the same size as the Rosario polity, or perhaps a bit smaller. Some of the centers, especially those located rather close to other (more) major centers, may turn out to have been dependencies, perhaps similar to PH2 centers. Another class, consisting of 17 subregional centers (Lee 1974: 10), is characterized by its centers having one ballcourt. These centers would most likely fit in at the PH3 or sometimes PH2 level. Finally, some PH4 centers would be found among large hamlets (Lee 1974: 9–10). In sum, we have some valuable knowledge of the major outlines of political settlement hierarchies outside the Rosario Valley, but much remains to be done to flesh these out and widen the regional comparative scope.

In conclusion, a detailed examination of the civic-ceremonial architecture distributed around the Rosario polity (Figure 39) leads to a number of interesting conclusions concerning its political regime (the distribution of political functions across different localities). Judging from this line of evidence, the polity has a more hierarchical than pyramidal regime. Political functions are differentiated according to hierarchical level, with a greater range of functions at higher levels. While a hierarchical regime is congruent with information-processing efficiency requirements (Johnson 1978), other lines of evidence concerning the distribution of civic-ceremonial facilities around the polity in relation to population distribution do not suggest that such requirements were paramount. Besides having a much greater range and number of political functions than any other center, the capital center at Tenam Rosario has both a civic-ceremonial layout and one of its ballcourts, which appear qualitatively to be constituted as political microcosms of its hinterland.

With these conclusions about the Rosario polity's political regime now added to those about its degree of unitariness (Chapters 5 and 6), the next step is to look at distributions of elite and non-elite domestic buildings along with civic-ceremonial buildings in order to analyze the polity's political stratification patterns (Chapter 8).

8

Political stratification patterns

Detecting political stratification

Political stratification concerns the unequal distribution of political rewards and inequalities in access to political offices. How to define presence or absence of political stratification is a secondary methodological question here, rather than a primary substantive focus as in cultural evolutionary studies of the origins of ranking or (economic) stratification (Service 1971; Carneiro 1981; Earle 1978). For the Rosario polity, I begin with the working assumption that it had clear political stratification: a regime featuring political inequalities, with privileged access to political offices for some. A basic division into rulers and ruled, leaders and subjects, or elite and commoner groups characterized most ancient Mesoamerican polities, at least from the Late Formative Period onward. There is no reason to believe that the Rosario polity was exceptional. Beyond sweeping generalizations, three specific lines of evidence locally sustain this assumption. First, the clear presence in the settlement record of a political settlement-hierarchy (an uneven distribution of civic-ceremonial facilities) means that the residents associated with differently ranked centers have differing access to political offices and activities. Second, considerable variability exists in domestic architecture attributes indicating hierarchical inequalities in sociopolitical status. In simplest terms, there was probably a set of sumptuary status-related rules about the appearance of dwellings. Third, differential distribution of special luxury items well meets the expectations for a stratified sociopolitical system. These items include polychrome pottery, fine imported pottery, figurines, jade-greenstone celts, seashell pendants, and so forth, all viewed as sumptuary sociopolitical status markers. Given a defensible assumption that there was political stratification (and not egalitarianism) in the Rosario polity, the problem then becomes one of investigating its nature. Such an investigation requires more detailed thinking about stratification patterns, beyond the simple presence of rulers and subjects, and a closer look at some of the lines of evidence just mentioned.

I give virtually exclusive attention to domestic architectural variability, which is appropriate for studying the prevalence of group or individual stratification, degrees of ascription and achievement, and relative pressures of contenders on political offices. Housegroup and individual building scales are most useful because the focus is on political actors grouped in households or multiples of households. To get a sense of the number and kinds of political offices to which access was being sought, civic-ceremonial buildings become useful as indicators for political offices since they are likely to have been loci for important public-domain political (and ritual) activities. I have analyzed exhaustively the uneven distribution of civic-ceremonial facilities across centers (Chapters 5 and 7), and the hierarchy of civic-ceremonial plazas (the PH) used there can serve here as a hierarchical framework for political offices.

Artifactual evidence is not used in this analysis for a number of reasons. Full analysis of the surface collections has not yet been completed. Surface collections were not made systematically with an eye to functional identification, but rather as an aid for dating the sites. Quantities of functionally explicit items found on the surface (sumptuary items in this case) are minimal, making it unwise to hang an analysis on such slim evidence, where the vagaries of uneven discovery are so great. This is especially clear when one compares artifactual evidence to domestic architectural evidence, whose preservation and recovery present many fewer problems (Chapter 4).

To further discuss uses of domestic architectural data for a study of political stratification, attention focuses on El Rosario (as in Chapter 4) since it is reasonably representative and best-studied in terms of intrasite settlement. Three "fast and dirty" formal sociopolitical rank indicators are used to study El Rosario's individual domestic dwellings – platform surface area, average platform height, and platform volume (de Montmollin 1981). To these a fourth (equally rough) formal indicator may be added – platform length. The last indicator is especially convenient for valley-wide use and is quite resistant to vagaries of preservation and visibility. Arguably, these are not ideal indicators, but their use is compelled by the nature of the settlement record. Better architectural status indicators such as presence or absence of masonry-superstructure walls and corbel-roof vaulting (Kurjack 1978; Freidel and Sabloff 1984) are not found. Qualitative indicators do exist in the Rosario Valley, but often their distribution is so restricted that it is very difficult to use them for classifying sufficient numbers of buildings. Visibility problems are a factor since some (more plentiful and usable) qualitative indicators are best recovered through excavation (such indicators are starred in the following list). Examples of qualitative status-indicators are: well-made and elaborate stairways, balustrades flanking stairways, high quality of cut stone, standardized size of building stones, well-made stone superstructure walls (*?), elaboration of intraplatform layout (*?), and use of plaster (*). Other potential indicators are contextual, e.g., location in a housegroup which has a formal outdoor domestic altar or location in a housegroup with a relatively large number of dwellings. Domestic altars are too scarce to be very useful. By valley-wide standards, domestic altars were relatively abundant at El Rosario, where their distribution does not correspond particularly closely with the distribution of other high status indicators. Number of dwellings in a housegroup turns out not to be related invariably to high or low sociopolitical status, but rather to a combination of this and the operation of a domestic cycle (below). For immediate utility, besides formal platform-size indicators, the best, most easily recordable indicator is another contextual one – whether or not a domestic dwelling is located on a civic-ceremonial plaza. The presumption here is that the occupants of dwellings located on plazas were relatively high ranking – a simple proximity argument that closeness in space relates to higher access to the political activities and offices associated with a plaza.

Lengthier discussion of arguments linking platform dimensions and sociopolitical status of its occupants is provided elsewhere (de Montmollin 1981) in an attempt to establish that the chosen formal attributes (platform area, volume, height, and length) work reasonably well as sociopolitical rank indicators. Before touching briefly on the highlights of that discussion, it bears repeating that manipulation and comparison of such variables is defensible to the degree that certain prior assumptions hold true – climax–crash contemporaneity, single-phase construction (reducing equifinality), consistent recovery of buildings, and good form-to-function arguments (Chapter 4). How does platform floor area perform as an indicator of sociopolitical status? Taken by itself, this attribute is difficult to use because of ambiguities associated with whether floor area simply reflects group size or else group status pretensions. In the latter case, area would indeed be usable. But much hinges on unanswerable questions about whether one can assume a constant ratio of floor area per person across communities, regions, and sociopolitical status groupings. Platform height is a more interesting attribute in sociopolitical terms because it is virtually impossible to relate, commonsensically, to the number of occupants for which the building was intended, eliminating the ambiguity associated with floor area. Any raising of platform height above a minimum functionally necessary to protect the floor from runoff and sheet flooding and the walls from seepage would be pure embellishment (Agrinier 1979; Kurjack 1974: 51). Platform volume as an attribute indicating relative sociopolitical status for occupants has all the suspect qualities associated with volumetric analysis (Chapters 4 and 5). In sum, it seems fair to say that volume, a product of height times area, has some marginal utility for sociopolitical status classification since it will be responsive, at least in part, to status projection considerations rather than to functional (demographic) considerations. Since an exhaustive analysis of building and housegroup level variability for the entire valley is really most appropriate for a subsequent more fine-scaled study, here the simplest possible approach is adopted for dividing the set of domestic dwellings in a sociopolitically meaningful way. This requires another formal indicator – total platform length. Such an indicator develops out of the observation that the vast majority of the buildings recorded were less than approximately 8–10 m in length, making buildings longer than this relatively remarkable. A tendency towards greater length is also associated with a tendency for buildings to be higher than usual (over 1.0 m in height). An additional rationale for focusing on building length is that range buildings, quite clear-cut examples of elite residences, are most notable for their great length (usually 15 m or more and up to 40 m). Thus, it seems plausible to associate a tendency towards greater building-length with higher sociopolitical ranking. One of the main advantages of this indicator is how easy it is to use.

In sum, to separate out a set of dwellings with high-ranking residents, the indicators are the following: the building platform is 9 m or more in length and/or the building is located on a plaza. One building with the required attribute(s) suffices to put its entire housegroup into the high-ranking category, since whole housegroups are the minimal relevant unit of analysis for political stratification.

Group versus individual stratification

The question of group versus individual stratification concerns the size and composition of the social groupings (or actors) that operate within the political stratification system. Actors may be relatively large multihousehold corporate groups or individual household-size sets of people attached to or competing for political offices. In group political stratification, higher-ranking people in line for political offices tend to organize themselves in larger corporate groupings to a greater and clearer degree than lower-ranking people outside the arena of contention for office. With group stratification, kinship and hierarchical political complexity are combined in ways not foreseen in the old evolutionary *societas–civitas* distinction with its polar contrast between kinship and territorial principles (Service 1985: ch. 9). Kinship reckoning is not something whose importance can be evaluated in pan-societal terms. In group political stratification, it proves to be more important at higher sociopolitical levels. Group political stratification has often been found to be congruent with segmentary structure, while individual stratification is congruent with unitary structure. Here, the issue of group versus individual political stratification is a pivot for the third set of research questions. To what degree were Classic Maya political systems characterized by group political stratification and to what degree were they characterized by ascription in access to offices (3a)? Was ascriptive group stratification, if present, closely linked to a segmentary (de-centralized, undifferentiated, and loosely integrated) arrangement of districts (3b)?

Thus, my immediate aim is to find out to what degree, if any, the Rosario polity featured group political stratification. In settlement terms, clear group political stratification would show a pattern in which architecturally upscale dwellings are clustered in larger multibuilding groupings, probably (but not invariably) in close proximity to site or ward civic-ceremonial plazas. Such groupings of upscale dwellings should exceed the largest sizes of most of the downscale dwelling groupings. The largest sizes for the latter would possibly have been achieved at more advanced phases of a domestic cycle. Before turning to the pattern in the Rosario polity which suggests individual (not group) stratification, I will flesh out these settlement expectations by looking at a number of Maya and Mesoamerican examples.

Although it is temporally and culturally removed from the Rosario polity, a key example is the settlement pattern at Late Postclassic Quiche sites. In one of the best studied of these sites, Pueblo Viejo Chichaj, higher-ranking dwellings are grouped into coherently planned segments of several housegroups in size. In clear contrast to this, the more humble dwellings around the edges of the site are found in much smaller groupings (Ichon 1975). Subject settlement farther outside the elite settlement is not well known so that more work needs to be done to demonstrate that this pattern holds. The same general contrast exists at Utatlan, Iximche, and other Quiche sites, but again non-elite settlement outside the site centers is relatively understudied (Wallace 1977; Guillemin 1977; Fox 1978). The Quiche example is of key interest and importance here because ethnohistory clearly suggests that the political regime featured group stratification for a category of rulers and absence of group stratification for subjects (Carmack 1976, 1981; de Montmollin 1982b). Goody provides a generalized description of segmentary conquest-based dynastic regimes with group stratification (Goody 1966), of which the Quiche seem to be an example. Within the range of ethnohistorically documented Late Postclassic polities in Mesoamerica, the Quiche polities appear exceptional for the degree to which they display clear group political stratification. There is a strong conquest element in the Quiche case, either direct conquest by foreign immigrants or very strong reference by local elites to exotic Central Mexican values and legitimating ideology. As such, the Quiche material structurally is probably most relevant to Postclassic Period cultures in Northern Yucatan (with their Mexican conquest aspect) and less relevant to the Lowland Classic Maya. From another perspective, Quiche materials might eventually provide an interesting conquest analog for the Rosario polity, if the argument can be sustained that there was an Usumacinta Region Maya takeover of the Upper Tributaries (Chapter 3). Certainly, by the Postclassic Period, the Quiche and related Highland Guatemalan groups are of direct relevance in the Upper Tributaries (Blake 1985). These comparative and historical considerations aside, my brief discussion of the Quiche is not designed to develop a precise or specific analog for developments in the Rosario Valley. Rather, my aim here is to sketch out an ideal type of the kind of settlement record associated with a prehispanic Mesoamerican political regime known to have featured a high degree of group stratification.

Temporally closer to the Rosario polity, there is a reasonably clear Classic Maya archaeological example of this general kind of residential distribution, hypothetically relatable to group stratification. This is the range of domestic (non-palatial) settlement groupings found in the Copan Valley (Fash 1983; Webster and Abrams 1983; Willey and Leventhal 1979). In and around the capital of Copan, highest-ranking dwellings occur in the largest and most coherently planned domestic clusters, referred to as agglutinated housing units. Such a pattern is reflected, although opaquely, in the locally used site typology where the residential groupings become both larger and more elegant as one moves up the classification's categories (Leventhal 1981). Beyond its having a residential distribution which suggests group stratification, the Copan polity differs from the Rosario polity in its much more elaborate and highly decorated domestic architecture (including vaulted buildings and private inscriptions).

In some domestic settlement distributions from Classic Northern Yucatan, elite (vaulted) buildings were usually parts of larger aggregations of dwellings, not always very well laid out, but often with a large, common basal platform. Humbler dwellings appeared in clearly smaller groupings, even less planned than the vaulted building-clusters and often without a large, common platform (Kurjack 1974; Kurjack and Garza 1981). Hierarchically above even the vaulted buildings, were multirange palace buildings at some centers. Like the vaulted building-clusters, the palaces housed relatively large groups of people. Such patterning corresponds to what might result from a situation of group political stratification.

If they were indeed elite residences (Harrison 1968), the multicourtyard palace compounds at Classic Central Lowland Maya sites might indicate some degree of group stratification. This is especially clear if one contrasts the size of groups in each palace with the size of groups inhabiting even the largest domestic housegroups. Within domestic housegroups themselves, there was quite a range of sizes, but the general pattern was to have not much more than four dwellings (Tourtellot 1983). As the Rosario polity lacks Peten-like (or Northern Yucatan-like) palaces, the kind of variability distinguishing palace groupings from ordinary domestic groupings is less comparable than the pattern of variability in kinds and clustering of domestic buildings (found in the Copan Valley and Northern Yucatan).

A possible tendency towards group political stratification is seen in the distribution of domestic settlement in Classic Oaxaca in Highland Mesoamerica (Winter 1974; Flannery 1983). Compared to downscale housing, elite residences (termed palaces) tend to have more buildings and a more formal layout with enclosed courts. In a rather weak way, this resembles the contrasting pattern of residences for Quiche ruling and subject groups.

Finally, an interesting and quite divergent example from Highland Mesoamerica is the domestic settlement patterning at Classic Teotihuacan (Millon 1976, 1981). While there are apparently a few cases of more atomized residences occupied by lowest-ranking people, almost everyone seems to have lived in rather large apartment compounds incorporating twenty families or more. The compounds were presumably associated with a corporate form of economic and political organization. Teotihuacan does not appear to have group political stratification, as defined here, since the large, corporate, residential format cross-cuts the sociopolitical scale. In this sense, there is a clear contrast with the Maya and Oaxaca examples where large, corporate, residential groupings are most developed towards the upper end of the sociopolitical scale.

In contrast to group political stratification, there is individual (single household) political stratification. Concerning settlement, individual political stratification results in a pattern in which architecturally upscale housing occurs in clusters of a size that falls within the range for standard downscale housing. Often, this range may fall within the limits for a hypothetical nuclear-to-small extended-family domestic cycle, of the kind which is familiar ethnographically among the Maya (Vogt 1969) and other Mesoamerican Indian groups. For most Lowland Maya cases, this standard housegroup size-range seems to be roughly one to four buildings (Tourtellot 1983).

Besides the requirement that architectural sociopolitical status indicators be available, another general set of requirements must be met for the (survey-data based) comparisons of housing-cluster sizes to be effective. Sites examined need to have a cumulative growth pattern and a fairly sudden abandonment (a climax–crash development, Chapter 4), leaving exposed to view a variety of domestic-cycle stages or structural-political arrangements. For domestic-cycle dynamics or status-related group size principles to be most detectable, there has to have been a fair amount of horizontal settlement growth (adding dwellings) rather than vertical growth (building up existing dwellings). Finally, a proximity assumption must be broadly valid as a bridging argument. It has to make a difference in social and political terms whether dwellings are set very close together in a planned fashion or whether they are set farther apart in a less strictly planned way. More specifically, the proximity assumption proposes that closely planned packing of dwellings indicates that the residents are corporately related. The strength of corporate links varies positively with the degree of proximity and the coherence of the layout for dwelling groups. And a further assumption in this case is that the corporate groupings work largely towards political ends against other corporate groupings (as illustrated by the ethnohistoric Quiche case). The converse of the proximity assumption is that a loose, unplanned spread of buildings usually means that the residents in the buildings are not corporately related, for political ends.[1] False proximity may be a problem in the sense that adjacency of dwellings may not always denote corporate political co-operation. False proximity may be produced by settlement growth over time in a restricted area, filling-in available space with housing. Confronted with this kind of equifinality problem, all I can do is try to find specific alternative lines of evidence allowing a distinction between false and corporately-determined proximity. When these and other requirements are taken into account (and hopefully met), surface survey evidence becomes useful for addressing the issue of group versus individual stratification by looking for presence or absence of the kind of patterning that occurs in the Quiche, Copan, Central Lowland Maya, Northern Yucatan, and Oaxaca cases. Relying on prior arguments (Chapter 4), I proceed as if the climax–crash and horizontal settlement growth requirements have been met. I can further discuss the proximity assumption with reference to concrete evidence from the Rosario settlement record.

With the necessary background in hand, I can now consider how the Rosario polity's domestic settlement compares with the contrasting settlement-pattern expectations for group and individual political stratification. At first glance, the Rosario pattern is more congruent with individual stratification. There is no clear tendency for upscale housing to be found in dramatically larger and more coherent groupings than downscale housing. Such an assertion can be checked with reference to El Rosario. There, no clear grouping of buildings exceeds the upper range of four buildings, congruent with a domestic cycle interpretation. In apparent contra-diction to this are the closely juxtaposed housegroups which do occur in the site's more densely occupied parts, especially in the area between the two pyramids in Section A (Figure 41). There, close-set housegroups (only some of which are particularly high status) are also quite close to civic-ceremonial plazas. But these are interpretable most easily as cases of false proximity, the probable result of a filling-

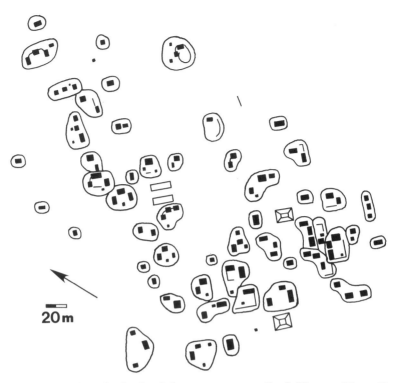

Figure 41   El Rosario: Section A (housegroups are outlined) [Key: see Figure 7]

in process. The overall layout of the close-set housegroups is still one of separate units jammed up against each other rather than a co-ordinate, jointly planned, assemblage of buildings. In this sense, the densest housing pattern at El Rosario looks less planned than the pattern found in some of the denser neighborhoods at Tenam Rosario (see below). Therefore, the conclusion remains that there are no clear residential groupings of salient size and status at Tenam Rosario.

Looking at the specifics of domestic settlement distribution at other major Rosario polity sites allows me to refine the argument a little bit. The one set of buildings in the valley that would be most functionally equatable with a palace in the Lowland Maya sense is the unique group of three range buildings on top of the mini acropolis at Tenam Rosario (Chapter 7, Figure 9). In its physical layout, this assemblage of buildings does not much resemble Lowland palaces. If anything, the acropolis group's design is that of a paradigmatic three-building domestic housegroup with altar, writ large and set atop a platform which is gigantic by local standards. Judging from the number and size of rooms on the range buildings, the estimated number of residents would exceed that of the largest three-building domestic housegroups by only two to three times, not a great difference. This is especially clear if one compares the impressive size differences between the Copan polity's elite agglutinated residential clusters (for example, those within the Sepultura and El Bosque zones near the Copan ceremonial center) and the scattered rural housegroups throughout the valley (Fash 1983, 1986).

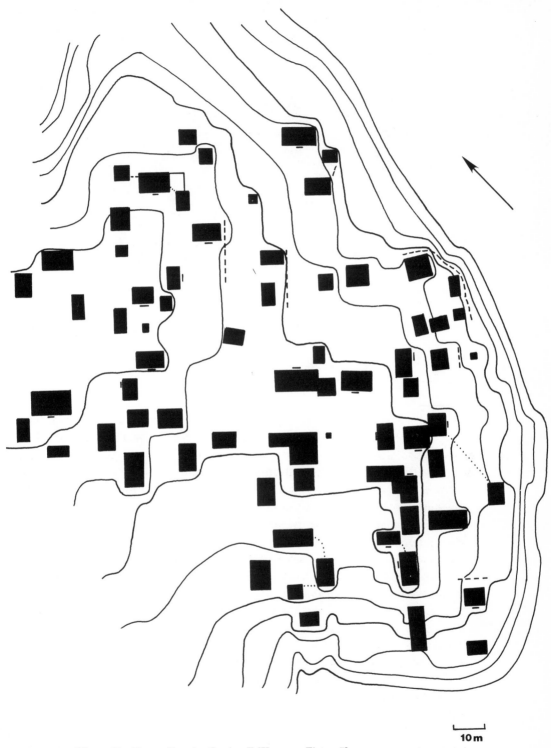

Figure 42   Tenam Rosario: Section E [Key: see Figure 7]

10 m

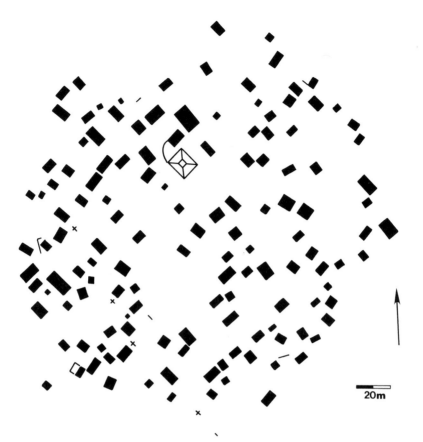

Figure 43   RV194 [Key: see Figure 7]

Outside the palace, the upscale domestic housing on the Tenam Rosario mesatop is quite closely packed by Rosario Valley standards (Figure 8; there are 32 dwellings per ha versus a general average of about 8.5 for other sites). There are also indications that some housegroups were laid out in a relatively planned manner with reference to one another (Section E has two of what appear to be streets, Figure 42). However, much of what appears to be ward-scale planning is a function of similar building orientation (between 40 and 50 degrees west of magnetic north, found everywhere in the valley) and of the crowding within the restricted space on the mesatop. Other sites with similar space restrictions often have an almost equally coherent look – especially RV194 (Figure 43), RV196 (Figure 44) or parts of El Rosario (Figures 7 and 41) and RV30/37 (Figure 10). And these other sites, although large, are fairly unexceptional in terms of the elaborateness of their domestic buildings. In none of these sites does one find the intricate network of closely interconnected patios that characterizes the large and elegant elite residential agglutinations in the Copan Valley (e.g., CV36 in the Sepultura zone, to the east of Copan – Webster and Abrams 1983: fig. 1). Because the instances of densely packed housegroups at Tenam Rosario and other sites in the Rosario settlement record show no clear evidence of supra-housegroup planning in their layout, I

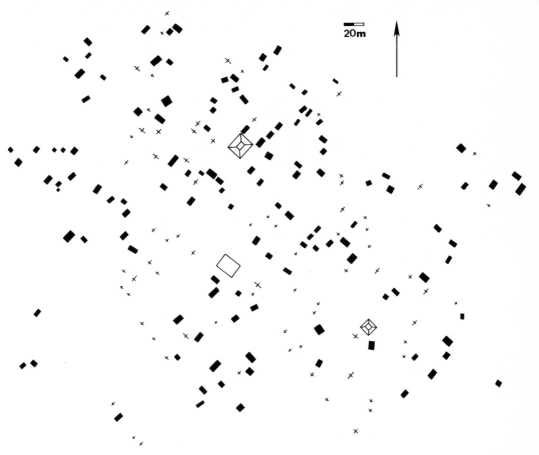

Figure 44   RV196 [Key: see Figure 7]

would conclude that these are discrete standard-sized (1–4 dwelling) housegroups packed closer together than usual, in false proximity.

As mentioned earlier, no Peten-style multicourtyard palace compounds occur in the Rosario polity, with the rather unconvincing exception of the group of range buildings atop a mini acropolis at Tenam Rosario. Nor are there vaulted masonry buildings. Only range buildings really stand out within the general run of residential buildings, but there is no indication that exceptionally large numbers of people lived in range buildings (alone, or in groups with associated regular dwellings).

The general conclusion has to be that group political stratification was absent from the Rosario polity. Settlement patterning is more congruent with individual household levels of affiliation among the contenders within the political stratification system. Lack of group political stratification would thus contrast with the cases reviewed – the Copan Valley, the Central Maya Lowlands, the Yucatan Peninsula, the Valley of Oaxaca, and the Quiche Highlands.

Ascription versus achievement

A difficult task is to study the variations in the mode of access to the offices distributed in a political stratification system. Logically, access varies from strict ascription to complete achievement (or contract), with a closely related continuum from determinacy to indeterminacy in succession principles to political office (Goody 1966; Burling 1974). Such variation in modes of access relates to continua already studied in research question 3b: Was ascriptive group stratification, if present, closely linked to a segmentary (decentralized, undifferentiated, and loosely integrated) arrangement of districts? Variations in the mode of access to political offices having to do with the contrast between ascription and achievement may be examined with reference to the domestic settlement record. As we have just discovered, virtually all the housing in the Rosario Valley, at whatever sociopolitical status level, falls within a range of one to three (very occasionally four) dwellings per housegroup. From this departure point, it becomes interesting to use the range of variability in the number of dwellings per housegroup as a means of appreciating the degrees of ascription versus achievement that characterizes the political stratification system.

Stringent requirements must be met to carry out an analysis of settlement survey data that compares the number of dwellings per housegroup and architectural indicators of relative political position. These are the same requirements as those for group and individual political stratification (above). Taking the requirements as met, I base my analysis of ascription versus achievement on the following line of reasoning. For early modern mortuary studies, a common procedure has been to chart the life cycle position of interred individuals and then to check whether burial goods or treatment are congruent with either an ascriptive or achievement-based arrangement for distributing these values (Brown ed. 1971). A roughly similar line of reasoning may be followed in a two-step analysis using architectural evidence from settlement survey. The first step is to attempt a demonstration that there was a close relation between the number of dwellings in a housegroup and the phase reached in a domestic cycle (Goody ed. 1962; Fortes 1962). If this relation exists, then one domestic building would indicate a beginning phase in the cycle, while two or more would indicate increasingly advanced phases of growth and replacement (Figure 45). At the upper numerical limit for dwellings per housegroup, fissioning would occur and new spatially distinct housegroups would be established. The second analytical step is to check the distribution of architectural status indicators across the different stages of the domestic cycle. Simply put, in an ascriptive situation indicators of high political position would be associated with all domestic cycle stages (just as prestigious grave goods and treatments would be found with some individuals across the full age and sex range in a mortuary program produced by an ascription-based society). In a more achievement-based arrangement, indicators of high political position would be concentrated at more advanced domestic cycle stages (just as prestigious grave goods and treatments would be concentrated among older male individuals in a mortuary program produced by an achievement-based society).

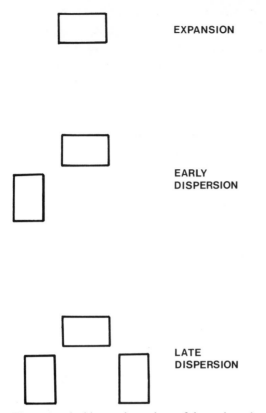

Figure 45   Architectural correlates of domestic cycle phases

I carry out both of these steps with reference to evidence from El Rosario, where cycling and stratification questions have received close study (de Montmollin 1981, n.d.c). For the first step (trying to show a relation between the number of dwellings at a housegroup and the stage reached in a domestic cycle), two major possibilities have to be explored.

The Domestic Cycle Hypothesis [H1] proposes that the sole source of variability in the number of dwellings per housegroup is the fact that the housegroups have attained different stages in the domestic cycle, at their maximal point of occupation.

The Ranking Hypothesis [H2] proposes that the sole source of variability in the number of dwellings per housegroup is the fact that there are distinct sociopolitical-rank divisions within the community. Each ranked sociopolitical division has housegroups with a different and conventional maximum number of dwellings.[2]

H2 has a general resemblance to the notion of group stratification, with a close (even determinate) relation between sociopolitical ranking and corporate, residential group size. But an important difference is that H2 operates within a much more restricted range of group size (one to four dwellings) while group stratification involves much larger aggregations.

To estimate relative validity of H1 and H2, one fairly straightforward test implication presents itself. For H1 to hold, there should be little correlation between a higher number of dwellings in a housegroup and a higher position on a sociopolitical-rank scale for its dwellings. For H2 to hold, there should be a strict correlation between the two factors. A variety of rank indicators are used to construct sociopolitical-rank classes for housegroups (de Montmollin n.d.c). Cross tabulations of the distribution of housegroups according to sociopolitical rank-class and number of dwellings show a spread across the rank classes of housegroups with different numbers of dwellings (details of the tests are in de Montmollin n.d.c). The absence of an invariant correlation between high position on the sociopolitical-rank scale and a higher number of dwellings per housegroup disconfirms H2 and supports a modified version of H1. Essentially, the conclusion is that domestic cycling operates in all rank classes, with higher ranks showing some tendency to advance farther in the cycle. In light of this, I can move on to the second step which requires an assumption that a domestic cycle produced much of the observed variability in the number of dwellings per housegroup.

In attempting to distinguish between strongly ascription-oriented and strongly achievement-oriented patterns of political stratification, two polar-opposite positions may be considered (with a probable continuum of variation between them).

The Ascription Hypothesis [H3] proposes that there is a closely determined hereditary mode of access to high ranking in the political stratification system.

The Achievement Hypothesis [H4] proposes that there is a large degree of achievement in the mode of access to high ranking in the political stratification system.

Unfortunately, test implications for H3 and H4 use the same lines of evidence as the test for distinguishing between H1 and H2. It becomes a matter of reinterpreting the material from a different perspective, not an ideal thing to do. To repeat the reasoning drawn from mortuary analysis, if ascriptive access were important, architectural indicators of higher sociopolitical rank would be freely associated with all stages of a domestic cycle (housegroups of all sizes). Ascribed sociopolitical status would allow groups even at an early stage in their development cycle to occupy higher positions. If achieved access were important, indicators of higher sociopolitical rank would be associated almost invariably with the maximal stages of the domestic cycle (housegroups with three or four dwellings).

The results of tests already described for H1 and H2 clearly suggest that there was a strong degree of ascription for determining access to high sociopolitical ranks. At the very least, the patterning precludes a condition of absolute achievement at El Rosario. As this is not a matter of absolutes, future development for this line of analysis will have to include the comparative study of other sites, to see where they lie along the ascription versus achievement continuum. In the meantime, another extremely summary test can be applied to the total aggregate of sites from the Rosario polity. This involves separating out housegroups directly associated with civic-ceremonial plazas as a very special set inhabited by highest-ranking political practitioners. Following the reasoning used above, I compare the sizes of housegroups directly contiguous with plazas to the sizes of housegroups away from

Table 20. *Dwellings per housegroup – averages*

	Housegroups									
	On plaza; high status		Off plaza; high status		Off plaza; low status		Off plaza; high/low status		On/off plaza; high status	
	no.	avdw	no.	avdw	no.	avdw	no.	avdw	no.	avdw
Polity	40	1.70	297	2.22	2,092	1.62	2,389	1.70	337	2.16
	*54	2.06							*351	2.19
Upper section	12	1.67	45	1.98	531	1.60	576	1.63	57	1.91
	*30	1.88							*61	1.95
Zorrillo	6	1.83	15	1.93	164	1.78	179	1.79	21	1.90
Nuestra Señora	4	1.50	12	1.92	154	1.49	166	1.52	16	1.81
Chihuahua	—	—	5	2.20	74	1.58	79	1.62	5	2.20
Momón	2	1.50	13	2.00	139	1.54	152	1.58	15	1.93
Lower section	27	1.70	205	2.21	1,494	1.62	1,699	1.69	232	2.15
	*31	1.87							*236	2.17
Rosario	6	1.33	46	2.11	400	1.72	46	1.76	52	2.02
Santa Inés N.	8	1.88	101	2.11	643	1.55	744	1.62	109	2.09
Santa Inés S.	11	1.64	46	2.43	323	1.58	369	1.69	57	2.28
borderline	2	2.50	12	2.58	128	2.25	140	1.85	14	2.57
Tenam	1	2.00	47	2.49	67	1.79	114	2.07	48	2.48
Rosario	*7	3.29							*54	2.59

* includes range buildings [each of the 19 range buildings is assigned a value of two dwellings, except where there is evidence for three rooms, in which case the range receives a value of three dwellings; there are 13 one-range groups, 1 three-range group, and 3 ranges attached to 3 domestic dwelling groups]
avdw   average number of dwellings per housegroup

plazas (also distinguishing between high- and low-ranking housegroups in this latter set). Residents in the high-ranking housegroups away from plazas are viewed as important participants in the political regime, although their possible association with political offices is not quite as clear as it is for residents of housegroups directly associated with plazas.

Results are lumped on a polity-wide scale and averages are used (Table 20). This is justifiable in the sense that dwellings per housegroup averages are reasonably constant across the polity's districts and not much variability is masked by lumping. A roughly equal number of dwellings per housegroup for the special (elite) and the subject housegroups would be produced by ascriptive conditions (based on the reasoning used for H3 and H4 at El Rosario). Such a pattern would suggest that elite residents are distributed across a full range of housegroup sizes representing all stages in the domestic cycle. In effect, there is a rough equality in average numbers of dwellings for elite and subject housegroups, an equality which is greatest when comparing plaza-associated housegroups (without range buildings) to the rest of the housegroups (Table 20). Expanding the pool of elite housegroups to include range buildings or higher-rank housegroups away from plazas results in a tendency for the elite housegroups to be slightly larger on average than subject housegroups (Table 20), perhaps pushing towards an achievement pattern. But, as there is still a full range of domestic cycle stages evident in this pool of elite housegroups, I cannot argue that there was a particularly high incidence of achievement in access to high sociopolitical rank. The only pattern likely to be produced by a largely achievement-oriented system is one where all or virtually all elite housegroups were in the final stages of a domestic cycle.

My examination of ascription versus achievement in the Rosario polity shows that the former is more likely to have been the dominant principle for access to political office.[3] To move the argument along briskly, I have kept discussion at a general summary level, in keeping with a problem orientation requiring a concentration on relatively large-scale regional (polity and district) settlement patterning. Alternatively, a problem orientation which required a concentrated focus on smaller community, ward, or household-scale settlement (perhaps a form of Household Archaeology – Wilk and Rathje 1982) would dwell much longer on the details of the bridging arguments required for detecting ascription versus achievement.

Contenders for office

The pressure of contenders on a supply of political offices and the distribution of contenders in relation to offices are central factors in political dynamics within ancient complex polities which lack professionalized bureaucracies (and routinized access to office). The shifting balance between contenders and offices contributes to such key political phenomena as fission or cleavage. Such a theme is covered in research question 3c: Was ascriptive group stratification, if present, closely linked to growth in the number of districts, through simple cleavage processes, and was this arrangement linked to a higher tendency to fission? While dynamics are clearly quite hard to seize with single-period settlement evidence (Chapter 4), what I can do is to make some structural static synchronic comparisons of the quantitative relation between contenders for political office, political offices, and subject population, across the Rosario polity's districts. From this patterning, I can then speculatively suggest what the potential pressures were and whether they differed in intensity from one district to another.

For a summary analysis, a number of very approximate archaeological correlates for political offices, contenders, and subjects can be mobilized. Relations among their values are then compared among districts (Table 21). Pyramid structures are taken as rough indicators of numbers of political offices – with small pyramids equal to one office and large pyramids equal to two offices.[4] Clearly these are not exact equivalencies, but simply expedient calculations meant to give relative values usable for comparisons (at least within the confines of the Rosario polity). Numbers of contenders for political office are equivalent to the numbers of dwellings included in housegroups located on plazas, and any housegroups located away from plazas

Table 21. *Numbers of political offices, contenders, and subjects*

	Large pyramid	Small pyramid	Total offices	Contenders (elite dwellings)*	Subjects (dwellings)
Zorrillo	2	9	13	42	292
Nuestra Señora	0	9	9	37	229
Momón	1	0	2	29	214
Chihuahua	0	3	3	11	117
Upper section	3	19	27	119	852
RV164†	8	9	25	140	120
Rosario	0	8	8	105	689
SIN	2	9	13	240	995
SIS	2	4	8	130	511
borderline	1	0	2	36	228
Lower section	5	21	31	511	2,423
Polity	16	49	83	770	3,395
Polity +	8	40	58	630	3,275

* range buildings included
† figures refer only to the capital center of Tenam Rosario, not to its catchment
+ not including Tenam Rosario

but which have at least one dwelling equal to or longer than 9 m. Numbers of subjects are equivalent to all the dwellings from housegroups not included in the elite category. The most meaningful comparisons are those effected among districts with reference to ratios such as the number of contenders per political office, the proportion of population in the contender class, and the number of subjects per contender (Table 22).

It makes ample sense to compare the contender per office ratio for different districts, using the rationale that a relatively high ratio could signify that there was a greater degree of pressure and potential for competition and conflict, at least within the elite or office-seeking group. In the Rosario polity, a considerably higher ratio exists in the lower as compared to upper section (about four times greater) which suggests a more stressful situation there with reference to providing political offices for all contenders. Such stress potential is not contradicted by earlier findings: that the lower section was more segmentary in its political structure than the upper section (Chapters 5 and 6). Pockets within each section have generally similar ratios (except Momón). Thus within each separate section, no marked differences appear in the pressures created by demand for political office at the pocket scale. All upper pockets (except Momón) are not beset as consistently by the problem of matching offices to contenders as are lower pockets. The strong intra-section uniformity for the contender-office ratio among pockets differs from the diversity among pockets in degrees of unitariness (Chapters 5 and 6) and forms of political regimes (Chapters 7).

Table 22. *Ratios of contenders, subjects, and political offices*

	Contenders per political office	Proportion of contenders*	Subjects per contender
Zorrillo	3.2	0.13	7.0
Nuestra Señora	4.1	0.14	6.2
Momón	14.5	0.12	7.4
Chihuahua	3.7	0.09	10.6
Upper section	4.4	0.12	7.2
RV164†	5.6	0.54	0.9
Rosario	13.1	0.13	6.6
SIN	18.5	0.19	4.1
SIS	16.3	0.20	3.9
Lower section	16.5	0.21	4.7
Polity	9.3	0.18	4.4
Polity+	10.9	0.16	5.2

* contender totals include range buildings (as do total population figures used for calculating proportion of contenders)
† figures refer only to the capital center of Tenam Rosario, not to its catchment
+ not including Tenam Rosario

As a measure, the proportion of population in the contender class resembles what Mayanists sometimes refer to as the elite fraction (Adams 1974; Adams and Smith 1977). But here my main interest lies not so much in determining the elite fraction's absolute size, as in comparing it from one part to another of a political system. The lower section has a higher proportion of its population in the contender class than does the upper section (in keeping with the lower section's higher contender per office ratio). By viewing the contender and the non-contender groups as roughly equivalent to tribute receivers and payers (mentioned in tribute-flow arguments, Chapter 5), it can be argued that a higher burden existed in the lower section compared to the upper section. This is the reverse of a conclusion reached earlier, in which the Tribute Load Index (TLI) for the upper section was higher.[5] A good degree of uniformity exists in the proportion of population in the contender class for the sets of pockets within each separate section, indicating that (along this measure) the burden imposed on tribute payers within each pocket does not vary greatly until one crosses a section boundary.

The subject per contender ratio is similar in some ways to Tributary Base Size (TBS) (Chapter 5). But instead of dividing the total universe of dwellings among a number of civic-ceremonial centers, the idea behind the subject per contender ratio is to divide a part of the universe of dwellings among a subset of these same dwellings considered to be occupied by elite members. In a very general sense, what is being measured here is the size of the support population available to leaders.[6] Quite clearly, the subject per contender ratios are determinately linked with the proportion of population in the elite fraction. Thus it follows from earlier comparisons of elite fractions that there is a higher subject per contender ratio in the upper than in the lower section, and that there are fairly uniform ratios within the two sets of pockets in each separate section. Absolute differences in the subject per contender ratios are difficult to interpret and they are not large (Table 22). Only Chihuahua is an outlier, which is less aberrant when one recalls that Tenam Rosario was closely associated and no doubt drew heavily on its subject population (note how the combined Tenam Rosario-Chihuahua ratio drops sharply). Summing up, there is a slightly greater average size for the support group that can be mobilized by individual political contenders in the upper section as opposed to the lower section. One might infer from this that there was a more vigorous scramble for support within the lower section and its constituent pockets, to go along with the more intensive pressure on the supply of political offices.

Concerning raw, political power-relations between the two sections (viewed as monolithic aggregates), the difference in subject per contender ratios is less important than the difference in TBS, which favors the lower section by a wide margin. But it may not always be most appropriate to view such districts as monolithic aggregates. Thus, the subject per contender ratio, though crude, aids understanding of politically relevant similarities or differences between sections. In this case, it suggests that the lower section's overall demographic size advantage may have been offset to some degree by its greater internal stresses. In the lower section, more rulers or potential rulers were dividing fewer available supporters among themselves. In general terms, my analysis of the number and distribution of contenders for political office tends to reinforce earlier findings (Chapters 5–7): that there was a greater degree of decentralization, segmentariness, and pyramidality in the lower section as compared to the upper section.

Elite forced settlement

In line with the idea that elite groups were internally segmented, it proves interesting to examine the proportion of the total contender-pool that actually resides at paramount centers (Figure 46), interpreting the differences through the idea of politically forced settlement at the elite rather than subject level (Chapter 5). The reasoning underlying elite forced settlement is that one of the available control policies for reducing intra-elite competition is for higher-ranking elite members to concentrate lower-ranking elite members into central political control points. Like subject forced settlement, elite forced settlement is a relevant concept for understanding how Classic Maya political systems worked. With reference to elite forced settlement, it pays to broaden the terms of discussion a little bit and to take a general look at the various ways in which Maya elite settlement distribution has been, and can be, interpreted. This is because distribution of elites is an issue of central importance for understanding political structure and organization in ancient Maya polities and its interpretation presents some intriguing problems. Indeed, on a still more general plane, in cultural geography one finds a thorough discussion of some of the possible relations between the spatial distribution of elite settlement and problems of political and especially economic control (C. Smith 1976).

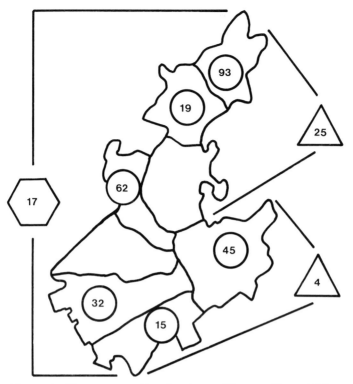

Figure 46   Elite paramount forced settlement [Key: see Figure 16b]

Although this work is based in part on Maya ethnographic materials from Highland Chiapas and Guatemala, which might make it relevant in a direct-historical way, its utility for my purposes is weakened by the formalist economics and monolithic socioeconomic class assumptions on which the analysis rests. Nevertheless, the idea of constructing generalizations about the spatial distribution of elites in relation to issues of political structure is a potentially good one for aiding archaeological bridging arguments.

Returning to Classic Maya elites and their distributions, from the perspective of their feudal model for society and politics, Adams and Smith have argued that:

> The relatively small size of the Maya elite would appear remarkable if the elite were envisioned as inhabiting the urban centers only and obtaining support from a spatially separate rural "peasantry" – an arrangement fraught with obvious difficulties of control. On the other hand, a feudal plan of dispersal of the elite throughout the region in centers…would incorporate one of the major advantages of a feudal arrangement: the enhanced ability of a small elite to control a very much larger subject population, as compared to other, more centralized systems of political control, which frequently require proportionally larger elite groups. (Adams and Smith 1981: 346)

Dispersal of subject settlement presents problems for centralized political control (Chapter 5), for which the elite dispersal plan described by Adams and Smith proposes one solution. Rather than bringing subjects to control centers (as in a forced settlement policy), the control centers (i.e., their elite personnel) bring themselves to the subjects. In the feudal elite dispersal model, the elites react to conditions presented by the subjects. In the forced settlement model, the subjects react to elite demands. Instead of being diametrically opposed ways of interpreting elite distribution with reference to subjects, these contrasting possibilities probably represent alternative strategies of control for elites dealing with subjects. It may or may not be possible to develop test implications contrasting the settlement effects of a forced settlement versus an elite dispersal policy. Very dispersed subject and elite settlement could be the result of a failed (or weakened) forced settlement policy by elite members on subjects or by elite members on other lower-ranking elite members. Or it could be the result of a feudal elite dispersal plan. Equifinality problems loom large with reference to the settlement evidence, and a diachronic perspective, although difficult to obtain at the required regional scale, would be very important for judging the stability of a very dispersed subject and elite settlement pattern. Even if total testability has not yet been attained on this issue, the contrast is still useful as a signpost towards better understanding of Maya settlement and politics.

As mentioned, an elite forced-settlement model contrasts with the feudal-plan model. Elite forced settlement is another interpretive tool for trying to understand elite settlement dispersal, one suggested by studies in political anthropology which concern themselves with fissioning among complex polities (Cohen 1981; Southall 1956; Fallers 1956). The logic is that dispersal of elites over a territory causes centralized control problems because members of the elite are not a monolithic entity set against an equally monolithic subject mass. Rather, the elite group is divided against itself and for purposes of top-down control it becomes more sound to concentrate elite members in a smaller number of more closely set places. Again, this is probably not an either/or proposition. Politically, it would have been necessary to balance both needs: to spread out elite members for purposes of keeping a close watch on scattered subjects and to concentrate elite members for purposes of intra-elite internal supervision and control. The second perspective on elite dispersal, while not framed specifically in terms of forced settlement, underlies interpretations of political structure in Classic Maya settlement in Northern Yucatan (Kurjack and Garza 1981; Garza and Kurjack 1984).

Evidently, knowing something about the composition of elite groups and their links with subjects is a prerequisite for unravelling the conceptual options concerning elite settlement and its relation to subject settlement. Without going into the details, the best (ethnohistoric, iconographic, and occasionally archaeological) evidence which is relevant to Lowland Maya elites suggests that factionalism and internal fissioning within the elite stratum were important (Webster 1976a; Cowgill 1979; Freidel 1986; Fox and Justeson 1986; Farriss 1984; Edmonson 1982, 1986). Consequently, the need to carry out forced settlement centralization within segmented elite groups must have been extremely important. That intra-elite conflict and contention may have been more of a problem than monolithic elite versus subject horizontal cleavages is also clear from some general overviews of ancient complex polities and their development (Service 1975; Wright 1986).

A somewhat different approach to the interpretation of both elite and subject residential dispersion deals with patterns within single settlements and uses one such settlement (Cerros) as a paradigm (Freidel 1981a). Nucleation or dispersal are seen as social inventions rather than results of environmental constraints on subsistence systems (Freidel 1981a: 372–374). On the face of it, densities of housing within single settlements seem to be more subject to social than to subsistence determinants, especially compared to regional settlement dispersal which is more easily relatable to carrying capacity (Trigger 1968). Since many archaeologists tend to think regionally when discussing Lowland Maya settlement dispersal, the intrasite focus is a problem if one is trying to settle the question of ecological versus social determinants. Beyond such (analytical scale) problems, the political mechanics set out in Freidel's argument are interesting.

> What would be the advantages of dispersed residential organization to a community housing social and economic unequals? Clearly, socioeconomic disparity is one of the important problems with which complex societies must deal. The normal pattern in nucleated complex communities is spatial segregation into distinct districts or neighborhoods reflecting economic or social class. Spatial segregation inhibits casual face-to-face interaction between social unequals and permits an upper class monopoly on information. While inevitably involving more legwork, spatial dispersion can accomplish the same objectives ... Indeed spatial dispersion of residence has a certain advantage over spatial segregation. If the social elite is embedded in dispersed communities, the illusion of egalitarian organization may be perpetrated and the sociopolitical identification of inferiors as a class discouraged. (Freidel 1981a: 375–376)

Substantively speaking, the association made between nucleation and spatial segregation of socioeconomic groups does not apply to either Teotihuacan or Mayapan, two of the best known Mesoamerican nucleated complex communities (Freidel even mentions the latter case himself, 1981a: 376). The association's universal validity must be questioned. There is no convincing demonstration that the end points of the two phenomena (or continua) – nucleation versus dispersal and spatial segregation versus interdigitation of socioeconomic groups – have to combine in the ways suggested. Even more importantly, the argument is implicitly framed in terms of a two-tone horizontal cleavage between monolithic class divisions, which is a problem since (as already argued) the most important lines of political cleavage probably ran vertically between internally stratified segments. Thus, the reason given for the dispersal of elite settlement – a need to maximize control of the masses by giving them the illusion of an egalitarian system – is provocative, but not convincing. Instead, with reference to dispersed patterns of elite and subject settlement, problems of control and co-ordination presented by the wide dispersal of potentially separatist elite groups would likely have been more important. Accordingly (in the elite forced settlement model), dispersed elite settlement would represent a failure by the higher-ranking elite groups to practice effective forced settlement centralization on lower-ranking elite groups.

Choosing between the several options for interpreting the spread of elite settlement presents enduring problems. What we have agreement on now is the apparent fact that Maya elite residences and facilities were unusually dispersed by Mesoamerican standards. Yet, were they so unusually dispersed, leaving out the too often cited cases of highland hyper-nucleation such as Teotihuacan? Few discussions are precise about what alternative dispersed or nucleated settlement patterns might look like on the ground. Setting these difficulties aside with the bromide that more developed bridging arguments are required, let me return to the theoretically more pressing variety of ideas about the determinants for elite dispersal. Current appreciation of the patterning is too vague to successfully identify the precise mix of determinants, but the appreciation is probably sufficient to defend the working hypothesis that there was a variable mix of determinants operating in various times and places rather than a single universal determinant. The prescription that follows from this is that each case must be approached with these and any other likely determinants in mind, so that evidence can be collected that bears on the relative strengths of the determinants.

It thus proves useful to approach one's cases with some systematic idea about the leading possibilities in the relation between political control and settlement distribution. Here, I recapitulate three such leading possibilities. First (according to the general or subject forced settlement model), highly dispersed subjects present control problems for various segments of the ruling group (but not in the sense of horizontal class conflict). There is a push and pull of subject population towards or away from the poles of control occupied by members of the ruling group. Rulers practice a forced settlement policy while subjects adopt a dispersal tactic. Second (according to the elite forced settlement model), the ruling group is hierarchically segmented (along the lines of a conical clan) producing a push and pull of elite population around superior control centers (structurally similar to the push and pull of subjects around the same centers). Higher-ranking rulers practice forced settlement on lower-ranking rulers while these adopt dispersal tactics. A third possibility, related to the first two, is that subject settlement nucleation is affected by the competition between segments of the ruling group for control of the same subjects. All of the pushing and pulling described here goes on simultaneously within a set of hierarchically nested territories.

Lagging behind in terms of probability (because they rely on horizontal cleavage models of sociopolitical stratification) are two other possibilities. First (according to the feudal plan), elite members disperse themselves among the dispersed subjects in order to control them (Adams and Smith 1981). Second (according to the elite dispersal as social invention model), the elite members disperse themselves among dispersed subjects more or less in order to make the subjects feel good about themselves (Freidel 1981a).

The settlement distribution phenomena here are relative, and appreciating them only makes sense in a comparative framework. In dealing with arguments about the determinants of elite or subject nucleation versus dispersal, the methodological (equifinality, contemporaneity, and form–function) problems are enormous. But progress occurs with the onset of conceptual clarity and flexibility about the political meaning of settlement distributions, analytical clarity about what kinds of settlement we are looking at (subject housing, elite housing, civic-ceremonial buildings), and analytical clarity about what settlement scale we are working at (housegroup, site, district, polity, culture area).

I now turn to the particulars of elite forced settlement in the Rosario polity. Most notable is the contrast between Tenam Rosario's high degree of elite forced settlement and its low degree of general (mostly subject) forced settlement (compare Figures 46 and 16). Greater elite forced settlement at the upper section PH2 center compared to the lower section PH2 center more closely parallels the pattern for subject forced settlement at these two centers.

Several overall conclusions emerge from the analysis of political stratification patterns in the Rosario polity. Concerning group versus individual stratification there is little or no settlement evidence for the operation of principles of group stratification in access to political office. This distinguishes the Rosario polity from some other Late Classic Period Maya polities where the presence of group stratification is a possibility. For the Rosario polity, this finding renders moot the questions of whether group political stratification was associated particularly closely with segmentary and decentralized political structure (question 3b) and of whether group political stratification was linked closely to tendencies towards fissioning (question 3c). But these questions do retain their validity for those other Maya and Mesoamerican cases which evidence some degree of group political stratification. As concerns modes of access to values and offices in the political stratification system, there was a fair amount of ascription in the Rosario polity system. Comparative relations between contenders, political offices, and subjects generally match earlier findings (Chapters 5–7) that the Rosario polity was internally diverse and that there was a more unitary and hierarchical system in the upper as compared to the lower section. Finally, the pattern of elite forced settlement suggests a greater degree of unitariness at the polity scale than did the pattern of subject forced settlement, as well as the same higher degree of unitariness in the upper compared to the lower section.

After my analysis of its settlement record to characterize the Rosario polity's position along several continua of variation concerning political structure (Chapters 5–8), the next step is to document the polity's position along a final structural continuum having broadly to do with economics (Chapter 9).

9

Mechanical versus organic solidarity

The mechanical–organic solidarity distinction finds distant inspiration in Durkheim's studies on the division of labor in society (Chapter 2; Durkheim 1933). Mechanical arrangements feature economically autarchic constituent units, limited exchange, and independence of parts. Contrarily, organic arrangements have a great deal of economic specialization among constituent units, extensive exchange, and interdependence of parts. It then follows (or does it?) that mechanical arrangements tend to be less solidary and less cohesive than organic ones, especially as scale increases. Aspects of the Rosario settlement record may be used to address the fourth set of research questions. What was the degree of mechanical versus organic economic solidarity that characterized Classic Maya society (4a)? If there was markedly mechanical economic solidarity, how closely was this associated with segmentary political structure (4b)?

My analysis of the mechanical–organic continuum in the Rosario polity must be quite a summary one, in keeping with a primary focus on politics (rather than economics), and to remain within the limitations imposed by very sketchy archaeological evidence concerning the presence or absence of economic specialization. However, at least some preliminary conclusions can be reached about the position of the Rosario polity and its districts along the mechanical to organic solidarity continuum. However imperfect, these conclusions are worthwhile in order to give at least some economic underpinning to the predominantly social and political factors investigated so far.

Certain patterns, which are potentially recoverable through archaeological survey methods, allow a distinction to be made between mechanical and organic solidarity. These patterns shed light on the question of relative community (site)-scale involvement in basic agricultural production activities. In general terms, a uniform degree of involvement for all communities occurs in a situation of mechanical solidarity. Uneven degrees of involvement potentially occur with more organic forms of solidarity, since communities with less than full involvement in agriculture need to engage in some kinds of craft or other non-agricultural activities. This in turn sets up a potential for organically interdependent relations with the more fully agricultural communities.

With these interests in mind, I consider three methods for determining degrees of economic specialization: catchment analysis concerning site population to catchment productivity ratios, comparative site catchment composition in terms of resource mix, and comparative kinds and amounts of craft related artifacts on the site surfaces. While all three methods may be considered in principle, it turns out that only the first is viable here (and even then, with some modification to the reasoning). Consequently, my primary effort is directed at exploring the relation between population and catchment productivity (in terms of population-resource ratios).

Catchment analysis (Flannery 1976) has proved a popular method for getting information about the presence or absence of economic specialization from settlement distribution maps. Accepting certain standard assumptions about pre-industrial (non-market) agricultural space use, standard-sized catchment areas may be drawn around a series of sites and resulting estimated catchment productivity compared to population (Brumfiel 1976; Steponaitis 1981; Peebles 1978).

A constant relationship between site population and catchment productivity would suggest a mechanical redundance for community level involvement in basic agriculture. Such a constant standard would have to occur at the same level in a site hierarchy derived independently of site size. A widely variable catchment productivity to site population ratio, within a given level in the site hierarchy, would be a possible indicator of a tendency towards organic economic solidarity. The latter case would be clearest if it could be shown, through other lines of evidence, that sites which exceeded the standard agricultural possibilities of their catchments were dependent on craft-production activities. The sites compared would have to be at the same political hierarchical level in order to filter out any possible vertical tribute-flow effects on site size in relation to catchment productivity – effects of the kind suggested by studies in the Basin of Mexico (Steponaitis 1981; Brumfiel 1976). It would also be necessary to filter out the possible effects on site population to catchment productivity ratios of uneven stages reached in a site growth cycle (Steponaitis 1981: 341, 345).

While such methods are elegant and interesting, two factors bar their direct application to the Rosario settlement record – scale of coverage and the dispersed spread of settlement. The survey coverage encompasses such a small area that the travel-time minimization logic which underlies catchment analysis is difficult to apply (the plateau effect mentioned earlier). Additionally, the almost continuous sprawl of settlement within the survey area makes it impractical to try to draw catchment circles around separate sites (even after factoring out smaller sites). There are rarely more than a few hundred meters between sites and even small catchment circles of one kilometer radius would be impossible to work with.

To overcome the difficulty raised by close packing of sites, districts may be used as the unit of analysis and compared for their population size and its relation to agricultural resource distribution. Redundancy in the relation between the two would be taken as evidence for mechanical economic solidarity and a clear differentiation could begin to suggest a more organic economic solidarity. Aspects of the variability in environmental composition among pockets were discussed earlier when sorting out possible political as opposed to economic determinants for population density (Chapter 6, Table 8). The proportion of Valley Floor (vf) and Valley Floor Eminence (vfe) area within the total area was used as a crude but simple-to-use indicator of the relative resource endowment in districts. Upper Hillside and Hilltop Zones may be subtracted from the total area to factor out the possible effects of uneven survey coverage along the valley edges. Higher proportions of vf-vfe relative to total area indicate a relatively richer resource base (Chapter 6, Figure 21).

In an earlier discussion of the differentiation subcontinuum, I briefly referred to the question of whether the environmental composition (vf-vfe to total area) of the various districts was determined primarily politically or economically (Chapter 6). The question (as formulated) is difficult to answer here, but the issue it raises is inspired by the example of Kaua'i (Earle 1978) where it is possible to see politically determined boundaries drawn so as to cross-cut environmental zones, thus including a standard complement of zones within each political unit. Other examples suggestive of the same arrangement, often on a much larger scale, would be Andean vertical archipelagos (Murra 1972), or hinterlands for Late Aztec centers in the Texcoco region (Parsons 1971: 225–226), or Classic Lowland Maya coastal realms (Hammond 1975b: ch. 7, drawing an analogy to English strip parishes). The eventual aim of this kind of political determination for environmental resource composition is to achieve a degree of autarchy within the districts or, in other words, mechanical economic solidarity among them. Persisting with the question for a moment, what are the criteria for determining whether or not environmental composition of districts was politically or economically determined? In a case of politically determined environmental composition, boundaries are designed to incorporate equal quantities and/or proportions of environmental resources, such as riverine frontage, valley-bottom lands, lower hillside, and so forth. In a case of economically (or at least non-politically) determined environmental composition, boundaries merely follow existing topographic or other constraints, with no effort to modify them so as to even out environmental composition.

It makes little sense to use such distinguishing criteria for the Rosario settlement record because of the uncertainty associated with drawing up district boundaries. All that can be said is that the districts, as I have defined them, do not seem to over-ride topographic divisions and/or even out proportional (or absolute) amounts of favored valley-bottom lands (Figure 21). Only a limited degree of uniformity in the resource composition of districts was achieved. But there is no convincing way to show to what degree the resource endowments for districts were politically determined. Given the valley's linear and clearly modular topography (with the pockets as sub-basins), it is difficult to see how the divisions could be much different from what they appear to be, or even how the boundaries could be altered to bring the vf-vfe to total area ratios more into line with one another.[1] At any rate, the Hawaiian and Andean cases cited above are much more clear-cut in the possibilities they present for political manipulation of environmental composition than are the Rosario districts.

For the Rosario polity, perhaps a better question would be whether there were political or economic determinants of the relation between population and resource endowment in the districts. This is the general logic behind the catchment approach outlined above. I began to address this question with reference to the degree of differentiation in TBS among districts (Chapter 6). It turned out that relative differences in population density (Figure 23) did not always match rigorously differences in relative resource endowments. The most dramatic example was Chihuahua, which had a very light population density compared to its rich resource endowment. At the very least, economic determinants were not the sole ones operating to produce differences in population densities for Chihuahua and some of the other pockets. Political implications of these density and resource endowment disparities were explored with special emphasis on what the resulting differences in TBS could mean in terms of unitary versus segmentary structure (see Chapter 6).

Let me now consider some of the more economic implications of variation (or lack of it) among districts in the relation between total population that is allowed by total resource endowment and the actual population recorded.[2] To tackle this problem, the range of land types under consideration is widened to include Lower Hillside and then a total resource endowment figure is generated. Omitting Upper Hillside filters out effects of uneven survey coverage along the valley edges. Since this zone is agriculturally marginal and lightly settled, leaving it out has little impact on the analysis. Two to four *Resource Units* (abbreviated to RU) are assigned to each hectare of Valley Floor and one RU to each hectare of Valley Floor Eminence or Lower Hillside. The RU values are not based on any exact appreciation of either modern or ancient productivities, but they are meant to generate reasonably plausible figures for comparing different zones. The higher valuation for Valley Floor lands is logical since there is a good chance that these lands could be continuously cropped, whereas the Lower Hillside probably had to be short-fallowed. Also, the soil moisture conditions in the Valley Floor were advantageous compared to the Lower Hillside which was thus more vulnerable to year-to-year irregularities in rainfall.

Total RU scores for districts give a relative sense of their potential catchment productivity. Scores may then be compared to total population values among the same districts. A comparison of the RU per dwelling ratios among districts provides a check on how evenly population is distributed in relation to agricultural resources (Figure 47). The upper section (without Chihuahua) has an RU per dwelling advantage (which narrows as one increases the RU score for Valley Floor lands). At any rate, there is not a great difference between the two sections, and differences among the pockets within each one are quite modest. Thus, there was probably a roughly even distribution of population in relation to agricultural resources between the two sections, and especially among the pockets within them. Chihuahua is the clear exception to this conclusion (see discussion below).

That there was an even distribution of population relative to agricultural resources differs somewhat from the conclusion reached earlier when relative differences in population densities were compared to relative differences in resource endowment, with the latter judged through a vf-vfe area to total area ratio (Chapter 6, Figures 21 and 22). In the earlier analysis, greater emphasis was placed on the

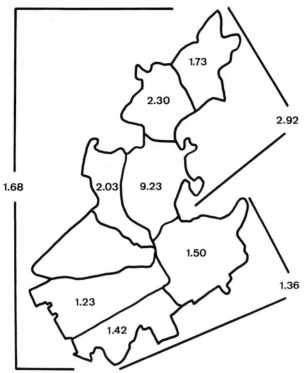

Figure 47a   Resource Units per dwelling with two RU per hectare of Valley Floor (vf) [Key: see Figure 20b]

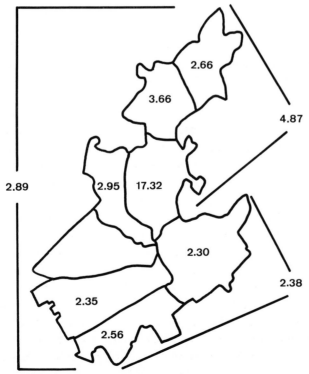

Figure 47b   Resource Units per dwelling with four RU per hectare of Valley Floor (vf) [Key: see Figure 20b]

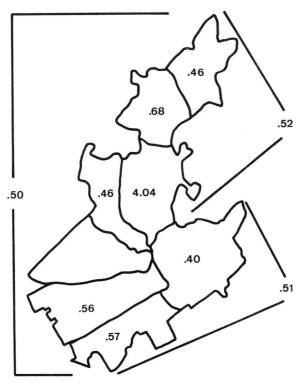

Figure 48   Hectares of Valley Floor (vf–vfe) per dwelling minus Upper Hillside [Key: see Figure 20b]

disparities from the relative densities that would be expected given economic determinants for population density. It made sense to emphasize any differences among the districts when the aim was to look for political determinants for settlement densities and population size. In this analysis, the measuring instrument for environmental resources is different and it evens out disparities among districts. Also, with different analytical aims, what disparities there are loom less large concerning their implications for economic specialization.

Another measure of the relation of population to agricultural resources in the districts is hectares (ha) of prime Valley Floor (vf) and Valley Floor Eminence (vfe) area available per dwelling (Chapter 6, Figure 24). Here the measures are recalculated slightly to leave out dwellings from the Upper Hillside, which helps to eliminate some possible distorting effects of uneven survey coverage along the valley edges (Figure 48). This brings the results even closer to a uniform spread of population in relation to catchment productivity (compare Figures 24 and 48) and lends additional support to conclusions reached when comparing RU per dwelling ratios.

Judging from both lines of analysis, it does not appear that population-resource disparities existed which would have been sufficient to require some districts to support themselves by (specialized) non-agricultural means. Yet, the pocket scale may be too large to allow detection of non-agricultural specialization in the distribution of population with reference to agricultural resources. Specialization may have occurred at the community or ward or household scale. Detecting it would require individual site catchment analysis or better still intensive surface "pickup" at individual sites. So my analysis leaves open the question of smaller-scale specialization. At a minimum, there must have been a group of tribute receivers who did not have to give much (if any) of their time to toil in the fields (the residences of this group were discussed earlier, Chapter 8). The results of my summary analysis at the district scale can be extended to suggest a generalized set of agricultural activities performed by most subject households and low levels of full-time non-agricultural craft specialization.

Among pockets, the exception to the population-resource distribution uniformity is always Chihuahua, according to all measures. Its low population in relation to catchment productivity does not suggest low involvement in basic agricultural production but rather the opposite. Underuse of Valley Floor lands (relative to valley-wide norms) is a pattern that almost demands explanation in terms of Chihuahua's proximity to the capital at Tenam Rosario. It is tempting to think that Chihuahua was an agricultural reserve for the large group of rulers at Tenam Rosario (de Montmollin 1985c). Perhaps the regular sort of peasants were kept off the lands in Chihuahua so that it could be farmed in larger than usual estates for the residents of Tenam Rosario. Puleston (1973: 213, 228–229) and Tolstoy (1982) have also used agricultural reserve arguments for cases where favored lands are relatively undersettled, compared to other favored lands, or else to less favored lands (the cases are Tikal and Oaxaca, respectively). On the other side of Tenam Rosario from Chihuahua, such a policy may also have been pursued in Rosario, as suggested by this pocket's slightly lower population densities compared to the other lower pockets. Also, in comparison to other lower pockets, a more rigorous avoidance of Valley Floor lands seems to occur in Rosario, leaving unusually large expanses of unsettled prime lands (similar to those in Chihuahua).

It seems improbable that a factor contributing to Chihuahua's deviation from norms was that it had reached an early stage in a growth cycle (Chapters 10 and 11). Still another possible factor contributing to Chihuahua's low density is the forced resettlement of its population into Tenam Rosario. But, that this was not a major factor contributing to Chihuahua's low settlement density is suggested by the very high proportion of elite residences at Tenam Rosario (Chapter 8, Figure 46) and by its unimpressive concentration of subject population (Chapter 5, Figure 16). Tenam Rosario would have had to be much larger to contain even part of the subject population that could have been supported by Chihuahua's very rich resource endowment. In sum, the pattern of markedly lower than expected settlement density in Chihuahua and slightly lower density in Rosario can best be attributed to a policy aimed at freeing Valley Floor lands for a land tenure regime featuring large estates. This policy would have been promoted by the elite group at Tenam Rosario, located in the dead center of this agricultural reserve zone.

A second method for determining degrees of economic specialization involves studying the composition of site catchments and comparing their agricultural and non-agricultural resource mixes (Zarky 1976). Replication of such mixes is another indicator of mechanical solidarity (with similar degrees of involvement for communities in basic agricultural production). Alternately, a variety of combinations of environmental zones and/or localized resources in the various site catchments is an indicator of differential involvement for communities in basic agricultural production, with potentially more organic economic solidarity. It is not feasible to apply this approach to the Rosario settlement record, because the approach is badly handicapped by problems mentioned earlier. These are small scale of coverage and high site-density. Additionally, an apparent redundance of non-agricultural resources within the surveyed valley robs the exercise of much utility. A peripherally relevant datum would be the variability in agricultural resource composition of different districts (Table 9 and Figure 21). My earlier analysis of this variability, in relation to settlement density and total population size (Chapter 6), does not support the idea that there was economic specialization and organic economic solidarity.

A third and final method for determining degrees of economic specialization is to trace the kinds and amounts of craft-related artifacts on site surfaces (Brumfiel 1980; Redmond 1983; Blanton *et al.* 1982; Kowalewski and Finsten 1983; Feinman *et al.* 1984). In a mechanical arrangement, equal-sized sites would have similar ranges of craft-related items (e.g., various lithic implements, spindle whorls, remains of lithic manufacture, and so forth). A more organic arrangement would result in a more uneven distribution of craft-related items. Certain specialized sites would have evidence for crafts out of proportion to their population size. This is fine in the abstract, but the small numbers of artifacts (let alone craft-related ones) found on the surface in the Rosario Valley made it impossible to pursue this line of evidence.[3] Additionally, the unsystematic artifact-recovery techniques (used for dating purposes in the first instance) do not lend themselves to greatly extrapolated conclusions about functional specialization. For what little it is worth, the patterning in the artifact collections from the survey gives little indication of major localized craft activity concentrated in any specific sites.[4]

One exception to the generalization that there was little economic specialization among sites and districts is suggested by architectural evidence for some sort of specialized resource exploitation concentrated in the Midvalley Range (Figure 5). This consists of circular buildings scattered along rugged, forested hillsides (de Montmollin 1985a: ch. 7). The distribution of specialized circular buildings does not suggest organic economic specialization because it is peripherally located in relation to the bulk of the settlement, and the circular buildings are best interpreted as seasonally used facilities. The proximity of the Midvalley Range concentration of circular buildings to Santa Inés North and Momón (as well as to Tenam Rosario) may suggest a degree of specialization for these areas. But the pattern remains difficult to interpret because of the limited coverage of Upper Hillside around the edges of the valley. This makes it presently impossible fully to appreciate how relatively concentrated circular buildings were in the Midvalley Range as opposed to some of the other steep and rugged valley edges.

In conclusion, the search for patterning in the distribution of craft-related artifacts and economic facilities is frustrating. Nagging doubts remain about whether economic redundancy and apparent lack of specialization is a real phenomenon or an artifact of the research methodology used. For the present, the argument that there was a generally more mechanical than organic mode of economic solidarity in the Rosario polity will have to do. A final, equally difficult, analytical step remains. I need to document the Rosario polity's position on the political–organizational continuum between segmenting and non-segmenting polities (Chapter 10).

10

Segmenting versus non-segmenting organization

Social statics and dynamics

The tendency of polities to segment or cohere is an aspect of political organization (dynamics). At the segmenting end of a continuum, polities show a tendency to break apart into constituent districts, while at the non-segmenting end, polities are less prone to break apart, maintaining their cohesiveness over long(er) periods (Chapter 2). It is particularly difficult to determine where the Rosario polity fits along this continuum, and to answer the fifth research question concerning the tendency of Maya polities to segment. In working around the edges of the problem, I examine several themes (listed in decreasing order of generality): structure (social statics) versus organization (social dynamics) and how one moves from the former to the latter, inferring diachronic (possibly cyclical) developments from synchronic evidence, and the relation of the Rosario polity's breakdown to the Classic Maya Collapse.

To reiterate an earlier point (Chapter 2), I draw a distinction between organization and structure. *Structure* (social statics) consists of relatively enduring and abstract norms, principles, or institutions for arranging and regulating relations among societal actors. *Organization* (social dynamics) is a contingent situational set of activities and pragmatic behaviors on the part of societal actors (after Firth 1964). My prior analysis has concentrated on structure (Chapters 5–9), with a problem orientation tailored closely to the chronological possibilities and limitations of settlement data (Chapter 4). A climax–crash view of settlement development allowed interpretation of patterns detectable from single-period settlement maps, according to principles of political structure. To get at questions of organization with such material is exceedingly more difficult. For example, segmentation may be a rather abrupt process masked in the palimpsests on single-period settlement maps. Without repeating my earlier debates about the relative uses of structural and processual approaches, suffice it to say that each one has its own strengths and weaknesses and a study of political segmentation benefits from both approaches (Chapter 4).

In less than ideal circumstances, the nettle is grasped by depending on hypothetical relations between positions on the first four structural continua to infer positions on the continuum between segmenting and non-segmenting organization. Segmentary (decentralized) polities with pyramidal regimes, group stratification, and mechanical economic solidarity will tend to be found towards the continuum's segmenting end. Unitary (centralized) polities with hierarchical regimes, individual (contractual) stratification, and organic economic solidarity will tend to be found towards the non-segmenting end (Chapter 2). In this way of moving from social statics to dynamics, the middle range theoretical generalizations about structure and organization (set out above) are taken to be essentially sound.

The Rosario polity as a whole does not exhibit the expected combination of positions on the structural continua, but the divergence is not too serious. Its (mostly) unitary political structure, hierarchical regime, and individual (but ascribed) political stratification all suggest that the Rosario polity should be placed towards the organization continuum's stable non-segmenting end. The polity's mechanical economic solidarity suggests placement towards the unstable end, but this economic continuum is relatively more poorly documented. Therefore, positions on the first three continua (and the suggestion of organizational stability) should be given more weight (Chapter 11 includes more detailed discussion of these substantive conclusions).

An earlier discussion of the climax–crash perspective (Chapter 4) hinged on the hypothesis that the Rosario polity collapsed rather suddenly, around AD 950–1,000. The importance of collapse themes is determined by the inescapable fact that the polity's finale appears less mysterious than its development. The continuum between segmenting and non-segmenting organization has much to do with political collapse (although logically, it can also refer to growth and development processes). It would be premature to take the Rosario polity collapse as a radical disconfirmation of the generalizations which suggest that its unitary political structure should be relatively stable. That the Rosario polity may have been on the receiving end of geopolitical developments elsewhere in the Maya Lowlands reinforces the idea. This places some of the responsibility for collapse outside the polity. Another, more general, reason for not jumping to conclusions is that an evaluation of the Rosario polity's political structure and organization needs to be checked by controlled comparison with other Maya polities. It becomes unhelpful, dogmatic falsificationism (Gándara 1981) to require that all positions on the various continua correspond exactly to theoretical expectations in each and every individual case (seen in isolation). At a minimum, it would make sense to compare polities that collapsed quickly to polities that endured for relatively long periods. Since no prehispanic Maya or Mesoamerican polities were completely collapse-proof, it becomes a matter of judging and comparing their relative durations. Controlled comparison would set up the possibility of identifying any consistent correlations between kinds of political structure and organizational propensities towards fragmentation.

Let me now examine the issue of statics to dynamics with reference to the specific research questions that have guided analysis of the Rosario polity. Question 2c, concerning the implications of pyramidal regimes for political stability, is moot for the Rosario polity as a whole (until it can be compared to other polities), since the polity was found to have a more hierarchical than pyramidal regime. However, there is relevant internal variation in which the lower section appears to have a slightly more pyramidal regime than the upper section (Chapter 7). This pattern raises interesting questions for future research aimed at discovering differences in political stability between the two sections and evaluating their relation to political structural differences (through controlled comparison).

Another processual question (3c), concerning the relation of ascriptive group stratification to growth in the number of districts (through cleavage) and to a higher tendency to fission, is also moot for the Rosario polity pending comparison to other polities. Nor is there internal variation setting up the possibility of smaller (section)-scale comparison, since group stratification clearly is absent in all the districts. Changing the terms of the question, differences in the pressure of contenders on the supply of political offices in each section (Chapter 8) provide some variation to work with. If a relatively higher number of contenders per political office indicates a greater degree of pressure on political resources and a greater potential for conflict, such a potential was considerably higher in the lower section as compared to the upper section (Chapter 8, Table 22). From this static datum, we can infer that there was a greater (dynamic) potential for the lower section to break apart. Again, this inference would have to be tested by more direct means, but at least it is possible to use the static information to develop some ideas about the political system's weak and potentially unstable points.

Finally, question 5, concerning the links between segmentary political structure and strong secessionist tendencies among districts, is moot for the Rosario polity, without other polities against which to compare and calibrate it. At any rate, the Rosario polity does not appear to be markedly segmentary on most of the indices used. However, relevant internal variation does appear. It would be interesting to find out whether the lower section's segmentary structure made it less stable.

Another way of arguing from statics to dynamics involves looking at spatial patterning in the distribution of power. In segmentary polities, it is the districts on the polity's edges that most easily separate and form new polities or join a competing polity, since centralized control decreases as one moves outward from the center. In relatively non-segmenting unitary polities, centralized control is exercised more evenly throughout the polity's extent (Southall 1956; Chapter 2). The alert reader will realize that ability to test this is severely hampered by the often-mentioned plateau effect. Distances in the Rosario Valley are too short to make a difference for delivering sanctions and/or exercising control. If only for future reference when working at larger scales, the settlement pattern implications of concentric control patterns may be sketched out. A polity with consistent segmenting tendencies will have its peripheral paramount centers attaining a relatively great political importance (seen in the civic-ceremonial complex) when compared to other paramount centers closer to the center. Finding such a settlement pattern, one might argue that the polity had fissioning potential. Alternately, a polity without segmenting tendencies will have peripheral paramount centers of normal or lesser importance when compared to interior centers and from this static patterning it might be argued that there was potential for stability and cohesion.[1] While the plateau effect would tend to invalidate this as a test, the observed pattern of alternating centralized and decentralized pockets (Chapter 11) does not consistently meet either of the expectations.

Development cycles

To help us move from social statics to dynamics with large-scale settlement evidence, an important concept is the possibility that differences in settlement patterns reflect stages in the operation of a development cycle. The reasoning needed is generically similar to that used by cultural evolutionists (Service 1971). In a nutshell, different ethnographic groups are taken by cultural evolutionists to represent different stages in an evolutionary sequence of development from simple to complex structure and organization. Here, my reasoning diverges from this belief in the sense that there is no exclusive commitment to linear onward and upward evolutionary schemes. Instead, I consider at least the possibility of cycling, implying back and forth flux. Also, I heed a pertinent critique of cultural evolutionist reasoning, to the effect that in turning statics into history there is an underestimation of how much the social forms under study have been affected by interaction with contemporaneous social groups of similar or different levels of development (Wolf 1982). Since this problem applies just as well to cyclical interpretations, the criticism is useful as a brake on the tendency to interpret all variation as representing stages rather than structural differences. Finally, it is worth emphasizing that conceptualizing a static data set as a freeze-frame of the variety of stages in an ongoing (cyclical) process owes much to seminal thinking about the domestic cycle and its effects on synchronically perceived patterns of household composition and residence (Fortes 1962; Goody 1962).

Cyclical interpretations of Maya development (Chapter 2) propose that there was a periodic alternance between relatively large and complex forms of political structure and relatively small and simple forms (Jones 1979; Freidel 1983a; Farris 1984; Sanders 1981). Much of the inspiration for this perspective comes from the ethnohistory of Northern Yucatan, especially the successive rise and fall of centralizing megapolities (empires) at Chichen Itza and Mayapan. Not coincidentally, etic cyclical interpretations of Maya political development correspond fairly well to emic Maya theories of history and politics. This results from the apparently good fit between Maya views of their political development and its actual unfolding. The latter is understood from archaeological analysis and etic historiography applied to the native sources. Increasingly acute dynamic interpretations of emic Maya notions of cyclical time and history and their impact on political behavior are now available (Bricker 1981; Edmonson 1979, 1982, 1986; Puleston 1979). Also relevant to cyclical developments in Maya prehistory are possible climate cycles (Folan, Gunn *et al.* 1983). That there was a close temporal correlation between the two kinds of cycles (climatic and political) and that the climate cycles may provide a compelling background for the political cycles (without providing a comprehensive explanation for them) seems a sensible working hypothesis.

Of greatest relevance to my analysis is the example provided by a typology of political systems in immediate pre-Contact Period Yucatan (Roys 1957). Three types of political systems co-existed among 16 provinces. One type had centralized leadership with a ruler (*halach uinic*) living at a capital. Another consisted of a fairly loose confederacy of local rulers (*batabs*), generally sharing a patronymic. The final type consisted of very loose alliances of diverse *batabs* who only united in response to serious outside threats. The types are treated synchronically in much the same way that social anthropologists constructed synchronic typologies of household composition or post-marital residence rules, searching for norms (before Fortes introduced the domestic cycle). Looking at the typology through the lenses provided by domestic cycle interpretations (Fortes 1962; Goody ed. 1962), it makes sense to hypothesize that the political types represent stages in a cycle between centralized and decentralized structure (de Montmollin 1980; see also Farriss 1984: 148, 241, for the more radical suggestion that Roys' typology breaks up a continuum of political arrangements which are in a situation of constant dynamic and not necessarily cyclical flux).

Similar reasoning is applicable to patterns of variation at three scales of settlement in the Rosario Valley – household, site, and region. At the same time, it helps to maintain a fairly sceptical attitude (inspired by Wolf's critiques of stage typologies) and use some approximate tests for deciding whether differences are primarily stage-related or structural. While these are not always mutually exclusive options, it proves interesting to try to differentiate between them.

An earlier investigation of cycling at the household scale analyzes settlement from El Rosario (Chapter 8; de Montmollin n.d.c). I repeat the essential arguments here because they so clearly exemplify a procedure of moving from statics to dynamics through distributional arguments applied to the settlement record. One starts with the observation that all the housegroups at El Rosario (and indeed elsewhere in the valley) have between one and four dwellings. The climax–crash assumption (Chapter 4) is mobilized to justify comparison and analysis of variability among housegroups (discounting palimpsest effects).[2] The Domestic Cycle Hypothesis proposes that the major source of variability in the number of dwellings per housegroup is the fact that housegroups had attained different stages in a domestic cycle. An alternative Ranking Hypothesis proposes that the sole source of variability in the number of dwellings per housegroup is a set of sumptuary restrictions on the size of households according to which ranked sociopolitical stratum they belong. The assumption is that members of higher-ranking strata would be allowed larger household sizes. For the Domestic Cycle Hypothesis to be accepted, there should be no strict correlation for housegroups between a high number of dwellings and high sociopolitical ranking (details in de Montmollin n.d.c). At El Rosario (and throughout the valley) there is a slight tendency for high numbers of dwellings and high sociopolitical status to co-occur. But the numerous exceptions, part of a spread across sociopolitical ranks of housegroups with different numbers of dwellings, lead to the conclusion that a modified Domestic Cycle Hypothesis is more plausible than the Ranking Hypothesis. In sum, an analysis of the settlement record at El Rosario (and other sites) gives us some clues as to whether it represents the end product of domestic (housegroup-scale) cycling processes.

Although its substance is different from the household-scale arguments just reviewed, a site (or community) cycling argument uses a similar rationale including climax–crash assumptions and distributional analyses. Differences among sites may indeed be structural for a set of contemporaneously operating sites. Or else a contributing factor to the same differences might be the stage reached in a site growth cycle. While choosing between the alternatives is difficult when using single-period distribution maps (Chapter 4), all is not entirely without hope. Simple distributional arguments are available to help determine whether differences among sites correspond to different stages reached in a growth cycle. A Site Growth Cycle Hypothesis proposes that, as sites grow and develop (get larger populations), they take on a greater political importance (a whiff of information-processing efficiency logic enters here [Johnson 1978]). Assuming a climax–crash form of settlement history, the operation of site growth cycling should produce a settlement record in which site comparisons show several indicators of a regular relationship between demographic size and political importance. These indicators are: constant TDI (Figure 15), constant TLI (Figure 15), constant pyramid-population ratios for sites, and close correspondence between PH rank (Table 2) and site demographic-size rank. None of the indicators appear, except possibly the last one (Figures 12–14). On this evidence, differences among sites are not accounted for primarily by different stages reached in a growth cycle. It is more likely that the sites' structural positions in a political system underlie the differences among the sites.[3] It is an interesting puzzle to try to distinguish whether structural factors, cycle-stage factors, or combinations of these are producing differences among sites. But ultimately the question may be dropped (or placed in a black box) in order to move forward with a synchronic comparative analysis of what the site differences imply (Chapter 6).

Shifting from the site to the regional (district) scale, the attempt to distinguish between cycle-stage and structural determinants for differences among districts draws on a similar rationale to that used for studying site (or domestic) cycling. A Regional Growth Cycle Hypothesis proposes that, as districts grow and develop (acquiring larger populations), they become either more or less centralized and unitary. The direction of the trend is less important than its consistency, so there is no pressing reason to try to choose between these options.[4] Assuming a climax–crash settlement history, if this growth cycle hypothesis were valid, a comparison of districts would show that the sets of small underdeveloped districts and large developed districts are found at the opposite ends of the centralization subcontinuum. Comparisons approximately meet this expectation. Smaller districts are grouped towards the centralized pole (Zorrillo, Nuestra Señora, Chihuahua, Momón, upper section). Larger districts are grouped towards the decentralized pole (Rosario, Santa Inés North, Santa Inés South, lower section).[5] This could indicate a trend of development from initial centralization to eventual decentralization, possibly leading to ultimate breakdown. Whether this apparent development is part of a unidirectional sequence or a proper cycle is impossible to tell because the climax–crash perspective has a built-in simplifying assumption that one will see growth rather than decline stages in a cycle. The ethnohistoric sources that inspire some of the cyclical interpretations of Postclassic Maya political developments lend support to cycling as a serious possibility to be investigated for the Classic Period. Archaeological testing difficulties aside, the synchronic distributional study supports the idea that the stage reached in a (unidirectional or cyclical) development sequence could have been a determinant of differences in centralization among districts within the Rosario polity.

But the correlation between population size and degree of centralization may be related to a variety of factors besides developmental stage (Chapter 11). One of the reasons for rejecting a cycle-stage interpretation is the small likelihood that districts within the unitary Rosario polity had the autonomy to go through a cycle without being importantly affected by their structural position within that polity. Faced with such ambiguity about whether cycle stage or some other more structural factors contribute most importantly to perceived differences in centralization among districts, it again makes most sense to place growth and development in a black box. Then, one can go on to compare and assess structural political implications of differences in district settlement patterns.

The Rosario polity and the Maya collapse

By far the most dramatic event visible in the diachronic sequence of the Rosario Valley settlement record is the political and demographic collapse between the Late/Terminal Classic Period and the Early Postclassic Period. On the other side of the Late/Terminal Classic Period, there is an apparent settlement hiatus in the Early Classic Period which has had the natural effect of turning attention towards the polity's collapse rather than its growth. Evidently, the Rosario polity's demise at the very end of the Classic Period is another instance of the larger Maya collapse phenomenon, which is so perennially interesting to Mayanists (Culbert 1974; Culbert ed. 1973; Sabloff and Andrews eds. 1986; Chase and Rice eds. 1985; Lowe 1985). A study of the Rosario polity does not provide big answers to the big questions that Mayanists have previously asked about The Maya Collapse. Rather, the aim here is to argue for continuing reformulation of the Maya collapse problem(s), before briefly reviewing possible factors contributing to the Rosario polity collapse.

Understanding Maya collapse(s) would benefit greatly from controlled comparison. Mesoamerican prehistory is replete with collapses of varying degrees of severity, and these invite detailed comparative study in order to isolate immediate causes from more generic causes. Possible generic causes relate to the fact that no Mesoamerican polity ever lasted more than a few hundred years, meaning that there may have been a tendency to collapse built into the political structure of Mesoamerican polities. Whether or not such generic features can be identified, we must begin to acquire a better understanding of Mesoamerican political structural aspects that might encourage or impede political collapses. One giant step forward is to discard the idea that polities which can be typed as states (rather than chiefdoms) have somehow attained a high level of stability (Service 1971; Wright 1977). This may be so in a relative sense (compared to chiefdoms), but clearly instability in such things as succession to high office continues to be a problem for states (however defined). In fact, for Mesoamerica one of the key structural political aspects (strongly suggested by ethnohistory) is the kind of intra-elite conflict that leads to instability and fissioning tendencies at the political apex. Such tendencies would make a polity subject to breakdown from within and/or vulnerable to outside disruption. Concepts such as this one from middle range political anthropological theory may eventually prove more fruitful than more abstract (reductionist) concepts such as hypercoherence from systems theory (Flannery 1972) or information-processing overload from information theory (Blanton *et al.* 1981). But, whatever level of abstraction one works at, a key reason for stressing controlled comparisons is the value of looking at cases of polities (or networks of polities) that collapsed and cases of polities that endured, at least relatively longer, at the end of the Classic Period.

Often, when Mayanists have tried to relate the Maya Collapse to collapses elsewhere in Mesoamerica, the argument has been cast according to this format: collapse event *x* in Central Mexico occurs and then has a backwash effect leading to collapse in the Maya area (Willey 1977; Morley *et al.* 1983). This invokes what are referred to as external causes for the collapse (Sabloff 1973). To break out of this format, it would be interesting to have more analytical studies relating Maya collapse(s) to other Mesoamerican collapses, in something like the controlled comparison framework advocated here. Good starting points are the tri-regional study by Blanton and others (1981) or a comparative effort by Cowgill (1979). Another example of a move in this direction is the attempt to fit the Late Classic Lowland Maya collapse into a diachronic sequence of centralization and decentralization phases seen as part of a great cycle (Freidel 1983a). Reformulating the Maya collapse problem as part of a great cycle is most interesting and raises the possibility of controlled comparison for whole cycles not just collapses. The interesting parallels and divergences between the Maya cycle and the central-ization–decentralization cycling that occurred in and around the Basin of Mexico (Sanders *et al.* 1979) and the Valley of Oaxaca (Blanton *et al.* 1982) become an issue.

A focus on such cycles of political centralization and decentralization requires a critical shift in the unit of analysis from whole culture areas (as homes of civilizations) or from individual sites (both units towards the extremes of a settlement-scale continuum) to units of intermediate scale and greater relevance to political analysis – the polity or the network of interacting polities (Price 1977; Renfrew and Cherry eds. 1986). Here, another major difficulty associated with earlier Maya Collapse studies presents itself (especially with reference to studies in the 1973 conference volume [Culbert ed. 1973], but also to some subsequent treatments [e.g., Culbert 1977; Hosler *et al.* 1983; Morley *et al.* 1983: ch. 5]). The arena for collapse is the Maya culture area while the phenomenon which collapses is Maya civilization, both concepts of extreme nebulosity for political analysis. Internal causes relate to things happening in the Maya culture area (or at least its Lowland portion), while external causes come from outside the culture area, usually Central Mexico or the Gulf Coast Putun area (Sabloff 1973). But, as one begins to think in terms of the numerous polities that existed in the Lowland Maya culture area during the Classic Period, it becomes necessary to conceptualize additional scales of political interaction. Consequently, there can be phenomena (or causes) internal to a polity (such as the Rosario polity), phenomena internal to a network of interacting polities (such as those in the Upper Grijalva Tributaries), phenomena internal to the whole Maya culture area (several networks of interacting polities), and, finally, phenomena internal to a still larger entity, incorporating several linguistic-culture areas (or civilizations) within Mesoamerica. In fairness, some earlier studies did take such nested levels of interaction into account, at least implicitly (e.g., Cowgill 1979; Edmonson 1979; Freidel 1983a; Marcus 1976; Bove 1981). And explicit recognition of the need for comparative work at something like the polity and polity network scales has recently blossomed as a natural outgrowth of the evident variability revealed by intensified research on the political trajectories of many centers within the Maya area, especially from the Late Classic onward (Freidel 1985: 295, 304–308; Sabloff 1986: 114–115; and see more narrowly focused, sometimes polity-specific studies in Sabloff and Andrews eds. 1986; Chase and Rice eds. 1985; plus the very impressive studies from the Copan Valley – Webster 1985a, 1985b; Fash 1986).

The need to calibrate the scale for political analysis is centrally relevant to why the Rosario study cannot be fitted easily into earlier Maya Collapse formulations. For example, my (tiresome) emphasis on the need to respect variability among polities and on the inappropriateness of generalizing about middle range theoretical issues from the vantage of a single-polity (or single-site) case study, without some form of controlled comparison, becomes entirely pointless if the unit of analysis is either Maya civilization or a single Maya site. In the latter case, one gets the previously familiar (but thankfully vanishing) arguments cast according to this format: the Maya collapse viewed from site X (or test pits X, Y, and Z). Factors of local scale and importance are extrapolated to serve as explanations for what happened to Maya civilization in general. In those instances, the individual case study, no matter how small its scale, serves as a microcosm for a much larger-scale problem.

Certainly there are local factors in the Rosario polity that need to be defined and related to its own collapse. Examples of these are: extreme pressure on the land base (with an estimated maximum density of 400 persons per sq km, at least in the core area); a possible climatic drying trend interacting with the first factor (fitting into larger-scale reconstructions of climatic cycling for Mesoamerica – Folan, Gunn *et al.* 1983); fouling of the water supply leading to epidemics (G. Lowe, personal communication 1983); and a problematic high level of elite contention and decentralized structure in parts of the polity, especially the lower section (Chapter 8). Even if they were better documented than they are, it would make little sense to propose such factors as invariable causes for the collapse of Maya civilization everywhere it occurred (i.e., the Maya Collapse as viewed from Valley *X*). One has to understand clearly that the relatively small Rosario polity's temporally late collapse was occurring on one of the very edges of the Lowland Maya linguistic and elite interaction sphere, off the edge of the Usumacinta zone network of polities (Figure 1). It is even possible that the Rosario polity (and other Upper Tributaries polities) had some sort of colonial dependency relation to large Usumacinta zone centers such as Yaxchilán and Bonampak and their polities, further in towards the Maya heartland (Chapter 3; Figure 1). Based on the criteria of lateness, smallness (?), and fringe dependency, the Rosario polity is not a key case from which to extrapolate for traditional Lowland Maya Collapse studies. Furthermore, are there even such things as key cases, entirely representative and microcosmic? Probably not, but on a continuum of most to least microcosmic, the Rosario polity has to lie towards the least microcosmic end. One needs to appreciate the Rosario polity's collapse in relation to the fact that it was a peripheral part of the Maya world, whose more central zones were in a collapsing condition for the last 150–200 years of the Late Classic Period. It is easy to imagine (and less easy to document, but see Marcus 1976; Bove 1981; Lowe 1985) that this collapse worked itself through networks of polities.[6] Thus, factors external to the Rosario polity, and having to do with the collapse process in other more central or else more precociously decadent parts of the Maya world, have to loom large in an explanation of how and why the Rosario polity collapsed. In this style of explanation, the Rosario polity collapsed because it was too intimately (hypercoherently – Flannery 1972) linked politically (and ritually) to a wider network of Lowland Maya polities or because it was too economically dependent on exchange links with such polities. Thus it withered away when the other Maya polities were disrupted by political and economic collapse.[7]

Arguments about the Rosario polity's dependent status with reference to developments elsewhere in the Maya area follow the format: collapse event *x* happens in Area *X* and has a backwash effect on Area *Y*. While this formula is probably inadequate when used to link up Central Mexican and Maya collapse episodes (at a supra-civilization scale), it would seem to be more applicable for linking the Rosario polity (and Upper Tributaries polity network) to the more central Maya Lowlands. The required, critically close, political (and indeed economic) relations are more plausibly found at this smaller scale. Furthermore, nothing entailed by this kind of argument prevents one from making a controlled comparison of the Rosario polity and other Lowland Maya polities. For, at the end of a long research road, there is a more autonomous role for the Rosario polity, as one case study in controlled comparisons aimed at isolating the structural features that either inhibited or promoted collapse in the decentralization phases of Mesoamerican developmental cycles.

In conclusion, as a preliminary attempt to balance the internal and external factors in the Rosario polity collapse, I present the following "just so story." Political collapse in the Rosario polity followed from overdeveloped (hypercoherent) links with the already collapsing central polities in the Maya Lowlands, through a kind of backwash effect. This was exacerbated by local weaknesses in the political system, such as the lower section's high potential for elite conflict over access to political office and its relatively low degree of centralization. The backwash effect occurred to a large extent in the ideological sphere, with a breakdown of the native theory for running the polity. There are two possibilities. If the ideological backwash leaves some room for sectarian argument about the theory, this is compatible with a situation featuring local elite conflict. But if there is total general agreement about the native political theory's breakdown (along the lines suggested by Puleston 1979), this leads to a quiet end, not with a bang, but a whimper. The latter process is much more difficult for us to imagine, but certainly in the realm of possibility for the Maya (Puleston 1979; Bricker 1981; Edmonson 1982, 1986). At any rate, the external backwash effects were probably more political–ideological than economic (exchange-related). Depopulation in the Rosario Valley was related more closely to local environmental phenomena, as the agricultural system was balanced on a knife edge and unable to absorb political–ideological shocks. Finally, the strong local impact of the collapse can be judged from the fact that, except for a relatively minor amount in the Early Postclassic Period, no significant settlement activity occurs in the Rosario Valley up to recent times. As far as it is possible to judge, this is also generally the case for the Upper Tributaries, except for a few isolated pockets of Postclassic and Colonial settlement (Blake 1985: ch. 9; Lee 1984). In its having a severe near total abandonment following a great demographic climax, the Rosario Valley and Upper Tributaries perhaps most closely resemble the Puuc Zone of Yucatan, among the Maya collapse cases available for comparison.[8]

At this point of collapse, we reach the end of the step-by-step archaeological documentation of where the Rosario polity can be situated within a bundle of continua of variation (Table 1). It now remains to recapitulate the political characterization of the Rosario polity and to take the analysis a step further by further exploring relations between positions on the several continua and relations of some of these positions to other variables more external to the political system – environment, demographic size and cycling, and spatial location (Chapter 11). To set the substantive results in wider archaeological context, it also remains to re-examine general theoretical and methodological issues revolving around the choices made in constructing a study of an ancient complex polity (Chapter 11).

11

Archaeological study of Maya polities

Conceptualizing an ancient polity

I selected bundled continua of variation in place of societal typologies in order to conceptualize the Rosario polity as an example of an ancient complex polity. Why was this? By so doing, some difficulties associated with societal typologies could be avoided. The full range of these difficulties concerned: resistance of whole societies (or polities) to typological analysis; difficulties of choosing scale and locating boundaries for societal types; undue reification of society; undue reification of societal types; inappropriately categorical thinking (for the study of continuous variation); inability to account for change from one type to another; a priori techno-environmental determinism (entailed by using a typological approach for societies but not for their physical environments); real rather than nominal definitions (Service 1985) for types, with assumed co-variation of several attribute levels and elimination of worthwhile research problems; and, finally, dubious extrapolation from documented attribute levels to undocumented attribute levels (Chapter 2).

The bundled continua approach derives from work done in political anthropology. The central premise is that it is "useful to place phenomena on a continuum, with the expectation that to do so will make it possible to locate cluster points" along several of the aligned continua (Easton 1959: 239). Reasons for the recurring clusters may then be sought. With such an approach, awkwardly multivariate societal types are broken down into more easily studied constituent variables. The existence of continuous as well as discontinuous variation is allowed for by avoiding a priori polar-categorical thinking. The object of study is given a nominal rather than a real definition (Service 1985), thus avoiding an essentialist approach which seeks to identify and discuss the true aspects of phenomena. An example of an essentialist approach to politics for ancient complex polities would be that which seeks to identify archaeologically *the* origins of *the* state and then to place these in an explanatory context. In contrast, a non-essentialist approach to the same general subject would select a conceptualization of politics (and political complexity) which meets the following broad requirements. First, the conceptualization should touch on interesting issues. What is interesting is, of course, a relative thing, but from my anthropological–archaeological viewpoint, I class as interesting many of those issues that exercise political anthropologists. Second, the conceptualization should be analytically flexible and it should allow one to document (at least some of) its elements in the archaeological record.

In line with such a non-essentialist approach, I constructed five continua in order to study the Rosario polity (Table 1). The first continuum between segmentary and unitary political structure concerns the nature and inter-relation of districts. This continuum is further broken down into three major and two minor subcontinua: decentralization versus centralization, replication versus differentiation, low versus high integration, *societas* versus *civitas*, and upward versus downward delegation of authority. A second continuum between pyramidal and hierarchical political regimes deals with decision-making (executive) and decision-implementing (administrative) aspects. A third set of dimensions incorporates varieties of political stratification (group versus individual stratification, ascription versus achievement) concerning access to political offices. A fourth continuum between mechanical and organic solidarity covers basic economic underpinnings (outside the strictly political sphere). And, finally, a fifth continuum between segmenting and non-segmenting political organization deals with cohesion among districts, with special reference to problems of territorial integrity and growth in political scale. The five continua are aligned with one another according to prevailing Grand Theory views about the relations between the variables they cover (Table 1). At one end of the spectrum lie unitary (centralized, differentiated, integrated, *civitas*) political structure, a hierarchical regime, ascribed individual stratification, organic economic solidarity, and non-segmenting political organization. At the opposite end lie segmentary (decentralized, replicated, unintegrated, *societas*) political structure, a pyramidal regime, ascribed group stratification, mechanical economic solidarity, and segmenting political organization.

A political portrait of the Rosario polity

With a detailed analysis of the five continua of variation in hand (Chapters 5–10), I am now in a position to paint a comprehensive portrait of the Rosario polity's political structure and organization. Where possible, some potential reasons for particular forms of political structure and organization are sketched out. The specific research questions molded to the continua of variation (Table 1) provide a framework for discussion. Additionally, Tenam Rosario, as a political microcosm of its hinterland, is viewed in comparative Mesoamerican perspective, and the possibilities for controlled comparison of the Rosario polity with other Maya polities are sketched out.

Let me begin, then, with the issues raised in question 1: To what degree did Classic Maya political structure feature a decentralized, replicated, and loosely integrated arrangement of districts? The investigation of the segmentary to unitary continuum was centrally important and it received the most detailed attention. The principal focus was on three subcontinua, having to do with centralization (Chapter 5), differentiation (Chapter 6), and integration (Chapter 6). The most closely documented is the first of these. Analysis of the other two is largely dependent on re-interpreting results attained when studying centralization. In these conclusions, the continuum from segmentary to unitary political structure is considered as a whole, with most emphasis on centralization (and the terms unitariness and centralization are used somewhat interchangeably).

The Rosario polity as a whole shows a tendency towards unitary structure with reference to several archaeological measures (Figure 15) compared across a political settlement-hierarchy (or PH, Table 2). The measures suggesting unitary structure are: tribute drawing centralization (declining TDI values down the PH); tribute imposition centralization (some decline in TLI values down the PH); differentiation of tribute base size (TBS); and vertical integration (declining TDI values down the PH, some decline in TLI values down the PH, and a hierarchical political regime featuring vertical differentiation and thus specialization of political functions at different PH levels). To set against such tendencies towards unitariness, there is a slight tendency towards more segmentary structure with reference to the following measures: paramount forced settlement (some increase in paramount forced settlement values down the PH); and aggregate forced settlement (some increase in aggregate forced settlement values down the PH). With respect to centralization indices, the Rosario polity seems to be more unitary in terms of indirect control (tribute drawing and imposition centralization) rather than direct control (forced settlement centralization). Conclusions about the Rosario polity's degree of unitariness (or any other of its political characteristics) can eventually be compared to conclusions about other Maya polities. An emphasis on comparison flows naturally from the fact that we are dealing with continua and differences of degree rather than absolutes. This makes it important to contrast and compare a number of cases to get an idea of some of the determinants that contribute to the differences.

For the moment, to get this all-important comparative perspective, smaller district-scale analytical units are available within the Rosario polity. These are the sections and pockets. To compare these districts with a view to understanding the variability that they display, a useful tack is to study their spatial disposition with reference to one another. Such spatial disposition is equivalent in some senses to a political framework or environment within which the districts operate (subsequently referred to as the *spatial-structural political environment*). Additionally, several other factors are potentially related to differences and similarities among the districts. These factors are scale (of population rather than territory), physical environment, and stage reached in a development cycle.[1] Scale, physical environment, and cycle-stage are outside the political system, while the spatial-structural political environment is evidently more political and within the system. Since the confronting of differences in unitariness with differences in these factors is part of an explanatory effort, why are the political (and economic) variables treated in the other four continua not also considered here as factors affecting (or being affected by) differences in centralization among districts? Doing so would correspond more closely to Easton's (1959) research program for political anthropology, which comprises a kind of model for my study (see discussion below). The reason for not bringing these other political variables into the analysis at this point is a simple practical one. With few exceptions, it turns out that the variables from the other four continua do not show enough district-to-district variation in their values to provide an effective avenue for controlled comparison with variations in degrees of unitariness among districts. Clearly, however, these variables have a (greater) chance of showing disparate values when the Rosario polity and other Maya polities come to be compared. Thus, they should become more useful for controlled comparisons at the polity scale.

Let me now move on to a review and analysis of the similarities and differences in unitariness between sections. Where appropriate, I check section-scale findings against the pocket-scale patterning of similarities and differences. The upper section shows a consistently more unitary structure than the lower section, most evidently in the degrees of paramount forced settlement centralization and vertical integration. Differences between the sections are less marked concerning the degrees of tribute drawing and tribute imposition centralization and the differentiation of tribute base size. Differences are thus stronger with reference to direct as opposed to indirect control. How can differences between sections be related to demographic scale, physical environment, cycle-stage, or spatial-structural political environment?

There is a clear demographic-scale difference between sections, with the lower section having at least three times more population. This population size difference is much more marked than any difference in territorial size. Additionally, territorial dimensions are probably too small to directly shape political structure because of the plateau effect in which distances are too short to present spatial efficiency problems. Essentially there is a pattern in which the demographically larger lower section is clearly less unitary in its structure than the smaller upper section. At the pocket scale, the correspondence between differences in population size and political structure (seen for the sections) begins to break down. There is no longer as regular a relation between larger population size and more segmentary structure.

How might the section-scale correspondence between size and political structure be accounted for? Does the fact that there are more people to govern in the lower section make it harder to maintain closely centralized unitary control? Does this contribute to its relative political segmentariness? Information theorists might answer affirmatively (Johnson 1978, 1982). The reasoning would be that, both sections having similar numbers of political hierarchy levels, one has much more population to be governed and therefore experiences greater information-management problems. These problems then lead to a more decentralized structure, a low degree of centralization being associated with poor management. But the information-theoretic scenario is probably too one-dimensional to account for political structural differences of the kind considered here. These differences involve more than just information-managing efficiency. Even if one stays within the general framework of information theory, the addition of energetics complicates matters:

> The general model called for decrease in centralization with system
> growth, but the [Oaxaca] phases...had both growth and
> more centralization...integration and centralization can both be augmented
> relative to previous states of the system when the growth in size is very

great. In other words, with a sufficiently large increase in energy, which having more people would provide, the organization... can afford to be more centralized. (Kowalewski *et al.* 1983: 50)

Furthermore, by moving away from the information-theory perspective altogether, it becomes possible to argue that this perspective is based on an analogy to the operation of business corporations which is inapplicable to ancient complex political systems (R. McC. Adams 1981: 76–78). Could there also be an equivalent of the spatial plateau effect which applies to population scale considered here? Is it possible that below a certain scale, population differences might be too small to have clearly problematic implications for information-processing? As there are probably no straightforward cross-culturally valid principles to apply (*contra* Johnson 1982), there is room for diversity of viewpoints on these questions. At one extreme, information-processing problems seem to become important as soon as you have six people (Johnson 1978)! Here, I am suggesting that differences of thousands of people[2] may not produce enough in the way of information-processing problems to be a relevant factor accounting for differences in centralization.

For a better political understanding, population scale and political structure have to be considered in terms of elite population as well as general population. Most of my discussion of elite population and its distribution is subsumed under the theme of political stratification (Chapter 8, and below). Here I touch only briefly on the question of elite population as it affects the relation between demographics and political unitariness. The lower section is larger-scale in both the absolute and relative sizes of its elite population group (Tables 21 and 22). The elite population difference between sections probably contributes more importantly to differences in their degrees of centralization than any general population differences. The proportionally much larger elite group in the lower section would present proportionally greater obstacles to effective centralization. On a related issue, the much greater degree of elite forced settlement at the upper section PH2 center compared to the lower section PH2 center matches the other trends in the evidence which suggest a greater degree of centralization in the upper section.

Are there environmental distinctions between sections which might contribute to differences in their political structure? The environmental distinctions between the upper and lower valley are not major qualitative ones, with reference to such factors as vegetation, soil, mineral resources, building materials, or (altitude-related) climate zones. However, clear differences of degree exist in agricultural resource endowments (Chapters 6 and 9). The lower section has a much greater absolute and relative amount of favored valley-bottom lands. But the effects on political structure are indirect. Such environmental differences have an impact only in the sense that they permit differences in population. And raw population differences are probably not critically important in accounting for the structural differences between the sections.

A possible factor shaping settlement (and thus structural) differences observed between sections is a district-scale developmental cycle propelled by demographic growth. In such a cycle, regular trends towards either greater or lesser centralization would occur as districts pass through the cycle stages. If such a cycle were suddenly cut off in its growth phase (using a climax–crash perspective), the two sections might have reached different stages in the cycle, accounting for the observed differences between them.[3] The question of regional developmental cycling was addressed earlier with emphasis on the difficulties of inferring dynamics from statics (Chapter 10). Suffice it to repeat here that even if cycling were a factor (and at the district scale it may have been), any cycle-related differences probably lasted long enough to have structurally affected the political system's operation. It seems unlikely that any differences in centralization among districts would automatically disappear as they reached the same stage in a demographic growth cycle.

Does the spatial-structural political environment account for differences in degree of centralization between sections? One feature to look at is the kinds of polities located on the polity's northeast and southwest sides.[4] On the northeast, there is a rugged area which appears to have relatively light settlement and marginal agricultural resources. This is a kind of buffer area extending towards the Morelos polity (Figure 2). In contrast, the Rosario polity's southwest edge borders on what appears to be a heavily populated area, with large expanses of flat valley-bottom and prime agricultural resources running through to the Ojo de Agua polity (Figure 2). That this last polity was centralized is tentatively indicated by its capital center's civic-ceremonial magnitude (Bryant and Lowe 1980). The lower section's relatively greater segmentariness (especially marked in Greater Santa Inés) may then be attributable in part to the fact that it is wedged between two centralized political entities: the Ojo de Agua polity and a district comprising the Rosario polity's heartland which includes Tenam Rosario and the Rosario Pocket. In contrast, the upper section is bounded on only one side by a centralized political entity, the same Rosario polity heartland. The political entity to its northeast, the Rosario-Morelos buffer, appears to be relatively decentralized and segmentary.

A pattern of alternating centralized and decentralized districts emerges more sharply at the pocket scale. An alternating pattern is most clearly defined for paramount forced settlement centralization, less clearly defined for tribute imposition centralization, and least clearly defined for tribute drawing centralization. It follows that this pattern is also not as clearly defined for integration measures since these are the same ones used to chart tribute centralization. From northeast to southwest, the sequence of alternating segmentary and unitary pockets is: unitary Zorrillo, segmentary Nuestra Señora, unitary Chihuahua-Momón-Tenam Rosario, unitary Rosario, and segmentary Santa Inés North-South. Political structure at either end of this chain matches the section-scale contrast, with unitary structure at the northeast end and segmentary structure at the southwest end. The alternating pattern for pockets does not seem to be accounted for solely by different stages reached in a demographic growth cycle since population size (as a rough indicator of stage reached in the cycle) does not vary in a completely regular way with degree of centralization (Chapter 10). Perhaps a more important factor accounting for an alternating pattern in degree of unitariness is an inhibiting political backwash effect exercised on their neighbors by districts with unitary political structure. The reasoning behind this is that it is more difficult for districts which have unitary neighbors on both sides of them to develop towards unitariness than it is for districts with unitary neighbors on only one side or on no side at all. Admittedly, this attempt to account for a settlement distribution pushes inference to its limits. And only a small number of cases serve to identify the spatial pattern of alternation in centralized and decentralized districts on which the inference is based. At the section scale, it would be helpful to evaluate the pattern's presence or absence through further survey in neighboring polities.

An alternating centralization-decentralization pattern for the pockets allows me to set aside (at least for this case) the notion that a segmentary polity can be distinguished from a unitary polity by the presence in the segmentary polity of more unitary districts towards the polity's edges, in keeping with a concentric drop in control outward from the center (Chapter 2). Since there seems to be a spatial plateau effect operating, the present case is not an adequate test for the general principle.

The second set of research questions concerns varieties of political regimes. For question 2a, concerning to what degree Classic Maya polities had a pyramidal regime (with replication of political functions at different hierarchical levels), the answer is that the Rosario polity as a whole had a more hierarchical than pyramidal regime. This emerges most clearly when using what are probably the most effective indicators of political hierarchy (the PH and the Civic-Ceremonial Volume Hierarchy [VH]) and the most effective indicator of political function (the Structure Diversity Index [SDI]). Within the polity, the lower section has a more pyramidal regime than the upper section. The pockets show some variability ranging from Santa Inés North at the pyramidal end to Zorrillo at the hierarchical end (details in Chapter 7).

A hierarchical political regime in a system with four levels of hierarchy is in line with predictions from information-theoretic approaches (Johnson 1973, 1978). However, a study of the pyramidal–hierarchical continuum involves something more than counting levels. It brings out differences of degree in political specialization at distinct levels within regimes; an example would be the differences between the upper and lower sections within the polity. Additionally, it is feasible to challenge the information-processing efficiency premises that underlie managerial approaches. This can be done by examining two aspects of the settlement record. These are the distribution of civic-ceremonial buildings with reference to population and the relation between the complexity of site settlement morphology and civic-ceremonial elaboration. In both cases (more so for the first), there were uneven patterns casting doubt on whether information-processing efficiency was a prime determinant of political structure in the Rosario polity (Chapter 7).

Question 2b concerns the possible scale limitations of pyramidal regimes, with special reference to the size of the political community. The question is moot for the Rosario polity as a whole since it evidences a hierarchical regime. But controlled comparisons with other polities having differing degrees of pyramidality and different population sizes should produce worthwhile answers. Presently, some comparisons are possible between sections within the Rosario polity. The more pyramidal regime in the lower section shows no signs of having greater scale limitations since it is larger in population and has essentially the same number of districts and PH levels. The same general conclusions also apply at the pocket scale. But all these findings should be treated sceptically because of the small numbers of cases for comparison and the possibility that the demographic scale is too small to matter (a demographic plateau effect).

Question 2c concerns the implications of a pyramidal regime for political stability, and it is also a line of investigation awaiting controlled comparison with other polities. At the section scale, a theme for further investigation concerns whether the relatively more pyramidal lower section was more stable, less stable, or equally stable when compared to the upper section (Chapter 10).

The third set of research questions revolves around political stratification. For question 3a, concerning to what degree Classic Maya political systems were characterized by group political stratification and ascription in access to political offices, the answer is that group political stratification was absent in the Rosario polity (Chapter 8). Instead, domestic residential patterns suggest that the actors contending for political office were constituted at a more individual household level. Associated with this, there was more ascribed than achieved access to political offices (Chapter 8). This system of individual political stratification may be contrasted with that in other cases where the domestic residential pattern (and occasionally ethnohistory) suggests group political stratification: the Late Classic Copan polity, Late Postclassic Highland Quiche polities, the Late Classic Central Maya Lowland polities, and Late Classic Northern Yucatec polities.

For question 3b, concerning whether ascriptive group stratification was closely linked to a segmentary arrangement of districts, there is an oblique answer for the Rosario polity. This is that individual (but ascriptive not contractual) stratification was associated with more unitary than segmentary political structure. But, as always, the possibility exists of shedding further light on the issues raised through a controlled comparison of the Rosario polity and other polities that provide examples of group or individual political stratification. After evaluating the position of these other polities on the segmentary to unitary continuum, it becomes possible to use a four-way matrix in which relationships between modes of political stratification and degrees of centralization could be evaluated.

Broadening the terms of question 3b leads to a consideration of elite population (however constituted) and its size and distribution around the political system. Relevant concepts are elite forced settlement and the elite fraction or the proportion of the population included in the elite (Chapter 8). Elite forced settlement is as interesting to consider as general (elite plus commoner) forced settlement. Elite forced settlement is measured as the proportion of the total elite group from its district or polity residing at a capital center. The importance of elite forced settlement has to do with the key notion that elite groups were not monolithic, but contained within themselves a potential for fission and conflict (Chapters 5 and 8).

The logic behind elite forced settlement is that one of the policies available to higher-ranking elite members for controlling lower-ranking elite members entails concentrating them into their own political control centers. In the Rosario polity, the degree of elite forced settlement at the capital, Tenam Rosario, is three times greater than the degree of general forced settlement (compare Figures 46 and 16). Less divergent (compared to general forced settlement patterns) is the greater elite forced settlement at the upper section PH2 center compared to the lower section PH2 center (compare Figures 46 and 16). This pattern falls in line with many other lines of evidence that suggest a greater degree of political centralization in the upper section. The lower section has almost twice as large an elite fraction (Table 22) and nearly five times as large a total elite population (Table 21) as the upper section. The larger elite fraction in the lower section probably does contribute importantly to the greater decentralization of its political structure, not so much because of information-processing problems, but because the larger elite group in the lower section presents greater problems for centralization and control (Chapter 8).

The final question (3c) in the third set is processual: Was ascriptive group stratification, if present, closely linked to growth in the number of districts and was this linked to a higher tendency to fission? This is a moot question for the Rosario polity as a whole, given the complete absence of group stratification. But, again, the issues raised can be pursued in a line of investigation featuring controlled comparison with other polities. Testing difficulties associated with this question are considerable and indirect means are required to address it (Chapter 10). Suffice it to mention again that the lower section has a contender per political office ratio about four times higher than the upper section's (Table 22). Following the argument that contender-office relations are critical sources of strain in a political system (Chapter 2; Goody 1966; Burling 1974; Lloyd 1965, 1968), it appears that there was potentially more stress in the lower section because of the greater difficulty in providing political office for all those seeking it. This kind of pressure would be congruent with the greater degree of decentralization in the lower section and might underlie a greater tendency to fission.

The fourth set of questions having to do with the continuum between mechanical and organic economic solidarity receives short shrift for practical and conceptual reasons (Chapter 9). To question 4a, concerning the degree of mechanical versus organic economic solidarity that characterized Classic Maya polities, the answer for the Rosario polity is that there was generally more mechanical than organic solidarity. With reference to measures of economic specialization among the districts, measures which check for relative degrees of involvement in basic agricultural activities, there is no variation of the kind that could be usefully related to variation in political structure. The variation among the economic measures which is of most direct political relevance is that which suggests that Chihuahua, and perhaps part of Rosario, formed a relatively undersettled agricultural reserve around the capital at Tenam Rosario (Chapter 9; de Montmollin 1985c).

Question 4b tries to relate the mechanical–organic continuum to the first and best-studied continuum which has to do with degrees of segmentariness: If there was a markedly mechanical economic solidarity, how closely was this associated with segmentary political structure? The answer for the entire Rosario polity is that mechanical economic solidarity was associated with a more unitary than segmentary political structure. But like so many of these questions applied at the polity scale, controlled comparison with other polities is required to explore further the issues raised. Understanding the relation between modes of economic solidarity and kinds of political structure is a central issue for interpretation of Maya sociopolitical structure and organization, especially in comparison to that of Highland Mesoamerica (Sanders and Price 1968; Sanders 1962, 1963; Webb 1973; Coe 1961, 1965; Parsons and Price 1971; Price 1978). But in studying the Rosario polity, this issue has been skirted in order to concentrate on understanding political structure.

Question 5, concerning whether segmentary Classic Maya political structure entails strong secessionist tendencies, is a moot question with reference to the Rosario polity as a whole, again requiring controlled comparison with other polities. To answer this question directly requires diachronic evidence of the kind that is unavailable in the single-period Rosario settlement record. To circumvent the problem, social dynamics have to be inferred from social statics. In this light, the positions occupied by the Rosario polity on the four structural continua broadly suggest that it should lie towards the stable, non-segmenting end of the continuum. Within the polity, the lower section should have been more unstable than the upper section since it has a more segmentary political structure (Chapter 10).

The Classic Maya Collapse problem (Culbert ed. 1973) is strongly evoked by the general theme of secession (related to political stability and durability) and by the Rosario polity's apparent drastic decline at the end of the Terminal Classic Period (Chapter 10). Since it concerns a single, marginal, and (colonially) dependent polity, the Rosario case cannot be used to propose factors relevant to explanations for the collapse of Maya civilization as a whole (the multitude of polities occupying the Maya culture area in the Classic Period). More realistically, the Rosario polity is one of numerous polities which collapsed over a 150–200 year span, probably in different ways and in response to different mixes of factors (Sabloff and Andrews eds. 1986; Chase and Rice eds. 1985; Lowe 1985). The following local (internal) factors probably contributed to the Rosario polity collapse: extreme pressure on the land base, a climatic drying trend, fouling of the water supply, and problematically high levels of elite contention. Some similar factors probably operated within the Upper Tributaries polity network (keeping in mind that Tenam Rosario was the likely capital of the network). In all probability, external political and economic factors were even more important. This is suggested by the likely linkage of the Rosario polity and other Upper Tributaries polities with Lowland Maya polities closer to the center of the Maya Lowlands. Political and economic disruptions among the latter polities would have rippled out to the Upper Tributaries fringe, with a backwash effect exacerbating any local problems. What seems least uncertain in all this is the severity of the collapse suggested by the lack of recovery (up to the present day) in the Rosario Valley and most other parts of the Upper Tributaries. This pattern contrasts with many other parts of the Maya Lowlands and Highlands where post-collapse Postclassic Period societies were vigorously present.

Cross-cutting many of the themes that emerged in studying the five continua are the findings from a study of the civic-ceremonial zone at the capital Tenam Rosario (Chapter 7, Figure 9; de Montmollin 1988). Tenam Rosario's civic-ceremonial zone shows enough coherence in its layout to indicate a master plan. No other major center in the Upper Tributaries has anything approaching this degree of planning (Chapter 7; Lee *et al.* n.d.). In fact, a comparison of civic-ceremonial layout at Tenam Rosario and Tr-152, which is closest in the relative size of its civic-ceremonial zone, highlights the latter's relatively disorganized layout, which apparently grew over a long time span (Bryant 1984). At Tenam Rosario, a dual replication pattern includes two large plazas of similar layout, each with an associated ballcourt of similar general design. These assemblages flank an apical palace complex. Attached to the edges of this highly structured arrangement are three or four smaller plazas. The apical character and position of the palace complex convincingly casts doubt on the possibility of multicephalous confederative rulership (*multepal* – Roys 1962; Freidel 1983a) such as might be expected in a segmentary polity. By themselves, the two plazas might indicate dual power sharing (even moities). But the unique palace complex between them makes this unlikely. What is most interesting about variability among the plazas is that their layout may represent a political microcosm of Tenam Rosario's hinterland. Developing the idea of a political microcosm, a hierarchical arrangement of the Tenam Rosario plazas may be related to the polity's districts and their centers (in the PH). In this scheme, the palace complex sits at the top of the Tenam plaza hierarchy and represents the whole polity and the PH1 center (Tenam Rosario) itself. The two large replicated plazas occupy a second level in the Tenam plaza hierarchy and represent the two sections and their PH2 centers at the capital. Finally, the three or four small peripheral plazas occupy a third level in the Tenam plaza hierarchy and represent the four pockets and their exclusively PH3 centers at the capital (the pockets with PH2/3 centers are represented by the two large replicated plazas). Interesting implications arise from a political microcosm pattern in Tenam Rosario's civic-ceremonial zone.

Given three levels of political hierarchy within the capital itself, there are two ways in which these can be fitted into the polity-wide PH (Figures 40a and 40b). All the Tenam levels may be placed hierarchically above the PH2 centers, which adds two levels to the overall hierarchy and results in a rather staggering six levels above the basal community! Alternately, only the topmost Tenam level may be placed hierarchically above PH2 centers, making Tenam second level plazas hierarchically equivalent to PH2 centers and Tenam third level plazas hierarchically equivalent to PH3 centers. Pursuing the second possibility, it becomes interesting to consider how the three Tenam levels might intermesh with the hinterland PH. One possibility is that the office holders at different rungs of the Tenam hierarchy are relatively detached from office holders out in the hinterland. From this perspective, Tenam Rosario is structurally equivalent to a pocket (judging by its number of plazas) or a section (judging by the number of hierarchical levels). A second possibility is that there was a close (kin or patron-client) relationship between office holders at Tenam plazas and at the hierarchically equivalent PH centers. A third possibility is that there was a rotation of office holders between Tenam plazas and their equivalent PH centers. The three possibilities lie along a continuum, concerning the strength of the integrative personal links between office holders at the capital and hinterland centers. The links are strongest in the third kind of arrangement. Interestingly, elite rotation represents an alternative policy to either subject or elite forced settlement for purposes of reinforcing centralized control. Rotating elite settlement schemes are a part of the general feudal model for Lowland Maya polities (Adams 1981).

The notions of a political microcosm at Tenam Rosario and of close links between specific Tenam plazas and specific hinterland centers are both hypothetical. Demonstrating their validity is not easy (Chapter 7). However, both notions (especially the first) are currently attractive ways of appreciating the striking patterning that springs to view when one looks at Tenam Rosario's civic-ceremonial layout. An additional and equally striking pattern has been detected by Agrinier in the disposition of sculptured markers on Tenam Rosario's principal ballcourt (Agrinier n.d.; Figure 9). In brief (a more detailed discussion appears in Chapter 7), each of the seven markers seems to correspond to a particular center: Tenam Rosario itself, both PH2 centers, and the four PH3 centers. This makes the ballcourt a kind of single-building political microcosm embedded within the larger multiplaza microcosm. Carrying speculation a bit further, the clarity of patterning in Tenam Rosario's civic-ceremonial zone may be a case in point for a principle mentioned earlier. This concerns the hypothesis that the Rosario polity was a colonial offshoot from the Maya Lowland Usumacinta zone (Agrinier 1983) and the principle that colonial sociopolitical structure tends to adhere particularly strictly to idealized norms espoused by the dominant colonizing society (Chapter 3). Thus, the ordered arrangement of Tenam Rosario's civic-ceremonial zone (and of one of its ballcourts) may be an effect of this principle.[5] If one accepts such a hypothetical scheme, the much higher degree of formal planning at Tenam Rosario compared to other neighboring regional centers also suggests that Tenam Rosario was a central focus of colonial control within the set of polities occupying the northern Upper Tributaries (Figure 2).

A final interesting property associated with Tenam Rosario's civic-ceremonial core as a political microcosm is the clear linear-concentric dropoff in architectural impressiveness and, by inference, political importance from the center to the edges. This can be seen as one moves out from the center constituted by the apical palace complex to the hierarchically less important plazas which occupy increasingly peripheral positions. Such a pattern is quite different from the hinterland's territorial-settlement hierarchy which has a nested rather than concentric arrangement. It may be that the quasi-concentric plaza arrangement at Tenam Rosario's core is designed to convey a clearer and sharper representation of the concept of hierarchy than is possible in the politico-territorial arrangement which is reproduced in microcosmic form. Also impressive is the way in which the political arrangement is fixed in a relatively massive architectural idiom. Similarly the mapping of the political system in the principal ballcourt (Agrinier n.d.) is less ambiguous concerning the relative hierarchical position of the various centers, particularly with reference to the superiority of PH2 centers over the PH3 centers in their sections (details in Chapter 7). The ballcourt arrangement is clearly less massively fixed than the entire civic-ceremonial layout, but it is nonetheless impressive. Looked at in functional terms, the clarity and fixity (resistance to easy or quick transformation) of the civic-ceremonial layout (and perhaps the ballcourt) could be seen as another integrative aspect of the capital, Tenam Rosario. In less instrumental terms, Tenam Rosario's civic-ceremonial layout and principal ballcourt might be appreciated as varieties of simplified ancient Maya models whose aim was to fix some principles and reduce the ambiguity (and disorder) in the real functioning political system. In a sense, these would be similar to the models in an archaeological analysis such as this one, models which have the same general aims of reducing disorder (although they are constructed with entirely different motivations).

In sum, the following substantive conclusions emerge from the study of civic-ceremonial layout and contents at Tenam Rosario. First, the presence of a clearly apical acropolis-palace complex suggests centralized rather than decentralized rule. Second, Tenam Rosario's layout shows a relatively high degree of political centralization in several ways, viewed in light of its hinterland's territorial and settlement structure. The Rosario polity's regional hierarchical and territorial (district) arrangement appears to be reproduced in microcosm within the capital's civic-ceremonial zone and within the larger of its two ballcourts. Taken together with the presence of a paramount palace complex, this suggests a high degree of political centralization. Even more simply, no other center in the polity shows the same civic-ceremonial size and complexity as Tenam Rosario, a clear indicator of high political centralization. Little or no replication of elaborate Tenam Rosario plaza forms is found in any subordinate center, which suggests centralized political structure in the sense that a unique set of activities is carried out only at the capital and not distributed down the hierarchy. Finally, the apparent reproduction of a full three-level political hierarchy within Tenam Rosario is an indicator of centralization, suggesting that political functions at all levels are centrally carried out at the capital.

A relatively high degree of political centralization, according to the preceding criteria, is not matched by any major demographic centralization. Tenam Rosario has only six percent of the total number of housemounds from the valley, while it has larger percentages of the total number of plazas, civic-ceremonial buildings of various kinds, and civic-ceremonial construction volume. In other words, political centralization does not entail a particularly high degree of forced settlement for the (subject) population at the capital (Chapter 5).

What are some wider implications of Tenam Rosario's qualities as a capital? Principal themes of interest are architecturally expressed political microcosms at capital centers and multiple levels of political hierarchy within (and outside) capital centers. That they might contain a political microcosm is an interesting possibility to keep in mind when examining the civic-ceremonial plans of Mesoamerican

Table 23. *Comparison of Mesoamerican capitals with political microcosms*

| | Monte Alban | | Utatlan | Mayapan | San Gervasio | Tenam Rosario |
	Early I	IIIb				
centralization*	low	high	low	low	low	high
conquest/ colonization	+	—	+	+	+	+
forced settlement	high	low	high	high?	low	low
capital population (in 1,000's)	5	24	10	12	?	1.5
capital area (ha)	65	650	250	420	100+	17
polity population (in 1,000's)	15	79	50	?	8	20
polity area (sq km)	2,200	2,200	750	67,000	400	50
% population at capital	34	31	high	?	low	6

Sources   Monte Alban: Blanton 1978; Feinman *et al.* 1985. Utatlan: Carmack 1981; Fox 1978, 1987. Mayapan: Pollock *et al.* 1962; Roys 1957. San Gervasio: Freidel and Sabloff 1984.

* Absence of an apical (or any) palace facility at Early I Monte Alban tentatively suggests a decentralized (perhaps confederative) political structure. Late Classic (IIIb) Monte Alban has a clearly apical palace facility on the main plaza's North Platform, which suggests a relatively centralized elite political structure. A replicated intrasite settlement pattern at Greater Utatlan matches ethnohistorically documented elite decentralization in the Quiche political system. Ethnohistoric accounts and the repetition of elite facilities both suggest that the ruling group at Mayapan was relatively decentralized. San Gervasio has replicated elite residences which, supported by analogies to Mayapan and Landa's general descriptions, underpin an argument for decentralized elite political structure.

capitals. Evidently, this line of investigation is easiest with clearly planned centers. Otherwise, two major problems occur. First, microcosms may be difficult to detect if a long and complicated development history has blurred an architectural layout. Second, the absence of an architecturally expressed microcosm may not always indicate true absence of such a concept, but rather its failure to be expressed in the design and layout of civic-ceremonial architecture. In spite of these and other potential difficulties, it proves interesting to compare in a preliminary way some of the possible cases of political microcosms at Mesoamerican capitals: Late Formative Monte Alban, Late Classic Monte Alban, Late Postclassic Utatlan, Middle Postclassic Mayapan, and Late Postclassic San Gervasio (Cozumel).

These capitals are selected for comparison because they show archaeological evidence of civic-ceremonial planning which is relatable either through survey data or ethnohistoric evidence to their hinterland's territorial structure. Thus, the selection seems enough for rudimentary controlled comparison (where the single attribute held constant is the presence of a political microcosm). To get a better understanding of how (and why) the political microcosm operates, it makes sense to look at some other attributes of the political structure and historical context relevant to these centers. Such attributes are: the degree of political centralization (as evidenced in the presence or absence of single palaces at the capital), the degree to which the capital takes shape as a part of a foreign elite conquest and/or colonization, the degree to which there is major, forced population-settlement or resettlement from the hinterland into the capital, and the polity's scale (Table 23).

The cases have differing degrees of apical centralization, as shown by the presence or absence of single palaces at the capital (Table 23). For the four relatively decentralized cases, a functionalist argument is possible to the effect that equally matched districts were represented in the capital as an expression of their collective stake in running the polity. For the cases with high centralization, the reasoning changes in that the microcosmic reproduction of the subordinate districts at the capital reinforces their close control from the central capital. This last interpretation is the one used for Tenam Rosario.

In four cases, a political microcosm may have been constructed as part of a foreign (elite) conquest and/or colonization of the polity (Table 23). In the Utatlan and perhaps Mayapan cases, the capital may itself come to serve as a metropolitan center for conquests outside its polity. A relation between clear planning (a political microcosm) and a foreign (elite) conquest and/or colonization is interesting when viewed in light of the principle that a colony tends to clearly reproduce the conceptual order of its metropolis (Foster 1960; Chapter 3).

A strong relation between forced resettlement (i.e., a primate settlement pattern) and a political microcosm holds in half of the cases (Table 23). This pattern might be interpreted as the result of an attempt by rulers literally to reproduce the polity in the central place, with subject people and all. In contrast, a political microcosm associated with only a low degree of forced resettlement can be interpreted as the result of an elite strategy featuring a more figurative reproduction of the polity, with greater emphasis perhaps on concentration of elite residence, leaving many subject people out in the hinterland. The question of how much of a polity's political system is actually contained in its capital recurs when one examines the idea that there may be several levels of political hierarchy at a capital center (see discussion below).

If political microcosms can be viewed as mechanisms for political integration, then they seem to be viable over a wide range of polity sizes (Table 23) and there seems to be no scale limitations or requirements.

Generally, the political microcosms selected here for comparison appear in association with a variety of political structures and strategies. Consequently, the political microcosm sketched out for the Rosario polity is best understood as one of a number of possible Mesoamerican political arrangements. To fill out these sketchy conclusions, comparison would have to be improved by increasing the number of cases (both with and without microcosms), widening the number of attributes considered, and strengthening the linking arguments.

Besides political microcosms, another wider implication of the study of Tenam Rosario's civic-ceremonial layout is that the presence of several levels of political hierarchy at a capital is a possibility worth considering when interpreting Mesoamerican (or other) settlement patterns. This is not an entirely novel observation for Mesoamerican archaeology since a pattern of intrasite hierarchical levels has been discussed for Teotihuacan (Cowgill 1983: 316, 331–332, 339–342) and Monte Alban (Blanton *et al.* 1982: 62, 110). But both of these sites are so very large and internally complex that they virtually compel this kind of interpretation. What has been less apparent is that the same line of analysis should also be kept in mind for smaller sites, especially the many Maya sites with multiple plazas of disparate sizes and contents.

Entertaining the possibility of a political hierarchy within a capital strongly affects how one is going to interpret political structure through settlement analysis. This perspective takes one sharply away from the pioneering archaeological views of settlement-administrative hierarchies in which political functions are seen to be efficiently distributed over a landscape, with basically one political level per site (Johnson 1973). This calls to mind Renfrew's discussion of hierarchical political systems and settlement in the light of Greek city-states, notably Melos. In contrast to the standard [Johnsonian] version of state settlement systems, Renfrew describes a variant in which "There is no doubt that the state did indeed have a decision-making hierarchy...But this was evidently not embodied in any clear system of spatial hierarchy...population [was] effectively concentrated in a single, urban centre" (Renfrew 1982: 281). He calls these arrangements primate states. From a Mesoamerican perspective, these primate states occupy one end of a continuum, in which the capital is a total representation of the political system, including all the political positions and all the population, both subject and elite. With respect to these issues, it helps (where possible) to consider separately the elite and subject population on the one hand, and political positions on the other hand. The Johnsonian model of state territorial organization lies somewhere near the other end of a continuum from primate states. It places only the uppermost levels of political hierarchy and only a (variable) proportion of the commoner and elite population at the capital. To the degree that they have internal hierarchies of political positions, the capitals with political microcosms analyzed here (Table 23) are somewhere towards the middle of what is perhaps best seen as a bundle of continua. Such capitals concentrate upper levels of political hierarchy within them, but lower political levels may be divided between the capital and subordinate centers out in the hinterland. Distribution of commoner and elite population between the capital and the subordinate centers can vary, as in the standard Johnsonian case and in contrast to the primate state model. As understanding of these variants increases, a subsequent step will be to appreciate the variability in terms of such factors as efficiency, necessary evolutionary trajectories, or cultural prior structure.

A methodological implication here is that supplementing intrasite analysis of capitals with the results of a regional analysis of their hinterlands has clear synergistic benefits for addressing questions about political structure. That a major capital has to be seen in its regional context is a truism brought home by numerous regional settlement studies carried out in Mesoamerica. But, in regional settlement analysis, it may not be advisable to adopt the very common approach of reducing the capital to a larger than usual dot on a settlement distribution map and comparing it to subordinate sites in purely quantitative terms (population size, area, or construction volume). Rather, the qualitative and quantitative interpretation of the capital's internal structure needs to be pushed to the limit to better understand a region's political structure. Reversing the direction of the argument, political intrasite analysis needs to be conducted with close reference to regional data (from the hinterland). Finally, to the degree that appropriate evidence is available, it also helps to perform some kind of qualitative intrasite analysis on subordinate sites. Doing so increases the chances of producing more effective comparative evaluations of the sites' political importance (compared to solely quantitative studies of site population size). Suggestions such as these for a better methodology are hollow unless it is clearly understood that their implementation is closely determined by the availability of an appropriately detailed settlement record, which can be recorded by regional survey methods. At a minimum, there is a need for datable and functionally identifiable civic-ceremonial buildings and facilities, contrastable with a range of domestic buildings (ideally, these should be further divisible along status lines). Within Mesoamerica, the high degree of architectural preservation required is most commonly present in many parts of the Maya area, but this area's forested lowlands are also among the most difficult environments in which to achieve block survey coverage and date domestic buildings from surface evidence. Perversely, the more easily surveyed Mesoamerican Highlands often suffer from a low degree of architectural preservation and visibility. As a result, acquiring the data for dual track intrasite and regional settlement analysis has been and will continue to be costly and difficult, but the intellectual rewards of such analyses are potentially enormous.

Given a comprehensive characterization of a single ancient complex polity such as the one I have just presented, where does research proceed? The future research potential of controlled comparison (Eggan 1954) of the Rosario polity to other similarly (ideally, better) surveyed Classic Period Maya polities has been a constant theme. The key point is that for work at a middle range of theoretical abstraction in political studies, it is impossible to use single-polity case studies in order to solve problems, no matter how typical the cases are felt to be. Instead, one has to work with a cluster of case studies in controlled comparison, to bring out important and possibly causal correlations between positions on a number of continua.

Thus, one of the next steps here is to take the characterization of the Rosario polity and compare it to roughly similarly constructed characterizations for other politics that resemble or diverge from it, along the several continua. A brief and partially developed example of this procedure was the comparison of political microcosms and their correlates. This particular comparison was somewhat uncontrolled in the sense that it ranged all over the Mesoamerican landscape and sequence, but the basic principle of controlled comparison (a search for concomitant variation) was adhered to. As another more limited example, a comparison of the Rosario polity to the Copan polity would focus on the facts that the latter polity seems to have group stratification, while the former has individual (household) stratification. It would then become a matter of seeing whether there are differences or similarities in other attributes such as population scale, degree of centralization, political regime, and so forth. A consistent trend of differences would point to linkages of the other attribute levels (or positions on continua) with the mode of stratification. Similarities along the other continua would point to the mode of stratification's varying somewhat independently of these other structural factors.

All this is easier said than done. Not only does the characterization of the Rosario polity still need substantial elaboration and improvement, but there is also a lot of basic fieldwork (including systematic settlement survey) and re-analysis of results required in this and other parts of the Maya area (and Mesoamerica). Attempting to understand Classic Maya political structure and organization is nothing if not a long-term project.

Middle range studies

Now that I have set out a series of substantive conclusions about politics in the Rosario polity, I will shift gears to take a final critical look at how my study of this ancient complex polity has been constructed. As a general rule, a self-critique of conceptual and methodological choices is definitely worthwhile (Chapter 1). There is great interest in exploring how and why selections have been made from the variety of theoretical and methodological options available for attacking a difficult subject such as ancient complex polities. This has to be at least as interesting as the inevitably imperfect and transitory substantive conclusions we can draw about these polities. The following discussion revolves around the theme that there is a need to steer a middle course between highly abstract generalization and nominalist particularism in constructing a study of politics in ancient complex polities.

Earlier, I related the notion of middle range abstraction to different kinds of analogies – substantive specific (single-case) analogies, substantive composite analogies, and extra-disciplinary theoretical analogies. These types of analogies lie along a continuum from the particular to the abstract (Chapters 1 and 2). Also, I briefly related the notion of degrees of abstraction to bridging arguments, contrasting highly abstract generalizing approaches with more particularizing approaches (Chapter 1). At this point, I will expand the discussion to give a fuller and more general idea of what it means to operate at a middle range of abstraction. For example, the concepts used for elaborating the bundled continua of variation occupy what can be termed a middle range of theoretical abstraction. To begin, middle range here does not refer to bridging arguments intermediate between theory and data (Binford 1977, 1983a). But does it refer instead to the middle range in middle range theory derived from sociology for archaeologists (Raab and Goodyear 1984; Yoffee 1979: 29)?

> Middle-range theory is principally used … to guide empirical enquiry. It is
> intermediate to general theories of social systems which are too remote
> from particular classes of social behavior, organization, and change to
> account for what is observed and to those detailed orderly descriptions of
> particulars that are not organized at all. Middle-range theory involves
> abstractions, of course, but they are close enough to observed data to be
> incorporated in propositions that permit empirical testing. (Merton 1968:
> 38, cited in Raab and Goodyear 1984: 257)

While the bundled continua used here are based on generalizations derived
mostly from Africanist political studies and fall into a middle range of abstraction,
there is a less immediate emphasis on testability than in Merton's characterization
of middle range theory. Raab and Goodyear's own emphasis on archaeological
testability emerges most clearly in their citing of work by Johnson (1982), Wright
and Johnson (1975), and Peebles and Kus (1977) as examples of middle range
theory (Raab and Goodyear 1984: 284–285). Indeed, such information-theory-
based studies adequately exemplify middle range theory if a testable form of propositions is the major criterion. But the studies cited are less identifiable as middle
range theory in light of two other equally valid criteria: applicability to subject
matter addressed, and applicability to the specific cases dealt with. On both counts
these exemplary studies are reductionist, operating at an arguably inapplicably high
level of abstraction, closer to general than to middle range theory.

Applicability must relate to a general subject of study, which in the present
case(s) is clearly politics. For the examples cited by Raab and Goodyear, the
following questions become relevant. Is it useful or interesting to reduce political
phenomena to the effects of information-processing efficiency considerations
(ultimately relating back to human brain capacity)? Is information theory a good
tool for political analysis applied to ancient complex polities? The answers have to
be no. The more central aspects of politics having to do with power and competition
are better handled by action theory (Barth 1959; Bailey 1970; Vincent 1978) or
symbolic theory (Cohen 1979) or structural-functionalism (Balandier 1970; Mair
1962), for example, than they are by information theory.

Another side of abstraction, in the sense of applicability, involves the dichotomy
between extreme nominalism and extreme broad-brush cross-cultural comparative
generalization. This is well known from anthropological polemics. The general
question concerns how applicable theoretical concepts are to the case at hand.
Again, with reference to the examples cited by Raab and Goodyear, applicability
problems exist for information-theoretic approaches in general archaeology. Since
these approaches have been developed with close reference to ancient Near Eastern
evidence, one needs to ask whether they are usefully extendable beyond Near
Eastern contexts. For example, information theoretic approaches do not seem to be
straightforwardly applicable to ancient Mesoamerican polities. This is because
ancient Near Eastern polities featured an unusual amount of state regulation and

management of the economy, and an unusually full development of professional bureaucracies (in Weber's sense, see Gerth and Mills eds. 1946: ch. 8), compared to Mesoamerican polities. Therefore, ancient Near Eastern political systems, with their heavy dependence on administrative efficiency, may not be the best arena for developing theoretical analogs of direct interest for studying Mesoamerican polities (or even Hawaiian polities, in the case of Peebles and Kus 1977). Failure to consider this applicability problem characterizes some influential analyses of Mesoamerican developments (Blanton *et al.* 1981; Spencer 1982). Further and even more general applicability problems for the information-theoretic approach derive from its being ultimately based on studies of modern business corporations. Principles generated from this kind of study are too narrowly ethnocentric for direct application to ancient non-western polities, perhaps even including ancient Near Eastern polities (if we are to believe R. McC. Adams 1981: 76–78).

Thus, the examples cited (by Raab and Goodyear) are less than full examples of middle range theory since they show only one of its properties: archaeologically testable form. In contrast, I would propose that the bundled continua used here more closely resemble adequate middle range theory because they incorporate concepts and explanatory ideas that are not overly reductionist for a study of politics in ancient complex polities. In light of best available generalizations, the bundled continua touch on matters that go to the core of what was etically (and, to a large degree, emically) important in ancient polities: intra-elite conflicts, intra-elite power relations, and hierarchical political control of subject population distribution. Checked against available Maya and Mesoamerican ethnohistoric analogies, the bundled continua seem broadly appropriate to the case at hand. The African case materials from which the generalizations that underpin the bundled continua of variation are constructed are arguably more structurally similar to ancient Maya polities than are the ancient Near Eastern polities or modern business corporations that provide the case materials for generalizations underlying information theory approaches. Furthermore, moving to the other (more particularistic) end of the spectrum, studies of African polities are also more relevant to ancient Maya polities than are the studies of politics within the closed corporate Maya peasant communities which are encapsulated within modern nation-states (Vogt 1969: ch. 11–12). Such studies of the modern Maya underlie direct-historical analogies (Vogt 1968, 1983; Gifford 1978), which are in turn justified by a Genetic Model of cultural development (Vogt 1964a; Marcus 1983c). But from the basically structural-functionalist perspective on politics I use here, close cultural–historical or genetic links cannot be sufficient to over-ride the clear structural distinctions between ancient Maya polities and modern peasantries (de Montmollin n.d.d).

The two kinds of applicability, to theme and case material, are the main virtues of the bundled continua approach as middle range theory, rather than any overwhelmingly superior archaeological testability. But the latter has not been ignored (Chapters 4–10). For example, the bundled continua of variation are better rendered into testable form than are societal types. The nuts and bolts of archaeological testing and bridging arguments return us to the Binfordian middle range, but squarely in the methodological, not the theoretical, domain.[6] Because of the hyper-austerity and banality that characterizes totally testable archaeological models for ancient complex polities (Chapter 2), testability cannot possibly be the sole or final criterion for judging a study of politics in such polities.

Having specified how the bundled continua lie in a middle range of theoretical abstraction, I should identify from what higher-order general theory the middle range continua derive. So far, this question has been largely set aside, except for brief comments about a Grand Theory consensus concerning why the several continua are aligned a certain way (Table 1). Such a Grand Theory consensus lies well up in the intellectual ozone, consisting of a hallowed and rather remote set of ideas about social evolution and the tendency of sociopolitical entities to range between small and simple, and large and complex forms. These ideas find modern nineteenth-century roots in Herbert Spencer (Carneiro ed. 1967) and feed successor structural-functionalist, systems, and information-theoretic approaches.

Another high-order theory that informs the bundled continua of variation is what I will call a culturally modified action theory of politics. This high-order theory operates at a lower level of abstraction and is more centrally interesting for a study of ancient complex polities than Grand Theory. Let us look more closely at what a culturally modified action theory of politics consists of. The theory combines both abstract and specific components. The abstract component consists of action theory pure and simple (Vincent 1978), covering generally recurring principles of political behavior that account for a good part of why polities operate and develop as they do. In political anthropology, examples of action theory principles are found in expositions of the game theoretic underpinnings of factional conflict and patron-clientism (Barth 1959; Bailey 1970). Examples of some general principles of politics applied to the Rosario polity are given in the forced settlement arguments about the tendency of elites to seek to exercise direct supervision and control over subjects and about the tendency of subjects to try to subtract themselves from this control (Chapter 5). Another example applied to the Rosario polity concerns the greater tendency of districts to secede in group political stratification systems because of divided loyalties (Chapters 2 and 8).

In essence, a raw action-theory perspective is somewhat analogous to formalist approaches in economic anthropology – with Political Man substituted for Economic Man. Raw action-theory also incorporates the position of strict methodological individualism (Ahmed 1976; de Montmollin n.d.b). Such a position proves to be awkwardly reductionist for the study of ancient complex polities since it operates according to the assumption that individual behavior always creates institutional structure. The consequence is that complex political arrangements are inappropriately reduced to the sum of individual components.

But action theory can begin to dodge problems of reductionism and becomes enriched when it takes into account that general political behavioral principles are heavily constrained by structural (institutional) or cultural conditions (Ahmed 1976). To emphasize this for political anthropology is broadly similar to adopting a substantivist position in economic anthropology. It also moves one towards a position of modified methodological individualism. And this position is more appropriate for a study of ancient complex polities since it acknowledges a reciprocal relation between individual behavior and institutional structure (Ahmed 1976; de Montmollin n.d.b). Emphasis falls on the study of norms and institutions, with a firm recognition that not everyone is an equal player in the political arena. Taken to an extreme, a focus on structural principles proper to each case can end up in nominalism (and relativism) or at least in a failure to seek and identify any general principles of political behavior common to many structurally different political systems. But the best of both worlds is a combination of the generalizing tendencies in action theory with a close attention to cultural–structural context. Not surprisingly, I believe that much of the Africanist political anthropology I have used to develop the bundle of continua (Table 1) and the research questions used here contains the desired combination of general principles of political behavior and attention to individual polities and their institutions. Particularly useful are historically-oriented structural-functionalist studies of succession to high office (Goody 1966), political centralization and decentralization (Fallers 1956), political stratification (Fallers 1973), varieties of political regimes (Southall 1965), and modes of access to elite groups along with intra-elite dynamics (Lloyd 1965, 1968). Examples of structural (institutional) factors in my analysis of the Rosario polity are the characterization of the polity as having vertical rather than horizontal (class) sociopolitical cleavages, individual versus group political stratification, and a political microcosm at its capital. All of these are institutional features (in the broadest sense) and channel individual and group political behavior.

A mix of the general and particular characterizes many anthropologically-informed Mesoamerican ethnohistoric studies (Carrasco *et al.* 1976, Carrasco and Broda eds. 1978; Collier *et al.* eds. 1982; and others). In future, the same tempering of action theory or formalist (political or economic) analysis with a cultural–structural or substantivist perspective needs to be brought more fully into Mesoamerican and Maya archaeological interpretations. This is especially necessary for studies of Formative or Classic polities (temporally preceding the ethnohistorical cases). Presently, most archaeological interpretations tend to lie towards the abstract action-theory (or formalist economics) end of the spectrum (Blanton *et al.* 1981, 1982; Kowalewski *et al.* 1983; Kowalewski and Finsten 1983; Alden 1979; Steponaitis 1981; Spencer 1982; Feinman 1986; Feinman *et al.* 1984; Santley 1984, 1986; Rathje 1973, 1975; Phillips and Rathje 1977; and many others). To repeat a key point, the formalist quality of such studies is thrown into doubt by the simple application of a (substantivist) evolutionary-historical or discontinuist logic derived from such theoreticians as Polanyi (1977), Service (1975), Wolf (1982) or Giddens (1985). Following such a logic, one cannot expect to find fully capitalist economies and politically modern nation-states during the Formative or Classic Periods preceding the Postclassic Period since the latter period features clearly non-capitalist and pre-nation-state polities. Consequently, formalist economics or raw action-theory should be ruled out of court as analytical approaches because they have been designed specifically for the study of modern polities and economies.

There are two reasons why formalist analyses have been used relatively frequently in archaeological studies of Mesoamerican and Maya ancient complex polities, as well in studies of such polities in the Old World (Renfrew 1982; Johnson 1973; Freidman and Rowlands 1977; Claessen and Skalnik eds. 1978). First, there is the theoretical tendency to discount substantivist logic and seek the most generalizing approach possible. In relation to this, it seems difficult to deny that the tendency to generalize widely (and indeed to tackle the great questions discussed earlier, Chapter 1) is linked to a universal desire among archaeologists to achieve maximum impact (and possibly relevance) for their own studies.

The second reason that formalist approaches have not been resisted to a greater extent is more academically interesting. It has to do with our limited capacity to use a rather austere archaeological record in order to mount and support more specific (substantivist) arguments. This is best understood in Mesoamerica by considering the contrast between purely archaeological appreciations of the Formative and Classic Periods and archaeological–ethnohistorical appreciations of the Postclassic and Contact Periods. The archaeologically-based conceptualizations of political structure and organization for the polities in the earlier periods tend to be very simplistic indeed, usually based on some kind of societal typology (Chapter 2).[7] In contrast, for the later period, with the clear addition of ethnohistorical inputs, conceptualizations of polities appears to be much more subtle and nuanced (sometimes to the point of glorious near incomprehensibility – e.g., the Aztec Arrangement as presented by Van Zantjwick 1985). The overall impression gained from this contrast is that there is a very smooth progression from Formative chiefdoms to Classic states followed by a collapse to Postclassic political entities of some sort which are cyclically unstable. In other words, both the evolutionary progression and the simple typological conceptualizations for polities break down.

One way to account for this puzzling contrast is to argue that it corresponds to an actual substantive-historical phenomenon. For example, one finds that a balkanization process (Blanton *et al.* 1981, 1982; Marcus 1983d) is invoked to account for the transition from relatively large coherent Classic period polities, seen as essentially similar to modern nation-states, to small, incoherent, warring Postclassic kingdoms (which are radically dissimilar to ethnically irredentist Balkan states, if truth be told). Probably a better way to appreciate (rather than dismiss or spuriously resolve) this puzzling contrast is to conclude that the archaeologically documented evolutionary progression and political typology need reworking. In other words, politics may have been as complicated in the Formative and Classic Periods as we know it was in the Postclassic Period. And what has held us back is the failure to appreciate this, abetted by the relative austerity of the archaeological evidence and by the predilection of theoretically inclined Meso-americanists for broad generalization.

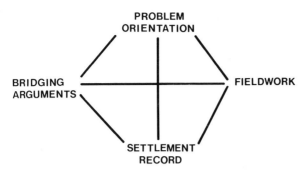

Figure 49   The web of research

The web of research

Whether or not one pitches a study of politics in ancient complex polities at the abstract or particularistic end of the spectrum can be attributed to any number of causes, in addition to those already reviewed. Some of these causes have to do with the fact that there are several other stages or phases in the research process besides the selection of a problem orientation, and these may impinge on the problem orientation itself. One useful stage scheme for research, generally followed here (and see also de Montmollin 1987), has been suggested by Easton (1959) for political anthropology. Briefly, in Easton's terms, this involves the following steps (with my own labels for the steps included in parentheses). First one isolates important sociopolitical variables and constitutes them non-typologically as a set of continua (problem orientation). Then one identifies changes in these variable values along continua (fieldwork, bridging arguments). Tests are then carried out to check for synchronically co-occurring variable values or for diachronically co-occurrent changes in variable values (bridging arguments and analysis). Finally, any co-occurrences are accounted for (if possible) in terms of higher-order theoretical considerations (drawing explanatory conclusions). Although this or something like it is a reasonably comprehensible format with which to present research results, it is certainly inaccurate to see problem orientation only as a chronological first step in the research process from which all others follow in lock step.

In the course of virtually any searching settlement study of an ancient complex polity, an archaeologist becomes entangled in a fascinating web of reciprocal relations between the settlement record's qualities and possibilities, fieldwork methods, bridging arguments (observational theory), and problem orientation (Figure 49). This scheme leaves out the drawing of explanatory conclusions because my aim is to consider most closely how it is that studies are put together, before substantive conclusions come to be drawn. Ideally, the aim is to continue working towards a close congruence between all these elements, a congruence which should be evident and discussed in the presentation of research results.

But, the world being an imperfect place, incongruities may have to be tolerated or even appreciated. For example, it often proves more interesting to give problem orientation some autonomy from the first three elements. Why should there be autonomy for problem orientation? If one does not allow some autonomy, the result can be an excessive theoretical austerity associated with totally testable models (Chapter 2). Examples show how this works in practice. Simpler and more elegant theoretical schemes than the one I used can be nailed down archaeologically in the Rosario Valley. One could attribute great importance to the number of levels in the (political and/or administrative) settlement hierarchy as an aspect of politics and look at change in the number of levels through time and space. With reference to the levels of settlement hierarchy, one could then talk about egalitarian versus stratified systems, or chiefdoms versus states, looking for presence or absence of these societal types. Or one could focus on size-complexity comparisons as the key to political analysis and come to some hard conclusions about the relations between population size and the number of levels of hierarchy. But all of these tactics, involving models which verge on the totally testable, suffer from excessive austerity in relation to the richness of issues that could be addressed in studying an ancient Maya polity.

Being less austere than the totally testable models sketched above, the bundled continua do leave a number of untested but interesting loose ends (some of which should lead to further research): pressure of numbers of contenders on the supply of political offices (Chapter 8), economic patterns and their relation to political structure (Chapter 9), and differences in strategies of control used to achieve centralization – forced settlement versus more indirect control exercised through having a flux of people and tribute in and out of political centers (Chapter 5). The last loose end is one of the most interesting. The two control strategies cannot always be readily distinguished with settlement survey (or even excavation) evidence. But no clear benefit, other than a possible aesthetic one for the style of presentation, results from leaving such archaeologically intractable loose ends out of the picture. In this case, rather than presenting forced settlement as the one and only determinant for archaeologically perceived patterns in degrees of settlement nucleation because it is relatively more accessible to archaeological testing, it makes more sense to mention forced settlement and flux as possible alternate strategies (with different degrees of testability).

Within the web of relations (Figure 49), several other relations repay closer examination. These relations are those between: settlement record and fieldwork, settlement record and bridging arguments, settlement record and problem orientation, and problem orientation and bridging arguments.

For the settlement record–fieldwork relation, I have already covered the particulars for the Rosario Valley in some detail (Chapter 4). More generally, a comparison between Highland Mesoamerican and Lowland Maya settlement records proves interesting, with a focus on how their different settlement records allow different kinds of fieldwork. The comparison indicates that the settlement record–fieldwork relation is quite substantively different in each area. Without going into detail (see de Montmollin 1985a: ch. 5), suffice it to say that a major contrast in settlement records is one between high visibility and poor (architectural) preservation in the highlands and low visibility and good (architectural) preservation in the lowlands. One obvious effect of this on fieldwork concerns the extension and rapidity of survey allowed. Using settlement-survey methods, highland sherd scatters are incomparably quicker to locate, map, and date than are lowland architectural assemblages (buried in the jungle and with little surface pottery for dating). While these and other differences are well known, it is strange that such differences have rarely been properly taken into account when comparing research processes and results from these two areas. This is especially important when one considers the knock-on effects on settlement analysis (bridging arguments) of the different kinds of field data sets allowed by radically different settlement records. On the one hand, an extensive architectural data set recoverable in lowland survey allows a much more searching set of bridging arguments concerning the relative political importance of settlements. This in turn helps to avoid dubious a priori equations of a settlement's relative demographic size with its relative political importance (Chapter 5). On the other hand, the highland regional perspectives will allow a wider range of political analyses concerning population distribution than those allowed with much more restricted, lowland single-site perspectives. In sum, understanding that the nature of the archaeological record will vary in different areas and impose knock-on effects on fieldwork and then on interpretations would seem to be an essential step for either detailed comparative work or even for general overviews in Mesoamerica and in other parts of the world (Ammerman 1981).

As we have seen, the settlement record–fieldwork relation impinges on the settlement record–bridging arguments relation. The latter is of central interest in studies of relatively large ancient complex polities and usually quite difficult to handle (Chapters 4–10). I have already provided detailed discussion about difficulties associated with linking politics and (single-period) settlement evidence. Such difficulties include contemporaneity, equifinality, scale of coverage, uneven preservation and recovery, and form to function, among others (Chapter 4). Some of the difficulties are close to being intractable. For example, contemporaneity problems in regional settlement data cannot be solved by a shift in fieldwork tactics to small-scale excavation without raising several new problems. These are: a narrowing of spatial coverage and theoretical interest, large and unwarranted amounts of extrapolation, and a (possibly unwitting) commitment to strict methodological individualism, of the kind implicitly associated with household archaeology (see below). Other difficulties are more tractable in the sense that they are self-inflicted by under-appreciation of the analytical (bridging argument) possibilities of a particular settlement record. For example, correctable problems arise in the construction of settlement hierarchies and in the handling of relatively complete and complex domestic and civic-ceremonial architectural evidence (Chapters 5 and 7; de Montmollin 1985a: ch. 5). It is hoped that the reader will have some initial basis for judging the analysis of politics in the Rosario polity in terms of whether good advantage has been taken of the possibilities presented by the settlement record. Eventually, these judgements will prove easier when bridging arguments presented here can be confronted with an extensive presentation of the settlement evidence from the valley (in de Montmollin n.d.a).

The settlement record–problem orientation relation is also quite difficult to handle at times, having much to do with the in many ways unbridgeable distinction between structure (social statics) and organization (social dynamics). I have already provided detailed discussion of indirect methods for studying issues of political structure and organization with evidence from a static settlement record (Chapters 4 and 10). An essential point that emerges from this is the need to avoid programmatic absolutism of the kind which says that archaeologists only study process (change) in ancient complex polities or alternately that archaeologists only study structure (stable continuities). With an understanding that such options are part of a range of possibilities, a better aim is to match the problem orientation with the qualities of the available data set(s). Concerning the entire archaeological record (not just settlement), an interesting question is whether the relative paucity of the record with reference to political issues imposes and helps to maintain an overly austere and too highly generalizing problem orientation. As I argued earlier with reference to totally testable models and the differences between archaeological and ethnohistorical perspectives on Mesoamerican polities, the answer would seem to be yes.

Finally, the problem orientation–bridging arguments relation concerns how a theoretical framework is operationalized. Here, this involves generating evidence appropriate for answering the set of research questions about political structure and organization (Chapter 2). The linkage between problem orientation and bridging arguments is not airtight and there is some autonomy for problem orientation. To take an example, the research questions are framed in general terms having to do with Classic Maya political structure and organization. Evidently, framing the questions with more specific reference to the Rosario polity would have provided a closer fit between problem orientation and bridging arguments. But, the general nature of the questions is attributable to the problem orientation's being formulated to set up the possibility of controlled comparison (Eggan 1954), with the Rosario polity as one case for comparison. Working at a middle range of theoretical abstraction, understanding and explanation are built up through continuing controlled comparison. As comparisons proceed, it may turn out that all the Maya polities compared show identical characteristics, so that it would be possible to extrapolate from one of them to all the rest. But, clearly, this is not a pattern to be assumed at the outset. It seems to be an unlikely possibility on the basis of informal comparison between the Rosario, Copan, and Tonina (Ocosingo Valley) polities, for example. In the meantime, I have been able to make some controlled comparisons at a smaller scale within the Rosario Valley (with districts as cases for comparison). Interesting results emerged (above), but this scale is too small to provide comprehensive answers to the research questions as formulated.

Scales of analysis

The idea that it is best to steer a middle course between abstract generalization and nominalist particularism in constructing a study of politics in ancient complex polities can be pursued effectively with reference to the choice of scales of analysis. Particularly interesting in this respect are the relations between different analytical scales and fundamental theoretical positions of methodological individualism or holism (de Montmollin n.d.b). This line of thinking is particularly appropriate in a settlement-oriented approach, where questions of spatial (and by inference sociopolitical) scale loom large. The Rosario Valley has a very well preserved settlement record when compared with that of many other ancient complex polities. Because of this, there is a particular clarity in the way that the Rosario settlement record offers several settlement scales for analysis. These scales consist of the valley, the section, the pocket, the site or center, the ward, the domestic housegroup or civic-ceremonial plaza, and the domestic building or civic-ceremonial building (Figure 6). Some of these nested spatial-settlement scales correspond approximately to nested social scales. The surveyed valley corresponds to a polity core. The sections and pockets correspond to districts. The sites correspond to communities. The wards correspond to lineages. The housegroups correspond to (small) extended families. The single domestic buildings correspond to nuclear families and individuals. Therefore, by selecting particular spatial scales to work with, one (wittingly or not) lays special emphasis on particular social scales. Given a problem orientation designed to study political structure and organization in an ancient complex polity, my main goal has been to analyze patterning that is perceivable at the polity and district scales. Patterning at site or smaller scales has been correspondingly underanalyzed; much of the relatively underutilized data consist of architectural and locational attributes recorded on well preserved individual buildings. Concerning what analysis I did do at these smaller scales, my focus on political structure meant that civic-ceremonial buildings and plazas received fuller attention than domestic dwellings and housegroups.

In terms of settlement scale, my study of settlement and politics has been built from the top down rather than from the bottom up. Generally speaking, in a top-down approach, the settlement record is viewed from a shifting aerial prospect. By contrast, in a bottom-up approach the settlement record is viewed inside-outward from a fixed-point prospect (Figure 50; Binford and Sabloff 1982). Additionally, a top-down approach involves laying particular emphasis on larger rather than smaller settlement scales. The latter are not ignored, however. To take an example, for the Rosario polity small-scale analyses have been carried out elsewhere using domestic building and housegroup-scale data from El Rosario (de Montmollin 1981, n.d.c). Such analyses have focused on questions about building functions leading to questions about domestic cycling and sociopolitical stratification patterns within a single (large and complex) settlement. But here I have treated these studies as early steps on the way to studying a more centrally relevant set of problems of the general kind and scale accessible with a regional data base. In light of this, I have dwelt only briefly on small-scale data and arguments since my main goal was

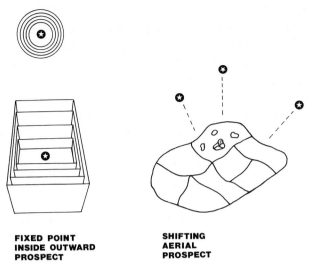

**FIXED POINT
INSIDE OUTWARD
PROSPECT**

**SHIFTING
AERIAL
PROSPECT**

Figure 50   Perspectives on settlement (for nested *chinese boxes*, see Hammond 1975b)

to move on to more centrally interesting later stages. In other words, more effort has been given to the upper end of a hierarchically ranked chain of interdependent arguments.

To take a specific example, in discussing forced settlement some idea was required of which were the dwellings among the small (clearly non-civic-ceremonial) mounds scattered around the valley. Rather than focusing heavily on that problem, I made reference to a longer study that deals with the issue for El Rosario (de Montmollin 1981) and the results of that study, based on surface data at the individual building and housegroup scale, were used as a functional typology (dwellings, outbuildings, walkways, altars, circular buildings) extendible to the whole valley. This facilitated brisk movement towards a more pressing argument concerning forced settlement, a political determinant of regional settlement nucleation and dispersal. Another aspect of forced settlement, the important contrast between commoner and elite forced settlement (Chapter 8), required further excursion into the individual building and housegroup-scale data set in order to partition dwellings (and housegroups) into elite and commoner categories. Again, I based my relatively sketchy effort on earlier studies of El Rosario (de Montmollin 1981, n.d.c) and perceived these as a way station on the road to hierarchically more important subsequent analysis concerning different (elite and subject) varieties of forced settlement.

For other problem orientations, the questions of building function or of architectural expressions of sociopolitical status might be central, consuming much more time and thought, and standing at the hierarchical apex of the chain of arguments (or hypotheses). One well-executed example of this general orientation is Tourtellot's discussion of Lowland Maya household settlement patterns (Tourtellot 1983, based on his analysis of Seibal settlement). In effect, this is an example of household archaeology with heavy emphasis on bridging arguments. Another example is a settlement pattern study of Cozumel Island which devotes extensive attention to building function, especially compared to the attention given to regional patterns (Freidel and Sabloff 1984). This rigorously executed study of politics and economics in Postclassic Yucatan clearly builds its arguments from the bottom up. The underlying reasoning appears to be that there is a hierarchy of bridging arguments which starts from the smallest-scale unit and builds upward to larger-scale units. Larger-scale arguments cannot be made until the smaller-scale problems (such as individual building function) have been thoroughly resolved. The outline of such a position has been set out by one of the co-authors of the Cozumel study (Sabloff 1983; Binford and Sabloff 1982). Closely allied to an emphasis on middle range theory (in the Binfordian sense), such a view seems too methodologically determined.[8] Methodological determinism in the Binfordian approach has been criticized from various perspectives (e.g., Bailey 1983; Raab and Goodyear 1984). Its problems include a lack of substantive theoretical problem-orientation, overemphasis on the scientific security of methodology, confusion between methodological and substantive theories, and so forth. My main criticism here is that, taken to an extreme, such methodological determinism entails that the resolution of all theoretical problems has to start with some of the smallest-scale analytical units such as individual buildings or housegroups (in the Maya case). This, in turn, requires an inappropriate position of strict methodological individualism (de Montmollin n.d.b).

Strict methodological individualism consists of a basic assumption that study is possible only at the individual level. Analysis is actor-centered, "with man as externalized to, and confronting, society... determined to 'better his chances' or 'maximize' them by consciously or unconsciously, 'manipulating' or 're-ordering' society and its symbols" (Ahmed 1976: 3). Strict methodological individualism has several general defects (after Ahmed 1976: 9–11). Academic ethnocentrism leads to the uncritical application of free market or social contract models cross-culturally (or cross-temporally, one might add). Ethnographic reductionism leads to the use of one segment of a society to stand for the whole. Theoretical reductionism leads to the characterization of complex societies as simple aggregates of freely acting individuals. And, finally, synecdochic analysis leads to the use of one social (or political) stratum in a society to represent all strata. All of these general defects are identifiable in the strict methodological individualism which underlies (formalist) studies of prehispanic Mesoamerican polities and economies. The defects can be remedied by working at a variety of sociospatial scales, not just the smallest scales. Additionally, account must be taken of the sharply stratified nature of ancient Mesoamerican polities (Carrasco *et al.* 1976) and/or the complex corporate mosaic arrangements within them (Van Zantjwick 1985). Applying these remedies leads to a position of modified methodological individualism.

In modifed methodological individualism, the basic assumption is that analysis must still focus on the individual, while placing his activities within a framework of sociopolitical and cultural structures. And these structures must be studied at a variety of sociospatial scales. There is nothing straightforward about this. Within a position of modified methodological individualism, there is a range of choices about how to view a set of important political issues. Some of these issues concern the degree to which social, political, and ideological structures place constraints on individual political actions of subjects and rulers, the degree of monolithic unity within groups of rulers, and the degree of monolithic unity among subjects.

In correcting the defects of strict methodological individualism, modified methodological individualism does not need to go to the opposite extreme, the structural determinism of methodological holism. Methodological holism is the basic assumption that study is best conducted at the level of the collectivity; "man is born into a matrix of interacting and largely fixed social patterns... Accordingly his capacity to manipulate the symbols of society around him is limited to the extent determined by the needs of society for change" (Ahmed 1976: 4). Methodological holism is particularly inappropriate for political analysis of ancient Mesoamerican or other polities because it illogically reifies social collectivities by attributing motives and agency to them. Reification problems are relative, varying in severity. Reifying whole polities, societies, or cultures is probably worse than reifying smaller segments within polities such as communities, lineages, or households. The smaller the grouping, the more plausible it is to assume that it might act as a unified agent at times. But the assumption is always going to base itself on an inexact organic metaphor for a superorganic social grouping.

So far, I have criticized methodologically inspired bottom-up approaches to settlement studies of ancient complex polities. A similar strict methodological individualism underlies a more theoretically driven bottom-up approach labelled Household Archaeology by its proponents (Wilk and Rathje 1982; Rathje 1983).[9] Many rationales have been proposed for Household Archaeology (these are reviewed in detail elsewhere – de Montmollin n.d.b). One very general set of claims runs as follows. The masses are the "fiber of all societies, ancient and modern," "all societies are composed of households" and, therefore, looking at "the history of specific households... can add to the search for meaning in general patterns of human behavior" (Rathje 1983: 24). These claims are combined with the notion that the time has come for Household Archaeology because it represents the final "move downward in specificity" in a historical progression in American archaeologists' selection of units of analysis. This is a progression from "whole culture areas" to "the settlement and variability between settlements" (Wilk and Rathje 1982: 617). The general suggestion arising from these and other statements is that Household Archaeology provides a kind of golden road towards explaining ancient societies (and polities).

Why doubt this? The claim for universality and basal importance of (small family) household organization is overextended and contradicted by ethnographic and ethnohistorical evidence. To claim that (small family) households are both ubiquitous and vitally important in every time and place is to take a formalist line and to suppress the importance of institutional variability among ancient complex societies. Taking a more substantivist interest in the question would instead lead one to stress such constrasts as group versus individual political stratification (Chapter 8). Substantivists would also look for the possibility that corporate groups larger than the small family were basally important in certain cases. Important New World examples of this are the Aztec polity's *calpullis* (Hicks 1986), the Inca polity's *ayllus* (Murra 1972), and Teotihuacan's apartment compounds (Millon 1981). More theoretically, the behavioral science approaches which are selected for studying households are way over towards the extreme generalization end of the spectrum and thus unattractive to archaeologists who want to work at a middle range of abstraction. This is a point much more pointedly and humorously made in Flannery's parable about the Golden Marshalltown where an old timer complains about the relentless law and order generalizations propounded by the same group of archaeologists who are largely responsible for Household Archaeology (Flannery 1982). In light of the present discussion, such behavioralism forces one into a very reductionist, strict methodological-individualist position. And this position is an inappropriate one from which to build an appreciation of the fascinating cultural and sociopolitical variability that lies at the heart of an archaeological–anthropological study of ancient complex polities.

With reference to the second rationale, that households are a unit of analysis whose time has come, Household Archaeology may be last on the scene, but a historical progression should not be confused with a theoretically logical progression. The historical progression in Americanist archaeology (as elsewhere) is one in which increasingly detailed focuses are adopted as a result of increases in available information. There is an inexorable filling-in of the gaps in knowledge which makes (spatially) broad-brush comparisons increasingly unattractive (and unmanageable). But Wilk and Rathje's account of a shift from culture area to site and intersite analysis is incomplete. It leaves out other analytical settlement scales such as the district and polity (Figure 6) which have come increasingly to the fore in recent interpretations (crystallized for Mesoamerica by Blanton *et al.* 1981). Such scales are not replaceable through some inexorable historical process by the household scale of analysis and explanation. Finally, and to redress the balance a bit, it would not be fair to conclude from this that Household Archaeology is an entirely worthless enterprise; this is far from the case. Its main failing is that it does not live up to the expectations of its proponents as the new golden road to understanding in archaeology, perhaps especially in the archaeology of complex polities with multiple, nested sociospatial scales.

To recap, the sticking point for either methodological or theoretical bottom-up approaches is that it is theoretically unwise to reduce the whole of an ancient complex political system to the sum of its smallest-scale building blocks: freewheeling individuals. Such a position of strict methodological individualism is overly reductionist and limiting for studying the kinds of political phenomena found in Classic Maya or other ancient complex polities.

In addition to general theoretical disagreements about the appropriateness of small-scale bottom-up approaches and their strict methodological individualism, there is a practical reason for avoiding programmatic bottom-up approaches to settlement analysis. This is that such approaches are unnecessarily limiting. Particularly in their methodologically driven forms, they do not allow for the possibility that theoretically interesting and empirically well-grounded work can be done at larger community or regional scales, without prior definitive resolution of smaller-scale problems. For example, it is clear enough that arguments about domestic building function and status correlates in the Rosario polity are not as strong as they might be and that no unambiguous bridging arguments have been found (on the doubtful assumption that these could ever be found). But the larger-scale arguments about forced settlement, centralization, and other aspects covered by the bundled continua do not stand or fall entirely on whether perfection has been achieved in the earlier and subordinate arguments (hypotheses) about building function and so forth. As long as these lower-order small-scale arguments are roughly adequate, it should be possible to proceed onward to larger-scale issues which constitute the central theoretical focus in a top-down approach to constructing a study of settlement and politics.[10]

In spite of real and enduring difficulties associated with lower-order small-scale arguments, the above considerations lead me to the conclusion that a top-down approach emphasizing large-scale study is the best for acquiring an understanding of political structure and organization in ancient complex polities. Whether or not one agrees with this conclusion, it is good to keep in mind the general notion that important analytical and theoretical choices arise when selecting a sociospatial scale of analysis for settlement studies aimed at questions of political structure. Ideally, choice of scale has to be clearly appropriate to a problem orientation; but, both the problem orientation and the choice of scale have to be grounded in a clear understanding of the theoretical and analytical implications of strict methodological individualism, modified methodological individualism, or methodological holism (de Montmollin n.d.b).

Conclusions

In presenting a study of politics and settlement in a Classic Maya polity, I have touched on many general problems that arise when studying ancient complex polities. It becomes clear in every such enterprise that important and interesting choices arise at each step of the research process. Archaeologists have to make choices in forming a problem orientation, conceptualizing the object of study, developing a fieldwork methodology, developing an analytical methodology (a set of bridging arguments to link concepts and the archaeological record), and drawing explanatory (or other kinds of) conclusions. In many cases, having to make these choices is interesting precisely because the procedures are not straightforward and we find ourselves confronted with several seemingly plausible options. More often than not the correct options are not revealed to us from a tried-and-tested body of archaeological research. This differs from the case for more mature or perhaps ossified disciplines, and it means that archaeologists require continuous scepticism about their own work. Continuing effort is needed to fashion well-thought-out justifications for selecting one or another option, and such effort proves necessary and useful at virtually every step in the research process.

To illustrate this, let me consider two perspectives from which to view the question of choice in archaeological research. The first perspective leads to a view of matters in terms of monolithic approaches in archaeology. From this perspective one chooses to label oneself or another archaeologist as an exponent of Marxist, structuralist, post-structuralist, critical, cognitive, cultural–ecological, feminist, systems, processual, new, cultural–historical, or some other brand of archaeology. Then debates arise about which of the brands is (or works) better. While they strike many sparks and the tracts are exciting to read because of their rhetorical punch and welcome bursts of passion, such debates fall short in their (presumed) aims of providing guidance for comprehensive archaeological research.[11]

Why do the debates about the different brands of archaeology fail to produce sufficiently comprehensive insights for constructing sustained archaeological research? One major drawback is the tendency to treat the brands of archaeology monolithically. There is a good analogy here to party political manifestos (or platforms). In these, fairly complicated (and often internally contradictory) sets of policies (or planks) require a simple dichotomous yes/no reaction from the electorate. Because of the similarly monolithic approach to the objects of choice in archaeological debate, the several steps (or phases) in a research process become hopelessly welded together. Ideally, for the debates to be more enlightening, the steps should be separated in order to discuss both their intrinsic worth and how well they mesh with the other steps.

Furthermore, such monolithic archaeological debates give relatively short shrift to the key factor that allows us to understand the heated differences among practitioners of the different archaeological brands. This, of course, is problem orientation. The difficulty is not that we lack assertive broad-brush statements about the aims of archaeology, about what archaeology is (or should be). Rather, the difficulty lies in the absence of a sustained consideration of the preferred problem orientation's relative worth in relation to a host of other factors. One of these factors is the archaeological (ethnohistorical, physical anthropological, linguistic, ethno-graphic, and historical) record which is relevant to the particular subject at hand, in this case the study of politics in one or more particular ancient complex polities. Another factor concerns the other possible problem orientations, while yet another is the prior research history for the subject of study. Finally, a whole set of other factors concern the steps in the research process besides problem orientation – fieldwork, analysis (bridging arguments), and drawing conclusions. Ideally, a searching discussion of a particular problem orientation that underlies one of the general positions in archaeology should critically cover the relation of the selected problem orientation to all the factors listed above. The world being a complicated place, in effect my requirement that specific subjects of study, bodies of evidence, and research histories be covered, actually precludes the possibility of meaningful discussions of problem orientation that would cover all archaeological possibilities.

This has to be the case, as there is no conceivable way that a single problem orientation could do justice to the variability in these factors.

I can illustrate the general point about problem orientation by looking briefly at two programmatic positions in archaeology. I shall do this from the point of view of someone primarily interested in the politics of ancient complex societies. This is a broad enough interest (e.g., compared to a specific interest in the Maya) that it is not unreasonable to require that an all-purpose approach have some relevance to it. At one end of a spectrum, in early New Archaeology, one finds statements that archaeology (as anthropology) deals with and explains cultural similarities and differences (Binford 1972). This is fair enough, but culture (the object of study) is conceptualized here in a way that gravely impedes an archaeological study of politics in ancient complex polities. A problem orientation aimed at explaining ancient complex polities simply and purely in terms of the interaction between their cultural and behavioral subsystems (viewed in light of a layer cake model – with ideological, sociopolitical, and technoeconomic levels) is open to criticism on several grounds. From my perspective, the most important of these is that the layer-cake behavioral model is wrongly formulated for studying politics. In contrast, a wealth of conceptual and empirical material is available in political anthropology for purposes of putting together a more analytically promising conceptualization of politics in ancient complex polities. In Maya (and Mesoamerican) terms, a rich data base (encompassing archaeological, linguistic, social anthropological, physical anthropological, ethnohistorical, and historical materials) cries out for the middle range combination of generalization and particularism found in political anthropology.

Towards the other extreme of a spectrum, in critical archaeology (Miller and Tilley eds. 1984), one finds notions that archaeology is politics, that it should be politically useful labor (aimed at producing more equitable political regimes), that it should rescue the individual from systemic anonymity. As a set of problem orientations, these assertions are so different from those proposed in New Archaeology, that any debate about the research processes in New Archaeology and critical archaeology can only be understood by analogy to what goes on in the House of Commons. Rhetoric reigns, party political points are scored, and no one changes their minds through the force of the arguments. To take the discussion down to a less abstract level, it is also quite obvious that these critical archaeology assertions have virtually no connection with the attempt to understand politics in ancient complex polities (or actually, in any empirically appreciated polities). The issues raised may be more or less widely interesting in the archaeological subculture, but they are too generalizing, monolithic, prescriptive, and quite simply wide of the (empirical) mark for the anthropological–archaeological study of ancient polities which I advocate here. At best, the issues that concern critical archaeologists could be inserted at the drawing conclusions (lessons) stage of an anthropological–archaeological study of ancient politics. At worst, the extreme presentist notion that the contemporary archaeologist does, and should do, no more than create ancient complex polities in the light of modern concerns is markedly obscurantist in its implications. There is always some truth in the ideas that present concerns shape archaeological problem orientation. But the extreme position that they are only determinants of what archaeologists can think and say about the past is absurd and flatly contradicted by the rich (and ever growing) bodies of evidence and the complex research histories related to ancient complex polities (or even to many more recent polities studied by political anthropologists). Both the evidence and the ways it has been handled through time clearly show that politics in ancient complex polities was different from contemporary political forms (whether actual or Utopian), even if awareness of these forms has colored archaeological interpretation. The idea that we cannot reconstruct the past as it really was is also quite sound. But it does not provide a licence for failing to respect and deal with the fascinating evidence that suggests some of the ways in which past politics differed from present politics.

My intention here is not to single out the (old) New Archaeology or the critical archaeology approaches for special criticism. Each of these conveniently represents one of the end points on a spectrum that runs from positivistic to anti-positivistic approaches. It seems that if one is guided by an interest in ancient complex societies, generally similar (and negative) conclusions can be drawn about the presentations of problem orientations in the several other brands of archaeology: Marxist, structuralist, post-structuralist, cognitive, cultural–ecological, feminist, systems, processual, and cultural–historical, among others.

There is a second perspective on choice in archaeological research which requires one to climb off the soapbox and surrender some rhetorical weapons. This is essentially the perspective I have tried to use in studying the Rosario polity, with varying degrees of effectiveness. Compared to the first perspective, this second perspective takes a much less monolithic view of approaches to archaeological research. The research process is broken down into steps or components, and the web-like linkages between them are appreciated and explored (Figure 49). An initial (and continuing) interest is to match the problem orientation as closely as possible to the scope and possibilities of the evidence, the archaeological and other kinds of records available for studying specific subjects – in this case, political structure and organization in an ancient Maya polity. This matching procedure also involves identifying the kinds of problems which the evidence does not allow us to pursue very effectively. With reference to problem orientation, for the reasons sketched out above, it is not really possible or necessary to align oneself with one of the reigning monolithic approaches in archaeology, at either the positivistic or the non-positivistic end of the spectrum. Rather, problem orientations can be chosen with a number of factors in mind: the data record, other possible problem orientations, research history, and the other research steps.

From this perspective, there can be no golden road to understanding ancient complex polities. Rather, there is a quite complicated research process that requires difficult choices at many steps along the way to drawing the least erroneous conclusions that we can manage, given present resources and understanding. In making choices, at virtually every step, I have tried to follow a middle-of-the-road strategy which is informed by an anthropological perspective on archaeology. This middle range strategy requires that one avoid extreme generalization or extreme particularism. The strategy obviously derives from the controlled comparative tendency in anthropology in which respect for diversity lies between total denial of differences and total relativistic nominalism. The preceding study is meant to show that it is a sensible strategy for dealing with the archaeology of political structure in ancient complex polities. In conclusion, then, while it is not a golden road to understanding ancient complex polities, an anthropological approach to their archaeology proves to be the most interesting way of getting to the most interesting results.

2 Thinking about Maya political structure

1 As tedious as they sometimes seem, terminological clarifications are useful.

   Political: in political anthropology usage, the terms *administrative* and *bureaucratic* are sometimes associated with the policy-implementing side of politics as distinguished from its policy-making or executive side (Easton 1959; M. G. Smith 1956, 1966). As it is unhelpful to draw administrative versus executive distinctions in theoretical discussions of ancient Mesoamerican polities and usually impossible to do so in archaeological testing (Chapter 7), the term *political* is used here to denote both aspects of politics without distinction.

   Structure and organization: the terms *structure* and *organization* are used in the following way (after Firth 1964). Structure refers to relatively enduring and abstract norms, principles, or institutions for arranging and regulating the relations among actors and groups in a society. Organization refers to a contingent, situational set of concrete activities and pragmatic behaviors on the part of societal actors and groups. It proves important for archaeological settlement analysis to make such a distinction between structure (statics) and organization (dynamics).

2 In an admirably detailed book, which appeared as this study was going to press, John Fox uses Southall's segmentary state concept as a kind of societal type in order to aid his interpretation of Postclassic Maya state dynamics and settlement, with special attention to developments in the Maya Highlands (Fox 1987: table 6.2). Fox's intriguing study is highly recommended to those interested in Maya settlement and politics.

3 With respect to the idea that hierarchical levels and distribution of political functions are related in complex ways, a recent cross-cultural study of sedentary prestate societies noted that:

> only a weak relationship was found between administrative complexity and chiefly tasks. Thus leaders at the top of more hierarchical political systems did not necessarily perform a wider range of activities. This weak relationship may be the consequence of the fact that leaders in more hierarchical organizations are concerned primarily with the coordination of responsibilities that have been delegated to their subordinates. (Feinman and Neitzel 1984: 77)

This suggests a non-hierarchical regime, although not precisely a pyramidal regime, in Southall's scheme (1956).

4 From the same substantivist perspective, similar historical–evolutionary logic may be applied to the other institutional components in the comparison between African and Mesoamerican polities (group stratification, vertical rather than horizontal cleavages, estates, corporate segments). All of these components can be inserted into reasonably clear historical sequences. In contrast, more abstractly defined factors such as scale, complexity, and integration need not be inserted quite as strictly in unidirectional sequences. These factors may be more successfully viewed within cyclical developmental frameworks (Blanton *et al.* 1981, 1982).

5 Another problem associated with the earlier New Archaeology approach which Wylie notes

is that the inductive versus deductive contrast drawn between the contexts of discovery and validation is not a sharp one, with inductive and ampliative arguments also required at the testing or validation stage (Wylie 1985: 87). Awareness of this difficult problem has not yet impinged on Maya or Mesoamerican studies.

4 Linking Maya politics and settlement

1 Small sites (with one to three dwellings) do not loom very large in the polity core. They contain less than 1 % of all dwellings.

Pocket	No. Small Sites	No. Dw	% Total Dw
Zorrillo	8	20	6
Nuestra Señora	9	14	5
Chihuahua	5	8	6
Momón	11	21	9
Rosario	2	4	x
Santa Inés N.	6	15	x
Santa Inés S.	2	4	x
All	43	86	x
Midvalley Range★	27	45	26

Dw dwelling
  x under 1 %
★ not included in analyses (Chapters 5–10)

2 The stone-robbing argument is tenuous as it requires that fairly subtle distinctions in the condition of housemounds be detectable after a millennium of postabandonment exposure to the natural elements. Human interference is much less of a problem here because of the virtual abandonment of the site and valley from the Early Postclassic Period onward. An underlying assumption for stone-robbing arguments is that there would have been a strong motivation to re-use stone materials from abandoned buildings (for practical or ideological reasons or both). Ideological strictures against disturbing abandoned and/or economically or politically based decisions not to re-use material from abandoned buildings would sabotage such an assumption and the argument it underlies. No definitive evidence supports one or the other set of possibilities. However, it seems reasonable to provisionally accept the stone-robbing argument.

3 A point of terminological clarification is that all occurrences of dwellings, whether single or multiple, are labelled "housegroups". There is no separate label for single isolated dwellings.

4 Eventually, fuller testing requires controlled comparison of comparative climax–crash settlement data sets. Copan Valley settlement (Fash 1983, 1986; Webster 1985a) and Ocosingo Valley settlement (Becquelin 1982) are good candidates for comparison. Also, settlement records without an obvious major Postclassic crash should be brought into the controlled comparisons to improve the chances of judging proposed relations between structural principles and organizational collapse. Possible cases of this type are the Northern Yucatan Peninsula (Kurjack and Garza 1981; Freidel 1981b) and Highland Guatemala (Fox 1978).

5 Surface form refers here to the basal platform or wall footing. It is likely that upper walls (probably cane, wattle and daub, or *corazón de piedra* [wattle and rubble] variants, with occasional plaster coating) or roofing materials (probably thatch or palm) were refurbished

within a basal platform's use-life. To better check the contention of single platform building phases for El Rosario it would be helpful to carry out excavations in the volumetrically largest housemounds (mostly in central Section A – Figures 7 and 41), as these are physically the most likely places in which to discover multiple construction stages.

6 Equifinality difficulties at a large scale may be set aside by the soft option of leaving developments up to the final settlement patterns in a black box. The black box works well enough for roughly identical settlement patterns. But when the settlement patterns under comparison are dissimilar, and one is trying to distinguish between structural and cyclical determinants for the dissimilarities, the black box is no help.

5 Centralization

1 Settlement and social-scale correlations suggested here are those between single dwellings and nuclear families, between multidwelling housegroups and small extended families, between wards and lineages, and between sites and communities. Such simple correlations between settlement scales and social scales might well be questioned. The ones listed here are well illustrated but certainly not validated by modern Maya settlement patterns (Vogt 1969: ch. 7–8; Gifford 1978; Fash 1983). Unlike the first two authors cited, I have no monolithic commitment to a patrilineage model for Classic Maya social structure. My only claim is a broad and instrumental one that more closely settled people tend to be more closely related sociopolitically. The relations may be expressed in a (patrilineal or other) kinship idiom. Or else relations may be expressed in an administrative-territorial idiom, in a patron-client idiom, in a status-related (horizontal class) idiom, in a craft-guild-related idiom, or in an employer-employee idiom, to mention just a few possibilities. Starting with kinship, the possible bases for co-residential group solidarity are listed here in what I take to be a decreasing order of probability for the Rosario polity. But I would also add the proviso that these are not completely mutually exclusive as possibilities. Ancient complex polities need not be limited to a single monolithic idiom for expressing relations within and among co-residential groups.

2 The PH must be based on criteria which are as independent as possible from the criteria used to evaluate control exercised from a center (this chapter) or from the criteria used to evaluate political function (Chapter 7). All of this is to avoid circular argument. Therefore, the PH does not exhaust all the possible interpretations that might be wrung from civic-ceremonial buildings and the classification criteria are kept as simple and as few as possible. The minimalist approach to selecting criteria for the PH leaves a number of attributes still available for other classifications:

  a the volume of individual civic-ceremonial buildings or plazas [used for the TDI and TLI – this chapter]

  b the existence of some functional differences among civic-ceremonial building types (e.g., pyramid versus range building versus high platform, although the pyramid versus ballcourt contrast is used for PH levels 1–3 versus level 4) [used for the Structure Diversity Index – Chapter 7]

  c the composition of individual plazas (except for multipyramid requirement for PH1 and PH2 versus PH3 and PH4) [used for the Structure Diversity Index – Chapter 7]

  d the layout of individual plazas

  e the number of dwellings falling within the span of influence of a plaza or associated with a center [used for forced settlement indices, TDI and TLI – this chapter]

  f the spatial relation of the plaza to associated dwellings (embedded versus disembedded arrangements)

  g the presence or absence of dwellings on the plaza itself

  h distribution of centers over different regional scales: polity, section, pocket [used for studying vertical and horizontal differentiation – Chapter 6] i the associated site morphology (number of intrasite divisions) [used for measuring administrative burden – Chapter 7]

As indicated, many of these attributes are used for other kinds of analytical tools (Chapters 5–10).

3 As portions of two lower-valley pockets were not completely surveyed (19% of Santa Inés North and 31% of Santa Inés South – de Montmollin n.d.a.: ch. 5), some cases are necessarily missing in the polity-wide, lower valley, Santa Inés North, and Santa Inés South site-size distributions. However, unsurveyed areas were relatively small and the general shape of the distributions would probably not be greatly changed by adding missing cases.

4 Competition among elite groups for control of commoners evokes aspects of Central Place Theory. Particularly relevant is the $k = 7$ administrative pattern where subordinate settlements are drawn in towards higher-order poles of political control (C. Smith 1974). But the forced settlement sketch does not entail a particular hexagonal territorial arrangement, nor does it require the necessary emergence of effort-minimizing locational arrangements for political centers.

5 Freidel's statement (1981b: 314) that there are "many allusions to foreigners gathering local populations into communities" in prehispanic Yucatan is not supported by the two secondary sources that he cites – Scholes and Roys 1968 [1948] and Roys 1957. Scholes and Roys' study of the Chontal Indians has many references to Spanish *congregación* activities (sometimes aided by Indian rulers – see also Farriss 1984: 98, 150, 175), but only a single reference to prehispanic forced settlement (discussed here). Freidel has misread a comment by these authors to the effect that conciliatory procedures were commonly used by foreign rulers in prehispanic times (Scholes and Roys 1968: 79, with examples, 79–80) to mean that settlement nucleation procedures were commonly used. Roys' careful study of settlement and political organization in Yucatan (1957) provides few explicit references to prehispanic forced settlement, but provides a wealth of detail about postconquest Spanish nucleation policies.

6 Civic-ceremonial architectural evidence could be used to indicate economic centers only in a very residual way, where it was proposed that civic-ceremonial plazas also serve as exchange localities (market places). Such is the argument in Freidel's pilgrimage-fair model (Freidel 1981a).

7 Narrowing the focus to look at settlement analysis, it becomes evident that all arguments against the relevance of economically-based individual household decisions to settle in centers undermine the worth of rank-size analysis, where rank-size relations are shaped by voluntaristic (household-level) attraction to economic services or employment prospects. Arguments for a large degree of top-down political compulsion over household settlement undermine the relevance of even a modified form of rank-size analysis, where relations are shaped by attraction to political services. In fact, overemphasis on voluntaristic commoner settlement strategies implicitly occurs in most attempts to recast economic geographic forms of locational analysis in more political terms (administrative services, tribute transport, and information-processing), to make them more anthropologically relevant to precapitalist polities (e.g., Johnson 1977; Steponaitis 1978, 1981; Alden 1979; Spencer 1982; Blanton *et al.* 1982). In political anthropology terms, such approaches are still at the formal or transactionalist theory end of the continuum (Winckler 1969; Vincent 1978).

8 Parenthetically, another way of measuring degrees of forced settlement does not rely directly on measuring the proportions of population at the capital center. This approach leads one to search for evidence that settlement at capital and other important sites is introducing marked inefficiencies into the distribution of population with reference to regional agricultural resources. This requires a regional perspective over a polity, not just a focus on carrying capacity problems in a major center's immediate hinterland (as in Brumfiel 1976; Steponaitis 1981). Where evidence does bear on the question, as in the Teotihuacan and Monte Alban

cases, major regional- (or polity-) scale inefficiencies do appear (Sanders *et al.* 1979; Bell *et al.* 1986; Gorenflo and Gale 1986; Kowalewski 1980). This line of analysis is used only lightly for the Rosario Valley (Chapter 9; de Montmollin 1985c), because the valley's small scale displays a kind of plateau effect whereby distances are too short to make transport cost factors very relevant, if at all. Interestingly, even the much larger Valley of Oaxaca survey area (2,150 sq km) seems to display a plateau effect with reference to certain kinds of spatial analyses (Kowalewski *et al.* 1983: 47).

9 Since there was incomplete coverage of the two lower-valley pockets – Santa Inés North and South [note 3 above], how does this affect forced settlement centralization measures? If we use the reasonable assumption that there were no PH3 or PH2 centers in the unsurveyed sectors, then the effect of omitted sites from the unsurveyed sectors should be to increase somewhat the relative proportion of population at these PH3 and PH2 centers for the lower section, for Santa Inés South, and for Santa Inés North (with consequent reduction in relative proportions at PH4 centers and PH5 sites). Since some analytical mileage is derived from relatively low degrees of paramount forced settlement centralization for the lower section (versus the upper section), and for Santa Inés South and North (versus other pockets), these hypothesized effects of incomplete survey in Santa Inés South and North tend to strengthen rather than vitiate the arguments. Polity-wide calculations are affected in the sense that there would be some inflation of relative proportions for PH1, PH2, and PH3 centers at the expense of PH4 centers and PH5 sites. The effects of incomplete survey on the relative proportions of population at PH4 centers compared to PH5 sites in the affected districts (Santa Inés South and North) are negligible, if one can assume that these proportions were roughly identical in the unsurveyed and in the surveyed areas.

10 Another case of relatively high PH3 and PH5 population is Chihuahua, with Tenam Rosario as its PH3 center (0.60 of the population at Tenam Rosario and 0.32 at PH5 sites). Chihuahua's relatively high PH5 population proportion (0.80 without Tenam Rosario or 0.32 with) may be related to its having been an agricultural reserve for Tenam Rosario (de Montmollin 1985c).

11 For Mayanists, the variability in settlement nucleation in different parts of the Rosario polity brought out in an analysis of degrees of forced settlement is interesting when juxtaposed to certain ethnographic analogy-based interpretations of Maya settlement dispersal (Vogt 1964a, 1964b, 1968, 1983). Such interpretations rely on a Genetic Model which denies the importance of ecological or environmental determinants for settlement dispersion, and presents settlement patterns as an immutable cultural characteristic:

> The basic type of Maya settlement pattern is one of dispersed hamlets (where the bulk of the population lives) surrounding ceremonial centers (of various types and sizes) that are either occupied and controlled by religious officials (priests) or at least serve as foci for ritual activity for the people living in hamlets (Vogt 1964a: 23)...My hypothesis is that this basic Maya settlement plan evolved as an ideal pattern at the proto-time level, or shortly thereafter, and that the Maya have tended to follow it in basic plan ever since – geographical and historical circumstances permitting. The pattern could be actualized with varying degrees of elaboration. It probably began with ceremonial centers that were simple caves in hills or waterholes, reached an extreme of elaboration in the Late Classic sites, and has since become less complex (Vogt 1964a: 24)...The exceptions [to the settlement type] are due either to very special geographic circumstances...or to heavy pressure exerted on the Maya from other cultural groups. An alternative explanation for the nature of Maya settlements...they simply reflect important ecological factors and have little or nothing to do with basic cultural patterns that have persisted in the genetic unit. (Vogt 1964a: 25)

Besides dispersed settlement and empty ceremonial centers, the analogies include *cargo* (religious and civic office) ladders for integrating the dispersed settlement and can be collectively termed the *cargo analogy*. Most archaeological reaction to the cargo analogy has revolved around whether or not the ethnographic analogies proposed really seem to work for the Classic Maya and the general consensus is that they do not work (the debate is summarized in Vogt 1983; see Becquelin 1973; Price 1974; Haviland 1966a, 1966b, 1968; and finally Sabloff 1983: 418, for a reasonable argument that the cargo analogy has not been given a fair test). The notions of relatively empty ceremonial centers, or of wide access to political and ceremonial offices, do not seem to be supported by the Classic Period archaeological evidence. Surprisingly, however, nowhere in the archaeological discussion is there reference to the unique theoretical approach to regional settlement distribution determinants that is incorporated in the cargo analogy. In the analogy, the present highland Maya dispersed settlement pattern is viewed as a systemic (after Kroeber) component of their culture. Persistence of such a settlement pattern is accounted for by a cultural predisposition among the Maya to live in widely scattered settlements, at least since *ca.* 2,000 BC (a proto-time level when the component crystalized). Cultural predisposition seems to be an unlikely sole determinant for regional settlement distribution, which is so sensitive to a variety of other ecological and especially political and economic determinants. While there may indeed be some cultural components whose continuing existence can be accounted for by the cultural imperatives used in a Genetic Model (Marcus 1983c, 1983d), it seems particularly unlikely that regional settlement patterns could be numbered among these components.

It is clear that the Genetic Model gives major importance to environmental determinants as shapers of the original (or *proto*) dispersed settlement. In this sense the argument falls within the environmental to political chain of reasoning (Chapter 1). But the persistence of dispersed settlement after the proto-time period is definitely shaped by cultural preference and not by continuing adaptation to the physical environment, a clear divergence from mainline cultural ecology (Sanders 1966). It is indeed curious that the only viable alternative to a genetic–cultural explanation for enduring settlement dispersal is an environmentally determinist one, since this leaves out a range of social and political determinants for settlement of the kind included in forced settlement models and presumably quite relevant to ancient complex polities. What is also curious about discussions of the cargo analogy by its supporters and critics is the way in which polar multivariate and idealized settlement-types are the conceptual units mobilized – e.g., Maya versus non-Maya regional settlement-types or ceremonial centers versus cities. In light of the forced settlement approach used here, I propose that it would make much more sense to use continuum-oriented thinking in these discussions and attempt to chart the diachronic and synchronic empirical variability in settlement variables such as nucleation [proportion of population residing at a capital] within and outside the Maya area.

12 Besides the methodological difficulties stressed here (contemporaneity and equifinality) there are some more substantive theoretical difficulties and ambiguities associated with the attempt to link political power and prestige directly with civic-ceremonial bulk or monumentality. For example, to set against the notion that there is a direct link between prestige and elaborate public monuments, there is the notion that hyper-monumentality corresponds to periods of political insecurity and uncertainty for the groups erecting the monuments. Marcus (1974) argues this with reference to the quantities of sculptured monuments erected in different periods at Monte Alban. Or, as another example of a shifting relationship between political prestige and monument building, consider that:

> massive monumental architecture projects were especially important to politically aggressive communities with up to 50,000 people, while established city states with over 50,000 inhabitants downplayed monumental architecture in favor of more useful

public architecture such as marketplaces, streets, aqueducts, irrigation facilities, and military fortifications. (Sidrys 1978:8)

Finally, interpretations of secularization trends from the Maya Classic to Postclassic Periods propose changing relations between political power and public monumentality – i.e., a close relation in the Classic Period and a distant relation in the Postclassic Period (Rathje 1975; Freidel and Cliff 1978). All these examples, correctly argued or not, are necessary "cautionary tales" serving to qualify the direct link argument by proposing temporally, structurally, and perhaps culturally shifting relations between political power and monumentality. Even so, for comparisons effected within the Rosario polity in the Classic Period (as opposed to grander cross-cultural and cross-temporal comparisons), the basic assumption that greater monumentality indicates greater political power and prestige is probably roughly adequate.

13 There are variant ways of organizing the inputs into the TLI calculation. Each has somewhat different implications.

Civic-ceremonial mass	Divided by	Number of dwellings
1 all PH1–4 centers	/	all sites
2 all PH1–4 centers	/	all PH5 sites
3 PH1–2 centers	/	all sites
4 PH1–2 centers	/	all sites except PH1–2 sites
5 PH3 centers	/	PH3, PH4, and PH5 sites
6 PH3 centers	/	PH4 and PH5 sites
7 PH4 centers	/	PH4 and PH5 sites
8 PH4 centers	/	PH5 sites

14 Abrams' very comprehensive study of palace construction at Copan comes to a similar conclusion that "elite construction was not a drain on the labor pool, and that elite construction demands created little if any stress on the infrastructure of Late Classic Copan society" (Abrams 1987:496; see also Webster 1985b:392). A similarly slight per capita burden of civic-ceremonial construction activities is also suggested by a calculation that Period IIIA civic mound volume in the Valley of Oaxaca represents one week's work for every male during his lifetime (Kowalewski and Finsten 1983:422).

15 The two PH2/3 centers are best left out of the comparisons because their TLI automatically increases when they are viewed as PH3 rather than PH2 centers.

6 Differentiation and integration

1 The revised Chihuahua total also includes a few dwellings from RV119, a Preclassic civic-ceremonial center with associated Late/Terminal Classic domestic settlement.

2 Unsurveyed area is included in the territorial size estimates discussed for both Santa Inés South and North, on the assumption that population density in the unsurveyed area generally matched that found in the surveyed area. Also, there is probably a slight undersurveying of Rosario on its south side, but the impact of this on the ratio calculations should not be too great.

3 The valley-bottom area considered here also includes valley-floor eminences and area covered by sites (so that the valley-bottom area would be somewhat reduced in an alternative set of calculations). This measure is affected to some degree by relatively how much of the sloping valley-edge was surveyed (or included within a pocket, in the case of Santa Inés North). Somewhat lesser coverage of the valley edges (in lower versus upper pockets) would

slightly increase the average value for the affected pockets. Since there were apparently very few structures well up into the more steeply sloping valley-edges that were surveyed (in the upper valley) or spot checked (in the lower valley), uneven coverage of these areas would not have a drastic effect on calculations. At any rate, it is possible to consult Figure 48 (relating to analysis in Chapter 9) where the hectares of vf-vfe per dwelling are recalculated to leave out dwellings from the Upper Hillside, reducing some of the problem.

4 To achieve more of a common standard of TBS across the two sections, it is possible to amalgamate Zorrillo and Nuestra Señora, and then Momón and Chihuahua (with the Tenam Rosario population added in) [Zorrillo-Nuestra Señora = 590; Momón-Chihuahua = 566].

5 The upper section is a possible partial exception, since the Nuestra Señora PH3 TDI value is higher than the PH2 TDI value, but the Nuestra Señora capital (RV6) is a wild card, virtually a vacant ceremonial center.

6 Such results are subject to the caution that the individual TBS for PH4 centers is relatively more sensitive to undercounting due to incomplete survey along the edges than is the TBS for PH3 centers. So there is a tendency for greater inflation of PH4 TLI values, which strengthens the patterning I am commenting on.

7 A continuing problem that weakens these and other tests of the co-variation between specialization and integration is the great difficulty in finding sound independent measures for the second of these dimensions. Integration has to be inferred from specialization and there is no clear test of their relation.

7 Political regimes and microcosms

1 Some of the centers have no associated dwelling buildings (4), or else no large enough wards (4). Neither of these kinds of centers are included in the analysis.

2 A solution to the problem of possible replication of plazas (and associated functions) within a multiplaza center is to examine building types at each plaza, within the relatively small number of multiplaza centers (11), to check for replication or absence of replication among plazas. Replication would tend to invalidate the PCI as a sensitive measure of political specialization at a center, while some differentiation among plazas would enhance the PCI. The comparisons (de Montmollin 1985a: ch. 11) show absence of replication at multiplaza centers, enhancing the PCI's validity.

3 The high PS in Momón is quite aberrant, not just by upper section standards.

4 This would be even clearer if one were to find another ballcourt within the unsurveyed portion of Santa Inés North since this would bring the ballcourt PS for that pocket down to the lower-valley norm.

5 Still another interesting feature of the ballcourt is that disc no. 3, in the centre of its playing alley (representing the central authority in the Rosario polity – Agrinier n.d.), was probably intentionally smashed in prehispanic times. The other six discs on the ballcourt (representing the authorities in subordinate districts) were left intact, sustaining only natural damage. This is a tenuous, but intriguing, line of evidence suggesting sudden political breakdown, possibly occurring earlier at the polity's center than in its hinterland.

6 The sites found in the reconnaissance have not been differentiated as between the Late Classic and the Late/Terminal Classic Periods. A working assumption (based on rapid examination of the collections, but certainly subject to revision through further collecting and ceramic analysis), is that the sites classed as Late Classic in the reconnaissance also fall into the Late/Terminal Classic Period, during which occupation reached its maximum in the Rosario Valley and surrounding valleys as well. Consequently, Late Classic Period regional centers outside the Rosario Valley are referred to as Late (Terminal) Classic Period centers.

8 Political stratification patterns

1 Methodologically speaking, I have used simple visual inspection to evaluate degrees of proximity. In this case, it would be absurd overkill to use formal spatial techniques (such as nearest-neighbor analysis) since the distances of interest are not too subtly small to escape the naked eye.

2 There are several variant possibilities associated with H2, which are treated elsewhere (de Montmollin n.d.c).

3 The variation between ascribed and achieved modes of access to political office also relates obliquely to the subcontinuum between *societas* which features ascribed and/or kinship-based political relations and *civitas* which features achievement and/or contract-based political relations. This is one of the minor subcontinua incorporated into the segmentary–unitary continuum (Table 1). My findings, that ascribed modes of access prevailed in the Rosario polity, generally support the idea that *societas* relations were important there, but with an emphasis on the ascribed rather than the kinship aspect of *societas*. My findings, that achieved access was less important, are directly relevant to the issue of *civitas*. The achievement system referred to in the tests is the one that precedes ascribed systems in a cultural evolutionary scheme (Service 1971; Freid 1967). This should be clear enough from my use of the logic of mortuary analyses developed with reference to North American evidence about achievement-based tribal or ascription-based chiefdom societies. The achievement or contract system referred to in the *civitas* concept used here (Chapter 2) is the system that follows ascribed systems in the Weberian historical sequence. Weber focuses on the relatively recent breakdown of ascribed relations in favor of personalized contract relations, the transition from traditional to rational/legal forms of legitimation (Gerth and Mills eds. 1946).

4 The distinction between small and large pyramids is the same as that used earlier (Chapter 7) for the Structure Diversity Index – i.e., 52 small pyramids (50–500 cu m) and 16 large pyramids (525–5,300+ cu m).

5 The difference in conclusions occurs mainly because of the importance of civic-ceremonial construction volume in the TLI calculation. This is more important than any effects of not dividing dwellings into classes of tribute payers and tribute receivers in the TLI. The TLI is still probably better as a measure of political centralization because it deals relatively directly with the evidence concerning political activity associated with civic-ceremonial buildings and plazas. The domestic housing criteria for the division into tribute payers and receivers (used in this chapter) are relatively more diffuse in what they are trying to measure and the resulting classification has broader social and cultural implications, beyond political structure.

6 The relative uses and merits of the TLI and the proportion of population in the contender class (elite fraction) as indicators of tributary imposition were compared in note 5. A similar kind of comparison can be made between the subject per contender ratio measure and the TBS. While both are interesting to use, the TBS (as was the case for the TLI) is less diffusely defined as a measure and more sensitive to purely political factors. Thus the TBS is a more politically realistic measure of the support group available to office holders. The subject per contender ratio also suffers from being an average and the product of a great deal of lumping that over-rides some spatial factors and possible hierarchical differences within the elite group.

9 Mechanical versus organic solidarity

1 The only possible example of such an alteration would be to combine the Chihuahua and Momón Pockets, which would bring the vf-vfe to total area ratio more into line with the others (Figure 21). And there is not much evidence to support the idea that this kind of combination was ever actually effected. The incomplete hierarchy in the Chihuahua Pocket is much more likely to have been capped by Tenam Rosario than by the Momón PH3 center.

2 Population allowed refers not to an absolute environmentally and/or technologically determined density standard (e.g., carrying capacity). Instead, it refers to a more politically and socially relative standard: the population density expected in a district if the total polity population were distributed evenly (according to resources) over it and other districts within the polity.

3 Beyond any preservation and visibility problems affecting the Rosario settlement record, clear artifactual evidence for craft specialization is rarely found in the Classic Maya Lowlands in general, even with extensive excavations to complement survey (Webster 1985b, with reference to the Copan Valley). In effect, it seems that most households were roughly similar economically, farming and a range of simple craft activities being the principal sources of livelihood.

4 The only site with very clear evidence for a high incidence of craft activity is an Early Postclassic center – La Mesa (RV140) – where there was some manufacturing of obsidian and chert implements. Another possible extraction (if not production) center is RV195 in Santa Inés South's southwest corner, where chert nodules occur on the surface.

10 Segmenting versus non-segmenting organization

1 Other variables need to be taken into account and factored out to make the test comparisons more effective. These include any interior versus periphery differences in environmental carrying capacities, and interior versus periphery differences in security or exposure to raiding.

2 The climax–crash assumption has a built-in simplifying subassumption that one will see primarily growth stages rather than decline stages in a cycle, since it is cut off in full flower. Consequently, this line of reasoning is not a thoroughly searching way of looking for the entire span of growth and decline implied by cyclical change (this also applies to subsequent analysis of cycles at the site and district level).

3 For comparison's sake, an interesting example from the Basin of Mexico concerns how site cycling may be perceived in a single-period settlement pattern:

> Once a village had reached the maximum size its catchment could reasonably support, any excess population would have to split off and form daughter communities. CH-4 and CH-8 may represent such daughter communities that were founded relatively late in the period and so were not occupied long enough to reach their maximum size. (Steponaitis 1981: 341, and see also 345)

4 Interestingly, the second option is vaguely similar to the notion that urban systems start off in primate form and develop towards mature lognormal form (Crumley 1976).

5 This pattern is not entirely clear-cut, with Chihuahua, Nuestra Señora, and Rosario being exceptional in various ways (Chapter 5).

6 My rather standard core-periphery perspective on the Maya area can be contrasted with a slightly different view:

> Marginal outposts of culture areas are fragile extensions of the societies that produced them. They tend to be extremely conservative, maintaining the traditions, notably material ones, of the center. At the same time, they are susceptible to strong outside influences, being both closer to the external forces and relatively far from the sustaining central ones. (Miller 1986: 200–201)

A view of peripheral zones as autonomous loci of developments (with reference to the center) because of exposure to outside influences makes sense in the context from which it comes, the East Coast of Yucatan, exposed as it was to Gulf Coast Putun groups from the Late Classic Period onward (Miller 1986; Sabloff 1977). However, it is difficult to extend the concept to an area such as the Upper Tributaries, which does not seem to have been exposed to strong non-Maya groups in the Classic Period.

7 On the subject of external factors, it is also relevant to mention that the Early Postclassic

Period in the Rosario Valley saw a marked shift towards Central Mexican obsidian sources, compared to exclusively Guatemalan sources in the Late/Terminal Classic Period and earlier (Clark n.d.). This small but clear datum suggests some sort of external Mexican involvement in the Rosario polity collapse or its immediate aftermath.

8 Although the precise timing of the Puuc decline relative to declines in other parts of the Maya area is under continuing discussion (Robles and Andrews 1986), the severity of the decline is not in question nor the lack of recovery virtually up to the present.

11 Archaeological study of Maya polities

1 Cultural factors are not stressed as causal elements for differences and similarities among districts. These factors are assumed to be rather constant within the Rosario polity. But wider-ranging comparisons of the Rosario polity to other polities (especially outside the Upper Grijalva Tributaries) would certainly have to take possible cultural differences into account.

2 The upper section with its approximately 1,000 dwellings has an estimated population of 5,000, while the lower section with about 3,000 dwellings has an estimated population of 15,000. Of course, these are maximum estimates for the Late/Terminal Classic Period and only close to being accurate if the climax–crash assumption about settlement history is valid.

3 The conceptualization of a synchronic, distributional data set as a snapshot of an ongoing process was pioneered in studies designed to evaluate the impact of a domestic cycle on censuses of household composition and residence rules (Fortes 1962; Goody ed. 1962).

4 Because of the linear arrangement of districts in the Rosario polity core (Figure 5), only the northeast and southwest ends are treated as political boundaries appropriate for comparison. The survey area's other sides are relatively rugged (and most probably lightly settled) and they border on a peripheral zone, surrounding the polity's core and pertaining to the polity.

5 A glance at the civic-ceremonial center plans for such major Usumacinta zone capitals as Yaxchilán, Bonampak, and Piedras Negras (Andrews 1975: figs. 57, 68, and 55) reveals no close similarities to Tenam Rosario in the contents and relative arrangements of plazas. But one generic resemblance is the presence at Tenam Rosario, Piedras Negras, and Yaxchilán of two ballcourts. Furthermore, at both Tenam Rosario and Piedras Negras, the two ballcourts are associated with two major civic-ceremonial architectural assemblages. Finally, civic-ceremonial structures at Tenam Rosario, Yaxchilán, Piedras Negras, and Bonampak tend to be oriented roughly 45 degrees west of north (while such an orientation can be explained away as corresponding to local topographic constraints, it is nevertheless a fairly unusual orientation by Lowland Maya standards). The lack of extensive and close resemblances between Tenam Rosario and the Usumacinta centers is not a disproof of the principle discussed by Foster (1960) since metropolitan norms are less likely to be clearly detectable than their colonial reproductions on a blank slate. In effect, the aggregated plaza plans for the long-lasting centers of Yaxchilán and Piedras Negras produce an exceedingly more complex (and less austere) pattern than Tenam Rosario's.

At any rate, some of the closest resemblances to Tenam Rosario's individual plaza patterns (especially Plazas 3 and 6, Figure 9) are found further afield in the Great Plaza at Tikal (Guillemin 1968), in the northeast Peten. Both have pyramids on three sides, with a range/palace on the south(western) side. Another parallel is with the Late Postclassic Central Quiche plaza plan replicated at several Highland Guatemala centers (Carmack 1981; Fox 1978, 1987). In this case, both have pyramids on at least two sides and a ballcourt on the south(west) corner. These last resemblances are puzzling. The similarities between Tenam Rosario and Quiche centers are not easily interpretable in terms of historical links, because of the gaps in space and time between the centers (but see Fox 1987: ch. 4). Similarities between Tenam Rosario and Tikal would seem to have a slightly greater chance of reflecting historical links. With reference to a similar theme on the opposite extreme of the Late Classic Maya world, Ashmore has argued for possible elite political links between the dependent Quirigua zone on the southeast Maya periphery and the dominant northeast Peten Lowlands, headed by Tikal (Ashmore 1986). Besides epigraphy and ceramics, another line of evidence for this is the presence in the former area of a Peten-style "triad group": a plaza with public-ritual buildings on all but the south side, which is often bounded by an elite residence (Ashmore 1986). This, of course, is the same general pattern found in Plazas 3 and 6 at Tenam Rosario. The question that comes immediately to mind is whether such triad groups are found in the Usumacinta zone, intermediate between the Rosario Valley and the northeast Peten. Among the three major Usumacinta capitals (Yaxchilán, Bonampak, and Piedras Negras) only the civic-ceremonial plan for Yaxchilán (Andrews 1975: fig. 57) displays a (dubious) example of the triad arrangement (i.e., what Andrews refers to as the southeast court of the second subgroup – 1975: 141).

Finally, concerning Tenam Rosario's larger ballcourt and ballcourts at other Usumacinta zone sites, Agrinier's analyses suggest that similarities are closest between the former and Ballcourt I at Yaxchilán (Agrinier 1983, n.d.). Most relevant to the notion of a political microcosm is the fact that both ballcourts have carved marker discs which feature portraits of rulers rather than ballplayers. Representations of the latter are very common in the Classic Maya Lowlands and would tend to be more congruent with interpretations of the ballcourt as a stage for ritual contests.

6 Others have pointed out the rather low-order methodological nature of much Binfordian middle range theory (Raab and Goodyear 1984; Bailey 1983; Willey and Sabloff 1980).

7 To simplify the argument, I leave out epigraphically-based studies of Classic politics which do introduce particularism, but tend at present to be rather divorced from the full spectrum of archaeological evidence and studies, especially for the Maya case (Chapter 3).

8 In fact, Binford himself has criticized such strict empiricist from-the-ground-up approaches as he sees them in the work of other reconstructionist archaeologists (Binford 1986: 461–464; referring to the work of Schiffer and Gould).

9 For methodological individualism as conventionally understood, the smallest-scale unit is, of course, the individual. But for the discussion here, I take some liberties in treating archaeological approaches which focus exclusively on households as examples of strict methodological individualism. This can be misleading in the sense that a focus on households as agents can be construed as a (low intensity) form of methodological holism. When households are treated as actors, the several individuals in the household are blended into a single-agency collectivity, in a process of reification which over-rides small group dynamics among individuals within households. Nevertheless, this deviation from convention seems justified when referring to issues in archaeological analysis where the smallest or irreducible analytical unit is only rarely the individual and much more commonly the household. Interesting as they are, prescriptive statements about the importance of the prehistoric individual for archaeology (Hodder 1986) have little bearing on this case since such statements have limited connection to archaeological (settlement) data, or especially to problems in the political analysis of ancient complex polities, my concerns here.

10 In this respect, I can also use the convenient analytical disclaimer that consistent errors of attribution will tend to cancel themselves out if the analysis focuses on comparisons and proportions rather than on absolute values (Chapter 4).

11 Viewed more cynically, the debates seem more successful in fulfilling their latent functions of providing an idiom for intradisciplinary political strife.

REFERENCES

Abrams, Elliot M. 1987   Economic Specialization and Construction Personnel in Classic
    Period Copan, Honduras. *American Antiquity*, 52: 485–499
Adams, Richard E. W. 1974   A Trial Estimation of Classic Maya Palace Populations at
    Uaxactun. In *Mesoamerican Archaeology: New Approaches*, edited by Norman
    Hammond, pp. 285–296. University of Texas Press, Austin
    1981   Settlement Patterns of the Central Yucatan and Southern Campeche Regions.
    In *Lowland Maya Settlement Patterns*, edited by Wendy Ashmore, pp. 211–257.
    University of New Mexico Press, Albuquerque
Adams, Richard E. W. (ed.) 1977   *The Origins of Maya Civilization*. University of New
    Mexico Press, Albuquerque
Adams, Richard E. W. and Richard C. Jones 1981   Spatial Patterns and Regional
    Growth Among Classic Maya Cities. *American Antiquity*, 46: 301–322
Adams, Richard E. W. and Woodruff D. Smith 1977   Apocalyptic Visions: The Maya
    Collapse and Medieval Europe. *Archaeology*, 30: 292–301
    1981   Feudal Models for Classic Maya Civilization. In *Lowland Maya Settlement
    Patterns*, edited by Wendy Ashmore, pp. 335–349. University of New Mexico Press,
    Albuquerque
Adams, Robert McC. 1981   *Heartland of Cities*. The University of Chicago Press,
    Chicago
Agrinier, Pierre 1979   *Late Classic Elite Vs. Non-Elite Domestic Variations from the
    Tenam Rosario Zone*. Paper presented at the XLIII International Congress of
    Americanists, Vancouver
    1983   Tenam Rosario: una posible relocalización del clásico tardío terminal Maya
    desde el Usumacinta. In *Antropología e historia de los Mixe-Zoques y Mayas.
    Homenaje a Frans Blom*, edited by Lorenzo Ochoa and Thomas A. Lee, Jr., pp.
    241–254. Universidad Nacional Autónoma de México, México
    1984   Densidad de problación contemporánea y del clásico tardío terminal en el valle
    de Santa Inés-Rosario, Chiapas. In *XVII Mesa Redonda*, vol. 1: 423–430. Sociedad
    Mexicana de Antropología, México
    n.d.   The Terminal Classic Ballgame in the Valley of El Rosario, Chiapas.
    Unpublished paper
Ahmed, Akbar S. 1976   *Millenium and Charisma Among Pathans: A Critical Essay in
    Social Anthropology*. Routledge & Kegan Paul, London
Alden, John 1979   A Reconstruction of Toltec Period Political Units in the Valley of
    Mexico. In *Transformations: Mathematical Approaches to Culture Change*, edited by
    Colin Renfrew and Kenneth L. Cooke, pp. 169–200. Academic Press, New York
Alvarez, A., Carlos 1982   Reconocimiento arqueológico en los valles cercanos a
    Las Margaritas, Chiapas. *Estudios de Cultura Maya*, 14: 145–177
Ammerman, Albert J. 1981   Surveys and Archaeological Research. *Annual Review of
    Anthropology*, 10: 63–88
Andrews IV, E. Wyllys 1965   Archaeology and Prehistory in the Northern Lowlands:
    An Introduction. *Handbook of Middle American Indians*, 2: 288–330

Andrews, George F. 1975 *Maya Cities: Placemaking and Urbanization*. University of Oklahoma Press, Norman

Arnold, Jeanne A. and Anabel Ford 1980 A Statistical Examination of Settlement Patterns at Tikal, Guatemala. *American Antiquity*, 45: 713–726

Ascher, Robert 1961 Analogy in Archaeological Interpretation. *Southwestern Journal of Anthropology*, 17: 317–325

Ashmore, Wendy 1981 Some Issues of Method and Theory in Lowland Maya Settlement Archaeology. In *Lowland Maya Settlement Patterns*, edited by Wendy Ashmore, pp. 37–69. University of New Mexico Press, Albuquerque

1986 Peten Cosmology in the Maya Southeast: An Analysis of Architecture and Settlement Patterns at Classic Quirigua. In *The Southeast Maya Periphery*, edited by Patricia A. Urban and Edward M. Schortman, pp. 35–49. University of Texas Press, Austin

Ashmore, Wendy (ed.) 1981 *Lowland Maya Settlement Patterns*. University of New Mexico Press, Albuquerque

Athens, J. Stephen 1977 Theory Building and the Study of Evolutionary Process in Complex Societies. In *For Theory Building in Archaeology*, edited by Lewis R. Binford, pp. 353–383. Academic Press, New York

Ayala, Maricela 1984 La estela 1 de Chihuahua o Tenam Rosario. In *Guía para el estudio de los monumentos esculpidos de Chinkultic*, by Carlos Navarrete, pp. 85–88 (Appendix C). Centro de Estudios Mayas, Universidad Nacional Autónoma de México, México

Bailey, Fred G. 1970 *Stratagems and Spoils: A Social Anthropology of Politics*. Blackwell, Oxford

Bailey, Geoff N. 1983 Concepts of Time in Quaternary Prehistory. *Annual Review of Anthropology*, 12: 165–192

Balandier, Georges 1970 *Political Anthropology*. Penguin Books, Harmondsworth

Barth, Frederic 1959 Segmentary Opposition and the Theory of Games: A Study of Pathan Organization. *Journal of the Royal Anthropological Institute*, 89: 5–21

Becquelin, Pierre 1973 Ethnologie et archéologie dans l'aire maya: analogies et évolution culturelle. *Journal de la Société des Américanistes*, 62: 43–56

1982 La structure de l'habitat dans la région d'Ocosingo. In *Tonina, une cité Maya du Chiapas*, vol. 2, ch. 4: 549–610, [figures are in vol. 3: 1,199–1,240]. Editions Recherche Sur Les Civilisations, Paris

Bell, Thomas L., Richard L. Church, and Larry Gorenflo 1986 Late Horizon Regional Efficiency in the Northeastern Basin in Mexico: A Location-Allocation Perspective. Unpublished paper

Binford, Lewis R. 1967 Smudge Pits and Hide Smoking: The Use of Analogy in Archaeological Reasoning. *American Antiquity*, 32: 1–12

1972 *An Archaeological Perspective*. Academic Press, New York

1977 General Introduction. In *For Theory Building in Archaeology*, edited by Lewis R. Binford, pp. 1–13. Academic Press, New York

1981 Behavioral Archaeology and the Pompeii Premise. *Journal of Anthropological Research*, 37: 195–208

1983a *Working at Archaeology*. Academic Press, New York

1983b *In Pursuit of the Past: Decoding the Archaeological Record*. Thames & Hudson, New York

1986 In Pursuit of the Future. In *American Archaeology Past and Future*, edited by David J. Meltzer, Don. D. Fowler, and Jeremy A. Sabloff, pp. 459–479. Smithsonian Institution Press, Washington

Binford, Lewis R. and Jeremy A. Sabloff 1982 Paradigms, Systematics, and Archaeology. *Journal of Anthropological Research*, 38(2): 137–153

Blake, T. Michael 1984 La detección de la organización social utilizando la arquitectura doméstica. In *XVII Mesa Redonda*, vol. 1: 471–478. Sociedad Mexicana de Antropología, México

1985   *Canajasté: An Evolving Postclassic Maya State*. Unpublished Ph.D. dissertation, University of Michigan

Blanton, Richard E. 1976   Anthropological Studies of Cities. *Annual Review of Anthropology*, 5: 249–264

1978   *Monte Alban: Settlement Patterns at the Ancient Zapotec Capital*. Academic Press, New York

1980   Cultural Ecology Reconsidered. *American Antiquity*, 45: 145–150

1983   Advances in the Study of Cultural Evolution in Prehispanic Highland Mesoamerica. *Advances in World Archaeology*, 2: 245–288

Blanton, Richard E., Stephen A. Kowaleski, Gary Feinman, and Jill Appel 1981   *Ancient Mesoamerica: A Comparison of Change in Three Regions*. Cambridge University Press, Cambridge

1982   Monte Alban's Hinterland, Part 1: The Prehispanic Settlement Patterns of the Central and Southern Parts of the Valley of Oaxaca, Mexico. *University of Michigan Museum of Anthropology Memoirs*, no. 15

Bove, Fred J. 1981   Trend Surface Analysis and the Lowland Classic Maya Collapse. *American Antiquity*, 46: 93–112

Bray, Warwick 1983   Landscape with Figures: Settlement Patterns, Locational Models, and Politics in Mesoamerica. In *Prehistoric Settlement Patterns*, edited by Evon Z. Vogt and Richard M. Leventhal, pp. 361–374. University of New Mexico Press, Albuquerque

Bricker, Victoria R. 1981   *The Indian Christ, the Indian King: The Historical Substrate of Maya Myth and Ritual*. University of Texas Press, Austin

Brown, James A. (ed.) 1971   Approaches to the Social Dimensions of Mortuary Practices. *Society for American Archaeology Memoir*, no. 25

Brumfiel, Elizabeth 1976   Regional Growth in the Eastern Valley of Mexico: A Test of the "Population Pressure" Hypothesis. In *The Early Mesoamerican Village*, edited by Kent V. Flannery, pp. 234–249. Academic Press, New York

1980   Specialization, Market Exchange, and the Aztec State: A View from Huexotla. *Current Anthropology*, 21: 459–478

Bryant, Douglas D. 1984   The Early Classic Period at Ojo de Agua, Chiapas, Mexico. In *XVII Mesa Redonda*, vol. 1: 391–398. Sociedad Mexicana de Antropología, México

Bryant, Douglas D. and Gareth W. Lowe 1980   Excavaciones en las ruinas de Ojo de Agua, Municipio de Trinitaria, Chiapas, en 1980. Report to Instituto Nacional de Antropología e Historia. MS on file, New World Archaeological Foundation, San Cristóbal

Bullard, William R. 1960   The Maya Settlement Pattern in Northeastern Peten, Guatemala. *American Antiquity*, 25: 355–372

Burling, Robbins 1974   *The Passage of Power: Studies in Political Succession*. Academic Press, New York

Carmack, Robert M. 1976   La estratificación social quicheana prehispánica. In *Estratificación social en la Mesoamérica prehispánica*, by Pedro Carrasco, Johanna Broda, *et al.*, pp. 245–276. Secretaría de Educación Pública-Instituto Nacional de Antropología, México

1981   *The Quiche Maya of Utatlan*. University of Oklahoma Press, Norman

Carneiro, Robert 1981   The Chiefdom: Precursor of the State. In *The Transition to Statehood in the New World*, edited by Grant D. Jones and R. Kautz, pp. 37–73. Cambridge University Press, Cambridge

Carneiro, Robert (ed.) 1967   *The Evolution of Society: Selections From Herbert Spencer's "Principles of Sociology".*The University of Chicago Press, Chicago

Carr, Robert F. and James E. Hazzard 1961   Map of the Ruins of Tikal, El Peten, Guatemala. *Tikal Reports*, no. 11 (Philadelphia)

Carrasco, Pedro 1978   La economía del México prehispánico. In *Economía política e ideología en el México prehispánico*, edited by Pedro Carrasco and Johanna Broda, pp. 15–76. Editorial Nueva Imagen, México

   1982   The Political Economy of the Aztec and Inca States. In *The Inca and Aztec States: 1400–1800*, edited by George A. Collier, Renato I. Rosaldo, and John D. Wirth, pp. 23–40. Academic Press, New York

Carrasco, Pedro, Johanna Broda, *et al.* 1976   *Estratificación social en la Mesoamérica prehispánica.* Secretaría de Educación Pública-Instituto Nacional de Antropología e Historia, México

Carrasco, Pedro and Johanna Broda (eds.) 1978   *Economía política e ideología en el México prehispánico.* Editorial Nueva Imagen, México

Chang, Kwang-Chih 1967   *Rethinking Archaeology.* Random House, New York

Charlton, Thomas H. 1981   Archaeology, Ethnohistory, and Ethnology: Interpretive Interfaces. *Advances in Archaeological Method and Theory*, 4: 129–176

Chase, Arlen F. and Prudence M. Rice (eds.) 1985   *The Lowland Maya Postclassic.* University of Texas Press, Austin

Cheek, Charles 1986   Construction Activity as a Measure of Change at Copan, Honduras. In *The Southeast Maya Periphery*, edited by Patricia A. Urban and Edward M. Schortman, pp. 50–71. University of Texas Press, Austin

Chi, Gaspar Antonio 1941   Relación histórica sobre las costumbres de los indios de Yucatán [orig. 1582]. In *Peabody Museum Papers*, no. 18: 230–32

Claessen, Henri J. M. and Peter Skalnik (eds.) 1978   *The Early State.* Mouton, The Hague

Clark, J. Grahame D. 1951   Folk-Culture and the Study of European Prehistory. In *Aspects of Archaeology*, edited by W. F. Grimes, pp. 49–65. Edwards, London

Clark, John E. n.d.   Lithic Artifacts From the 1983 Rosario Valley Survey. Unpublished MS on file, New World Archaeological Foundation, San Cristóbal

Cline, Howard F. 1949   Civil Congregations of the Indians in New Spain, 1598–1606. *Hispanic American Historical Review*, 29: 349–369

Coe, Michael D. 1961   Social Typology and Tropical Forest Civilizations. *Comparative Studies in Society and History*, 4(1): 65–85

   1965   A Model of Ancient Community Structure in the Maya Lowlands. *Southwestern Journal of Anthropology*, 21: 97–114

   1974   Comment on Prof. Sanders' Paper. In *Reconstructing Complex Societies*, (Supplement to the Bulletin of the American Schools of Oriental Research, no. 20), edited by Charlotte B. Moore, pp. 116–118. Massachusetts Institute of Technology Press, Cambridge

Coe, William R. 1959   Piedras Negras Archaeology: Artifacts, Caches, and Burials. *Museum Monographs, University of Pennsylvania*

Cohen, Abner 1979   Political Symbolism. *Annual Review of Anthropology*, 8: 87–113

Cohen, Ronald 1981   Evolution, Fission, and the Early State. In *The Study of the State*, edited by Henri J. M. Claessen and Peter Skalnik, pp. 87–115. Mouton, The Hague

Cohen, Ronald and Elman R. Service (eds.) 1978   *Origins of the State: The Anthropology of Political Evolution.* ISHI, Philadelphia

Collier, George A., Renato, I. Rosaldo and John D. Wirth (eds.) 1982   *The Inca and Aztec States: 1400–1800.* Academic Press, New York

Cowgill, George L. 1975   On Causes and Consequences of Ancient and Modern Population Changes. *American Anthropologist*, 77: 505–525

1979 Teotihuacan, Internal Militaristic Competition, and the Fall of the Classic Maya. In *Maya Archaeology and Ethnohistory*, edited by Norman Hammond and Gordon R. Willey, pp. 51–62. University of Texas Press, Austin

1983 Rulership and the Ciudadela: Political Inferences from Teotihuacan Architecture. In *Civilization in the Ancient Americas*, edited by Richard M. Leventhal and Alan L. Kolata, pp. 313–343. University of New Mexico Press, Albuquerque

1986 Archaeological Applications of Mathematical and Formal Methods. In *American Archaeology Past and Future*, edited by David J. Meltzer, Don D. Fowler, and Jeremy A. Sabloff, pp. 369–393. Smithsonian Institution Press, Washington

Cowgill, George L., Jeffrey H. Altschul, and Rebecca S. Sload 1984 Spatial Analysis at Teotihuacan: A Mesoamerican Metropolis. In *Intrasite Spatial Analysis in Archaeology*, edited by Harold Hietala, pp. 154–195. Cambridge University Press, Cambridge

Crumley, Carol 1976 Towards a Locational Definition of State Systems of Settlement. *American Anthropologist*, 78: 59–73

Culbert, T. Patrick 1974 *The Lost Civilization: The Story of the Classic Maya*. Harper & Row, New York

1977 Maya Development and Collapse: An Economic Perspective. In *Social Process in Maya Prehistory*, edited by Norman Hammond, pp. 510–530. Academic Press, New York

Culbert, T. Patrick (ed.) 1973 *The Classic Maya Collapse*. University of New Mexico Press, Albuquerque

de Montmollin, Olivier 1979a Offertory Practices Associated with Domestic Structures at El Rosario. Unpublished paper

1979b Informe de las excavaciones realizadas en El Rosario (Tr-142) en 1979. Report on file, New World Archaeological Foundation, San Cristóbal

1979c Comparison of Exchange and Marketing Systems in the South Tzeltal Region (Chiapas) and the Valladolid Region (Yucatan). Unpublished paper

1980 An Ethnohistoric Perspective on the Political Organization of Late Postclassic Yucatan. Unpublished paper

1981 Functional Classification of Domestic Structures Using Survey Information from the Terminal Classic Period Site of El Rosario, Chiapas, Mexico. Unpublished paper

1982a Sociopolitical Structure and Organization in a Terminal Classic Period Maya Polity of the Upper Grijalva Basin, Chiapas, Mexico: Research Proposal. Unpublished paper

1982b Dynamic Contentiousness among the Late Postclassic Central Quiche of the Guatemala Highlands. Unpublished paper

1984 Patrón de asentamiento y de comunidad en el sitio de El Rosario, Chiapas, México. In *XVII Mesa Redonda*, vol. 1: 415–422. Sociedad Mexicana de Antropología, México

1985a *Classic Maya Settlement and Politics in the Rosario Valley, Chiapas, Mexico*. Unpublished Ph.D. dissertation, University of Michigan

1985b Settlement Pattern Survey in the Rosario Valley, Chiapas, Mexico. *Working Papers*, no. 41 (Centre of Latin American Studies, Cambridge)

1985c *Patterns of Land Tenure in the Late Classic Period Rosario Valley, Chiapas, Mexico*. Paper presented at the XLV International Congress of Americanists, Bogotá

1987 Forced Settlement and Political Centralization in a Classic Maya Polity. *Journal of Anthropological Archaeology*, 6: 220–262

1988 Tenam Rosario – A Political Microcosm. *American Antiquity*, 53: 351–370 n.d.a.   Maya Settlement in the Rosario Valley, Chiapas, Mexico. *New World Archaeological Foundation Papers*, MS in preparation

n.d.b.   Settlement Scale and Theory in Maya Archaeology. Unpublished paper

n.d.c.   Domestic Cycling and Stratification at El Rosario, Chiapas, Mexico. Unpublished paper

n.d.d.   Ethnographic Analogy and Maya Archaeology. Unpublished paper

De Roche, C. D. 1983   Population Estimates from Settlement Area and Number of Residences. *Journal of Field Archaeology*, 10: 187–192

Dunnel, Robert C. 1980   Evolutionary Theory and Archaeology. *Advances in Archaeological Method and Theory*, 3: 35–99

Durkheim, Emile 1933   *The Division of Labor in Society*. The Free Press, Glencoe

Earle, Timothy K. 1976   A Nearest-Neighbor Analysis of Two Formative Settlement Systems. In *The Early Mesoamerican Village*, edited by Kent V. Flannery, pp. 196–221. Academic Press, New York

1978   Economic and Social Organization of a Complex Chiefdom: The Halelea District, Kaua'i, Hawaii. *University of Michigan Museum of Anthropology Papers*, no. 63

Easton, David 1959   Political Anthropology. *Biennial Review of Anthropology 1959*: 210–262

Edmonson, Munro S. 1979   Some Postclassic Questions about the Classic Maya. *Estudios de Cultura Maya*, 12: 157–178

1982   *The Ancient Future of the Itza: The Book of Chilam Balam of Tizimin*. University of Texas Press, Austin

1986   *Heaven Born Merida and its Destiny: The Book of Chilam Balam of Chumayel*. University of Texas Press, Austin

Eggan, Fred 1954   Social Anthropology and the Method of Controlled Comparison. *American Anthropologist*, 56: 743–763

Fallers, Lloyd A. 1956   *Bantu Bureaucracy*. University of Chicago Press, Chicago

1973   *Inequality: Social Stratification Reconsidered*. University of Chicago Press, Chicago

Farriss, Nancy M. 1984   *Maya Society under Colonial Rule*. Princeton University Press, Princeton

Fash, William L. 1983   Deducing Social Organization from Classic Maya Settlement Patterns: A Case Study from the Copan Valley. In *Civilization in the Ancient Americas*, edited by Richard M. Leventhal and Alan L. Kolata, pp. 261–288. University of New Mexico Press, Albuquerque

1986   History and Characteristics of Settlement in the Copan Valley, and Some Comparisons with Quirigua. In *The Southeast Maya Periphery*, edited by Patricia A. Urban and Edward M. Schortman, pp. 72–93. University of Texas Press, Austin

Feinman, Gary 1986   The Emergence of Specialized Ceramic Production in Formative Oaxaca. *Research in Economic Anthropology*, supplement 2: 347–373

Feinman, Gary, Richard E. Blanton, and Stephen A. Kowalewski 1984   Market System Development in the Prehispanic Valley of Oaxaca. In *Trade and Exchange in Early Mesoamerica*, edited by Kenneth G. Hirth, pp. 157–178. University of New Mexico Press, Albuquerque

Feinman, Gary, Stephen A. Kowalewski, Laura Finsten, Richard E. Blanton, and Linda Nicholas 1985   Long-Term Demographic Change: A Perspective from the Valley of Oaxaca, Mexico. *Journal of Field Archaeology*, 12: 333–362

Feinman, Gary and Jill Neitzel 1984   Too Many Types: An Overview of Sedentary Prestate Societies in the Americas. *Advances In Archaeological Method and Theory*, vol. 3: 39–102. University of New Mexico Press, Albuquerque

Firth, Raymond 1964   *Essays on Social Organization and Values*. Athlone Press, London

Flannery, Kent V. 1972   The Cultural Evolution of Civilizations. *Annual Review of Ecology and Systematics*, 3: 399–426

   1973   Archaeology with a Capital S. In *Research and Theory in Current Archaeology*, edited by Charles L. Redman, pp. 47–53. John Wiley & Sons, New York

   1976   The Village and its Catchment Area. In *The Early Mesoamerican Village*, edited by Kent V. Flannery, pp. 91–95. Academic Press, New York

   1982   The Golden Marshalltown: A Parable for the Archaeology of the 1980s. *American Anthropologist*, 84: 265–278

   1983   The Legacy of the Early Urban Period: An Ethnohistoric Approach to Monte Alban's Temples, Residences, and Royal Tombs. In *The Cloud People*, edited by Kent V. Flannery and Joyce Marcus, pp. 132–136. Academic Press, New York

Flannery, Kent V. (ed.) 1982   *Maya Subsistence: Studies in Memory of Dennis E. Puleston*. Academic Press, New York

Fletcher, Roland 1981   People and Space: A Case Study on Material Behavior. In *Patterns of the Past*, edited by Ian Hodder, Glynn Isaac, and Norman Hammond, pp. 97–127. Cambridge University Press, Cambridge

Folan, William J., Joel Gunn, Jack D. Eaton and Robert W. Patch. 1983   Paleoclimatological Patterning in Southern Mesoamerica. *Journal of Field Archaeology*, 10: 453–468

Folan, William J., Ellen R. Kintz, and Laraine A. Fletcher 1983   *Coba: A Classic Maya Metropolis*. Academic Press, New York

Foley, Robert A. 1981   Off-Site Archaeology and Human Adaptation in Eastern Africa. *British Archaeological Reports International Series*, 97

Ford, Anabel 1982   Los mayas en El Peten: distribución de las poblaciones en el periodo clásico. *Mesoamérica* (Antigua, Guatemala), 3: 124–144

   1986   Population Growth and Social Complexity: An Examination of Settlement and Environment in the Central Maya Lowlands. *Arizona State University Anthropological Research Papers*, no. 35

Fortes, Meyer 1953   The Structure of Unilineal Descent Groups. *American Anthropologist*, 55: 17–41

   1962   Introduction. In *The Developmental Cycle in Domestic Groups*, edited by Jack R. Goody, pp. 1–14. Cambridge University Press, Cambridge

Fortes, Meyer and E. E. Evans-Pritchard (eds.) 1940   *African Political Systems*. Oxford University Press, London

Foster, Brian L. 1977   Trade, Social Conflict, and Social Integration: Rethinking Some Old Ideas on Exchange. In *Economic Exchange and Social Interaction in Southeast Asia*, edited by Karl Hutterer, pp. 3–22. University of Michigan, Ann Arbor

Foster, George M. 1960   Culture and Conquest: America's Spanish Heritage. *Viking Fund Publication in Anthropology*, no. 27

Fox, James A. and John S. Justeson 1986   Classic Maya Dynastic Alliance and Succession. In *Handbook of Middle American Indians*, Supplement–Ethnohistory, 4: 7–33

Fox, John W. 1978   *Quiche Conquest*. University of New Mexico Press, Albuquerque

   1987   *Maya Postclassic State Formation*. Cambridge University Press, Cambridge

Freeman, Leslie G., Jr. 1968   A Theoretical Framework for Interpreting Archaeological Materials. In *Man the Hunter*, edited by Richard B. Lee and Irven DeVore, pp. 262–267. Aldine Publishing Co., Chicago

Freidel, David A. 1981a   The Political Economy of Residential Dispersion among the Lowland Maya. In *Lowland Maya Settlement Patterns*, edited by Wendy Ashmore, pp. 371–382. University of New Mexico Press, Albuquerque

   1981b   Continuity and Disjunction: Late Postclassic Settlement Patterns in Northern Yucatan. In *Lowland Maya Settlement Patterns*, edited by Wendy Ashmore, pp. 311–332. University of New Mexico Press, Albuquerque

1983a Political Systems in Lowland Yucatan: Dynamics and Structure in Maya Settlement. In *Prehistoric Settlement Patterns*, edited by Evon Z. Vogt and Richard M. Leventhal, pp. 375–386. University of New Mexico Press, Albuquerque

1983b Lowland Maya Political Economy: Historical and Archaeological Perspectives in Light of Intensive Agriculture. In *Spaniards and Indians in Southeastern Mesoamerica: Essays on the History of Ethnic Relations*, edited by Murdo J. MacLeod and Robert Wasserstrom, pp. 40–63. University of Nebraska Press, Lincoln

1985 New Light on the Dark Ages: A Summary of Major Themes. In *The Lowland Maya Postclassic*, edited by Arlen F. Chase and Prudence M. Rice, pp. 285–309. University of Texas Press, Austin

1986 Maya Warfare: An Example of Peer Polity Interaction. In *Peer Polity Interaction and Socio-Political Change*, edited by Colin Renfrew and John F. Cherry, pp. 93–108. Cambridge University Press, Cambridge

Freidel, David A. and Maynard B. Cliff 1978 Energy Investments in Late Postclassic Maya Masonry Religious Structures. *Institute of Archaeology* (University of California at Los Angeles), monograph no. 8: 184–208

Freidel, David A. and Jeremy A. Sabloff 1984 *Cozumel: Late Maya Settlement Patterns.* Academic Press, New York

Fried, Morton H. 1967 *The Evolution of Political Society*. Random House, New York

Friedman, Jonathan and Michael J. Rowlands 1977 Notes towards an Epigenetic Model of the Evolution of "Civilisation." In *The Evolution of Social Systems*, edited by Jonathan Friedman and Michael J. Rowlands, pp. 201–276. Gerald Duckworth and Co. Ltd., London

Gándara, Manuel 1981 Archaeology and Dogmatic Falsificationism: The Hawaiian Refutations. Unpublished paper

Garza, Silvia and Edward B. Kurjack 1980 *Atlas arqueológico del estado de Yucatán.* Secretaría de Educación Pública/Instituto Nacional de Antropología e Historia, México

1984 Organización social y asentamientos mayas prehispánicos. *Estudios de Cultura Maya*, 15: 19–28

Gerth, Hans H. and C. Wright Mills (eds.) 1946 *From Max Weber: Essays in Sociology.* Oxford University Press, New York

Giddens, Anthony 1984 *The Constitution of Society*. Polity Press, Cambridge

1985 *The Nation-State and Violence*. Polity Press, Cambridge

Gifford, James C. 1978 The Ancient Maya in the Light of Their Ethnographic Present. In *Cultural Change and Continuity in Mesoamerica*, edited by David L. Browman, pp. 205–227. Mouton, The Hague

Gilman, Antonio 1981 The Development of Social Stratification in Bronze Age Europe. *Current Anthropology*, 22: 1–23

Goldman, Irving 1970 *Ancient Polynesian Society*. University of Chicago Press, Chicago

Goody, Jack R. 1962 The Fission of Domestic Groups among the Lodagaba. In *The Developmental Cycle in Domestic Groups*, edited by Jack R. Goody, pp. 53–91. Cambridge University Press, Cambridge

1966 Introduction. In *Succession to High Office*, edited by Jack R. Goody, pp. 1–56. Cambridge University Press, Cambridge

1971 *Technology, Tradition, and the State in Africa*. Oxford University Press, London

Goody, Jack R. (ed.) 1962 *The Developmental Cycle in Domestic Groups*. Cambridge University Press, Cambridge

Gorenflo, Larry and Nathan Gale 1986 Population and Productivity in the Teotihuacan Valley: Changing Patterns of Spatial Association in Prehispanic Central Mexico. *Journal of Anthropological Archaeology*, 5: 199–228

Guillemin, Jorge F. 1968 Development and Function of the Tikal Ceremonial Center. *Ethnos*, 33: 1–35

1977   Urbanism and Hierarchy at Iximche. In *Social Process in Maya Prehistory*, edited by Norman Hammond, pp. 227–264. Academic Press, New York

Haas, Jonathan 1981   Class Conflict and the State in the New World. In *The Transition to Statehood in the New World*, edited by Grant D. Jones and Robert R. Kautz, pp. 80–102. Cambridge University Press, Cambridge

1982   *The Evolution of the Prehistoric State*. Columbia University Press, New York

Halpernin, Rhoda H. 1984   Polanyi, Marx, and the Institutional Paradigm in Economic Anthropology. *Research in Economic Anthropology*, vol. 6: 245–272

1985   The Concept of the Formal in Economic Anthropology. *Research in Economic Anthropology*, vol. 7: 339–368

Hammond, Norman 1974   The Distribution of Late Classic Maya Major Ceremonial Centers in the Central Area. In *Mesoamerican Archaeology: New Approaches*, edited by Norman Hammond, pp. 313–334. University of Texas Press, Austin

1975a   Maya Settlement Hierarchy in Northern Belize. *Contributions of the University of California Archaeological Research Facility*, 27: 40–55

1975b   Lubaantun, A Classic Maya Realm. *Peabody Museum Monographs*, no. 2

1981   Settlement Patterns in Belize. In *Lowland Maya Settlement Patterns*, edited by Wendy Ashmore, pp. 157–186. University of New Mexico Press, Albuquerque

Harris, David R. 1972   Swidden Systems and Settlement. In *Man, Settlement, and Urbanism*, edited by Peter J. Ucko, Ruth Tringham, and G. W. Dimbleby, pp. 245–262. Gerald Duckworth and Co. Ltd., London

Harrison, Peter D. 1968   Form and Function in A Maya Palace Group. *Proceedings XXXVIII International Congress of Americanists*, vol. 1: 165–172

1981   Some Aspects of Preconquest Settlement in Southern Quintana Roo. In *Lowland Maya Settlement Patterns*, edited by Wendy Ashmore, pp. 259–286. University of New Mexico Press, Albuquerque

Harrison, Peter D. and Billy L. Turner (eds.) 1978   *Pre-Hispanic Maya Agriculture*. University of New Mexico Press, Albuquerque

Haviland, William A. 1963   Excavation of Small Structures in the Northeast Quadrant of Tikal, Guatemala. Unpublished Ph.D. dissertation, University of Pennsylvania. University Microfilms, Ann Arbor

1966a   Maya Settlement Patterns: A Critical Review. *Middle American Research Institute (Tulane)*, publication 26: 21–47

1966b   Social Integration and the Classic Maya. *American Antiquity*, 31: 625–631

1968   Ancient Maya Lowland Social Organization. *Middle American Research Institute (Tulane)*, publication 26: 93–117

1969   A New Population Estimate for Tikal, Guatemala. *American Antiquity*, 34: 429–433

1970   Tikal, Guatemala, and Mesoamerican Urbanism. *World Archaeology*, 2: 186–197

1982   Where the Rich Folks Lived: Deranging Factors in the Statistical Analysis of Tikal Settlement. *American Antiquity*, 47: 427–429

Hawkes, Christopher 1954   Archaeological Theory and Method: Some Suggestions From the Old World. *American Anthropologist*, 56: 155–168

Hayden, Brian and Aubrey Cannon 1984   The Structure of Material Systems: Ethnoarchaeology in the Maya Highlands. *Society for American Archaeology Paper*, no. 3

Helms, Mary W. 1979   *Ancient Panama: Chiefs in Search of Power*. University of Texas Press, Austin

Hicks, Frederic 1986   Prehispanic Background of Colonial Political and Economic Organization in Central Mexico. *Handbook of Middle American Indians*, Supplement-Ethnohistory, 4: 35–54

Hill, James N. 1972   The Methodological Debate in Contemporary Archaeology: A
    Model. In *Models in Archaeology*, edited by David L. Clarke, pp. 61–107. Methuen
    and Company Ltd., London
  1977   Systems Theory and the Explanation of Change. In *Explanation of Prehistoric
    Change*, edited by James N. Hill, pp. 59–103. University of New Mexico Press,
    Albuquerque
Hill, James N. and R. K. Evans 1972   A Model for Classification and Typology. In
    Models in Archaeology, edited by David L. Clarke, pp. 231–273. Methuen and
    Company Ltd., London
Hodder, Ian 1982   *The Present Past: An Introduction to Anthropology for Archaeologists*.
    B. T. Batsford Ltd., London
  1986   *Reading the Past*. Cambridge University Press, Cambridge
Hodder, Ian and Clive Orton 1976   *Spatial Analysis in Archaeology*. Cambridge
    University Press, Cambridge
Holland, William R. 1964   Contemporary Tzotzil Cosmological Concepts as a Basis For
    Interpreting Prehistoric Maya Civilization. *American Antiquity*, 29: 301–306
Hosler, Dorothy, Jeremy A. Sabloff, and Dale Runge 1977   Situation Model
    Development: A Case Study of the Classic Maya Collapse. In *Social Process in
    Maya Prehistory*, edited by Norman Hammond, pp. 553–590. Academic Press,
    New York
Ichon, Alain 1975   Organización de un centro Quiché protohistórico: Pueblo Viejo-
    Chichaj. *Instituto Nacional de Antropología e Historia Publicación Especial*, 9
    (Guatemala)
Johnson, Gregory A. 1973   Local Exchange and Early State Development in
    Southwestern Iran. *University of Michigan Museum of Anthropology Papers*, no. 51
  1977   Aspects of Regional Analysis in Archaeology. *Annual Review of Anthropology*, 6:
    479–508
  1978   Information Sources and the Development of Decision-Making Organization.
    In *Social Archaeology*, edited by Charles L. Redman, Mary J. Berman, Edward V.
    Curtin, William T. Langhorne Jr., Nina M. Versaggi, and Jeffery C. Wanser, pp.
    87–112. Academic Press, New York
  1982   Organizational Structure and Scalar Stress. In *Theory and Explanation in
    Archaeology*, edited by Colin Renfrew, Michael J. Rowlands, and Barbara Abbott
    Segraves, pp. 389–421. Academic Press, New York
Jones, Grant D. 1979   Southern Lowland Maya Political Organization: A Model of
    Change from Protohistoric through Colonial Times. *Proceeding of the XXXII
    International Congress of Americanists* (Paris 1976), vol. 8: 83–94
Jones, Grant D. (ed.) 1977   *Anthropology and History in Yucatan*. University of Texas
    Press, Austin
Kowalewski, Stephen A. 1980   Population-Resource Balances in Period I of Oaxaca,
    Mexico. *American Antiquity*, 45: 151–165
  1983   Differences in the Site Hierarchies below Monte Alban and Teotihuacan: A
    Comparison Based on the Rank-Size Rule. In *The Cloud People*, edited by Kent V.
    Flannery and Joyce Marcus, pp. 168–170. Academic Press, New York
Kowalewski, Stephen A., Richard E. Blanton, Gary Feinman, and Laura Finsten 1983
    Boundaries, Scale, and Internal Organization. *Journal of Anthropological Archaeology*,
    2: 32–56
Kowalewski, Stephen A. and Laura Finsten 1983   The Economic Systems of Ancient
    Oaxaca: A Regional Perspective. *Current Anthropology*, 24: 413–441
Kurjack, Edward B. 1974   Prehistoric Lowland Maya Community and Social
    Organization – A Case Study of Dzibilchaltun, Yucatan, Mexico. *Middle American
    Research Institute (Tulane)*, publication 38

1978   The Distribution of Vaulted Architecture at Dzibilchaltun, Yucatan, Mexico. *Estudios de Cultura Maya*, 10: 91–102

1979   Introduction to the Map of the Ruins of Dzibilchaltun, Yucatan, Mexico. *Middle American Research Institute (Tulane)*, publication 47

Kurjack, Edward B. and Silvia Garza 1981   Precolumbian Community Form and Distribution in the Northern Maya Area. In *Lowland Maya Settlement Patterns*, edited by Wendy Ashmore, pp. 287–310. University of New Mexico Press, Albuquerque

Lee, Thomas A., Jr. 1974   *Terminal Late Classic Settlement Pattern Responses to Demographic and Ecological Pressures in Southeastern Chiapas: A Sociopolitical Model*. Paper presented at the XLI International Congress of Americanists, Mexico City

1984   Investigaciones arqueológicas recientes del Clásico, Postclásico, y Colonial Maya en Chiapas: resumen e implicaciones. In *XVII Mesa Redonda*, vol. 1: 113–130. Sociedad Mexicana de Antropología, México

Lee, Thomas A., Jr., T. Michael Blake, Susan Blake, Barbara Voorhies, and James White n.d.   Archaeological Reconnaissance of the Upper Tributaries Region of the Grijalva Valley, Chiapas, Mexico. *New World Archaeological Foundation Papers*, MS in preparation

Leone, Mark 1982   Childe's Offspring. In *Symbolic and Structural Archaeology*, edited by Ian Hodder, pp. 179–184. Cambridge University Press, Cambridge

1986   Symbolic, Structural, and Critical Archaeology. *American Archaeology Past and Future*, edited by David J. Meltzer, Don D. Fowler, and Jeremy A. Sabloff, pp. 415–438. Smithsonian Institution Press, Washington

Leventhal, Richard M. 1981   Settlement Patterns in the Southeast Maya Area. In *Lowland Maya Settlement Patterns*, edited by Wendy Ashmore, pp. 187–209. University of New Mexico Press, Albuquerque

1983   Household Groups and Classic Maya Religion. In *Prehistoric Settlement Patterns*, edited by Evon Z. Vogt and Richard M. Leventhal, pp. 55–76. University of New Mexico Press, Albuquerque

Lewarch, Dennis E. and Michael J. O'Brien 1981   The Expanding Role of Surface Assemblages in Archaeological Research. *Advances in Archaeological Method and Theory*, 4: 297–342

Litvak King, Jaime 1985   *Ancient Mexico, An Overview*. University of New Mexico Press, Albuquerque

Lincoln, Charles E. 1986   The Chronology of Chichen Itza: A Review of the Literature. In *Late Lowland Maya Civilization: Classic to Postclassic*, edited by Jeremy A. Sabloff and E. Wyllys Andrews V, pp. 141–196. University of New Mexico Press, Albuquerque

Lloyd, Peter 1965   The Political Structure of African Kingdoms: An Explanatory Model. In *Political Systems and the Distribution of Power*, edited by Michael Banton, pp. 63–112. Tavistock Publications, London

1968   Conflict Theory and Yoruba Kingdoms. In *History and Social Anthropology*, edited by I. M. Lewis, pp. 25–61. Tavistock Publications, London

Lowe, John W. G. 1985   *The Dynamics of Apocalypse: A Systems Simulation of the Classic Maya Collapse*. University of New Mexico Press, Albuquerque

Lowe, Gareth W. 1959   Archaeological Exploration of the Upper Grijalva, Chiapas, Mexico. *New World Archaeological Foundation Papers*, 2 (publication 3)

MacNeish, Richard S. 1981   The Transition to Statehood as Seen from the Mouth of a Cave. In *The Transition to Statehood in the New World*, edited by Grant D. Jones and Robert R. Kautz, pp. 123–154. Cambridge University Press, Cambridge

MacNeish, Richard S., Frederick A. Peterson, and James A. Neely 1972   The

Archaeological Reconnaissance. In *The Prehistory of the Tehuacan Valley*, 5: 341–495. University of Texas Press, Austin

Mair, Lucy 1962   *Primitive Government*. Penguin Books, Harmondsworth

  1977   *African Kingdoms*. Oxford University Press, Oxford

Marcus, Joyce 1974   The Iconography of Power among the Classic Maya. *World Archaeology*, 6(1): 83–94

  1976   *Emblem and State in the Classic Maya Lowlands*. Dumbarton Oaks, Washington

  1983a   Lowland Maya Archaeology at the Crossroads. *American Antiquity*, 48: 454–488

  1983b   On the Nature of the Mesoamerican City. In *Prehistoric Settlement Patterns*, edited by Evon Z. Vogt and Richard M. Leventhal, pp. 195–242. University of New Mexico Press, Albuquerque

  1983c   The Genetic Model and the Linguistic Divergence of the Otomangueans. In *The Cloud People*, edited by Kent V. Flannery and Joyce Marcus, pp. 4–9. Academic Press, New York

  1983d   A Synthesis of the Cultural Evolution of the Zapotec and Mixtec. In *The Cloud People*, edited by Kent V. Flannery and Joyce Marcus, pp. 355–360. Academic Press, New York

Martinez H., J. (ed.) 1929   *Diccionario de Motul. Maya-Español*. Mérida

McGuire, Randall H. 1983   Breaking Down Cultural Complexity: Inequality and Heterogeneity. *Advances in Archaeological Method and Theory*, vol. 6: 91–142

Meggers, Betty J. 1954   Environmental Limitations on the Development of Culture. *American Anthropologist*, 56: 801–824

Merton, Robert K. 1968   *Social Theory and Social Structure*, (third edition). Free Press, New York

Michelon, O. (ed.) 1976   *Diccionario de San Francisco (Yucatán)*. Akademische Druck-u. Verlagsanstaldt, Graz, Austria

Miller, Arthur G. 1986   From the Maya Margins: Images of Postclassic Power Politics. In *Late Lowland Maya Civilization: Classic to Postclassic*, edited by Jeremy A. Sabloff and E. Wyllys Andrews V, pp. 199–222. University of New Mexico Press, Albuquerque

Miller, Daniel and Christopher Tilley (eds.) 1984   *Ideology, Power, and Politics*. Cambridge University Press, Cambridge

Millon, Rene 1976   Social Relations in Ancient Teotihuacan. In *The Valley of Mexico*, edited by Eric R. Wolf, pp. 205–248. University of New Mexico Press, Albuquerque

  1981   Teotihuacan: City, State, and Civilization. *Handbook of Middle American Indians*, Supplement–Archaeology vol. 1: 198–243

Morley, Sylvanus G., George W. Brainerd, and Robert J. Sharer 1983   *The Ancient Maya* (fourth edition). Stanford University Press, Stanford

Morris, Craig and Donald E. Thompson 1985   *Huanuco Pampa: An Inca City and its Hinterland*. Thames and Hudson, London

Murra, John V. 1972   El "control vertical" de un máximo de pisos ecológicos en la economía de las sociedades andinas. In *Visita de la Provincia de Leon de Huánuco en 1562*, vol. 2, edited by John V. Murra, pp. 429–476. Universidad Nacional Hermilio Valdizán, Huánuco

Palerm, Angel 1954   Notas sobre las construcciones militares y la guerra en Mesoamérica. *Anales* (Instituto Nacional de Antropología e Historia) 8: 123–134

Parsons, Jeffrey R. 1971   Prehistoric Settlement Patterns in the Texcoco Region, Mexico. *University of Michigan Museum of Anthropology Memoirs*, no. 3

Parsons, Lee A. and Barbara J. Price 1971   Mesoamerican Trade and its Role in the Emergence of Civilization. In *Contributions of the University of California Archaeological Research Facility*, 11: 169–195

Peebles, Christopher S. 1978   Determinants of Settlement Size and Location in the Moundville Phase. In *Mississippian Settlement Patterns*, edited by Bruce D. Smith, pp. 369–416. Academic Press, New York

Peebles, Christopher S. and Susan Kus 1977   Some Archaeological Correlates of Ranked Societies. *American Antiquity*, 42: 421–448

Phillips, David A. and William L. Rathje 1977   Streets Ahead: Exchange Values and the Rise of the Classic Maya. In *Social Process in Maya Prehistory*, edited by Norman Hammond, pp. 103–112. Academic Press, New York

Plog, Fred 1973   Diachronic Anthropology. In *Research and Theory in Current Archaeology*, edited by Charles R. Redman, pp. 181–198. John Wiley, New York

Polanyi, Karl 1944   *The Great Transformation*. Beacon Press, Boston
   1957   The Economy as Instituted Process. In *Trade and Market in Early Empires*, edited by Karl Polanyi, Conrad M. Arensberg, and Harry W. Pearson, pp. 243–270. The Free Press, Chicago
   1977   *The Livelihood of Man*. Academic Press, New York

Pollock, Harry E. D., Ralph L. Roys, Tatiana Proskouriakoff, and A. Ledyard Smith
   1962   Mayapan, Yucatan, Mexico. *Carnegie Institution of Washington*, publication 619

Price, Barbara J. 1974   The Burden of Cargo: Ethnographic Models and Archaeological Inference. In *Mesoamerican Archaeology: New Approaches*, edited by Norman Hammond, pp. 445–465. University of Texas Press, Austin
   1977   Shifts in Production and Organization: A Cluster-Interaction Model. *Current Anthropology*, 18: 209–233
   1978   Commerce and Cultural Process in Mesoamerica. *New World Archaeological Foundation Papers*, 40: 231–245

Proskouriakoff, Tatiana 1962   Civic and Religious Structures of Mayapan. *Carnegie Institution of Washington*, publication 619: 86–140

Puleston, Dennis E. 1973   *Ancient Maya Settlement Patterns and Environment at Tikal, Guatemala: Implications for Subsistence Models*. Ph.D. dissertation, University of Pennsylvania. University Microfilms, Ann Arbor
   1979   An Epistemological Pathology and the Collapse, Or Why the Maya Kept the Short Count. In *Maya Archaeology and Ethnohistory*, edited by Norman Hammond and Gordon R. Willey, pp. 63–71. University of Texas Press, Austin

Raab, L. Mark and Albert C. Goodyear 1984   Middle-Range Theory in Archaeology: A Critical Review of Origins and Applications. *American Antiquity*, 49: 255–268

Rappaport, Roy A. 1977   Maladaptation in Social Systems. In *The Evolution of Social Systems*, edited by Jonathan Friedman and Michael J. Rowlands, pp. 49–71. Gerald Duckworth and Co. Ltd., London

Rathje, William L. 1973   Classic Maya Development and Denouement: A Research Design. In *The Classic Maya Collapse*, edited by T. Patrick Culbert, pp. 405–454. University of New Mexico Press, Albuquerque
   1975   Last Tango at Mayapan: A Tentative Trajectory of Production-Distribution Systems. In *Ancient Civilization and Trade*, edited by Jeremy A. Sabloff and Clifford C. Lamberg-Karlovsky, pp. 409–448. University of New Mexico Press, Albuquerque
   1983   To the Salt of the Earth: Some Comments on Household Archaeology among the Maya. In *Prehistoric Settlement Patterns*, edited by Evon Z. Vogt and Richard M. Leventhal, pp. 23–34. University of New Mexico Press, Albuquerque

Redmond, Elsa 1983   A Fuego y Sangre: Early Zapotec Imperialism in the Cuicatlán Cañada, Oaxaca. *University of Michigan Museum of Anthropology Memoirs*, no. 16

Relaciones de Yucatán 1898–1900   *Relaciones histórico-geográficas de la Gobernación de Yucatán*. Colección de documentos inéditos relativos al descubrimiento, conquista y organización de las antiguas posesiones españolas de Ultramar, segunda serie num. 11 y 13. Madrid

Renfrew, Colin 1974   Beyond a Subsistence Economy: The Evolution of Social Organisation in Prehistoric Europe. In *Reconstructing Complex Societies* (Supplement to the Bulletin of the American Schools of Oriental Research, no. 20), edited by Charlotte B. Moore, pp. 69–84. Massachusetts Institute of Technology Press

1975   Trade as Action at a Distance: Questions of Integration and Communication. In *Ancient Civilization and Trade*, edited by Jeremy A. Sabloff and Clifford C. Lamberg-Karlovsky, pp. 3–59. University of New Mexico Press, Albuquerque

1978   Trajectory Discontinuity and Morphogenesis, the Implications of Catastrophe Theory for Archaeology. *American Antiquity*, 43: 203–244

1982   Polity and Power: Interaction, Intensification, and Exploitation. In *An Island Polity: The Archaeology of Exploitation in Melos*, edited by Colin Renfrew and Malcolm Wagstaff, pp. 264–290. Cambridge University Press, Cambridge

1984   *Approaches to Social Archaeology*. Edinburgh University Press, Edinburgh

1986   Introduction: Peer Polity Interaction and Socio-Political Change. In *Peer Polity Interaction and Socio-Political Change*, edited by Colin Renfrew and John F. Cherry, pp. 1–18. Cambridge University Press, Cambridge

Renfrew, Colin and John F. Cherry (eds.) 1986   *Peer Polity Interaction and Socio-Political Change*. Cambridge University Press, Cambridge

Rice, Don S. and Dennis E. Puleston 1981   Ancient Maya Settlement Patterns in the Peten, Guatemala. In *Lowland Maya Settlement Patterns*, edited by Wendy Ashmore, pp. 121–157. University of New Mexico Press, Albuquerque

Rice, Don S. and Prudence M. Rice 1980a   The Northeast Peten Revisited. *American Antiquity*, 45: 432–454

1980b   1978 Introductory Survey of the Central Peten Savanna. *Contributions of the University of California Archaeological Research Facility*, 41: 231–277

Rivero T., Sonia E. 1978   Los Cimientos: análisis del patrón de asentamiento por localización espacial. *Estudios de Cultura Maya*, 11: 113–119

Robles C., Fernando and Anthony P. Andrews 1986   A Review and Synthesis of Recent Postclassic Archaeology in Northern Yucatan. In *Late Lowland Maya Civilization: Classic to Postclassic*, edited by Jeremy A. Sabloff and E. Wyllys Andrews V, pp. 53–98. University of New Mexico Press, Albuquerque

Rosenfeld, Henry 1965   The Social Composition of the Military in the Process of State Formation in the Arabian Desert. *Journal of the Royal Anthropological Institute*, 95: 75–86, 174–194

Roys, Ralph L. 1957   The Political Geography of the Yucatan Maya. *Carnegie Institution of Washington*, publication 613

1962   Literary Sources for the History of Mayapan. *Carnegie Institution of Washington*, publication 619: 25–86

Sabloff, Jeremy A. 1973   Major Themes in the Past Hypotheses of the Maya Collapse. In *The Classic Maya Collapse*, edited by T. Patrick Culbert, pp. 35–40. University of New Mexico Press, Albuquerque

1977   Old Myths, New Myths: The Role of Sea Traders in the Development of Ancient Maya Civilization. In *The Sea in the Precolumbian World*, edited by Elizabeth P. Benson, pp. 67–95. Dumbarton Oaks, Washington

1983   Classic Maya Settlement Pattern Studies: Past Problems, Future Prospects. In *Prehistoric Settlement Patterns*, edited by Evon Z. Vogt and Richard M. Leventhal, pp. 413–422. University of New Mexico Press, Albuquerque

1986   Interaction among Classic Maya Polities: A Preliminary Examination. In *Peer Polity Interaction and Socio-Political Change*, edited by Colin Renfrew and John F. Cherry, pp. 109–116. Cambridge University Press, Cambridge

Sabloff, Jeremy A. and E. Wyllys Andrew V (eds.) 1986 *Late Lowland Maya Civilization: Classic to Postclassic.* University of New Mexico Press, Albuquerque

Sahlins, Marshall D. 1958 *Social Stratification in Polynesia.* University of Washington Press, Seattle

1968 *Tribesmen.* Prentice-Hall, Inc., Englewood Cliffs, N.J.

1972 *Stone Age Economics.* Aldine Publishing Co., Chicago

Sanders, William T. 1962 Cultural Ecology of the Maya Lowlands: Part 1. *Estudios de Cultura Maya,* 2: 79–121

1963 Cultural Ecology of the Maya Lowlands: Part 2. *Estudios de Cultura Maya,* 3: 203–241

1966 Review of "Desarrollo Cultural de los Maya", edited by Evon Z. Vogt and Alberto Ruz. *American Anthropologist,* 68: 1,068–1,071

1967 Settlement Patterns. *Handbook of Middle American Indians,* 6: 53–86

1973 The Cultural Ecology of the Lowland Maya: A Reevaluation. In *The Classic Maya Collapse,* edited by T. Patrick Culbert, pp. 325–365. University of New Mexico Press, Albuquerque

1974 Chiefdom to State: Political Evolution at Kaminaljuyu, Guatemala. In *Reconstructing Complex Societies* (Supplement to the Bulletin of the American Schools of Oriental Research, no. 20), edited by Charlotte B. Moore, pp. 97–121. Massachusetts Institute of Technology Press, Cambridge

1981 Classic Maya Settlement Patterns and Ethnographic Analogy. In *Lowland Maya Settlement Patterns,* edited by Wendy Ashmore, pp. 351–369. University of New Mexico Press, Albuquerque

Sanders, William T. and Barbara J. Price 1968 *Mesoamerica, The Evolution of A Civilization.* Random House, New York

Sanders, William T., Jeffrey R. Parsons, and Robert S. Santley 1979 *The Basin of Mexico.* Academic Press, New York

Santley, Robert S. 1980 Disembedded Capitals Reconsidered. *American Antiquity,* 45: 132–145

1984 Obsidian Exchange, Economic Stratification, and the Evolution of Complex Society in the Basin of Mexico. In *Trade and Exchange in Early Mesoamerica,* edited by Kenneth G. Hirth, pp. 43–86. University of New Mexico Press, Albuquerque

1986 Prehispanic Roadways, Transport Network Geometry, and Aztec Politico-Economic Organization in the Basin of Mexico. In *Research in Economic Anthropology,* supplement 2: 223–244

Schact, Robert M. 1984 The Contemporaneity Problem. *American Antiquity,* 49: 678–695

Schele, Linda and Mary E. Miller 1986 *The Blood of Kings: Dynasty and Ritual in Maya Art.* Kimbell Art Museum, Fort Worth

Scholes, France V. and Ralph L. Roys 1968 *The Maya Chontal Indians of Acalan-Tixchel* (second edition). University of Oklahoma Press, Norman

Service, Elman R. 1971 *Primitive Social Organization* (second edition). Random House, New York

1975 *Origins of the State and Civilization.* W. W. Norton & Co. Inc., New York

1985 *A Century of Controversy: Ethnological Issues from 1860 to 1960.* Academic Press, New York

Sidrys, Raymond 1978 Archaeological Measurement of the Matter-Energy Flow in Mesoamerican Civilization. In *Institute of Archaeology* (University of California at Los Angeles), monograph no. 8: 1–39

Smith, Carol A. 1974 Economics of Marketing Systems: Models From Economic Geography. *Annual Review of Anthropology,* 3: 167–201

1976 Exchange Systems and the Spatial Distribution of Elites: The Organization of

Stratification in Agrarian Societies. In *Regional Analysis Vol. 2*, edited by Carol A. Smith, pp. 309–374. Academic Press, New York

Smith, Michael E. 1979 The Aztec Marketing System and Settlement Pattern in the Valley of Mexico: A Central Place Analysis. *American Antiquity*, 44: 110–125

Smith, M. G. 1956 On Segmentary Lineage Systems. *Journal of the Royal Anthropological Institute*, 86: 39–80

1960 *Government in Zazzau*. Oxford University Press, London

1966 A Structural Approach to Comparative Politics. In *Varieties of Political Theory*, edited by David Easton, pp. 113–128. Prentice-Hall Inc., Englewood Cliffs, New Jersey

1977 Conditions of Change in Social Stratification. In *The Evolution of Social Systems*, edited by Jonathan Friedman and Michael J. Rowlands, pp. 29–48. Duckworth, London

Southall, Aidan W. 1956 *Alur Society*. Cambridge University Press, Cambridge

1965 A Critique of the Typology of States and Political Systems. In *Political Systems and the Distribution of Power*, edited by Michael Banton, pp. 111–140. Tavistock Publications, London

Spencer, Charles S. 1982 *The Cuicatlán Cañada and Monte Albán: A Study of Primary State Formation*. Academic Press, New York

Spriggs, Matthew (ed.) 1984 *Marxist Perspectives in Archaeology*. Cambridge University Press, Cambridge

Steponaitis, Vincas P. 1978 Location Theory and Complex Chiefdoms: A Mississippian Example. In *Mississippian Settlement Patterns*, edited by Bruce D. Smith, pp. 417–453. Academic Press, New York

1981 Settlement Hierarchies and Political Complexity in Nonmarket Societies: The Formative Period of the Valley of Mexico. *American Anthropologist*, 83: 320–363

Steward, Julian 1942 The Direct Historical Approach to Archaeology. *American Antiquity*, 7: 337–343

1949 Cultural Causality and Law: A Trial Formulation of the Development of Early Civilizations. *American Anthropologist*, 51: 1–27

Tainter, Joseph A. 1977 Modeling Change in Prehistoric Social Systems. In *For Theory Building in Archaeology*, edited by Lewis R. Binford, pp. 327–351. Academic Press, New York

Taylor, Donna 1975 Some Locational Aspects of Middle-Range Hierarchical Societies. Unpublished Ph.D. dissertation, City University of New York. University Microfilms, Ann Arbor

Thompson, J. Eric S. 1970 *Maya History and Religion*. University of Oklahoma Press, Norman

1971 Estimates of Maya Population: Deranging Factors. *American Antiquity*, 36: 214–216

Tolstoy, Paul 1975 Settlement and Population Trends in the Basin of Mexico (Ixtapaluca and Zacatenco Phases). *Journal of Field Archaeology*, 2: 331–349

1982 Advances in the Valley of Oaxaca, Part 2. *Quarterly Review of Archaeology*, 3(4)

Toumey, C. P. 1981 Pattern and Scale in Archaeological Regions. In *Networks of the Past: Regional Interaction in Archaeology*, edited by Peter D. Francis, F. J. Kense, and P. G. Duke, pp. 467–476. University of Calgary Archaeological Association, Calgary

Tourtellot, Gair 1983 An Assessment of Classic Maya Household Composition. In *Prehistoric Settlement Patterns*, edited by Evon Z. Vogt and Richard M. Leventhal, pp. 35–54. University of New Mexico Press, Albuquerque

Trigger, Bruce G. 1968 The Determinants of Settlement Patterns. In *Settlement Archaeology*, edited by Kwang-Chih Chang, pp. 53–78. National Press, Palo Alto

1974 The Archaeology of Government. *World Archaeology*, 6: 95–106

van Zantwijk, Rudolph 1981 The Great Temple of Tenochtitlan: Model of Aztec Cosmovision. In *Mesoamerican Sites and World Views*, edited by Elizabeth P. Benson, pp. 71–86. Dumbarton Oaks, Washington

1985 *The Aztec Arrangement*. University of Oklahoma Press, Norman

Vincent, Joan 1978 Political Anthropology: Manipulative Strategies. *Annual Review of Anthropology*, 7: 175–194

Vogt, Evon Z. 1964a The Genetic Model and Maya Cultural Development. In *Desarrollo cultural de los mayas*, edited by Evon Z. Vogt and Alberto Ruz, pp. 9–48. Universidad Nacional Autónoma de México, México

1964b Summary and Appraisal. In *Desarrollo cultural de los mayas*, edited by Evon Z. Vogt and Alberto Ruz, pp. 395–403. Universidad Nacional Autónoma de México, México

1968 Some Aspects of Zinacantan Settlement Patterns and Ceremonial Organization. In *Settlement Archaeology*, edited by Kwang-Chih Chang, pp. 154–173. National Press, Palo Alto

1969 *Zinacantan. A Maya Community in the Highlands of Chiapas*. Harvard University Press, Cambridge

1983 Ancient and Contemporary Maya Settlement Patterns: A New Look from the Chiapas Highlands. In *Prehistoric Settlement Patterns*, edited by Evon Z. Vogt and Richard M. Leventhal, pp. 89–114. University of New Mexico Press, Albuquerque

Wallace, Dwight T. 1977 An Intra-Site Locational Analysis of Utatlan: The Structure of an Urban Site. *Institute of Mesoamerican Studies* (State University of New York-Albany), 1: 20–54

Webb, Malcolm C. 1973 The Peten Maya Decline Viewed in the Perspective of State Formation. In *The Classic Maya Collapse*, edited by T. Patrick Culbert, pp. 367–404. University of New Mexico Press, Albuquerque

Webster, David L. 1976a On Theocracies. *American Anthropologist*, 78: 812–828

1976b Defensive Earthworks at Becan, Campeche, Mexico: Implications for Maya Warfare. *Middle American Research Institute (Tulane)*, publication no. 41

1977 Warfare and the Evolution of Maya Civilization. In *The Origins of Maya Civilization*, edited by Richard E. W. Adams, pp. 335–372. University of New Mexico Press, Albuquerque

1985a Recent Settlement Survey in the Copan Valley, Honduras. *Journal of New World Archaeology*, 5(4): 39–51

1985b Surplus, Labor, and Stress in Late Classic Maya Society. *Journal of Anthropological Research*, 41: 375–399

Webster, David L. and Elliot M. Abrams 1983 An Elite Compound at Copan, Honduras. *Journal of Field Archaeology*, 10: 285–296

Wenke, Robert 1981 Explaining the Evolution of Cultural Complexity: A Review. *Advances in Archaeological Method and Theory*, vol. 4: 79–127

White, Leslie A. 1959 *The Evolution of Culture*. McGraw-Hill Book Co. Inc., New York

Wilk, Richard R. and William L. Rathje 1982 Household Archaeology. *American Behavioral Scientist*, 25(6): 617–639

Willey, Gordon R. 1974 Precolumbian Urbanism: The Central Mexican Highlands and the Lowland Maya. In *The Rise and Fall of Civilizations*, edited by Jeremy A. Sabloff and Clifford C. Lamberg-Karlovsky, pp. 134–144. Cummings Publishing Co., Menlo Park

1977 External Influences on the Lowland Maya: 1940 and 1975 Perspectives. In *Social Process in Maya Prehistory*, edited by Norman Hammond, pp. 58–75. Academic Press, New York

1979   The Concept of the "Disembedded Capital" In Comparative Perspective. *Journal of Anthropological Research*, 35: 123–137

1981   Maya Lowland Settlement Patterns: A Summary Review. In *Lowland Maya Settlement Patterns*, edited by Wendy Ashmore, pp. 385–415. University of New Mexico Press, Albuquerque

1986   The Postclassic of the Maya Lowlands: A Preliminary Overview. In *Late Lowland Maya Civilization: Classic to Postclassic*, edited by Jeremy A. Sabloff and E. Wyllys Andrews V, pp. 17–51. University of New Mexico Press, Albuquerque

Willey, Gordon R. and William R. Bullard 1965   Prehistoric Settlement Patterns in the Maya Lowlands. *Handbook of Middle American Indians*, vol. 2: 360–377

Willey, Gordon R. and Richard M. Leventhal 1979   Prehistoric Settlement at Copan. In *Maya Archaeology and Ethnohistory*, edited by Norman Hammond and Gordon R. Willey, pp. 75–102. University of Texas Press, Austin

Willey, Gordon R. and Jeremy A. Sabloff 1980   *A History of American Archaeology* (second edition). W. H. Freeman and Company, San Francisco

Winckler, Edwin A. 1969   Political Anthropology. *Biennial Review of Anthropology 1969*: 301–392

Winter, Marcus C. 1974   Residential Patterns At Monte Alban, Oaxaca, Mexico. *Science*, 186: 981–987

Wobst, H. Martin 1977   Stylistic Behavior and Information Exchange. *University of Michigan Museum of Anthropology Anthropological Papers*, no. 61: 317–342

Wolf, Eric R. 1959   *Sons of the Shaking Earth*. University of Chicago Press, Chicago

1982   *Europe and the People Without History*. University of California Press, Los Angeles

Wright, Henry T. 1977   Recent Research on the Origin of the State. *Annual Review of Anthropology*, 6: 379–397

1978   Towards An Explanation of the Origin of the State. In *Origins of the State*, edited by Ronald Cohen and Elman R. Service, pp. 49–68. Institute for the Study of Human Issues, Philadelphia

1986   The Evolution of Civilizations. In *American Archaeology Past and Future*, edited by David J. Meltzer, Don D. Fowler, and Jeremy A. Sabloff, pp. 323–365. Smithsonian Institution Press, Washington

Wright, Henry T. and Gregory A. Johnson 1975   Population, Exchange, and Early State Formation in Southwestern Iran. *American Anthropologist*, 77: 267–289

Wright, Henry T., Naomi Miller, and Richard Redding 1980   Time and Process in an Uruk Rural Center. In *L'archéologie de l'Iraq: Perspectives et limites de l'interprétation anthropologique des documents*, edited by Marie-Therese Barrelet, pp. 265–282. Centre National de la Recherche Scientifique (Colloque International no. 580), Paris

Wylie, Alison 1985   The Reaction Against Analogy. *Advances in Archaeological Method and Theory*, 8: 63–111

Yoffee, Norman 1979   The Decline and Rise of Mesopotamian Civilization: An Ethnoarchaeological Perspective on the Evolution of Social Complexity. *American Antiquity*, 44: 5–35

Zarky, Alan 1976   Statistical Analysis of Site Catchments at Ocos, Guatemala. In *The Early Mesoamerican Village*, edited by Kent V. Flannery, pp. 117–128. Academic Press, New York